W9-CKD-893

HARVARD STUDIES IN CLASSICAL PHILOLOGY

VOLUME 113

HARVARD STUDIES
IN
CLASSICAL PHILOLOGY

VOLUME 113

Department of the Classics, Harvard University
Cambridge, Massachusetts
Distributed by Harvard University Press
2023

THIS BOOK IS PRINTED ON ACID-FREE PAPER, AND ITS
BINDING MATERIALS HAVE BEEN CHOSEN FOR STRENGTH
AND DURABILITY.

LIBRARY OF CONGRESS CATALOGUE NUMBER: 44–32100

ISBN-13: 9780674295797

PRINTED IN THE UNITED STATES OF AMERICA

EDITORIAL NOTE

Harvard Studies in Classical Philology is published by the authority of the President and Fellows of Harvard College on behalf of the Department of the Classics. Publication is assisted by the generosity of the Class of 1856, as well as by other gifts and bequests. The guidelines for style and a statement of the editorial policy may be found at http://publishing. classics.fas.harvard.edu/submitting-article-hscp.

CONTENTS

῞ΕΡΥΜΑΙ AND ᾽ΕΡΥΚΩ

ANDREW MERRITT

Though occasionally encountered in prose (Herodotus, Xenophon, etc.), ἐρΰκω, together with its compounds ἀπερΰκω and κατερΰκω, is fundamentally an item of the Epic register.[1] The root ἐρῡκ-, which allows elision,[2] forms a present (ἐρΰκε/ο-),[3] future (ἐρῡξε/ο-), sigmatic aorist (ἐρῡξα-), and descriptively reduplicated aorist stem (ἐρῡκακε/ο-).[4] The basic meaning of ἐρΰκω is 'retain', either within or without a given physical or figurative space. Accordingly, besides general restraint or prevention, the verb refers to the steadying of men and horses (Il. 6.80,

I thank Alan Nussbaum, Michael Weiss, Hayden Pelliccia, Benjamin Fortson, Jay Jasanoff, and the anonymous reviewer for their roles in the formation of this article, the content of which is my full responsibility.

[1] LfgrE (= Snell et al. 1955–2010): vol. 2, 717–719.

[2] E.g., νύμφη πότνι᾽ ἔρυκε, Καλυψὼ δῖα θεάων (Od. 1.14); here and hereafter, I use West 2011 for the text of the Odyssey and West 2017 for the text of the Iliad. Further evidence that ἐρῡκ- is indeed a root is provided by the nominal derivative ἐρυκτῆρας, used by the fragmentary historian Myron (FGrHist [= Jacoby 1923–1958] 106 F 1) to describe a class of freedmen at Sparta ('Retainers'?). Other than the personal name ᾽Ερυξίμαχος (Pl. Symp.), the only other nominal derivative known to the author is κατερῡκτικός 'inhibitive' (PMag. Lond. 121.450).

[3] In addition, the Streckform ἐρῡκανόωσ᾽, which points to an ἐρῡκανάω (Hom. 1×), stands beside an ἐρῡκάνω (ἐρΰκανε, Od. 10.429) immediately derived from ἐρΰκω (cf. Hom. ἰσχανάω ← ἰσχάνω ← ἴσχω 'hold fast').

[4] On this unusual aorist type, see Chantraine 2013:385; in all likelihood, this ἐρῡκακε/ο- was artificially formed by analogy to ἄγε/ο- : ἀγαγε/ο- (as Alan J. Nussbaum pointed out to me). Given this artificiality and the nonprosaic profile of the verb generally, it is explicable that the temporal augment, which in Homer happens to occur only in this reduplicated form (e.g., ἠρΰκακε, Il. 5.321), is written with <H>. As in marginal prosaic cases of augmented ἀπερΰκω (ἀπήρῡξα, Xen. An. 5.8.25; ἀπήρῡκον, Polyb. 16.1.3), the temporal augment with eta may be explained by supposing that this infrequent, synchronically vowel-initial item would be subject to the same augmentation as certain other vowel-initial verbs (e.g., ἐσθίω : ἤσθιον). Consequently, this kind of augment does not provide decisive evidence for the shape of the root historically.

Il. 11.48), the suppression of emotion (*Od.* 11.105), the entertainment or detainment of guests (*Il.* 6.217, *Od.* 4.594), the confinement of women to their quarters (*Od.* 19.16), the holding or warding off of enemy forces (*Il.* 15.297), and the staying or blocking of their weapons (*Il.* 21.594).[5] In the abstract, therefore, ἐρῠ́κω expresses the interposition of force separating an object from the domain to which it might move. Analysis of this conceptual image requires an etymological account. Though ἐρῡκ- is for Homer a root, there is clear internal and comparative evidence that the final segment was suffixal. The primary evidence for this analysis is the vestigial class of thematic presents characterized by a kappatic element (e.g., ὀλέκω 'destroy'; τήκω '[cause to] melt'). While descriptively a root extension, this element is better understood as a present-stem formant, for that is precisely its function in ὀλέκω, which, like ὄλλῡμι, serves as the imperfective counterpart to ὠλόμην : ὤλεσα. Similarly, τήκω, though synchronically classed as a simple thematic present to a root τηκ-/τακ-[6], clearly bears the same erstwhile suffix. If, therefore, ἐρῠ́κω is similarly explicable as a metanalyzed *-ke/o- present,[7] the question now concerns the base from which that present had been formed.

The best approach seems to be the internal reconstruction of a situation in which, like ὀλέκω, the ancestor of ἐρῠ́κω still served as a present stem corresponding to an akappatic paradigm of synchronically the same root. Despite Chantraine's derivation from (ϝ)ἐρύω 'drag',[8] whose initial digamma, short upsilon, and remote semantics make a connection with ἐρῠ́κω unlikely, it is generally agreed that the root was that of ἔρῡμαι 'guard, protect, ward off, check'.[9] At first glance, there are three reasons for this association: (1) Homeric ἔρῡμαι's lack of initial

---

[5] LSJ (= Liddell and Scott 1996): 693.

[6] E.g., ἐ-τάκ-ην : τακ-ερός 'tender' vs. Lat. *tā-bēs* 'decay', OCS *ta-jǫ* 'melt': *teh_2- 'tauen', LIV² (= Rix et al. 2001):616.

[7] A similar analysis, for example, may be assigned to Gothic *filhan* 'hide, conceal' (< *pel-ke/o-) beside Lat. *pellis* 'skin' (< *pel-n-i-), Old Saxon *filmen* 'skin, membrane', etc. (Pokorny 1959–1969: vol. 3, 803–804).

[8] Chantraine 2009:358.

[9] *LfgrE*: vol. 2, 720–722; Schwyzer 1939:702; Frisk 1960–1972: vol. 1, 568; Risch 1974:279. The form ἔρῡμαι is the only unattested instance of the verb used in this paper and is intended solely as a means of referring to the lexeme.

digamma,[10] (2) its frequently long upsilon (e.g., ἔρῦτο : ἐρῦκ-), and (3) its occasionally equivalent sense of prevention. Though each argument offers a promising hypothesis, the evidence is complex.

Like ἐρύ̆κω, the Homeric forms of ἔρῦμαι begin with a vowel that lacks the effects of digamma, but, unlike the forms of ἐρύ̆κω, those of ἔρῦμαι appear to ablaut. While this occurs most notably in its athematic present (ἔρῦτο : ῥύ̆ατ᾽, Il. 18.515, Od. 17.201; cf. ἔρυσθαι : ῥῦσθαι; invariant perfect: εἰρύ̆αται, Od. 16.463 : εἴρῦτο, Il. 16.542),[11] root allomorphy is also encountered in the thematic present (ἐρύεσθαι : ἐρύετο, Il. 6.403 : ῥύ̆ετ᾽, Il. 16.799) and sigmatic aorist (ἐρύ̆σατο, Il. 5.344 : ῥύ̆σατ᾽, Od. 23.244). Given the absence of digamma,[12] the only way to make sense of this ablaut historically is to acknowledge that the anlaut was *h. On this basis, we may provisionally reconstruct for Homer's trivially psilotic ἐρῦ- a radical preform *herū-/hrū-.

Though the length of the final *ū constitutes a problem for which a solution will have to be proposed,[13] we may observe for the moment that this *herū-, given its disyllabicity, necessarily reflects an overtly suffixed stem whose analysis requires the isolation of an etymon *ser- 'guard, watch',[14] the aniṭ character of which is supported by the length of the root vowel in the Avestan τομός-type adjective hāra- 'watching over'[15] (< *sor-ó-). According to Jasanoff, this root formed two primary presents, one of the radical molō type (*sór-e : *sér-r̥s 'kept watch', e.g., YAv. ni-šaŋharatū 'shall beware', nī haraitē 'guards', Myc. o-ro-me-no 'watching', ἐπὶ ὄρομαι 'watch over', ὄρει· φυλάσσει Hsch.), and the other with suffixal *-u- (cf. *térh₂-u-/tr̥h₂-u-´ 'overcome, cross' > Hitt. tarḫu- 'conquer', Ved. tarute 'attains to' : Ved. tū́rvati 'overcomes').[16] The primary evidence for the latter is Avestan ni-šhauruuaiti 'watches',

---

[10] Schulze 1892:325–327; Solmsen 1901:244–248.

[11] The term "present" here is merely morphological; the appearance of primary endings is post-Homeric (e.g., ἔρῦται, Ap. Rhod. 2.1208).

[12] "L'absence de digamma dans le mot grec constitue une difficulté grave" (Chantraine 2009:359).

[13] "La question de la longueur de l'υ de ἔρυμαι, ἐρύκω pose un problème inextricable" (Wathelet 1968:111).

[14] 'aufpassen auf, beschützen' LIV²:534; Chantraine 2009:358–359.

[15] Bartholomae 1904:1806.

[16] Jasanoff 2003:75, 142.

which, like the molō-type reflexes above, displays the usual transference of the h_2e-conjugation to thematic inflection. However, as displayed most clearly by Vedic *tarute* 'attains to' (*RV* 10.76.2),[17] there also appears to have been a tendency to retain athematic inflection, as the middle endings evolved (e.g., ῥῦσθαι 'ward off').[18] In either direction, the general consequence is the same: the stem's final segment was analyzed as a semantically void addition to the root or as a part of the root itself—an event whose occurrence at some stage of the protolanguage is especially evident from the fact that Avestan and Greek attest nominal derivatives whose root shape corresponds to the erstwhile present stem (e.g., YAv. *pasuš.hauruua-* 'sheepdog', ἔφορος/Hom. ἐπίουρος 'overseer' < second compound member *-sorṵ-o- 'oversight'; cf. τήκω : τακερός above).[19] Accordingly, besides the thematic present reflected in Avestan, it is reasonable to suppose that the language ancestral to Greek and Indo-Iranian also formed from the same secondary root *seru- an athematic middle of basically the same sense (i.e., *séru-to 'guarded').

This verb is provisionally the immediate preform of Homeric ἔρῦμαι. The problem, of course, is the upsilon, which is long in so many formal and metrical contexts[20] that it cannot be dismissed as mere metrical lengthening.[21] Most importantly, if ἐρῦκω, with an invariably

---

[17] It is, however, possible that this hapax was artistically generated after *tarutr̥-* 'overcomer' (Gotō 1987:164).

[18] Jasanoff 2003:142.

[19] Additional evidence of this secondary root may be found in Latin *servus* 'slave', which arguably reflects a radical *e*-grade possessive derivative *serṵ-ó-* (cf. *leuk-ó-* 'having light, clear' [: λευκός 'white'] ← *lóṵk-o-* 'light, clearing' [OE *léah* 'meadow', Lith. *laũkas* 'field', etc.]) of the τόμος-type substantive *sórṵ-o-* evident in the abovementioned compounds. As Nussbaum 2017:241 observes, the product of possessive derivation from verbal abstracts may also be used to refer to the theme/patient (e.g., δορός 'leather bag' < *dor-ó-* 'cut thing'). Accordingly, *servus* < *serṵ-ó-* might originally have meant 'overseen, kept', which accords with the apparently *newaḫḫi* factitive reflected by *servāre* 'save, preserve' and the substitutively dethematic *serṵ-ie/o-* 'cause to be overseen' (cf. καθαρός 'pure' → καθαίρω 'purify') possibly reflected by Umbrian *šeritu* 'observe'.

[20] For example, forms like ἐρῦετο, *Il.* 6.403 and the frequent ἔρῦτο would be unusual given that, in a sequence of shorts, the locus of lengthening is usually the initial syllable (e.g., ἠγάθεος 'most holy', cf. ἀγακλεής 'famous') (Chantraine 2013:100).

[21] While all Homeric instances of the form ἔρυτο contain a long upsilon, ἔρῠτ' occurs once at Hes. *Theog.* 304.

long upsilon, is recognized as the historical derivative of ἔρῡμαι, the length of the upsilon must be inherent in ἔρῡμαι's ancestor *herū-. Though *herū- cannot directly reflect *seru-, what renders the latter the best candidate is of course the meaning 'protect'. The aspect of protection expressed by *ser(u)- seems to have been vision as an agentive activity—a meaning clearly reflected in ὁράω (<< *sor-eh₂-(i̯)e/o- 'watch'; cf. It. *guardare* 'look at' ← Frankish *wardōn* 'guard'). Indeed, the sense of observation, rather than protection, is manifest at *Od.* 16.462–463, where Telemachus asks Eumaeus whether the suitors are still on watch for him (perf. εἰρύαται).[22] However, many instances of ἔρῡμαι are semantically more dynamic than the visual 'watch, guard'. For example, the verb may be predicated of armor or animate beings that protect or avert through physical interposition of some enveloping substance or phenomenon, such as the mist or darkness used by Iliadic gods to protect their battlefield favorites.[23] While an extension from 'watch (for)/guard (against)' to physical protection and aversion ('defend/fend off') is conceivable, the protective/aversive semantics seem somewhat stretched in light of ἔρῡμαι's expression of restraint, as when Athena brings Dawn to a halt to prolong Odysseus's night of reunion (*Od.* 23.243–244).[24] Such stretching of general protective/ aversive sense is also encountered in Odysseus's initial experiences on Scheria. After his traumatic arrival, the exhausted hero heaps upon himself as many leaves as to shelter two or three men:

... φύλλων γὰρ ἔην χύσις ἤλιθα πολλή,
ὅσσον τ᾽ ἠὲ δύω ἠὲ τρεῖς ἄνδρας ἔρυσθαι
ὥρηι χειμερίηι, εἰ καὶ μάλα περ χαλεπαίνοι.

Od. 5.483–485

---

[22] ἦ ῥ᾽ ἤδη μνηστῆρες ἀγήνορες ἔνδον ἔασιν | ἐκ λόχου, ἦ᾽ ἔτι μ᾽ αὖθ᾽ εἰρύαται οἴκαδ᾽ ἰόντα; "Are the haughty suitors already home from their ambush, or instead still on watch for me heading home?" (here and hereafter author's translation).

[23] καὶ τὸν μὲν μετὰ χερσὶν ἐρύσατο Φοῖβος Ἀπόλλων | κυανέηι νεφέληι (*Il.* 5.344–345). "And him between his hands did Phoebus Apollo protect in a dark cloud."

[24] νύκτα μὲν ἐν περάτηι δολιχὴν σχέθεν, Ἠῶ δ᾽ αὖτε | ῥῦσατ᾽ ἐπ᾽ Ὠκεανῶι χρυσόθρονον. "Night long at world's end did she hold in place, and Dawn whose throne is gold did she detain at Ocean's edge."

For there was a heap of leaves very plenteous, as much as
to shelter either two or three men in wintry season, even
if it should be very severe.

This act is described in a simile summarized with ὡς Ὀδυσεὺς φύλλοισι
καλύψατο ("so Odysseus covered himself with leaves," *Od.* 5.491). When
on the next day Odysseus is roused by the cry of Nausicaa's maidser-
vants, he uses leaves to *conceal* his genitals (ῥύσαιτο):

ὡς εἰπὼν θάμνων ὑπεδύσετο δῖος Ὀδυσσεύς,
ἐκ πυκινῆς δ' ὕλης πτόρθον κλάσε χειρὶ παχείηι
φύλλων, ὡς ῥύσαιτο περὶ χροῒ μήδεα φωτός.

Od. 6.127–129

Having so spoken did divine Odysseus get up from the
bushes, and from the thick wood broke with stout hand a
young branch of leaves, that it might cover round the skin
the hero's genitals.

Though this use of ἔρῡμαι is arguably an amusing adaptation of battlefield language,[25] the eligibility of ἔρῡμαι's meaning 'protect' as the
source of a conception whose target is concealment (or shelter, *Od.*
5.484) requires a conceptual affinity with the basic act of covering.[26]
If the formally problematic *seru- entirely underlies the semantics of
ἔρῡμαι, one would have to postulate a degree of extension to encompass not only the physically protective meanings but the physical,
nonprotective sense 'stop' evident in Athena's forestalling of Dawn (*Od.*
23.243–244). Demanding such extension seems excessive.

Beyond the length of ἔρῡμαι's upsilon, the formal vindication of
the suspicion that we are dealing with more than just *seru- is the fact
that outside Homer there is definite evidence for initial /w/ in descriptively the same Greek verb. The most ancient evidence is Mycenaean
u-ru-to (PY An 657), which refers to watchers (*e-pi-ko-wo*) stationed on
the coast near Pylos. This form, the only example of the athematic stem

---

[25] Garvie 1994:114.

[26] For recent treatment of conceptual metaphor theory applied to Homeric poetry, see
Zanker 2019.

outside Epic, is generally interpreted as a third plural present indicative /wruntoi/.[27] Beyond the usual obscurities of Mycenaean, what is clear with respect to ἔρῡμαι is the identity of the meaning 'watch/guard' and the difference in anlaut. This difference is also found in Pamphylian, which attests a nominal derivative <ιρυμάλι>[28] 'surety' (cf. ῥῦσιον 'id.' [*Il.* 11.674] and ῥῦμα 'protection'), whose initial segment is represented by a letter that necessarily represents the reflex of */w/.[29] The evidence from Aeolic is even more compelling. A hitherto neglected form is εὐρύσαο 'you saved', used by Alcaeus to describe his brother's heroic service as a mercenary in the Middle East:[30]

> ἄεθλον μέγαν, <u>εὐρύσαο</u> δ' ἐκ πόνων,
> κτένναις ἄνδρα μαχαίταν βασιληΐων
> παλάσταν ἀπυλείποντα μόναν ἴαν
> παχέων ἀπὺ πέμπων …

Alc. 350.4–7

A great feat, and <u>you saved</u> (them) from troubles, having slain a fighting man whose height in royal palms was but one short of five cubits.

Though Alcaeus also uses Ionic (i.e., Epic) forms of ῥύομαι (e.g., ῥύεσθαι, 129.20), whose anlaut, if genuine Aeolic, would otherwise be represented with <β> (cf. βραϊδίως, 129.22), the form εὐρύσαο makes clear that the Aeolic root began with */w/—a fact equally clear from the

---

[27] See Chantraine 2009:358 and Beekes 2010:466. If this interpretation is correct, one would have to suppose that Mycenaean has analogically introduced /-ntoi/, for, as Risch 1958:415 notes, Homeric ῥῦατ' reveals the regular treatment. This note may be refined with the observation that the appearance of the allomorph -ατ' (i.e., -ατο), unless analyzed as a later generalization, is only possible because of an erstwhile laryngeal in the onset (i.e., *-u.h_x-n̥.to(i̯)). Since, as discussed below, the long upsilon must result from a laryngeal in the coda of the syllable preceding the desinence (i.e., *-uh_x-to(i̯)), the root allomorph of verse-initial ῥῦατ' is a metrically useful replacement for the expected ῥῠ- (: ἔρῠτο).

[28] *CIG* (= Boechk et al. 1828–1859):4342c2.

[29] Lejeune 1972:157–158.

[30] Text of Lobel and Page 1955:272.

inscriptional attestation of the personal name Εὐρυσίλαος on Lesbos.[31] Mention should also be made of the Thessalian toponym Εὐρύμεναί (e.g., Ap. Rhod. 1.597),[32] which, like the Boeotian Ἀλαλκομεναί (: ἀλεξε/ο- : ἀλαλκε/ο- 'defend'), appears to reflect the tendency to refer to settlements as protective positions (cf. NHG TN *Landshut* : *Hut* 'keeping, care, guard' < OHG *huota* 'id.'). Finally, Apollonius Dyscolus (*Adv.* 157.20) mentions βρυτῆρες as Aeolic for ῥῡτῆρες 'reins' (*Il.* 16.475). Although this word is often connected with (ϝ)ἐρύω 'drag',[33] it is at least equally likely that ῥῡτήρ is derived from ἔρῡμαι in light of its preventive/retentive sense (cf. Fr. *rêne* < VL *retina(m)* ← *retinēre*). In sum, whereas Homeric ἔρῡμαι only provides positive evidence for an Ionic root *herū-, other dialects point to *werū-.

As it turns out, comparative evidence can only support the latter. The most prominently associated set of forms is the family of Vedic *varūtár-* 'protector' (: *várūtha-* 'protection' : *várūtrī-*[34] 'protectress'). Like the reflexes of *seru- 'guard', Vedic *varū-* strongly suggests an erstwhile *u*-present, but, unlike *seru-, the *set* character of the primary root cannot be excluded. Given the unwontedness of /uː/ in the protolanguage, it is preferable to take Proto-Greek *werū- and Vedic *varū- back to an immediate *u̯eruh$_x$- 'protect'. As Rasmussen argues, the best way to account for this preform is to suppose that the outcome of laryngeal metathesis from *u̯erh$_x$-u- was reanalyzed as the root.[35] Accordingly, one may isolate an original root *u̯erh$_x$-, the primary evidence for which are the reflexes of Proto-Germanic *warjaną 'hinder,

[31] Cf. Ἐρυσίλαος, Chantraine 2009:359. Specht 1932:36–37's claim of remodeling on the basis of the compositional form εὐρυ- 'broad' is untenable especially in light of non-onomastic evidence of εὐρυ(σι)- as the dialectal variant of ἐρυ(σι)- (e.g., ἐρυσίπτολις, *Il.* 6.305 : εὐρύσαο). For an etymological attempt to associate εὐρύς and ἔρῡμαι, see de Lamberterie 1990: vol. 1, 232–243.

[32] Another name for this settlement was Ἐρυμναί (Str. 9.5.22), which is clearly derived from ἐρυμνός 'fortified' (Hes. +). This adjective is in turn identifiable as a possessive derivative of ἔρῡμα (*Il.* 4.137), which denotes protection or any kind of protective means.

[33] Chantraine 2009:360; Beekes 2010:468; cf. NHG *Zügel* : *ziehen* 'draw'.

[34] The entry in Grassmann 1996 has been erroneously printed with a short *u*. This error undermines Klingenschmitt 1982:233's proposal that the *ū* of *varūtár-* is attributable to rhythmic lengthening. I thank Benjamin Fortson for this point.

[35] Rasmussen 1989:100; i.e., HI > IH / C(R)_C; Weiss 2020:123–124.

defend'.[36] Given the formal ambiguities of this iterative-causative (i.e., *(h$_x$)u̯or(h$_x$)-éi̯e/o-),[37] there appear to be three possibilities for the etymology of the root. In principle, *warjaną may be derived from *u̯er- 'watch'.[38] If, however, we follow this course, we face the same problem of requiring substantial extension into the domain of physical protection and prevention. In light of this domain, another possibility, as proposed by Kroonen, is *h$_x$u̯er-.[39] This laryngeal-initial aniṭ root, which Lubotsky has plausibly reconstructed largely on the basis of Indo-Iranian and Balto-Slavic evidence (e.g., Vedic ápāvr̥ti- 'opening', ápāvr̥ta- 'opened' : vr̥ṇóti 'covers', Av. vərənao- 'id.', Lith. atvérti 'open', OCS zavrěti 'shut'),[40] has the advantage of accounting for the more dynamic meaning of the Germanic forms. Nevertheless, as we shall discuss below, although the semantic sphere of covering or enclosure is an apt domain for that of protection and restraint, the development of these meanings would require an assumption rendered unnecessary if we operate with a *u̯erh$_x$- in which those meanings are already present. In other words, the range of attested meanings, which involve both defense and prevention, makes a connection with our *u̯erh$_x$- a real

[36] E.g., Goth. warjan 'κωλύω', ON verja 'defend', OE werian 'hinder, check, restrain', Orel 2003:449.
[37] Vedic vāráyate 'hält auf, hemmt' under the entry 1. *u̯er- 'aufhalten, (ab)wehren' (LIV²:684), unless the length of its radical vowel is analogical, would reflect the iterative-causative to *h$_x$u̯er- 'einschließen, stecken, hineintun' (LIV²:227) or 1. *u̯el- 'einschließen, verhüllen' (LIV²:674).
[38] LIV²:685, 3. *u̯er- 'beobachten, wahrnehmen'; Lat. vereor 'fear', Goth. wars 'on guard', etc. Likely derived from this root is PGmc. *warđaz (Goth. daurawards 'doorkeeper', OE weard 'guard', etc.), from which was formed *warđōjaną (ON varđa 'guard', OE weardian, etc.). According to Orel 2003:448, *warđaz reflects a *u̯or-tó- which he designates as a participle. Given its radical o-grade, oxytony, and agentive semantics, this *u̯or-tó- may be analyzed as a possessive derivative of an accented radical o-grade abstract *u̯órto- derived from the -tó- verbal adjective to *u̯er- (cf. *n̥s-tó- [→ *r̥s-to- > Ved. ásta- n. 'home'] → *nós-to- [> νόστος 'return home'], García Ramón 2016, Höfler 2019). Otherwise, one would have to invoke a *u̯orđʰo- of unclear morphological analysis.
[39] Kroonen 2013:274; *h$_x$u̯er- 'einschließen, stecken, hineintun' LIV²:227.
[40] Lubotsky 2000:317–318. In particular, Lubotsky reconstructs *h$_2$u̯er- on the basis of comparison with ἀείρω 'raise'. Insofar as ἀείρω is understood as a verb of joining or attachment—a sense present in composition (cf. συναείρω 'bind together', Il. 10.499, συνήορος 'conjoined', Od. 8.99)—the reconstruction of *h$_2$u̯er-, subsequently supported by ἄορον· μοχλόν, πυλῶνα, θυρωρόν (Hsch.), may be justified (Beekes 2010:24).

possibility. The question of course is what this root and its secondary variant *$\underline{u}eruh_x$*- actually meant.

In light of the Greek, Indic, and Germanic evidence adduced so far, *$\underline{u}erh_x$-/$\underline{u}eruh_x$*- must have had a sense so physical as to encompass the attested meanings of protection and restraint. Given that both actions involve the imposition of a boundary, we may hypothesize that the root expressed some sort of closure or confinement. There are at least two sources of evidence for this meaning.

Evidence may be drawn from Vedic *ūrvá-* (*RV* +), which generally designates an enclosure for water, cattle, and even a prison for people.[41] Though traditionally derived from *vṛṇóti* 'covers',[42] the *aniṭ* character of this verb excludes such a derivation. For this reason, *$\underline{u}rh_x\underline{u}ó$*- in the sense of 'enclosed space' is a possible preform parsimoniously interpretable as an early derivative of our secondary root *$\underline{u}erh_x u$*- 'enclose, confine' (cf. *$g^w ih_3\underline{u}$-ó-* 'alive' ← *$g^w ih_3\underline{u}$-e/o-* << *$g^w ih_3$-u-* 'live'), whose prevocalic allomorph precluded laryngeal metathesis.[43]

Nevertheless, the etymological indeterminacy effected by the merger of the liquids in Indo-Iranian dialects requires particular caution when dealing with *ūrvá-* and possibly related material. In principle, *$\underline{u}l̥h_x\underline{u}ó$*- is also a possible preform. Assessment of *$\underline{u}l̥h_x\underline{u}ó$*- relies

---

[41] *sám anyā́ yánty úpa yanty anyā́ḥ samānám ūrváṃ nadyàḥ pṛṇanti | tám ū śúciṃ śúcayo dīdivā́ṃsam apā́ṃ nápātam pári tasthur ā́paḥ* || (*RV.* 2.35.3). "Some come together; others go directly (to the sea): (but) it is the same <u>vessel</u> that the rivers fill. The gleaming, shining Child of the Waters do the gleaming waters surround." *ná tvā gabhīrā́ḥ puruhūta síndhur nā́drayaḥ pári ṣánto varanta | itthā́ sákhibhya iṣitó yád indrá dṛḷhā́ṃ cid árujo gávyam ūrvám* || (*RV.* 3.32.16). "Not the deep river nor the surrounding peaks could obstruct you, much invoked one, when impelled just so from your comrades, Indra, you broke into the cattle <u>enclosure</u> though it was firmly fastened." *mahás cid agna énaso abhī́ka ūrvā́d devā́nām utá mártyānām | mā́ te sákhāyaḥ sádam íd riṣāma yáchā tokā́ya tánayāya śáṃ yóḥ* || (*RV.* 4.12.5) "(Release us) from even a great offense in close quarters, Agni, from the <u>enclosure</u> [=imprisoning] [sic] of gods and of mortals. Let us, your comrades, never be harmed. Extend luck and lifetime to kith and kin" (text of Aufrecht 1877; translation by Jamison and Brereton 2014).

[42] Mayrhofer 1986–2001: vol. 1, 245.

[43] Though Lithuanian *ùrvas* 'hole, burrow, cave' (cf. Latvian *urva* 'den') is sometimes connected with Vedic *ūrvá-* (Derksen 2015:483; with doubts, Smoczyński 2018: vol. 4, 1570–1571 with references), the phonological, morphological, and semantic indeterminacy of these Baltic data is prohibitive—an assessment for which I thank Miguel Villanueva Svensson.

especially on Greek data. In light of the forms of εἴλω 'press, shut' (e.g., ἔλσαν 'they pressed', *Il.* 11.413; ἐέλμεθα 'we are confined', *Il.* 24.662; ἄλεν 'they crowded in', *Il.* 22.12; cf. εἶλαρ 'defensive wall'), the *aniṭ* root listed under the entry 1. *$ṷel$-* 'einschließen, verhüllen'[44] is certainly justified. The second *$ṷel$-* 'drehen, rollen'[45] is another story. While Latin *volvō* 'roll' and Greek εἰλύω 'wrap' provide evidence that there was a secondary root whose originally final segment was the suffix of a *u*-present, it is doubtful that this present had been formed to 1. *$ṷel$-* or any other *aniṭ* root. Since the Homeric forms of εἰλύω 'enfold, enwrap' almost entirely display a long upsilon (# εἰλῠᾶται, *Od.* 20.352 excepted), it is likely that there was originally a *$ṷelh_x$-* 'wind, wrap' from which a *u*-present (> secondary root) had been derived. This suspicion is corroborated by the analysis of Latin *volva* (*vulva*) 'womb', which de Vaan connects with *volvō* in the sense of 'envelop'.[46] Unless this connection was sufficient for analogical interference, the sequence *-lw-* should point to an erstwhile intervening syllable. By comparison to *salvus* 'safe', whose etymon points to the application of the *palma* rule (< *$*salawo$-* < *$*slh_2uo$-*),[47] and *sollus* 'whole', whose etymon displays the Saussure Effect (*$*solwo$-* < *$*sol(h_2)ṷo$-*),[48] it is preferable to derive *volva* from a Proto-Italic *$*welawā$-* (< *$*ṷélh_xṷeh_2$-*), given the inoperability of a radical *o*-grade preform (i.e., *$*ṷólh_xṷeh_2$-* > †*volla*). Similarly, a radical zero grade cannot account for *volva*, though under the accent a zero grade may in fact explain *valvae* 'door-folds' (< *$*walawā$-* < *$*ṷl̥h_xṷeh_2$*, cf. *salvus* 'safe'). Accordingly, if *volva* and *valvae* point to radically variant dethematic *h_2*-stems, there is a distinct possibility that Vedic *ūrvá-* reflects that thematic base (i.e., *$*ṷl̥h_xṷó$-* 'enveloping').

More reliable evidence for *$*ṷerh_xu$-* in the sense 'enclose' may be drawn from the verbal adjective ῥυτός. Occurring but twice in the formula # ῥυτοῖσιν λάεσσι (*Od.* 6.267 and *Od.* 14.10), this epithet is semantically mysterious, as one may judge from the variety of

---

[44] LIV²:674.
[45] LIV²:675.
[46] De Vaan 2008:689.
[47] Höfler 2017; Weiss 2020:119.
[48] Nussbaum 1997.

translations.[49] In the first instance, ῥυτοῖσιν λάεσσι refers to the stone-fitted Phaeacian ἀγορή:

> ἔνθα δέ τέ σφ᾽ ἀγορὴ καλὸν Ποσιδήϊον ἀμφίς,
> ῥυτοῖσιν λάεσσι κατωρυχέεσσ᾽ ἀραρυῖα.

Od. 6.266–267

And there is their meeting ground round about Poseidon's fair shrine, fitted with quarried, <u>closely set</u> stones.

Though Garvie's rendering presupposes derivation from (ϝ)ἐρύω 'drag',[50] he observes that "the description is rather of the seating, or more probably of the wall that enclosed the ἀγορή."[51] This latter interpretation is supported by the second instance of the epithet, which describes an enclosure that Eumaeus has built to surround his hilltop αὐλή:

> τὸν δ᾽ ἄρ᾽ ἐνὶ προδόμωι πῦρ᾽ ἥμενον, ἔνθά οἱ αὐλή
> ὑψηλὴ δέδμητο περισκέπτωι ἐνὶ χώρωι,
> καλή τε μεγάλη τε, περίδρομος, ἥν ῥα συβώτης
> αὐτὸς δείμαθ᾽ ὕεσσιν ἀποιχομένοιο ἄνακτος,
> νόσφιν δεσποίνης καὶ Λαέρταο γέροντος,
> ῥυτοῖσιν λάεσσι καὶ ἐθρίγκωσεν ἀχέρδῳ

Od. 14.5–10

[Odysseus] found him sitting down in the forecourt, where by him was built a lofty courtyard, at a site seen on all sides, both big and beautiful, running round, which the swineherd himself had built for the pigs of his master gone away, apart from his lady and the old man Laertes, with <u>closely set</u> stones and coped it with wild pear.

---

[49] E.g., 'dragged', Garvie 1994:148; 'heavy', Wilson 2018:205; 'quarried', LSJ. Regarding this final example, I note that the old association with Latin *rūta caesa* 'timber and minerals of an estate' is formally untenable as this would require a relation to the cognate of ὀρύσσω 'dig', whose preform began with *h_3.

[50] This likely erroneous view is shared by Hesychius: ῥυτοί· ἑλκυστοί. λίθοι μεγάλοι, διὰ τὸ μέγεθος οὐ δυνάμενοι βασταχθῆναι.

[51] Garvie 1994:148.

In both passages, it is the present arrangement of the stones, not how they came to be there, that is important; the wall depends on stones held in place by their being fitted together and closely set.[52] This meaning may be compared to the sense expressed by πυκινός/ πυκνός 'compact', likewise used of stones. In the simile at *Il.* 16.212 describing the compact ranks of the Myrmidons, the phrase πυκινοῖσι λίθοισι is used to refer to the means by which the wall of a house is fitted together. At *Il.* 24.798 πυκνοῖσιν λάεσσι refers to the means by which the grave containing Hector's bones is covered. In both cases, πυκινός/πυκνός expresses an essential feature of an enclosure: that the material forming the covering or enclosure be sufficiently close together to keep some things in and others out (cf. πυκάζω 'cover closely' [Hom. +]).[53] It is no doubt for this reason that πυκινός may be attributed to an enclosure itself rather than merely the means by which it is an enclosure (e.g., δόμος, *Od.* 7.88; θάλαμος, *Od.* 23.229).[54] For another illustration of this "close" association in another root, we may observe that in the simile at *Il.* 5.89 describing a torrent rushing across a flooded plain,[55] the γέφυραι 'dams, dikes, embankments' are characterized as ἐεργμέναι, which in this case can only mean 'firm, compact' rather than 'confined' or 'enclosed' as would be expected of the perfect mediopassive participle to ἐέργω 'shut'.

If we compare the use of πυκινός/πυκνός and, in particular, of the participle ἐεργμένος to that of the verbal adjective ῥυτός 'close-set', the sense of ῥυτός is arguably attributable to a slight extension from 'covered, (en)closed' to 'close'—a semantic development actually

---

[52] Indeed, that such arrangement restrains them from dilapidation is credible in light of ῥῦτά (Hes. [*Sc.*] 308), whose meaning 'reins' arguably arises from the substantival use of ῥυτός in the sense that the horse is held back by things that are themselves 'held back' by the rider (i.e., restraints).

[53] In light of this sense of density, it may be possible to connect Hitt. u̯arḫui- / u̯arḫuu̯ai- 'raw, rough; unshaven; leafy; covered with forest', which Kloekhorst 2008:960–961 reconstructs as *u̯érh₂/₃u-i-, *urh₂/₃u-éi-s (i.e., *u̯rh₃u̯-i-), with the *u̯erhₓ-u- we are discussing.

[54] If Pokorny 1959–1969: vol. 3, 849 is correct in connecting the family of πυκνός with ἄμπυξ 'diadem, snood' and Avestan pusā- 'headband' under a root *puḱ- 'zusammendrängen, eng umschließen', the use of πυκνός and πυκάζω would be entirely explicable.

[55] τὸν δ' οὔτ' ἄρ τε γέφυραι ἐεργμέναι ἰσχανόωσιν. "Nor do the compact dikes hold it off."

manifest in the adjective *close* itself (← OFr. *clos* < Lat. *clausus* : *claudere* 'shut'). Accordingly, it seems entirely reasonable that ῥυτός reflects a *$\u{u}ruh_x$-tó-* derived from the secondary root *$\u{u}eruh_x$-* in the sense 'enclosed, confined, retained'.

On the basis of this *$\u{u}eruh_x$-*, much of the form, meaning, and relationship between ἔρῡμαι and ἐρῡ́κω can be explained if we recognize the general ease with which verbs of containing, enclosing, or covering develop the sense of restraint. For example, as discussed by Watkins,[56] Latin *arceō* developed from a verb of enclosure and containment[57] to one of prevention (cf. ἀρκέω 'ward off', Arm. argel 'prevention')— a pathway perfectly paralleled within Greek by εἴργω,[58] which in Homer, as discussed above, signifies enclosure but in Attic-Ionic prose has become synonymous with κωλύω 'hinder, prevent'. Moreover, Lubotsky notes that *vṛṇóti* has also developed the sense 'check, stop'.[59] Accordingly, whatever the exact meaning of *$\u{u}erh_x$-u-*, especially in relation to the formally and semantically similar *$h_x\u{u}er$-* (or *$h_2\u{u}er$-*) discussed above, it is highly likely that a semantic sphere encompassing confinement, enclosure, covering, and containment conditioned ramifications not only into the domain of 'protect, defend, avert', but also that of 'prevent, check, stop, hinder, restrain, detain'.

I therefore propose that in the first instance there was a root *$\u{u}erh_x$-* 'cover, enclose' that formed a *u*-present. Given that this category was originally characterized by *e* : zero root ablaut and the endings of the *h_2e*-series,[60] it is conceivable that *$\u{u}érh_x$-u-e : $\u{u}rh_x$-u-ér*, a protomiddle with the autobenefactive sense 'cover (for oneself), protect', was involved in the initial stage of a series of morphological developments, which, as argued by Jasanoff, affected *u*-presents generally.[61] Regarding the Pre-PIE *$\u{u}érh_x$-u-e : $\u{u}rh_x$-u-ér* specifically, we may suppose that the first of those developments was the bifurcation of our *$\u{u}érh_x$-u-/$\u{u}rh_x$-u-´* into a *h_2e*-conjugation active *$\u{u}érh_x$-u-e : $\u{u}rh_x$-u-ént* and a middle with

[56] Watkins 1970.

[57] Cf. Lat. *arca* 'box', *arx* 'Schloß', and Hitt. *ḫarzi* 'holds' (: *h_2erk*- 'halten' LIV²:273).

[58] As Jenny Strauss Clay has pointed out to me, ἐέργοι is a variant of καλύπτοι (Hes. *Theog.* 127).

[59] Lubotsky 2000:315.

[60] Jasanoff 2003:141–142.

[61] Jasanoff 2022/2023.

e-grade of the root, represented most often by the third singular *u̯érh$_x$-u-to 'protected'. Since this form would have been both frequent and subject to laryngeal metathesis resulting in *u̯éruh$_x$-to, it conceivably contributed to speakers' reanalysis of the root as a *u̯eruh$_x$- whose older active *u̯érh$_x$u̯-e : u̯ruh$_x$-ént (<< *u̯r̥h$_x$-u̯-ént),[62] now no longer that of a u-present, was renewed as a *u̯réu̯h$_x$-t : u̯ruh$_x$-ént corresponding to a new middle *u̯ruh$_x$-to : u̯ruh$_x$-n̥to (: ῥῦτο· ἐρύσατο, ἔσωσεν Hsch. : Myc. u-ru-to, Hom. ῥῦατ'), even as the old middle *u̯éruh$_x$-to, interpretable as deponent in accordance with Grestenberger's analysis,[63] continued to exist as a bearer of an older root allomorph.[64] It is arguably this allomorph that was selected for the formation of a *-ḱe/o- present[65] *u̯éruh$_x$-ḱe/o- 'put a lid on, restrain', the derivational transparency of which was in all likelihood preserved in Proto-Greek (*werū-ke/o- : *w(e)rū-, cf. again ὀλέκω : ὠλόμην : ὤλεσα).

Beside this *w(e)rū- and its derivative *werū-ke/o-, Proto-Greek must also have inherited the reflex of *ser-u- 'guard, watch',[66] which, as an original u-present protomiddle *sér-u̯-e : sr̥-u̯-ér, would also have had root ablaut and been renewed, in part, as an athematic middle, namely, a *sér-u-to eventually reanalyzed as a *séru-to (: ἔρῠτ' [Hes. Theog. 304]) derived from a root *seru- 'guard'. The reflex of this *seru-, namely, *heru-, would have strongly resembled *werū- in form as well as in meaning (*werū-to 'protected' : *heru-to 'guarded'). In the language ancestral to the variety of Ionic contributory to the Kunstsprache, this resemblance conditioned a conflation characterized by replacement

[62] Despite the lack of direct evidence for this active, it is, as already noted by Peters 1980:94, a fundamentally necessary postulate.

[63] Grestenberger 2016:123–125.

[64] I owe this point to Jay Jasanoff.

[65] The palatal quality of this morph's first segment is likely if one considers the ubiquitous *-sḱe/o- a hybrid of the sigmatic and kappatic present (Jasanoff 2003:133–134).

[66] Mention should also be made of the proposal of Hackstein 2002:123–131, who attempts to include all of the forms discussed here (i.e., ἔρῦτο, ὄρονται, etc.) in the set of reflexes of a *su̯erh₃- of unspecified meaning. Beside the invocation of the marginal metathesis observed in τρυ-φάλεια (< *kʷtru- < *kʷtur- 'four'; *sruh₃- < *su̯erh₃-) and the assumption of numerous analogies, the proposal severs the clear relationship with varūtár- and does not assess the evidence needed to disprove an originally */w/-initial root. The proposal of an original *su̯er-, which Bader 1971 argues to underlie both *ser- 'watch, guard' and *u̯er- 'observe', is similarly problematic.

of anlaut and retention of quantitative variation in *werū-'s stem-final vowel. Since the *herū-[67] of the resulting *herū-to was still interpretable as the base of the *-ke/o- present, the analogical anlaut replacement that had created ἔρῡμαι's ancestor also produced *herū-ke/o-, the immediate preform of Epic ἐρῠ́κω.

CORNELL UNIVERSITY

WORKS CITED

Aufrecht, Theodor. 1877. *Die Hymnen des Rigveda*. Vol 1. 2nd ed. Bonn.

Bader, Françoise. 1971. "Vocabulaire et idéologie tripartite des Indo-Européens: La racine *swer- 'veiller sur' en grec." *Bulletin de la Société de Linguistique de Paris* 66:139–211.

Bartholomae, Christian. 1904. *Altiranisches Wörterbuch*. Strasbourg.

Beekes, Robert. 2010. *Etymological Dictionary of Greek*. 2 vols. Leiden.

Boechk, August, et al., eds. 1828–1859. *Corpus inscriptionum Graecarum: Auctoritate et impensis Academiae Litterarum Regiae Borussicae*. 4 vols. Berlin.

Chantraine, Pierre. 2009. *Dictionnaire étymologique de la langue grecque: Histoire des mots*. 2nd ed. Paris.

———. 2013. *Grammaire homérique*. Vol. 1, *Phonétique et morphologie*. New ed. Paris.

Derksen, Rick. 2015. *Etymological Dictionary of the Baltic Inherited Lexicon*. Leiden.

Frisk, Hjalmar. 1960–1972. *Griechisches etymologisches Wörterbuch*. 3 vols. Heidelberg.

García Ramón, José Luis. 2016. "Les substantifs du type νόστος, φόρτος, χόρτος en grec et leur préhistoire." In *Nouveaux acquis sur la formation des noms en grec ancien: Actes du Colloque international,*

---

[67] We should also note that the shape of the e-grade root appears to have differed in other dialects. As discussed above, the strong form of the radical morph is εὐρυ- in what may be termed Aeolic (εὐρύσαο, Εὐρυσίλαος). Accordingly, one might suppose that, while Proto-Attic-Ionic (vel sim.) simply generalized the full grade of *heru- : hru-, the "Aeolic" version of the conflation may have consisted in the application of the first syllable of *heru- to the weak form of *werū- : wru- (i.e., *hewruto, cf. Εὐρῠμεναί).

Université de Rouen, ERIAC, 17–18 octobre 2013, ed. Alain Blanc and Daniel Petit, 203–224. Leuven and Paris.

Garvie, Alexander F. 1994. *Homer. Odyssey VI–VIII.* Cambridge.

Gotō, Toshifumi. 1987. *Die 'I. Präsensklasse' im Vedischen: Untersuchung der vollstufigen thematischen Wurzelpräsentia.* Vienna.

Grassmann, Hermann. 1996. *Wörterbuch zum Rig-Veda.* 6th ed. Wiesbaden.

Grestenberger, Laura. 2016. "Reconstructing Proto-Indo-European Deponents." *Indo-European Linguistics* 4:98–149.

Hackstein, Olav. 2002. *Die Sprachform der homerischen Epen.* Wiesbaden.

Höfler, Stefan. 2017. "Observations on the Palma Rule." *Pallas* 103:15–23.

———. 2019. "*Story of O*: On a Peculiar Substantivization Type in PIE." Paper delivered at the Fifth Indo-European Research Colloquium, Leiden University, March 21–22, 2019.

Jacoby, Felix. 1923–1958. *Die Fragmente der griechischen Historiker.* Berlin and Leiden.

Jamison, Stephanie W., and Joel P. Brereton, trans. 2014. *The Rigveda: The Earliest Religious Poetry of India.* Vol. 1. Oxford.

Jasanoff, Jay H. 2003. *Hittite and the Indo-European Verb.* Oxford.

———. 2022/2023. "PIE *$g^wíh_3 u̯e/o$- 'live', u-presents, and the Prehistory of the Thematic Conjugation." *Die Sprache* 55:61–81.

Klingenschmitt, Gert. 1982. *Das altarmenische Verbum.* Wiesbaden.

Kloekhorst, Alwin. 2008. *Etymological Dictionary of the Hittite Inherited Lexicon.* Leiden.

Kroonen, Guus. 2013. *Etymological Dictionary of Proto-Germanic.* Leiden.

Lamberterie, Charles de. 1990. *Les adjectifs grecs en -υς: Sémantique et comparaison.* 2 vols. Louvain-la-Neuve.

Lejeune, Michel. 1972. *Phonétique historique du mycénien et du grec ancien.* Paris.

Liddell, Henry George, and Robert Scott. 1996. *A Greek-English Lexicon: With a Revised Supplement.* 9th ed. Oxford.

Lobel, Edgar, and Denys Lionel Page. 1955. *Poetarum Lesbiorum fragmenta.* Oxford. Reprinted with corrections (Oxford, 1968).

Lubotsky, Alexander. 2000. "The Vedic Root *vr̥*- 'to Cover' and Its Present." In *Indoarisch, Iranisch, und die Indogermanistik: Arbeitstagung der Indogermanischen Gesellschaft vom 2. bis 5. Oktober 1997*

18   Andrew Merritt

in *Erlangen*, ed. Bernhard Forssman and Robert Plath, 315–325. Wiesbaden.

Mayrhofer, Manfred. 1986–2001. *Etymologisches Wörterbuch des Altindoarischen*. 3 vols. Heidelberg.

Nussbaum, Alan J. 1997. "The 'Saussure Effect' in Latin and Italic." In *Sound Law and Analogy: Papers in Honor of Robert S. P. Beekes on the Occasion of his 60th Birthday*, ed. Alexander Lubotsky, 181–203. Amsterdam.

———. 2017. "Agentive and Other Derivatives of 'τόμος-Type' Nouns." In *Verbal Adjectives and Participles in Indo-European Languages / Adjectifs verbaux et participes dans les langues indo-européennes: Proceedings of the Conference of the Society for Indo-European Studies (Indogermanische Gesellschaft), Paris, 24th to 26th September 2014*, ed. Claire Le Feuvre, Daniel Petit, and Georges-Jean Pinault, 233–266. Bremen.

Orel, Vladimir. 2003. *A Handbook of Germanic Etymology*. Leiden.

Peters, Martin. 1980. *Untersuchungen zur Vertretung der indogermanischen Laryngale im Griechischen*. Vienna.

Pokorny, Julius. 1959–1969. *Indogermanisches etymologisches Wörterbuch*. 2 vols. Bern.

Rasmussen, Jens Elmegård. 1989. *Studien zur Morphophonemik der indogermanischen Grundsprache*. Innsbruck.

Risch, Ernst. 1958. "L'interprétation de la série des tablettes caractérisées par le mot o-ka (PY AN 519, 654, 656, 657, 661)." *Athenaeum*, n.s., 36:40–65.

———. 1974. *Wortbildung der homerischen Sprache*. 2nd ed. Berlin.

Rix, Helmut et al. 2001. *Lexikon der indogermanischen Verben: Die Wurzeln und ihre Primärstammbildungen*. 2nd ed. Wiesbaden.

Schulze, Guilelmus [Wilhelm]. 1892. *Quaestiones epicae*. Gütersloh.

Schwyzer, Eduard. 1939. *Griechische Grammatik*. Vol. 1, *Allgemeiner Teil: Lautlehre, Wortbildung, Flexion*. Munich.

Smoczyński, Wojciech. 2018. *Lithuanian Etymological Dictionary*. 5 vols. Berlin.

Snell, Bruno et al. 1955–2010. *Lexikon des frühgriechischen Epos*. 25 vols. Göttingen.

Solmsen, Felix. 1901. *Untersuchungen zur griechischen Laut- und Verslehre.* Strasbourg.

Specht, Franz. 1932. "Beiträge zur griechischen Grammatik." *Zeitschrift für vergleichende Sprachforschung auf dem Gebiete der indogermanischen Sprachen* 59, no.3/4:31–131.

Vaan, Michiel de. 2008. *Etymological Dictionary of Latin and the Other Italic Languages.* Leiden.

Wathelet, Paul. 1968. "Les verbs ἐρύω et ἔρυμαι en mycénien et dans les formules de l'épopée grecque." *In Studia Mycenaea: Proceedings of the Mycenaean Symposium, Brno, April, 1966,* ed. Antonín Bartoněk, 105–111. Brno.

Watkins, Calvert. 1970. "On the Family of *arceō*, ἀρκέω and Hittite ḫark-." *Harvard Studies in Classical Philology* 74:67–74.

Weiss, Michael. 2020. *Outline of the Historical and Comparative Grammar of Latin.* 2nd ed. Ann Arbor.

West, Martin L. 2011. *Homerus. Ilias.* Vol. 1, *Rhapsodiae I–XII.* Reprint. Berlin.

———. 2017. *Homerus. Odyssea.* Berlin.

Wilson, Emily, trans. 2018. *The Odyssey.* New York.

Zanker, Andreas T. 2019. *Metaphor in Homer: Time, Speech, and Thought.* Cambridge.

VOWEL LENGTHENING IN ATTIC PRIMARY COMPARATIVES

GEORGIOS KOSTOPOULOS

I. BACKGROUND AND PREVIOUS PROPOSALS

A S A RULE, comparative adjectives of the type βελτίων and θάττων contained a long -ῑ-/root vowel in Attic, but a short one in Ionic and other Greek dialects.[1] The long vowel in such forms was apparently an Attic innovation,[2] though its origin has remained unclear.

Lagercrantz supposed that, in Attic, vowels were lengthened before the clusters *-kʰⁱi̯- and *-gi̯- (note: θάττων < *-kʰi̯-, μείζων < *-gi̯-).[3] Lengthening probably spread from one category of primary

---

For comments on earlier versions of this paper I am grateful to Martin Peters, Julián Méndez Dosuna, and the two anonymous reviewers. I also wish to thank Ryan Pasco and the editor of *HSCP* for suggesting several stylistic improvements to the final manuscript. Naturally, any remaining infelicities are my own responsibility.

[1] Cf., e.g., Att. θᾶττον vs. Hom. (v.l.) θάσσον (Lagercrantz 1898:38), Att. μείζων vs. Ion. μέζων, Att. κρείττων vs. Ion. κρέσσων. Cf. further Boeot. μεδδονος (*SEG* 32:450), Lesb. μεζονων (*IG* XII Suppl. 692.16), μέσδων (Sappho 111.7 Voigt), Cyr. μεζονος (*SEG* 26:1817.56–57), and Lagercrantz 1898:36–37, Jacobsohn 1908:344–345. For the quantity of -ι- in -ιον- in Attic and elsewhere, see La Roche 1884:17–18, Schulze 1892:300–301, Dieu 2011:123n126. Cf. further Hdn. Περὶ διχρόνων 291 Lentz, [τ]ὰ εἰς ων λήγοντα καθαρὰ συγκριτικά, ὁπότε παραλήγοιτο τῷ ι, ἐκτεταμένῳ αὐτῷ παραλήγονται ... Ἀριστοφάνης δὲ ἐν Ἀττικαῖς λέξεσιν Ἀττικοὺς ἱστορεῖ προφέρεσθαι ἐκτεταμένως. "When the penultimate syllable of comparatives in -ων ends in ι, that ι is long ... Aristophanes (of Byzantium), in his Ἀττικαί λέξεις, reports that (the iota) was pronounced long by the Athenians."

[2] The long vowel in the Vedic comparative suffix -ī́yas- is the result of an inner-Indic process; cf. Cowgill 1970:136, Schindler 1986:386–387, Jamison 1988:218, Dieu 2011:586–590, Barber 2013:152–153. The long root vowel in words such as Hom. θᾶσσον is an Attic feature that entered the Homeric and other non-Attic texts secondarily; cf. Jacobsohn 1908:344–348, Wackernagel 1915:124–125, Ruijgh 1975:92n4, Peters 1980:288–289n242, de Lamberterie 1990:573, Vessella 2007, Dieu 2011:125–131, Barber 2015.

[3] Lagercrantz 1898:36.

comparatives to the other, so the long -ῑ- in -ῐ́ων could be secondary after comparatives like μείζων and θᾱ́ττων.[4] Even if we leave aside the ad hoc nature of Lagercrantz's proposal,[5] the lengthening of a vowel only before *-$k^{(h)}i̯$- and *-$g̯i̯$- would be cross-linguistically unparalleled and phonologically poorly motivated. Furthermore, as shown in a recent study,[6] the scant evidence in support of Lagercrantz's theory is questionable. Also, Att. ὄττα 'voice' < *$u̯ok^ui̯a$, πίττα 'pitch' < *$piki̯a$, τριοττίς 'necklace with three pendants like eyes' < *-$ok^ui̯$-, and θρίττα 'Clupea alosa' < *$t^hrik^hi̯a$, which are apparently the only words containing *-$k̯i̯$- outside the comparative and the verbal domain, contain a short root vowel.[7]

Osthoff argued that the long vowel in κρείττων is analogical after its antonym, χείρων, whose -ει- is phonologically regular.[8] According to him, the vocalism of μείζων was influenced by χείρων on the basis of μέγιστος and the (hypothetical) superlative *χέριστος. Inscriptional ολειζων (: ὀλίγος) contains a secondary long vowel after its "begrifflichen Widerpart" μείζων.[9] Osthoff traces θᾶττων and ἐλᾶττων back to *$t^hank^hi̯$- and *$elank^hi̯$-.[10] These reconstructions would result in forms with long root vowels by regular sound change. However, θᾶττων and ἐλᾶττων most likely go back to *$t^hăk^hi̯$- and *$elăk^hi̯$- (see the literature in note 2). If so, the long -ᾱ- in those two forms should also be seen as secondary.

The relevant forms in -ων cannot have acquired a long vowel via consecutive analogical changes triggered essentially by χείρων.

---

[4] Cf. Kuryłowicz 1956:276, Peters 1980:289n242.
[5] For example, both *-$k̯i̯$- and *-$t̯i̯$- result in -ττ- in Attic. Why did lengthening occur only before *-$k̯i̯$-?
[6] See Batisti 2014:158–181.
[7] On ὄττα as a counterexample see Solmsen 1899:654, Thumb 1901:63 (Solmsen, unlike Thumb, is sympathetic to Lagercrantz's idea). Jacobsohn 1908:348n32, who generally follows Lagercrantz (as does Peters 1980:289n242), unconvincingly considers ὄττα a loanword from a northwest Greek dialect. On πέττω < *-$k̯ui̯$- (for "expected" †πείττω), etc., see Lagercrantz 1898:42.
[8] Osthoff 1910:191–195.
[9] Osthoff 1910:206–208.
[10] Osthoff 1910:46–63.

Similarly, *pace* Kuryłowicz,[11] χείρων and potentially (analogical) κρείττων and μείζων (or ἥττων) would not have been a firm enough basis for the creation of a rule that would generalize the long vowel in all primary comparatives—including those in -ἴων.[12] πλείων, μείων, etc. contain a diphthong[13] and are thus hardly relevant, since Attic comparatives like μείζων contained a long vowel.[14]

II. A NEW APPROACH

Comparatives and superlatives to *o*-stem adjectives are normally built with -ότερος and -ότατος when the stem vowel is preceded by a heavy syllable (e.g., δεινότερος, δεινότατος). When the syllable before the stem vowel is light, the form of the suffixes is -ώτερος and -ώτατος instead (e.g., σοφώτερος, σοφώτατος).[15] Saussure plausibly argued that the -ω- in σοφώτερος, etc. results from a process of vowel lengthening. The motivation behind this development was a disprefence for a

---

[11] Kuryłowicz 1956:276.

[12] Risch 1974:89 argues that the long vowel in κρείττων, μείζων, etc. results from over-generalization of the pattern full grade : zero grade that is seen in κρέσσων : κράτιστος. This is a questionable analogy and there were probably no root ablaut differences between the comparative and the superlative in Proto-Greek (cf. Rau 2014:329): κράτιστος contains a secondary zero grade after the positive. It is unlikely that the process reconstructed by Risch was based exclusively on κρέσσων : κράτιστος. For the theories of Brugmann, Rix, and Sihler, see the criticism in Osthoff 1910:48, Dieu 2011:124n127, and Nikolaev 2022:553.

[13] Cf. Dieu 2011, Nikolaev 2022. Note that secondary *ē* was shortened before *ŏ* in Attic and Ionic (see Peters 1980:87–90n40, Nussbaum 2017).

[14] Cf., e.g., Ruijgh 1975:92n3, *pace* Nikolaev 2022:559–560. Compare Att. fifth-century μἐζονὄν (*IG* I³ 231.a3–4), μἐζονο[ς (*IG* I³ 21.76), μἐζονος (*IG* I³ 425.45), ολἐζŏν (e.g., *IG* I³ 3.9; for the last form cf. further Dieu 2011:573, Nikolaev 2022:558). κρείττων is not attested in Attic inscriptions, but on the basis of μἐζον- and ολἐζον- we can safely conclude that it contained a long vowel and not a diphthong. If we assume that the change of Att. *ei* to *ē* before vowels was earlier than the lengthening in the type θἄττων, then the connection with πλείων, etc. could be maintained (cf. Dieu 2011:124, 130n137). However, the monophthongization of Att. *ei* in prevocalic position began in the Hellenistic period (cf. Threatte 1980:202–205, 302–303; Allen 1987:72–73, 83–84). Thus, the change *ei* > *ē* in, e.g., πλείων was certainly later than the lengthening in θάττων, etc.

[15] Cf., e.g., *Epimerismi Homerici* μ 66.52–54 Dyck, ἐὰν οὖν μακρὰ ᾖν ἡ παραλήγουσα, τὸ ο μένει … ἐὰν δὲ βραχεῖα, διὰ τοῦ ω μεγάλου. "If the penultimate syllable (of the positive) was long, o remained intact … if it was short, (the comparative was written) with omega."

sequence of three light syllables.[16] The same phenomenon, with slight differences, is also attested in Vedic.[17]

An alternative analysis of -ωτερο- and -οτερο- claims that the former originates in comparatives built to adverbs in -ω(ς) (e.g., σοφῶς), while the latter in comparative adjectives built to the nominal stem. At some later point, the two variants fell into a complementary distribution: -ωτερο- was used with stems like σοφο-, but -οτερο- with

---

[16] Saussure 1884. Secondary long *ō* from like-vowel contraction or compensatory lengthening was normally less open than inherited **ō* and was denoted by ου in, e.g., Attic-Ionic. Despite the fact that the process envisaged by Saussure is neither a contraction nor a compensatory lengthening, the lengthened **o* in σοφώτερος might be expected to be written ου; cf. the lengthening in, e.g., μείζων (but this process is comparatively late, see II.4).

However, in some cases, secondary long *ō* (and *ē*) was represented by ω (and η) even in dialects like Attic. Compare forms like Att. βασιλέως < βασιλῆος. The change in question, which is traditionally known as "quantitative metathesis," involves the desyllabification of the *e*-vowel with compensatory lengthening of the following segment. It is highly unlikely that the lengthened vowel was realized as open somehow due to the preceding η (Méndez Dosuna 1993).

Wackernagel's *Dehnungsgesetz*, i.e., the lengthening of the initial vowel in the second member of compounds, also yields open vowels when **o* or **e* are involved (cf., e.g., ὁμώνυμος, ὠμηστής). The most natural way to account for compositional lengthening is to assume elision (or desyllabification) of the final vowel in the first member, with compensatory lengthening of the first vowel in the second member (cf. Berenguer-Sánchez 2011, Batisti 2014:193–200; differently Bader 1972).

According to several scholars (see, e.g., Hermann 1923:48–49, Peters 1984:100*), Att.-Ion. ὦμος, ὦνος, κῶμος, and Διώνῡσος, with a secondarily lengthened *o*-vowel, are *lautgesetzlich*, despite κουρεύς, οὐρά, etc. This approach is not without problems, but it is arguably superior to the one that sees ὦμος, etc. as borrowings from a dialect with a system of five long vowels (see Batisti 2014:201–228 for discussion).

Like-vowel contraction and compensatory lengthening after loss of **h₁* or **h₃* result in η and ω in all of Greek (cf., e.g., ἦα < *(h₁)e-h₁es-m̥*, δίδωμι < *di-doh₃-mi*). Since the lengthening in -ωτερο-/-ωτατο- could be quite old and the chronology of this change relative to laryngeal loss and the first compensatory lengthening (cf. οὐρά̄ < *orsā*) is not known, it may not be illegitimate to compare -ω- from *-oh₃C-*, etc. with -ω- in -ωτερο-.

One final remark: whether ε and ο were close vowels, as is commonly believed, is far from clear (Allen 1987:63, 72, 89–90). Allen concludes that they were open and that, consequently, their long counterparts were η and ω.

[17] Insler 1997, Steriade 2018. In Greek, tribrachs were also avoided across word boundaries. Evidence for the dispreference of tribrachs in Greek also comes from meter. See further Steriade 2018. Cf. also Specht 1936.

stems of the type δεινο-. That was due to a dispreference for a sequence of three light syllables.[18] The speculation that -ωτερο- is deadverbial, though sufficiently valid,[19] cannot be substantiated. On the other hand, the proposal that -ωτερο- and -οτερο- were used complementarily, despite being unrelated to Saussure's lengthening, is perfectly plausible: according to Steriade, root allomorphs that were originally generated by Wackernagel's *Dehnungsgesetz* (e.g., -ω/οροφο-) were redistributed so as to avoid tribrachs in compounds.[20] Steriade showed recently that sequences of three light syllables were systematically avoided in Greek through various repair strategies. This strongly supports Saussure's analysis of -ωτερο-: vowel lengthening in secondary comparatives was probably one way, among others, to avoid a tribrach.[21] In light of Steriade's findings and the Vedic parallel, it would be unattractive to consider -ωτερο- deadverbial. As the simplest and most compelling way to analyze -ωτερο- vs. -οτερο-, Saussure's theory is to be preferred.

---

[18] Cf. Güntert 1910:34–35, Kuryłowicz 1954:257, Risch 1974:94.

[19] It has been suggested that the comparative suffixes Gmc. *-ōzan- and Slav. *-ějьš- are deadverbial (e.g., Kuryłowicz 1954). This is not implausible typologically, but the whole theory remains controversial (cf., e.g., Dieu 2011:299n362, Fulk 2018:218–219). Also, according to Szeptyński 2017:197–198, Slav. *-ějьš- is deverbal.

[20] Steriade 2018. When a secondary comparative was unmetrical in its original form, -οτερο- was apparently replaced by -ωτερο- in Homer; cf. ὀϊζῡρώτερον/-τατον, κακοξεινώτερος. However, -ω- in such cases may result from metrical lengthening and be analogical for -ου-: metrically lengthened <O> in the original may have been transcribed -ω- instead of (usual) -ου- under the influence of -ωτερο- (Hermann 1923:11; cf. Solmsen 1901:94n1). At any rate, suffix substitution for metrical reasons is also found in Hom. ἀνῑηρέστερον (but the use of -εστερο- with o-stems is not uncommon after Homer; Schwyzer 1939:535).

[21] Steriade 2018. Vowel lengthening as a repair strategy is rare to nonexistent outside the secondary comparative. Att.-Ion. and Koine ἱερ(ε)ωσύνη continues *hιερηϝοσυνᾱ, with "quantitative metathesis" *-ηο- > -εω- (and, later, contraction). Words such as μεγαλωσύνη have been modeled on ἱερωσύνη (Schulze 1892:144, 146). ἰδιώτης, ἡλικιώτης, etc. are probably irrelevant; see Leukart 1994:138n31, 186–187n154; Schwyzer 1939:500. On ἑτέρωθεν and the like see Steriade 2018. On -η/εδον- see II.2.

26 Georgios Kostopoulos

II.1. THE LACK OF LENGTHENING IN γλυκύτερος

Some scholars have analyzed -ωτερο- as deadverbial because vowel lengthening does not apply in comparatives of the type γλυκύτερος.[22] However, the alternation εὐρύτερος : *γλυκῦτερος could have been leveled out in Attic-Ionic.[23] -ύτερο- vs. *-ῡτερο- was a low type-frequency pattern.[24] "Unproductive alternations are gradually leveled or regularized …"[25] It seems that a similar process took place in Ionic (and *mutatis mutandis* in Attic). In that dialect, -ῐον- after light syllables (as in Hom. γλυκίων) is probably a replacement of earlier -ῑον- (cf. Hom. βραχίων); see further II.5.[26]

An alternative analysis would involve the assumption that fifth-century γλυκύτερος (etc.) has not been affected by Saussure's Tribrach Law (TL) because it was formed late.[27] There seems to be a tendency to replace comparatives built with the suffixes *-ioh- and (*)-i(h)on- (< *-ios-, *-ison-) with forms containing the root of the positive plus the suffix -τερο-.[28] It could be argued that γλυκύτερος was created when

---

[22] See, e.g., Güntert 1910:33, Kuryłowicz 1954:257. For the quantity of the upsilon, cf., e.g., Ar. Ach. 462, 467, 475; Lys. 79, 872, 889, 890 (meter: iambic trimeter). Compare also the fact that the type γλυκύτερος, unlike the type εὐρύτερος, is not attested in hexameter poetry; cf. Moorhouse 1949:161; Seiler 1950:38, 49. (This is also the case, e.g., for participles like φερόμενος; the only forms attested before the fifth century are metrically lengthened οὐλόμενος, γεινόμενος, and δῡνάμενος.)

[23] Cf. Moorhouse 1949:161 (*pace* Güntert 1910:33).

[24] Cf. Hom. εὐρύτερος, θηλύτερος (oppositive meaning; de Lamberterie 1990:877–878), πρεσβύτερος; Archil. ὀξύτερος (Hom. -τατο-); Thgn. ἰθύτερος, ὠκύτερος (Hom. -τατο-/-ιστο-); fifth-century ἀμβλύτερος, βρῑθύτερος, δριμύτερος, πρηΰτερος, τρηχύτερος; Hippoc. ἡδύτατος; third-century αἰπύτερος (thirteen adjectives) vs. fifth-century βαθύτερος, βαρύτερος, βραδύτερος (Theoc. βαρδύτερος), βραχύτερος, γλυκύτερος, δασύτερος, θρασύτερος, παχύτερος, πλατύτερος, ταχύτερος (ten adjectives).

[25] Bybee 2001:178. See also II.3 last paragraph.

[26] Devine and Stephens 1994:104 suggest that the stem vowel in γλυκύτερος was not lengthened "because u is intrinsically shorter than o." However, earlier in their book (page 64), they note that durational differences between vowels are not "metrically relevant" in Greek and "not a major factor in Greek speech rhythm."

[27] Schwyzer 1939:534.

[28] See Risch 1974:95. Almost all comparatives of the γλυκύτερος type had counterparts in -σσων/-ίων, see note 34 and Seiler 1950 (for some reason, for the type εὐρύτερος, the opposite is the case; we have only ἡδίων, πρειγον-, ὤκιστος). The new forms in -τερο- had

the constraint against tribrachs in the derivational domain had become violable and vowel lengthening (VL) had stopped being an active process. Two comparable cases would be κενότερος < *κενϝότερος and στενότερος < *στενϝότερος: the rule was already inactive when, for example, *κεν.ϝός became *κε.νϝός in Attic (cf. Att. κᾰλός < *κα.λϝός), so the tribrach in κενότερος and στενότερος remained intact.[29]

II.2. PARADIGMATICALLY UNSTABLE VIOLATIONS

Steriade believes that only certain TL violations were targeted— namely, those extending across the entire paradigm.[30] Saussure on the other hand, as it seems, did not hold the same opinion. According to him, the long vowel in the suffix -ηδον- originated in TL.[31] -ηδον- has the alternative form -εδον-. Saussure proposes that the initial long vowel of -ηδον- arose in words like τερηδών, -όνος (for older *τερεδών, -όνος), where the root syllable was light. The original form of the suffix was only found in words like τηκεδών.

---

the obvious advantage of morphological transparency: the morphological structure of γλυκύτερος was clearer than that of γλυκίων/γλύσσων in, say, the classical period.

[29] Cf. Hermann 1923:10–11. The usual explanation is that the loss of digamma happened after VL stopped being operative (e.g., Devine and Stephens 1994:104). This is probably true, but it is only part of the story, since the cluster was already tautosyllabic in Attic when ϝ was lost.

The fact that -ωτερο- is regularly found after light syllables in the classical period hardly supports the idea that VL was active until late: classical -ωτερο- could result from a rule "-οτερο- after heavy syllables, -ωτερο- after light syllables" that was based on earlier material. στενώτερος and κενώτερος are also attested in fifth-/fourth-century Attic and Ionic, but they are rare. If these regularized forms have not been introduced by later copyists (they are never found in inscriptions), they could be analogical on the model of σοφώτερος (vs. δεινότερος); cf. further, e.g., κυντερώτερος in Pherecrates (comp. κύντερος) and κυντατώτατα (superl. κύντατος) in Eubulus (cf. Hermann 1923:9, 11; Devine and Stephens 1994:104; Steriade 2018; differently Fortson 1995).

Similar to κενότερος and στενότερος are Hdt. ἐπιτηδεότατος (vs. earlier ἐπιτηδειότατος) and probably Hom. λᾱρώτατος (Simon. λᾱρότερον), if from *λαε/αρώτατος (cf. Dieu 2011:229–230). It is not clear whether Hdt. οἰκηότατος continues an earlier *οἰκηιώτατος with shortening after contraction (*pace* Schulze 1888:252n1). Such a development may be seen in fifth-/fourth-century κοιλοτερο- vs. Anac. κοΐλώτερα (< *κοϝι-).

[30] See Steriade 2018. Cf. the lack of lengthening in, e.g., ἀργύρεος, ἀργύρεον; compare ἀργυρέῳ, ἀργυρέους, fem. ἀργυρέη, etc.

[31] Saussure 1884.

The distribution reconstructed by Saussure is no longer visible in our texts. Also, recent advances in Indo-European nominal morphology suggest that the long vowel in -ηδον- may have nothing to do with TL.[32] In any case, the fact remains that, according to Saussure, in paradigms where, not all, but the majority of forms violated TL, lengthening should be expected: although the nominative singular *τερεδών was TL compliant, all other forms of the paradigm were TL violating (cf., e.g., *τερεδόνος, *τερεδόνα).

II.3. -ῑον- AS A CASE OF TL-INDUCED VOWEL LENGTHENING

Forms like γλυκίων and φιλίων violated TL in all case forms except in the nominative singular masculine/feminine (cf. γλυκίονος, γλυκίονα, γλυκίονες, γλύκιον, etc.).[33] Following Saussure (cf. II.2), one might expect TL-induced VL to apply in a (sufficiently old) paradigm where TL-violating forms were the majority. My conjecture is, therefore, that in forms like γλῠ̆κῐ̆ὄνος lengthening of the second vowel took place in compliance with TL, exactly as in σοφώτερος, etc. From there, the nominative singular also acquired a long -ῑ-.

The long vowel later spread to ἡδίων, etc. There are seven comparatives of the γλυκίων type in pre-fifth-century texts.[34] The type ἡδίων is represented by seven/eight items in the same period.[35] If we also count

---

[32] See Rau 2010:166–170 with reference to Nussbaum.

[33] The dative plural in -ίοσι (as in γλυκίοσι) does not come from *-ison-si (with a heavy penultimate syllable). In the locative/dative plural, the old form must have been *-isn̥-si: *-ison- goes back to Proto-Greek and perhaps Proto-Indo-European (see, e.g., Rau 2014:329, Nikolaev 2022:552–554). *-isn̥-si (or a later form of it) was early on replaced by *-iso-si, with *-o- generalized from the rest of the paradigm (cf., e.g., Schwyzer 1939:569, Barber 2013:149n8). The instrumental plural (/dual) in -φι would be rare with comparative adjectives. Also, -φι stopped being part of the spoken language rather early (before the late eighth century, but in post-Mycenaean times).

[34] These are Hom. γλυκίων, φιλίων, κακίων, βραχίων (II.5); adv. Hes. βράδιον; Alcm. θρασίων; and adv. Tyrt. μάλιον (for the last word, see Seiler 1950:67–68). Cf. also adv. Aesch. τάχιον, Xen. ἑκατονταπλασίων (this is a secondary formation; Seiler 1950:103–104), Aratus παχίων, and adv. Theoc. βάθιον (Etym. Magn. ἐλαχίων, λαλίων).

[35] These are Hom. αἰσχίων, κερδίων, ῥίγιον, ἀλγίων; epic κῦδίων (Iliu persis), Mimn. βελτίων, and probably λώϊον (Dieu 2011:206–210) and καλ(λ)ίων (Hom.+). Cf. further classical ἡδίων, ἐχθίων, ῥᾴων, perhaps ὕψιον (Seiler 1950:110), ὀνήϊον (Dieu 2011:236–238), and the adverbs πόρσιον and ἔγγιον (compare also Etym. Magn. τερπνίων, ὠκίων

the forms that are attested between the fifth and the third centuries, we find approximately fourteen with a heavy and eleven with a light first syllable. The difference between ἡδίων and (*)γλυκίων, therefore, could have been leveled out quite easily in Attic,[36] and all primary comparatives might have been rebuilt with the suffix -ῑον- regardless of the quantity of their root syllable.[37] The fact that less than half of the -ιον- forms attested violated TL fits well with the limited distribution of -ῑον- in Greek.

In the secondary comparative, the alternation between -ωτερο- and -οτερο- was preserved. Contrariwise, the -ῑον- : -ῐον- alternation in the primary comparative was leveled out. This is not surprising, as -οτερο- vs. -ωτερο- was a high type-frequency pattern and therefore more likely to be maintained. On the other hand, as noted already, unproductive alternations like the one in ἡδίων : γλυκίων are expected to be regularized.[38]

[Hom. ὤκιστος, Lat. *ōcius*, Skt. *áśīyas-*], πρεσβίων, and ψευδίων). Although **kaluii̯on-* (cf. Alcm. κάλιον) would contain a light first syllable in Attic at least, Att. στενότερος and κενότερος (< *-nu̯-) suggest that lengthening would not apply in καλλίων, even if that form acquired its secondary geminate at a late stage. Note that *muta cum liquida* clusters, which are frequently tautosyllabic in Attic, normally act as heavy in the context of TL (cf. Hermann 1923:8–11, Fortson 1995, Steriade 2018).

[36] There is a small number of forms with short -ĭ- in Attic dramatic writers. For attestations and discussion see Schulze 1892:300–301n4 and most importantly Diggle 1981:29–30.

[37] Forms like Att. acc. sg. βελτίονα originally contained a word-final tribrach. However, it is doubtful that, e.g., Att. βελτῑον- is phonologically regular. In TL-induced VL, the first short is never lengthened (though analogy might have played a role here). Also, according to Steriade 2018, TL did not apply outside derivational contexts (cf., e.g., ὄνομα, -ατος, μέγεθος, -εος, 1pl. mid. λεγόμεθα). Inflected words with word-final tribrachs (e.g., ἀργύρεος) show no evidence of TL either, probably because in such cases forms containing tribrachs were not the majority in the paradigm (II.2). In the inflectional paradigm of βελτίων/βέλτιον, as attested in the historical period, eight case forms contain a tribrach and five are TL compliant. Even if we assume that TL would normally apply in parts of the paradigm, the TL-compliant forms may have been too many and too frequent for the long vowel to be generalized. Compare the fact that -ῑον- may have been generalized in Ionic and other dialects (II.5).

[38] Bybee 2001:178. After I had finished writing this article, I was pleased to discover that the Dutch classicist Frederik Muller Jzn. had also connected the long vowel in -ῑον- with Saussure's TL (Muller Jzn. 1920:87–88). This was done in an entirely cursory way, but it is a welcome surprise to see that the main idea of this paper has been anticipated by another scholar.

II.4. The Long Vowel in the Type θᾱττων

The long vowel in -ῑων was part of the suffix, but the long vowel in, for example, θᾱττων was part of the root. An analogical process whereby the root vowel of the latter was lengthened on the basis of the long -ῑ- in the suffix -ῑον- would be difficult to imagine. However, if γλυκίων was at some point resegmented as γλυκῑ-ων after, say, θᾱττ-ων, it would become less difficult to understand how the type θᾱττων was created.[39]

In early Attic, θᾱττων was initially formed via the rule "to form the primary comparative, add -ον- to the root of the comparative." Now resegmented forms like γλυκῑ-ων, ἡδῑ-ων could give the impression that primary comparatives generally have a long vowel before -ων. On the basis of that misconception, the above rule was slightly modified: "to form the primary comparative, add -ον- to the root of the comparative and lengthen the presuffixal vowel."[40]

It is most likely that this modified version was added to the grammar after the generalization of -ῑ- in the primary comparative— i.e., at a time when both γλυκίων and ἡδίων contained a long iota. This would mean that LENGTHENING EXTENSION in θᾱττων followed not only RESEGMENTATION but also ῑ-GENERALIZATION. Now the generalization of -ῑ- was based on a rule "to form the primary comparative add -ῑον- to the root (of the positive)" (cf. note 47). This rule cannot have followed the resegmentation γλυκῑ-ων because it presupposes the existence of a suffix -ῑον-. Thus, the most plausible ordering is ῑ-GENERALIZATION → RESEGMENTATION → LENGTHENING EXTENSION.

II.5. Homeric βραχῑων

It has long been suspected that βραχῑων 'arm, upper arm' is an old comparative of the adjective βραχύς 'short'.[41] As argued by Diggle and

---

[39] Kuryłowicz 1956:276. The segmentation θᾱττ-ων is confirmed by the comparative Cret. πρειγον- (= πρεσβυτερο-), which is a secondary formation containing the base πρειγ- (cf. Cret. πρειγυς) plus the suffix -ον- (see Seiler 1950:60).

[40] In two prose inscriptions from Attica dating from the early fourth century, μείζων apparently has a short first vowel. The form is both times nom. sg. μεζων (see Threatte 1996:309).

[41] The upper arm was called 'shorter' vis-à-vis the forearm. The latter also included the hand, according to some ancient authors. For the semantics see further Ruijgh 1968:147–148; de Lamberterie 1990:166–167, 169–170; van Beek 2022:286–288.

others, the old meaning 'weaker, inferior' is probably attested in Eur. *Supp.* 478.[42] This important but little-known detail strongly supports the traditional etymology of βραχΐων (cf. further Hsch. βραχίων· βραχύτατος).[43] There is one major problem with the idea that βραχΐων is an old comparative. The -ι- of that word is always long in Homer, whereas comparative adjectives consistently have short -ῐ- in the two epics.[44] The middle vowel of βραχΐων cannot have been lengthened for metrical reasons: other comparatives never undergo metrical lengthening (ML), and this analysis is excluded at *Il.* 13.529. The last point is important in itself but more so in the present case because βραχΐων is only attested six times in Homer.[45]

The long -ῑ- in Hom. βραχΐων would be easy to understand in the context of the theory proposed in II.3. The dispreference for tribrachs as well as the remedial lengthening in secondary comparatives was

---

[42] See Diggle 1973:247–250, 1981:13.

[43] The fact that the hapax Hom. βράσσων ?'shorter' (Hsch. βρόσσονος· βραχυτέρου) functions as a comparative while the more recent form, βραχΐων, is a noun goes against Kuryłowicz's fourth law of analogy (for the historical priority of βράσσων cf., e.g., Ruijgh 1975:92–93, Nikolaev 2022:551; for the connection of βράσσων with βραδύς 'slow', cf. La Roche 1884:20; Seiler 1950:43, 56; de Lamberterie 1990:53). According to that "law," the more recent form usually has the primary meaning/function, and the older form a secondary meaning/function. However, it seems that in cases of "lexical split, the 'secondary function' is sometimes reserved for the old form ..., and sometimes for the new" (Kiparsky 2003:81). Kiparsky's exceptions to Kuryłowicz's fourth law are not considered real exceptions by several scholars (e.g., Hock 2003:447), but the important point here is that there are numerous cases like βράσσων vs. βραχΐων (cf., e.g., regularized *weaved* ← *wove* in the specialized meaning 'move from side to side'). How one analyzes these cases is a theoretical issue that has no bearing on the history of βραχΐων.

[44] Cf. Meyer 1878:14, Schulze 1892:300n1, Seiler 1950:42. Ruijgh 1968:147–148 defends the connection with βραχύς, but he suggests that βραχΐων contained the suffix -ιον- that was used to form sobriquets. This analysis should be accepted only as a last resort. In any case, according to Solmsen 1901:47–59, it is not clear whether the suffix in question had a long ῑ, since -ῑον- in Homer (as in Κρονΐονος) could be the result of metrical lengthening. The long iota in forms like Pi. Κρονΐων may be due to epic influence. See, however, van Beek 2022:347–350.

[45] Seiler 1950:42–43. In most passages, the assumption of ML would be acceptable. Seiler tentatively proposes that the quantity of the vowel at *Il.* 13.529 (where ML is excluded) was influenced by (supposedly) metrically lengthened βραχΐονος three verses later (*Il.* 13.532). However, this is improbable.

pan-Greek.[46] One can imagine that the pair (say) ἡδίων : γλυκίων also existed in other Greek dialects at some stage. For Ionic—i.e., the dialect closest to Attic—that would be a distinct possibility.

If -ῐον- instead of -ῑον- was generalized in Ionic, this probably happened via a rule of the sort "to form the primary comparative add -ῐον- to the root (of the positive)."[47] βραχίων must have become a substantive meaning 'arm' at an early date, since the old meaning is only attested once and, quite importantly, in a fixed expression (ἐκ βραχιόνων[48]). If βραχίων was not considered a comparative by most early Greek speakers, then this word would not be expected to be rebuilt or have its suffix substituted with -ῐον- in Ionic. Importantly, βραχίων contains (and always contained) a light first syllable, and according to section II.3, VL would normally occur in this word. Hom. βραχίων, then, can be seen as a genuine dialect form, a remnant from the time when TL-induced VL in primary comparatives also existed in Ionic.

The obvious conclusion that can be drawn from the above theory is that -ῑον- was found in both Attic *and* Ionic, and possibly in other Greek dialects.[49] Also, if the present analysis of βραχίων is accepted, originally only *some* primary comparatives showed -ῑον- in Attic (cf. Hom -ῐον- vs. -ῑον-)—probably those with a light first syllable. All this is exactly what was proposed above on the basis of the Attic data alone.

[46] For the former see Steriade 2018, for the latter see Hermann 1923:8–9. -ωτερο-/-ωτατο- is robustly attested in Attic-Ionic and is also found in, e.g., the Lesbian poets, Pindar, Alcman, Sophron, Theocritus, and others. Some inscriptional forms containing -ωτερο-/-ωτατο- are mid-fourth-century Lesb. ευνοωτατα (*SEG* 36:750.6), late fourth-century Arc. νεωτερων (*IG* V.2 357.A16), Dor. συμφορωτερον (*SEG* 15:397.3), and late third-century Boeot. νιωτερω (*IG* VII 2420.15).

[47] The type ἡδίων in Attic was based on the converse of that rule: "to form the primary comparative add -ῑον- to the root (of the positive)." This was a modification of the original rule used in Greek to form comparatives in -ιον-. That rule was preserved intact in Ionic despite the existence of new forms with -ῑον-, but it was modified in Attic.

[48] But this was not an unproductive pattern: cf., e.g., ἐξ ἀέλπτων, ἐξ ἀμηχάνων, ἐξ ἅπαντος (Diggle 1973:249). ἐκ βραχιόνων was probably a lexicalized phrase.

[49] There are five comparatives with long ῑ in non-Attic poetic texts from the archaic period. Of these, Archil. 11.1 West and Thgn. 811, [1175] West are at the end of a hexameter and are thus not decisive (cf., e.g., Peters 1980:254n211). The clearest cases are Simon. epigr. 142.3 Bergk κάλλῑον (but see also Seiler 1950:16; v.l. τοιοῦτον) and κύδῑον᾽ in *Iliu persis* fr. 4.2 Bernabé (the long -ῑ- here, if real, must be seen as analogical, since it is found after a heavy syllable).

III. SUMMARY AND CONCLUSIONS

The long -ῑ- in -ῑ́ων results from Saussure's Tribrach Law, according to which the second of three light syllables becomes heavy through vowel lengthening. The rule originally applied to forms like γλῠκῐ́ονες and γλῠκῐ́ονα, but, at a later stage, the long -ῑ- was generalized to the nominative singular and was extended to forms with a heavy first syllable (e.g., ἡδίονες). Finally, comparatives in -ῑ́ων were resegmented as γλυκῑ́-ων, ἡδῑ́-ων, etc., and this eventually led to the extension of the lengthening to comparatives like θᾱττ-ων.

Initially, forms like γλυκῑ́ων were not confined to Attic. They were also found in Ionic and perhaps in other dialects. Outside Attic, -ῑ́ων was generalized at the expense of -ῑ́ων. A relic of the old situation in Ionic is preserved in Hom. βραχῑ́ων '(upper) arm': this word is an old comparative but it was not recognized as such and did not participate in the leveling process. Thus, the long vowel here was preserved.

WORKS CITED

Allen, W. Sidney. 1987. *Vox Graeca: A Guide to the Pronunciation of Classical Greek.* 3rd ed. Cambridge.

Bader, Françoise. 1972. "Le traitement des hiatus à la jointure des deux membres d'un composé nominal en mycénien." *Minos* 12:141–196.

Barber, Peter J. 2013. *Sievers' Law and the History of Semivowel Syllabicity in Indo-European and Ancient Greek.* Oxford.

———. 2015. "Comparative Adjectives in Herodian." *Mnemosyne*, n.s., 68, no. 2:234–253.

Batisti, Roberto. 2014. *Ricerche sull'Allungamento di Compenso in greco antico: Fonetica, fonologia, dialettologia.* PhD diss., University of Bologna.

Beek, Lucien van. 2022. *The Reflexes of Syllabic Liquids in Ancient Greek: Linguistic Prehistory of the Greek Dialects and Homeric Kunstsprache.* Leiden.

Berenguer-Sánchez, José A. 2011. "Notas sobre la «ley de alargamiento de Wackernagel»." *Emerita* 79, no. 2:381–390.

Bergk, Theodor. 1882. *Poetae lyrici Graeci*. Vol. 3, *Poetas melicos continens*. 4th ed. Leipzig.

Bernabé, Alberto. 1996. *Poetarum epicorum Graecorum testimonia et fragmenta*. Pt. 1. 2nd ed. Stuttgart.

Bybee, Joan. 2001. *Phonology and Language Use*. Cambridge.

Cowgill, Warren. 1970. "Italic and Celtic Superlatives and the Dialects of Indo-European." In *Indo-European and Indo-Europeans: Papers Presented at the Third Indo-European Conference at the University of Pennsylvania*, ed. George Cardona, Henry M. Hoenigswald, and Alfred Senn, 113–153. Philadelphia. Reprinted in *The Collected Writings of Warren Cowgill*, ed. Jared S. Klein (Ann Arbor, 2006), 191–226.

Devine, Andrew M., and Laurence D. Stephens. 1994. *The Prosody of Greek Speech*. Oxford.

Dieu, Éric. 2011. *Le supplétisme dans les formes de gradation en grec ancien et dans les langues indo-européennes*. Geneva.

Diggle, James. 1973. "The *Supplices* of Euripides." *Greek, Roman, and Byzantine Studies* 14, no. 3:241–269.

———. 1981. *Studies on the Text of Euripides: Supplices, Electra, Heracles, Troades, Iphigenia in Tauris, Ion*. Oxford.

Dyck, Andrew R. 1995. *Epimerismi Homerici*. Pt. 2, *Epimerismos continens qui ordine alphabetico traditi sunt. Lexicon* ΑΙΜΩΔΕΙΝ *quod vocatur seu verius* ΕΤΥΜΟΛΟΓΙΑΙ ΔΙΑΦΟΡΟΙ. Berlin.

Fortson, Benjamin. 1995. Review of *The Prosody of Greek Speech*, by Andrew M. Devine and Laurence D. Stephens [= Devine and Stephens 1994]. *Bryn Mawr Classical Review*. https://bmcr.brynmawr.edu/1995/1995.10.09.

Fulk, Robert D. 2018. *A Comparative Grammar of the Early Germanic Languages*. Amsterdam.

Güntert, Hermann. 1910. "Zur Geschichte der griechischen Gradationsbildungen." *Indogermanische Forschungen* 27:1–72.

Hermann, Eduard. 1923. *Silbenbildung im Griechischen und in den andern indogermanischen Sprachen*. Göttingen.

Hock, Hans Henrich. 2003. "Analogical Change." In *The Handbook of Historical Linguistics*, ed. Brian D. Joseph and Richard D. Janda, 441–460. Malden, MA.

Insler, Stanley. 1997. "Vedic Denominatives to Thematic *a*-stems." In *Sound Law and Analogy: Papers in Honor of Robert S. P. Beekes on the Occasion of His 60th Birthday*, ed. Alexander Lubotsky, 103–110. Amsterdam.

Jacobsohn, Hermann. 1908. "Der Aoristtypus ἆλτο und die Aspiration bei Homer." *Philologus* 67:325–365, 481–530.

Jamison, Stephanie W. 1988. "The Quantity of the Outcome of Vocalized Laryngeals in Indic." In *Die Laryngaltheorie und die Rekonstruktion des indogermanischen Laut- und Formensystems*, ed. Alfred Bammesberger, 213–226. Heidelberg.

Kiparsky, Paul. 2003. "Analogy." In *International Encyclopedia of Linguistics*. Vol. 1, *AAVE-Esperanto*, ed. William J. Frawley, 77–83. 2nd ed. Oxford.

Kuryłowicz, Jerzy. 1954. "Remarques sur le comparatif (germanique, slave, v. indien, grec)." In *Sprachgeschichte und Wortbedeutung: Festschrift Albert Debrunner gewidmet von Schülern, Freunden und Kollegen*, 251–257. Bern.

———. 1956. *L'apophonie en indo-européen*. Wrocław.

La Roche, Jacob. 1884. "Die Comparation in der griechischen Sprache." *Jahresbericht des kaiserlich-königlichen Staats-Gymnasiums zu Linz* 33:3–25.

Lagercrantz, Otto. 1898. *Zur griechischen Lautgeschichte*. PhD diss., University of Uppsala.

Lamberterie, Charles de. 1990. *Les adjectifs grecs en -υς: Sémantique et comparaison*. Louvain-la-Neuve.

Lentz, August. 1868. *Herodiani technici reliquiae*. Pt. 2, fasc. 1, *Reliqua scripta prosodiaca pathologiam orthographica continens*. Leipzig.

Leukart, Alex. 1994. *Die frühgriechischen Nomina auf -tās und -ās: Untersuchungen zu ihrer Herkunft und Ausbreitung (unter Vergleich mit den Nomina auf -eús)*. Vienna.

Méndez Dosuna, Julián. 1993. "Metátesis de cantidad en jónico-ático y heracleota." *Emerita* 61, no. 1:95–134.

Meyer, Leo. 1878. "Die homerischen Vaternamen und einige verwandte Bildungen." *Beiträge zur Kunde der indogermanischen Sprachen* 4:1–21.

Moorhouse, Alfred C. 1949. "The Morphology of the Greek Comparative System: Its Rhythmical and Repetitive Features." *American Journal of Philology* 70, no. 2:159–170.

Muller, Frederik, Jzn. 1920. *Latijnsche woordverklaringen op semantisch-taalhistorischen grondslag*. Amsterdam.

Nikolaev, Alexander. 2022. "Notes on Greek Primary Comparatives." In *Verus convictor, verus academicus: k 70-letiju Nikolaja Nikolaeviča Kazanskogo*, ed. Maxim L. Kisilier, 549–563. St. Petersburg.

Nussbaum, Alan J. 2017. "The Homeric Formulary Template and a Linguistic Innovation in the Epics." In *Language and Meter*, ed. Dieter Gunkel and Olav Hackstein, 267–318. Leiden.

Osthoff, Hermann. 1910. "Zur primären Komparativ- und Superlativbildung." In *Morphologische Untersuchungen auf dem Gebiete der indogermanischen Sprachen*, vol. 6, by Hermann Osthoff and Karl Brugmann, 70–302. Leipzig.

Peters, Martin. 1980. *Untersuchungen zur Vertretung der indogermanischen Laryngale im Griechischen*. Vienna.

———. 1984. "Indogermanische Chronik 30a: VII Altgriechisch." *Die Sprache* 30, no. 1:67*–105*.

Rau, Jeremy. 2010 [2004]. "The Derivational History of the Greek Stems in -άδ-." *Münchener Studien zur Sprachwissenschaft* 64:137–173.

———. 2014. "The History of the Indo-European Primary Comparative." In *Das Nomen im Indogermanischen: Morphologie, Substantiv versus Adjektiv, Kollektivum; Akten der Arbeitstagung der Indogermanischen Gesellschaft vom 14. bis 16. September 2011 in Erlangen*, ed. Norbert Oettinger and Thomas Steer, 327–341. Wiesbaden.

Risch, Ernst. 1974. *Wortbildung der homerischen Sprache*. 2nd ed. Berlin.

Ruijgh, Cornelis J. 1968. "Les noms en -won- (-āwon-, -īwon-), -uon- en grec alphabétique et en mycénien." *Minos* 9:109–155. Reprinted in *Scripta minora ad linguam Graecam pertinentia*, ed. Jan M. Bremer, Albert Rijksbaron, Frederik M. J. Waanders (Amsterdam, 1991), 240–286.

———. 1975. Review of *Greek Dialects and the Transformation of an Indo-European Process*, by Gregory Nagy. *Lingua* 36, no. 1:85–100. Reprinted in *Scripta minora ad linguam Graecam pertinentia*, ed.

Jan M. Bremer, Albert Rijksbaron, Frederik M. J. Waanders (Amsterdam, 1991), 635–650.

Saussure, Ferdinand de. 1884. "Une loi rythmique de la langue grecque." In *Mélanges Graux: Recueil de travaux d'érudition classique dédié à la mémoire de Charles Graux*, 737–748. Paris. Reprinted in *Recueil des publications scientifiques de Ferdinand de Saussure*, ed. Charles Bally and Léopold Gautier (Geneva, 1922), 464–476.

Schindler, Jochem. 1986. "Zum Jüngstavestischen: Die femininen Komparative auf -iiaiiā̊." *Die Sprache* 32, no. 2:384–390.

Schulze, Wilhelm. 1888. "Zwei verkannte Aoriste." *Zeitschrift für vergleichende Sprachforschung* 29, no. 3/4:230–255. Reprinted in *Kleine Schriften*, ed. Wilhelm Wissmann, 2nd ed. (Göttingen, 1966), 330–349.

———. 1892. *Quaestiones epicae*. Gütersloh.

Schwyzer, Eduard. 1939. *Griechische Grammatik: Auf der Grundlage von Karl Brugmanns Griechischer Grammatik; 1. Band: Allgemeiner Teil, Lautlehre, Wortbildung, Flexion*. Munich.

Seiler, Hansjakob. 1950. *Die primären griechischen Steigerungsformen*. Hamburg.

Solmsen, Felix. 1899. Review of *Zur griechischen Lautgeschichte*, by Otto Lagercrantz [= Lagercrantz 1898]. *Wochenschrift für klassische Philologie* 16, no. 24:649–654.

———. 1901. *Untersuchungen zur griechischen Laut- und Verslehre*. Strasbourg.

Specht, Franz. 1936. "Griechische Miszellen: 6. Zur Vermeidung von Wörtern mit drei kurzen Silben." *Zeitschrift für vergleichende Sprachforschung* 63, no. 3/4:207–226.

Steriade, Donca. 2018. "Quantitative Rhythm and Saussure's Tribrach Law." In *Proceedings of the 28th Annual UCLA Indo-European Conference: November 11th and 12th, 2016*, ed. David M. Goldstein, Stephanie W. Jamison, and Brent Vine, 231–265. Bremen.

Szeptyński, Rafał. 2017. "Vocalic Elements and Prosody in Slavic Comparatives." *Indogermanische Forschungen* 122:189–205.

Threatte, Leslie. 1980. *The Grammar of Attic Inscriptions*. Vol. 1, *Phonology*. Berlin.

———. 1996. *The Grammar of Attic Inscriptions*. Vol. 2, *Morphology*. Berlin.

Thumb, Albert. 1901. Review of *Zur griechischen Lautgeschichte*, by Otto Lagercrantz [= Lagercrantz 1898]. *Anzeiger für indogermanische Sprach- und Altertumskunde* 12:63–65.

Vessella, Carlo. 2007. "Overlength and the System of Primary Comparatives in Homeric and Attic Greek." In *Greek and Latin from an Indo-European Perspective*, ed. Coulter George, Matthew McCullagh, Benedicte Nielsen, Antonia Ruppel, and Olga Tribulato, 131–139. Cambridge.

Voigt, Eva-Maria. 1971. *Sappho et Alcaeus. Fragmenta*. Amsterdam.

Wackernagel, Jacob. 1915. "Akzentstudien III." *Nachrichten von der königlichen Gesellschaft der Wissenschaften zu Göttingen. Philologisch-historische Klasse* 1914, no. 2:97–130. Reprinted in *Kleine Schriften*, vol. 2 (Göttingen, 1955), 1154–1187.

West, Martin L. 1989. *Iambi et elegi Graeci ante Alexandrum cantati*. Vol. 1, *Archilochus, Hipponax, Theognidea*. 2nd ed. Oxford.

XENOPHANES ON THE SOUL
ANOTHER CHAPTER OF ANCIENT PHYSICS

CHRISTIAN VASSALLO

S CHOLARSHIP OF THE LAST CENTURY has shown great interest in the
problem of the soul in early Greek philosophy, a slippery notion
that must come to terms with the doxographical accounts available
to us.[1] In addition to the more well-researched topic of psychology
in the Orphics, in Pythagoras and the Pythagorean tradition, and in
Heraclitus,[2] scattered studies from the past few years focused on the
same problem have been devoted to the Milesians, the Eleatics, the
Pluralists (especially Empedocles), and the early Atomists.[3] However,
scholars have not yet systematically studied the concept of the soul
in Xenophanes. In his groundbreaking work *Psyche*, Rohde did not
pay particular attention to Xenophanes.[4] This omission was likely
due, at least in part, to a certain trend of the doxographical accounts

I thank the Alexander von Humboldt-Foundation for its financial support. I am also
very grateful to Benjamin Harriman, David Konstan, and Alexander P. D. Mourelatos
for useful advice and constructive criticism on some difficult points of this paper. All
references to Xenophanes will follow Strobel and Wöhrle's 2018 edition, on which see
Mourelatos 2020. As for the fragments, i.e., Xenophanes' *ipsissima verba*, Strobel and
Wöhrle (SW)'s numbering will be preceded by Diels-Kranz (DK)'s.

[1] A well-balanced and well-documented survey on this point can be found in Sassi
2020:165–201.

[2] See, e.g., Edmonds 2014 on the Orphics; Huffman 2009 and Mansfeld 2018a on the
Pythagoreans; Schofield 1991, Long 2009, Betegh 2013, Mansfeld 2018c, and Vassallo 2020,
with further bibliography therein, on Heraclitus.

[3] See, e.g., Mansfeld 2018b on Anaximenes; Tor 2020 on Parmenides; Inwood 2009,
Trépanier 2020, and Betegh 2020 on Empedocles; Rechenauer 2009 on Democritus.

[4] Rohde 1903: vol. 2, 137–197; there is only a very fleeting nod to Xenophanes at
155–156, although it is unclear whether Rohde also refers to Xenophanes when he states
here that for the Ionian philosophers the soul was a part of nature, so that knowledge
of the soul starts from that of nature (see also the very brief hints to Xenophanes at
162–163n6, 258–259n3, 320–321n1).

concerning the soul, from Aristotle to Aëtius, as it will be clear shortly. A shallow approach to the whole tradition of this Presocratic philosopher, now available in its entirety thanks to the new edition of the testimonies on him by Strobel and Wöhrle, could lead to the conclusion that Xenophanes' "depsychologization" in the standard doxographical sources is a good reason to think that he had nothing positive to say on the topic. Since many sources, surprisingly, testify to the contrary, in this paper I will take another path. Specifically, I will systematically analyze all the bits of evidence at our disposal in order to help us better understand the possible meaning(s) of *pneuma* and *psyche* in Xenophanes. After contextualizing these witnesses, I will discuss Xenophanes' concept of the soul in terms of its physical and theological (and/or "pantheistic") characteristics that tradition, to varying degrees, has attributed to it. In particular, I will attempt to prove that speaking of a Xenophanean psychology is legitimate and that Xenophanes' psychology stems from the fundamental principles of his physics.

I. "DEPSYCHOLOGIZING" XENOPHANES

In the chapters of Book 4 of Aëtius's compendium devoted to the soul and its nature, no *doxographicum* on Xenophanes appears.[5] Xenophanes is already (seemingly) missing from chapter 2 of Book 1 of Aristotle's *On the Soul*, where all the psychological doctrines of his predecessors are examined. If we consider that Aristotle devoted an entire work (in one book) to Xenophanes and the criticism of his doctrines,[6] it could be natural to infer that he found nothing important on the topic in Xenophanes' thought. There is, however, a passage in the abovementioned chapter of *On the Soul* in which Aristotle discusses the psychology that philosophers more crude than others (τῶν δὲ φορτικωτέρων) upheld.[7] Among them, Aristotle includes Hippo and Critias: the first,

---

[5]   Aët. 4.2–7 Mansfeld and Runia (part 3, 1393–1525) = 4.2–7 (Ps.-Plut. + Stob.), DG (= Diels 1879) 386–393.

[6]   Diog. Laert. 5.25 Dorandi: Πρὸς τὰ Ξενοφάνους α′ (= Xen 6 & 140 SW = Arist. test. 1 Gigon).

[7]   Arist. *De an.* 1.2.405b2–3.

Aristotle notes, identified the soul with water (38 A 10 DK), the second with blood (88 A 23 DK). Aristotle then observes how, in the list of *doxai* he previously provided, the philosophers who had until then described the soul had resorted to all physical elements except the earth (πάντα γὰρ τὰ στοιχεῖα κριτὴν εἴληφε, πλὴν τῆς γῆς). And he adds the following:

ταύτην δ᾽ οὐθεὶς ἀποπέφανται, πλὴν εἴ τις αὐτὴν εἴρηκεν ἐκ πάντων εἶναι τῶν στοιχείων ἢ πάντα.[8]

But this [sc. earth] no one has suggested except in so far as one has said that the soul is composed of, or is identical with, all the elements.[9]

In general, Aristotle is believed to refer here specifically to Empedocles, to whom, shortly before, he had attributed an identical psychological conception, on which, moreover, Empedocles' "like to like" epistemological principle was grounded.[10] But, upon closer inspection, the conjunction ἤ in the passage above seems more than merely epexegetical. Rather, it suggests that Aristotle is here referring not to one, but to two psychological concepts that take the element earth into account: viz., that the soul is a compound (or product) of all elements (i.e., an entity "ontologically" distinct from them) and that the soul is identified with all the elements. Of course, there are those who, like Empedocles, combine these two perspectives. However, in the history of Presocratic thinkers, the only philosopher who reserved a primary role for the earth in his doctrine of principles and of the origin of beings was certainly Xenophanes. Of the two interpretive possibilities that the conjunction ἤ in this passage of *On the Soul* suggests, at least three fragments of Xenophanes' corpus seem to trace the second—viz., identifying ψυχή with πάντα (sc. στοιχεῖα)—back to him.[11]

[8] Arist. *De an.* 1.2.405b9–10.
[9] Translation: Hett 1957:29.
[10] Arist. *De an.* 1.2.404b11–15, with the quotation of 31 B 109 DK.
[11] So already Untersteiner 2008:cxxxix. It is worthwhile to note that the allusion to Xenophanes in the passage of *On the Soul* in question appears at the end of the brief list of "uncouth" doctrines mentioned above. As we know, in the *Metaphysics* (1.5.986b25–27) Aristotle employs a similar expression—μικρὸν ἀγροικότεροι—with regard to Melissus and, not by chance, Xenophanes (21 A 30 DK = Xen 7 SW, see also below).

Christian Vassallo

| 21 B 27 DK | ἐκ γαίης γὰρ πάντα καὶ εἰς γῆν πάντα τελευτᾷ. |
| (= Xen 197, 89 SW)[12] | For from earth come all things, and into earth all end up.[13] |

| 21 B 29 DK | γῆ καὶ ὕδωρ πάντ᾽ ἐσθ᾽ ὅσα γίνοντ᾽ ἠδὲ φύονται. |
| (= Xen 238 SW)[14] | Earth and water are everything that comes into being and grows.[15] |

| 21 B 33 DK | πάντες γὰρ γαίης τε καὶ ὕδατος ἐκγενόμεσθα. |
| (= Xen 89 SW)[16] | For all of us came about from earth and water.[17] |

According to Diels's reconstruction, these three fragments all belong to Xenophanes' *On Nature* (Περὶ φύσεως). But their interpretation is difficult due to two apparent aporias. First, their content does not seem entirely consistent: B 27 testifies in favor of a monistic physical theory (earth *qua* principle), while B 29 and 33 presuppose the existence of at least two elements—i.e., earth and water—which Porphyry (fr. 141bF Smith)[18] rather interpreted as symbols of dry (τὸ ξηρόν) and wet (τὸ ὑγρόν).[19] The other difficulty stems from the fact that Xenophanes' *On Nature* also includes well-known theological fragments.[20] The understanding of God that emerges from them seems inconsistent with a radically "physical" vision of the generation, or rather "formation," of life in the universe.

Before analyzing the psychological lexicon of the Xenophanean corpus in depth, we must take a closer look at frs. 27, 29, and 33 DK. If, as Gomperz already hypothesized[21]—and as I am inclined to believe as well—Xenophanes had a precise (if not systematic) physical view

---

[12] *Ap. Theodor. GAC* 4.5 ~ Sext. Emp. *Math.* 10.313 (= *DG* 284n).

[13] Translation: Laks and Most 2016: vol. 3.2, 41 [8 D 27].

[14] *Ap. Simpl. in Phys.* 189.1 Diels ~ Philop. *in Phys.* 125.30 Vitelli.

[15] Translation: Laks and Most 2016: vol. 3.2, 41 [8 D 25].

[16] *Ap. Sext. Emp. Math.* 10.314.

[17] Translation: Laks and Most 2016: vol. 3.2, 41 [8 D 26].

[18] Xen 157 SW (= *deest* DK).

[19] On all the hermeneutic problems raised by these fragments, I refer to Lesher 1992:124–134, Schäfer 1996:131–136, and Schirren 2013:358–360.

[20] 21 B 23–26 DK (= Xen 116, 86, 229 SW). See also below.

[21] Gomperz 1922:134–136.

of the world, earth and water in his thought could be considered not only as simple *physical elements*, but also as *principles* like those the Milesians theorized. Moreover, on the physical level, earth and water together could represent an early form of "pluralism" in the history of Presocratic philosophy. If everything comes from and can be broken down into earth and water, then even the soul, whatever it is, derives from and can be reduced to earth and water.

As we will see shortly, this inference, which offers a potential first definition of Xenophanes' soul, seems to contradict the testimony of Diogenes Laërtius, which states that Xenophanes thought that the soul (ψυχή) was breath (πνεῦμα).[22] This inconsistency can be resolved in various ways, but, for the moment, let us take a look using Aristotle's account of the *Prinzipienlehre* of his predecessors. As is well known, in the *Metaphysics* Aristotle points out that none of the *physiologoi* who postulated the existence of a single principle (viz., the Monists) identified that principle as the earth.[23] This choice—Aristotle argues— may be due to the fact that, unlike water, air, and above all, fire, the earth is composed of parts too large (διὰ τὴν μεγαλομέρειαν) to act as a principle of everything.[24] Aristotle evidently deems this thesis vulgar and therefore not philosophical: he ascribes it to the majority of men (οἱ πολλοὶ τῶν ἀνθρώπων), who believe that everything is earth (πάντα γὰρ εἶναί φασι γῆν), and notes that this popular tradition finds ample space in poetic texts, such as in Hesiod, for whom the earth was the first body to be generated.[25]

In light of the three fragments cited above, the problem of Xenophanes' absence in this context must be addressed: all the more so, since in Book 5 of the *Metaphysics* (5.4.1014b33), and in Book 2 of the *Physics* (2.1.193a21) as well, the *Prinzipienlehre* that selects the earth

---

[22] Diog. Laert. 9.19 Dorandi (= 21 A 1 DK = Xen 145 SW).
[23] Arist. *Metaph.* 1.8.988b28–32.
[24] Arist. *Metaph.* 1.8.989a5–6.
[25] Arist. *Metaph.* 1.8.989a9–12. Cf. Hes. *Theog.* 116–117, where, in fact, Chaos is said to have appeared first of all, then Earth.

as the original principle is expressly cited. Of the various attempts to explain this fact, at least two are worth mentioning.[26]

  a. According to Deichgräber, the contradiction is only apparent: Aristotle does not ascribe a specific physical doctrine to Xenophanes because he considers him a mere "theologian," who, on the one hand, did not grasp the difference between material and formal cause, and, on the other hand, argued only that the One is God in his speculation on the universe as a whole.[27] Deichgräber's thesis, in fact, only apparently solves the problem at hand and does not take into account the fact that the relationships between Ionic *physiologia* and ancient "theology" are not as clear as they might seem.[28]

  b. Cherniss's position is more convincing and deserves further analysis. Accepting in *Metaph.* 1.8.989a5 the *lectio* τῶν ὕστερον from tradition α of the manuscripts,[29] he maintained that "the limiting phrase in the present passage, οὐδεὶς τῶν ὕστερον, saves him from self-contradiction. This implies either that he did not consider Xenophanes' material principle to be earth (for Xenophanes is later than the Ionians included in τῶν ὕστερον) or that he thought Xenophanes posited more than one element."[30]

II. THE RIDDLE OF DIOGENES LAËRTIUS'S ACCOUNT

Identifying *psyche* with earth (and water) is certainly one of the plausible hypotheses that could help illuminate Xenophanean psychology.[31] But, based on the sources at our disposal, there is another possible definition of the soul according to Xenophanes: viz., soul as life-giving

---

[26] On this point, see the other witnesses recorded in 21 A 36 DK (= Xen 197, 205, 239, and 113 SW).

[27] Arist. *Metaph.* 1.5.986b18–27 (= 21 A 30 DK = Xen 7 SW). See Deichgräber 1938:13–14.

[28] See Graham 2013, who ascribes to the Ionians a "theology of nature" rather than a "natural theology."

[29] So now Primavesi 2012:495: οὐθεὶς γοῦν τῶν ὕστερον ἠξίωσε καὶ ἓν λεγόντων γῆν εἶναι στοιχεῖον, δηλονότι διὰ τὴν μεγαλομέρειαν.

[30] Cherniss 1976:229n50.

[31] See also, in this regard, Gal. *In Hipp. Nat. hom.* 1.2 (= 21 A 36 [IV] DK = Xen 113 ~ 70 SW).

breath or *pneuma*. As previously noted, we find this meaning of the soul in Diogenes Laërtius, and with a view toward my subsequent remarks on this definition, I outline below the wider context in which this peculiar *doxa* appears.

Φησὶ δὲ τέτταρα εἶναι τῶν ὄντων στοιχεῖα, κόσμους δ' ἀπείρους, οὐ παραλλακτοὺς δέ. τὰ νέφη συνίστασθαι τῆς ἀφ' ἡλίου ἀτμίδος ἀναφερομένης καὶ αἰρούσης αὐτὰ εἰς τὸ περιέχον. οὐσίαν θεοῦ σφαιροειδῆ, μηδὲν ὅμοιον ἔχουσαν ἀνθρώπῳ· ὅλον δὲ ὁρᾶν καὶ ὅλον ἀκούειν, μὴ μέντοι ἀναπνεῖν· σύμπαντά τε εἶναι νοῦν καὶ φρόνησιν καὶ ἀίδιον. πρῶτός τε ἀπεφήνατο ὅτι πᾶν τὸ γινόμενον φθαρτόν ἐστι καὶ ἡ ψυχὴ πνεῦμα.[32]

He holds that there are four elements of existent things, and worlds unlimited in number but not overlapping <in time>. Clouds are formed when the vapour from the sun is carried upwards and lifts them into the surrounding air. The substance of God is spherical, in no way resembling man. He is all eye and all ear, but does not breathe; he is the totality of mind and thought, and is eternal. Xenophanes was the first to declare that everything which comes into being is doomed to perish, and that the soul is breath.[33]

This passage undoubtedly raises many problems. One of the greatest difficulties is that it presents a jumble of seemingly disconnected themes: physical, cosmological, meteorological, and theological. It is not easy to determine how the final psychological *doxa* is connected on the philosophical level to what precedes it. Most likely, the *doxa*'s identification of *psyche* with *pneuma* reflects the influence of a later source. In fact, Untersteiner already suggested that a later source would prove useful here.[34] He referred to the use of the expression *psychikon pneuma* in ancient medicine, in particular in Diocles of Carystus (fourth century

---

[32] Diog. Laert. 9.19 Dorandi (= 21 A 1 DK = Xen 145 SW).
[33] Translation: Hicks 1970–1972: vol. 2, 427.
[34] Untersteiner 2008:cclxiv.

BC).[35] However, an analysis of the links between *psyche* and *pneuma* in different contexts is also helpful—for instance, in the meteorological section of the treatise *On the Cosmos* (third century BC?). There, Ps.-Aristotle says that the wind (ἄνεμος) comes from dry exhalations transformed into flow by the cold: in fact, wind is nothing more than a large, concentrated air current that is otherwise called *pneuma* (i.e., "breath").[36] But he then adds (postponing the discussion of this point to another occasion) that the term πνεῦμα may also belong to a completely different lexicon:

Λέγεται δὲ καὶ ἑτέρως πνεῦμα ἥ τε ἐν φυτοῖς καὶ ζῴοις καὶ διὰ πάντων διήκουσα ἔμψυχός τε καὶ γόνιμος οὐσία, περὶ ἧς νῦν λέγειν οὐκ ἀναγκαῖον.[37]

In another sense "breath" means that substance found in plants and animals and pervading everything, that brings life and generation; but about that there is no need to speak now.[38]

The meaning of this passage seems clear: *pneuma* is considered the *principle of life* for all beings. Unless the text is emended philologically,[39] the Stoic nature of such a definition of *pneuma* is quite evident. However, there is no need to insist on this point here, as it involves the *vexata quaestio* of ascribing the treatise *On the Cosmos* to a specific author. Rather, Ps.-Aristotle's evidence is useful in drawing a connection between Diogenes Laërtius's evidence on Xenophanes' soul and the well-known and much discussed fr. 2 DK of Anaximenes, handed down by Aëtius (Ps.-Plutarch) and predicated, as the doxographer himself attests, on the synonymity of air (ἀήρ) and "breath" (πνεῦμα):

---

[35] Cf. Diocl. Car. frs. 78 and 80 van der Eijk (= Anonym. Par. *De morb. ac. et chron.* 2; 5, pp. 10.16–27; 30.14–23 Garofalo), hereto van der Eijk 2000–2001: vol. 2, 160–162, 165–166.

[36] Ps.-Arist. *De mundo* 4.394b7–9.

[37] Ps.-Arist. *De mundo* 4.394b9–12.

[38] Translated by D. J. Furley in Forster and Furley 1955:367.

[39] So Reale and Bos 1995:286, who suggest either expunging καί before διὰ πάντων or, following Holwerda 1993:50, adding the participle <οὖσα> immediately after ζῴοις.

Ἀναξιμένης Εὐρυστράτου Μιλήσιος ἀρχὴν τῶν ὄντων
ἀέρα ἀπεφήνατο· ἐκ γὰρ τούτου πάντα γίνεσθαι καὶ εἰς
αὐτὸν πάλιν ἀναλύεσθαι· οἷον ἡ ψυχή, φησίν, ἡ ἡμετέρα
ἀὴρ οὖσα συγκρατεῖ ἡμᾶς, καὶ ὅλον τὸν κόσμον πνεῦμα
καὶ ἀὴρ περιέχει· λέγεται δὲ συνωνύμως ἀὴρ καὶ πνεῦμα.
κτλ.[40]

Anaximenes, the son of Eurystratus, the Milesian declared
air to be (the) principle of the things that exist, for
from this all things come to be and (back) to it they are
dissolved again. "Just as," he says, "our soul, which is air,
holds us together and dominates us, so also *pneuma* and
air contain the entire cosmos." (Air and *pneuma* are used
synonymously.) Etc.[41]

The authenticity of this witness is highly disputed. In the supposedly
Anaximenean fragment it transmits, there is a series of anachronisms
that make it impossible to assign these words to Anaximenes without
reservation. In particular, the use, on the one hand, of the term *kosmos*
in the sense of universe or order of the world and, on the other, the
analogy between microcosm and macrocosm are not attested before
Heraclitus (22 B 30 DK) and Democritus (68 B 34 DK), respectively.
Mansfeld, in particular, has recently focused on these anachronisms
and other evidence that seem to make this fragment irremediably
spurious.[42] Apart from the question of its authenticity, the passage also
contains an analogy between the directive role of the *soul* in relation to

[40] Aët. 1.3.3 Mansfeld and Runia (part 1, 201) = 1.3.4 (Ps.-Plut.), *DG* 278 (= 13 B 2 DK = As
35 Wöhrle).

[41] Translation: Mansfeld and Runia 2020: part 4, 2066.

[42] Mansfeld 2018b:169–170. By contrast, Sassi 2020:170 (with n11) is cautiously inclined
to accept the fragment's authenticity. According to Alt 1973, in Aët. 1.3, Anaximenes was
actually confused with Diogenes of Apollonia, but Mansfeld has criticized this hypothesis. On the other hand, Laks 2018:12n30, who does not rule out a priori an Anaximenean
concept of an "ensouled" (viz., "living") world, points out "that Alt is right to insist that
the outlook of Aëtius' entry on Anaximenes taken as a whole [...] points to the Peripatetic
background of Aëtius' notice, rather than a Stoic one." On this point, see also Betegh
2013:254–257.

the individual and that of the *air* in relation to the universe.[43] Although *indirectly*, this analogy exploits a similarity between the individual soul and a physical element (or principle) but does not make them the same thing. Since, as the doxographer interprets, for Anaximenes air and *pneuma* are synonymous, the evidence does not equate the individual soul with air and therefore does not identify an individual soul with *pneuma*. However, what Diogenes Laërtius says more succinctly about Xenophanes can perhaps be found in Aëtius's report on Anaximenes' psychology as well: i.e., *psyche* is *pneuma*, as the soul unifies and gives life to individuals just as "breath" (air) unifies and gives life to the entire universe. Thus, the philosophical reason behind Diogenes' *doxa* on Xenophanes is also explained: it is the synthesis of the physical, cosmological, meteorological, and theological information that precedes the *doxa* on the soul. It is possible, then, that both testimonies, Diogenes' on Xenophanes and Aëtius's on Anaximenes, have a common philosophical root. But while in Aëtius the soul in question is explicitly an individual soul (ἡ ἡμετέρα), not necessarily immortal but nevertheless inside the individual,[44] in Diogenes it oscillates ambiguously between an individual and a universal sense (and in this latter sense it could be considered a kind of World Soul). Hence, in light of the doxographical genesis of 13 B 2 DK, I believe that the identification of *psyche* with *pneuma* in 21 A 1 DK can certainly be attributed to the influence of a late source, which, following Mansfeld, I am inclined to consider, once again, of Stoic nature.[45]

We cannot rule out, however, the possibility that Xenophanes actually used the term *pneuma* in his writings (although he may have used it in a somewhat or entirely different sense from the term's meaning in the doxographical versions that overlap these usages). And, on the other hand, it seems possible, on the basis of the sources available to us, to reconstitute the link between the soul and (the concept of) *pneuma* in a strictly physical, rather than generically cosmological, sense. In order to examine the likelihood that Xenophanes used the term *pneuma*, we

[43] On this analogic procedure, see Lloyd 1966:235–236 and 254n2.
[44] See Schäfer 2009:58.
[45] See Mansfeld 2018b:170n10.

must discuss another Aëtian passage devoted to Xenophanes' physics and cosmology. In Aët. 3.4.4 Mansfeld and Runia,[46] *pneuma* refers to the physical phenomenon of the wind. Aëtius claims that, according to Xenophanes, the atmospheric phenomena occur because of the warmth of the sun (ἀπὸ τῆς τοῦ ἡλίου θερμότητος), which represents their "efficient cause" in Peripatetic terms. The clouds (νέφη) are generated in this way: the heat of the sun evaporates the moisture of the sea; the sweet part (τὸ γλυκύ) of seawater dissolves due to its particles and forms the clouds, which turn into fog (ὀμιχλούμενον), causing rain (ὄμβρους) after condensation and *exhaling the winds* (διατμίζειν τὰ πνεύματα). To confirm his attribution of this explanation of the atmospheric phenomena to Xenophanes, Aëtius cites the first part of line 1 of 21 B 30 DK (= Xen 345 SW). In this fragment, the sea is considered the source of water and, through water (and its transformations), also the source of winds, clouds, rivers, and rain.[47] The doxographer describes the *anemoi*—i.e., the winds of which Xenophanes speaks in the fragment—with the term *pneumata*.[48] Now, is there a link between such a physical understanding of *pneuma* and Xenophanes' concept of soul? In other words, is it possible to argue that for Xenophanes the soul, as well as the wind and other atmospheric phenomena, finds its origin in water, and in seawater in particular? Upon closer inspection, such a hypothesis is by no means unprecedented in early Greek philosophy. In a well-known passage from his *Stromata* (6.17.1–2), Clement of Alexandria highlights the soul's watery origin, as well as its link with moisture more generally, via a comparison between an Orphic fragment, *OF* 437 Bernabé,[49] and, cited immediately afterward, Heraclitus's fr. 36

---

[46] Mansfeld and Runia 2020: part 3, 1203–1204 = (Stob.) *DG* 371 (= 21 A 46 DK = Xen 217 SW).

[47] πηγὴ δ᾽ ἐστὶ θάλασσ᾽ ὕδατος, πηγὴ δ᾽ ἀνέμοιο | οὔτε γὰρ ἐν νέφεσιν <γίνοιτό κε ἲς ἀνέμοιο | ἐκπνείοντος> ἔσωθεν ἄνευ πόντου μεγάλοιο | οὔτε ῥοαὶ ποταμῶν οὔτ᾽ αἰθ<έρος> ὄμβριον ὕδωρ, |⁵ ἀλλὰ μέγας πόντος γενέτωρ νεφέων ἀνέμων τε | καὶ ποταμῶν ... (text by Laks and Most 2016: vol. 3.2, 52 [8 D 46]).

[48] Cf., e.g., Hdt. 7.16.7–9.

[49] ἔστιν ὕδωρ ψυχῆι θάνατος, χὐδάττεσσι δὲ γαῖα· | ἐκ δ᾽ ὕδατος <πέλε> γαῖα, τὸ δ᾽ ἐκ γαίας πάλιν ὕδωρ, | ἐκ τοῦ δὴ ψυχὴ ὅλον αἰθέρα ἀλλάσσουσα. Cf. also *OF* 436 Bernabé.

DK (= fr. 66 Marcovich).[50] Clement intends here to prove that the Greeks took ideas from each other and that they essentially said nothing new.[51] But, apart from this polemical intent, he also philosophically links the two fragments by interweaving the stages of the soul and that of the physical elements that make up its essence (i.e., water and earth): the soul "is generated" by water just as water "generates" from the earth, and, at the same time, the soul "dies," becoming water just as water "dies" and becomes earth. In other words, these physical elements are what everything comes from and to which everything returns.

This understanding of the soul leads us to hypothesize that Xenophanes, if he ever posited a link between the soul and *pneuma*, did so in relation to the foundations of his physical theory, based, as we have seen above, on the belief that everything derives from water and earth. We find further confirmation of the physical nature of the bond between the soul and *pneuma* in Xenophanes in the aforementioned testimony by Diogenes Laërtius with reference to the paraphrase of 21 B 24 DK (= Xen 86 SW). This version differs significantly from the one we read in Sextus Empiricus:[52] Diogenes says that God sees and hears everything, but he adds that God *does not breathe* (μὴ μέντοι ἀναπνεῖν). The verb ἀναπνεῖν is clearly derived from πνεῦμα. If Xenophanes had actually ascribed to it the Stoic definition of the soul as breath/*pneuma*, as used by Diogenes, then consequently Xenophanes would have understood the soul as an *exclusively human* characteristic. However, this claim is clearly not based in Stoic principles and only indirectly involves *pneuma*. On the grounds of this inference, some have advanced the hypothesis that this is sufficient evidence of a polemic against the Pythagorean concept of the individual soul and the idea that a Soul exists in the living World.[53] Although this conclusion cannot be ruled out a priori, I think it is more likely that the Xenophanean concept of

---

[50] ψυχῆσιν θάνατος ὕδωρ γενέσθαι, ὕδατι δὲ θάνατος γῆν γενέσθαι· ἐκ γῆς δὲ ὕδωρ γίνεται, ἐξ ὕδατος δὲ ψυχή. Cf. 22 B 76 DK (= fr. 66[e] Marcovich), B 12 DK (= fr. 40 Marcovich), and B 31 DK (= fr. 53 Marcovich).

[51] See Osborne 1987:5–7.

[52] Sext. Emp. *Math.* 9.144: οὖλος ὁρᾷ, οὖλος δὲ νοεῖ, οὖλος δέ τ' ἀκούει.

[53] See Schäfer 1996:200: "Das mag gegen die pythagoreische Ansicht einer symbiontischen Seele oder einer belebenden Weltseele gehen."

a God devoid of a soul links the question of Xenophanes' psychology to the field of mortality—that is, to the domain of the laws that govern how mortal beings and physical phenomena come to be and pass away again. Perhaps it is not a coincidence that Diogenes places Xenophanes' identification of soul and *pneuma* immediately after the *doxa* on the corruptibility of every becoming being (πᾶν τὸ γινόμενον φθαρτόν ἐστι), in a kind of cause-and-effect relationship. Read in this way (in the absence of any doxographical overlaps), Diogenes Laërtius's witness proves very useful. It is therefore necessary to test this reading, which highlights the physicality and mortality of the soul, by comparing it with various passages of the *Corpus Xenophanenum*.

III. AGAINST PYTHAGORAS?

We may begin with a witness by Maximus of Tyre that is not recorded in the Diels-Kranz collection. In *Dissertation* 38, which discusses whether a man may become good by divine destiny, Maximus recalls the case of the epic poet Aristeas. He maintained that his soul (τὴν ψυχὴν αὐτῷ), leaving his body, rose in flight, crossing all of Greece and beyond, until it reached the Hyperborean regions. In regard to these events concerning the soul (i.e., its reincarnations and its superior visions), Maximus points out, Aristeas was more convincing than Anaxagoras, Xenophanes, or some others who tried to explain reality (τις ἄλλος τῶν ἐξηγησαμένων τὰ ὄντα ὡς ἔχει). In fact, men have never clearly understood the transmigration of the soul (τὴν ψυχῆς περιπόλησιν) and the way in which it "sees" after the death of the body: however, they have always been convinced that the soul must "travel" in order to be able to report the supreme truths of the things it contemplated.[54] The testimony is evidently imbued with Middle Platonist influences. However, for the purposes of the present survey, it raises two points as interesting as they are problematic. The first point concerns the possibility of extending the reference to Anaxagoras,

---

[54] Max. Tyr. *Diss.* 38.3.g Koniaris (= Xen 78 SW). On Aristeas's legend and its importance for understanding the archaic Greek concept of soul, see Bremmer 1983:24–45; also Zhmud 2016.

Xenophanes, and the other (naturalist) philosophers. They seem to be called into question for their (common) theory of the transmigration of the soul (or, at any rate, of the life of the soul after the death of the body), although Maximus criticizes them for not having been as clear and convincing (πιθανώτερος) as Aristeas on this issue. The other point concerns the attribution of the concept of the soul's transmigration both to Anaxagoras and Xenophanes, which, in my opinion, reveals the shakiness of the evidence on this question. In the remaining evidence concerning Anaxagoras we do not find any source that can confirm this *doxa*, and yet we know that for him, life and death were nothing more than the union and separation of particles (59 B 17 DK). As for Xenophanes, the only passage known to us that takes metempsychosis into account (i.e., fr. 7 DK) is the excerpt of an elegy handed down by Diogenes Laërtius (8.36). But the interpretation of these lines is notoriously controversial, as it involves the problem of Xenophanes' attitude toward Pythagoras. In the elegy in question, according to Diogenes, Xenophanes testified that Pythagoras would be reincarnated several times (περὶ δὲ τοῦ ἄλλοτε ἄλλον αὐτὸν γεγενῆσθαι). After mentioning the incipit of the elegy,[55] Diogenes quotes the section of it that refers to a curious anecdote about Pythagoras's theory of *Seelenwanderung*:

καί ποτέ μιν στυφελιζομένου σκύλακος παριόντα
    φασὶν ἐποικτῖραι καὶ τόδε φάσθαι ἔπος·
"παῦσαι μηδὲ ῥάπιζ', ἐπεὶ ἦ φίλου ἀνέρος ἐστὶ
    ψυχή, τὴν ἔγνων φθεγξαμένης ἀίων."[56]

And they say that when he was once passing by a puppy that was being mistreated, | he took pity and said these words: | "Stop beating it, since this is truly the soul | of a dear friend which I recognized on hearing it cry out."[57]

---

[55] νῦν αὖτ' ἄλλον ἔπειμι λόγον, δείξω δὲ κέλευθον.

[56] 21 B 7 DK (= Xen 141 SW). Other sources of the fragment are *Sud.* 9.46 (= Xen 287 SW) and *Anth. Gr.* 7.120 (= Xen 334 SW).

[57] Translation: Laks and Most 2016: vol. 3.2, 71 [8 D 64], with some changes (for the consequences of these changes, see below).

From Rohde onward,[58] these lines have generally been considered a *Verspottung* of Pythagoras and his theory of metempsychosis. The context of this piece of evidence seems to encourage such a reading. Indeed, in this section of Book 8 of Diogenes Laërtius's *Lives*, some very biting and derisory judgments on Pythagoras and on the Pythagoreans in general are collected.[59] Without a doubt, the passage has an anti-Pythagorean character. Our concern is rather to understand whether it only wittily criticizes, as many texts do, Pythagoras's person or whether Xenophanes attempts to attack Pythagoras (and Pythagoreanism) on a more doctrinal level. In my opinion, a careful analysis of the fragment supports the second reading. To prove that this fragment is more than a fun anecdote, I would like to focus on the use of the term *psyche*. Xenophanes employs this term after careful consideration: his listeners would not have understood even the superficial aspects of his criticism if Pythagoras had not used that term himself, in one way or another, or if Xenophanes had not evoked the concept of the soul from early Pythagoreanism.[60] The philosophical point of this anecdote, therefore, lies not in the transmigration of the soul and its grotesque implications, but in the nature of the soul and its functions. It is the soul that is recognized and heard, not the friend as such (note the feminine τὴν ... φθεγξαμένης).

Indeed, in recent years, some scholars have tried to further explore this very aspect of the passage at issue. According to one line of interpretation, Xenophanes philosophically criticizes the Pythagorean concept of the individual soul in his attack on the *Seelenwanderung*, proposing the concept of soul-*pneuma* instead: more generally, this criticism of Pythagoras is only one aspect of Xenophanes' more general criticism of the popular conception of divinity, i.e., anthropomorphism, since, in fact, each "metempsychosis" is at odds with the

[58] Rohde 1903: vol. 2, 162n6. For a *status quaestionis*, I refer to Untersteiner 2008:122–125n.

[59] In addition to Xenophanes, Diogenes cites Timon of Phlius (fr. 57 Di Marco = *SH* 831), who is said to have criticized Pythagoras but also to have emphasized his solemn bearing, and then Cratinus's (frs. 6–7 Kassel-Austin), Mnesimachus's (fr. 1 Kassel-Austin), and Aristophon's (fr. 12 Kassel-Austin) *Verspottungen*.

[60] See Huffman 2009:35 and Zhmud 2012:152.

"metamorphosis" it entails.[61] On the other hand, it sounds blasphemous inasmuch as it claims to guarantee immortality for humankind, which is rather, according to Xenophanes, the true difference between men and gods.[62] This reading partly hits the mark, as the weak point of Pythagoras's *Seelenwanderung* (in Xenophanes' thought) is his claim to reconcile the contradiction between the soul's movement from one body to another and the permanence of its *individuality* (*Ego*). But it is unlikely that Xenophanes launches such criticism in order to espouse the alternative concept of the soul-*pneuma*. This concept, on the one hand, certainly offers a sound philosophical explanation for the mechanism of the *intelligibile in sensibili* but, on the other hand, is rather the result of Stoic contamination in Diogenes Laërtius's account on Xenophanes, as we said above. And even less convincing is the attempt[63] to connect Xenophanes' concept of the soul to 21 B 16 DK (= Xen 117 SW), a fragment of his *Silloi* that contains a kind of manifesto of Xenophanes' criticism of anthropomorphism: different peoples have various representations of divinity, according to their own genetic characteristics; i.e., the Ethiopians make them snub-nosed and dark, while the Thracians give them blue eyes and red hair.[64] But B 16 must be properly contextualized. Its source is Clement of Alexandria,[65] which means we should approach it with a good deal of caution. Indeed, Clement points out in his polemics that the Greeks give the gods a *human shape* and consequently *human passions* as well. He adds that even men in his own time represent the gods as they themselves are, and, in order to give an impression of this tendency, Clement cites the Xenophanean fragment in question. Immediately after this quotation, Clement adds that men do the same not only for the physical appearances of the gods, but for their souls (τὰς ψυχάς) as well: the barbarians represent them as fierce and violent, while the

---

[61] So Schäfer 2009:54–61, who also cites Fränkel's (1993:311–312) not entirely convincing attempt to solve this *aporia*.

[62] Schäfer 2009:64. Cf. the evidence collected in 21 A 13 DK (= Xen 12, 59, 61, 63 SW).

[63] Schäfer 2009:64–65.

[64] Αἰθίοπές τε <θεοὺς σφετέρους> σιμοὺς μέλανάς τε | Θρῆκές τε γλαυκοὺς καὶ πυρρούς <φασι πέλεσθαι>.

[65] Clem. Al. *Strom.* 7.4.22.1–2.

Greeks describe theirs as milder, as well as endowed with (human) passions. Therefore, Clement concludes, it follows that bad people have bad representations of God, but that good people have excellent representations of him. As we can see, first of all, the reference to the *psychai* is only in Clement, not in Xenophanes; secondly, the term *psyche* refers here to the "ethical" disposition of the gods (and, by consequence, of human beings) rather than to the individual soul and its nature.

Lesher, for his part, has highlighted the epistemological aspects of the anti-Pythagorean criticism in B 7, in the sense that the fragment targets "the preposterous idea that a particular dog can be known (ἔγνων) to be the *psyche* of a dear friend based on the sound of its voice" (viz., the voice of the soul, not that of the dog). According to this perspective, the criticism focuses on the link between body and soul, and more specifically on the chance of knowing the soul through the body.[66] This reading, in my opinion, can help us solve some of the problems at hand. In fact, I think that the criticism of the concept of the individual soul in the fragment targets not the link between body and soul *per se*, but rather the idea of a soul as an *autonomous* "center of perceptions" or *anima patiens*. If so, it is quite evident, in my opinion, that Xenophanes agrees in large part with archaic epic on this point.[67] As Snell has pointed out, ψυχή, "das Wort für Seele im späteren Griechisch, hat mit der denkenden, fühlenden Seele ursprünglich nichts zu tun."[68] The Homeric soul is a "soul" as such insofar as it "ensouls" the body: that is, it keeps the body alive. There is no trace, in the *Iliad* in particular, of a soul *qua* independent center of emotions and passions:[69] the soul is rather the source of life for the body, as long as death does not occur.[70] In the anecdote of B 7, we (apparently) see

---

[66] Lesher 1992:80.

[67] *Pace* Untersteiner 2008:126n, although the scholar seems to refer to the Pythagorean concept of the soul rather than to Xenophanes' psychology as it stands out from the (alleged) criticism against Pythagoras.

[68] Snell 2011:18.

[69] I refer, in particular, to Snell 2011:13–29 (esp. 18–19), in addition to Böhme 1929. See, however, the caveat in Bremmer 1983:14–24.

[70] Cf., e.g., *Il.* 21.569.

the soul defined as the center of perceptions through the description of the friend's soul that "feels" the beatings suffered by the dog in which it has been embodied. This phenomenon, which we may define as the "perceptive symbiosis" of body and soul, is inconceivable if—as I believe Xenophanes thought—the soul possessed merely "physicobiological" functions, which have nothing to do with psychological or spiritual affections. I think that this fact has some bearing on the interpretation of B 7 even if it were reduced to an anti-Pythagorean tirade.

If we use B 7, for instance, to reread B 15 (= Xen 116 SW), the "physico-biological" nature of the body-soul connection seems to be clearly confirmed. Quoted by Clement,[71] this fragment portrays how animals, if they had hands, would represent (by drawing or writing) the gods. Under normal circumstances, animals, since they lack hands (or perhaps a voice), have (i.e., manifest) no conception of gods. This is what makes animals' "souls" inferior to humans'. The fragment at issue also suggests that Xenophanes' soul must be merely the center of vegetative functions, or basically nothing more than animals usually have, although they are voiceless and underdeveloped in comparison to human beings. Such a concept of the soul is clearly *not independent* from the physical constitution of the body, especially from the organs that transmit and show feelings and/or thoughts. As I will discuss further below, this complex relationship between biology, physiology, and psychology can be extended to the main distinction between a soul *qua* "principle of life" and a soul *qua* "center of command" of vital functions and/or mental representations. In large part, underestimated and (partly) unexploited sources better explain this point.

IV. THE PHYSICAL SIDE OF XENOPHANES' PSYCHOLOGY

The few further pieces of evidence on Xenophanean psychology available to us, although late, do not seem to disprove the interpretive line followed thus far. Macrobius, for example, indicates in a brief aside that the soul overlaps with the physical elements in Xenophanes' thought: *Xenophanes ex terra et aqua* (sc. *animam esse dicit*). The broader

---

[71] *Strom.* 5.109.1.

context of this witness recorded in Strobel and Wöhrle's edition, which reproduces the entire sequence of the doxographical list (from Critolaus to Epicurus),[72] allows us to make a better comparison with the extended parallel passage in Aët. 4.3 Mansfeld and Runia, where, as already in Aristotle, Xenophanes' name is missing (see above, section I). It is hard to say whether this means that Macrobius relied on a source partly different from Aëtius. However, I am quite sure that the concepts of earth and water which, according to Macrobius, coincide with Xenophanes' soul refer directly to frs. 27, 29, and 33 DK (see above, section I): given that in the Latin language the word *anima* has a meaning very similar to the Greek πνεῦμα,[73] Macrobius clearly traces Xenophanes' concept of the soul back to the vital "breath" and the exhalation process which derive from the ongoing transition from wet to dry and vice versa.[74] Macrobius's doxographical source probably overinterprets the cited fragments, but even so it further proves, in my view, that Xenophanes' psychology was (primarily) a matter of physics.

Upon closer inspection, this claim is also confirmed by the *Turba philosophorum*, a very disputed and shaky source that should be taken into account only with extreme caution but should certainly not be overlooked. The original text of this work dates back to about AD 900. The Latin version circulated as early as the mid-twelfth century and is divided into two parts: one cosmological and the other alchemical.[75] The first part is devoted to the doctrine of the principles of nine Presocratics, the last of which is Xenophanes, here called Eximenus, discussed in *sermo* 9. In Strobel and Wöhrle's edition, this evidence is labeled Xen 304.[76] The passage, in reality, seems to have had only marginal importance for the question of the soul; it rather deals with

---

[72] Macrob. *In Somn.* 1.14.20 (= 21 A 50 DK = Xen 203 SW): *Critolaus Peripateticus constare eam de quinta essentia, Hipparchus ignem, Anaximenes aera, Empedocles et Critias sanguinem, Parmenides ex terra et igne, Xenophanes ex terra et aqua, Boethos ex aere et igne, Epicurus speciem ex igne et aere et spiritu mixtam.*

[73] See, e.g., Ernout and Meillet 2001:34 (s.v.).

[74] So Vitali 2000:130.

[75] For a new critical reconstruction of this text, see Lacaze 2018.

[76] *Turba phil.* 63–65 Lacaze (pp. 376–381) = 82–83 Plessner (~ 116.33–117.27 Ruska) & 117.28–118.5 Ruska. On the question of *sermo* 9's actual division into two parts, see Strobel and Wöhrle 2018:312n2.

the formation of the cosmos and God's role in it, through the arrangement of the four elements. At the end of his exposition, Eximenus urges the crowd not to destroy their soul and their money (*nolite ergo et animas et pecunias uestras destruere*), and not to be sad. As we can see, this witness does not exactly help us determine a philosophical definition for the soul. But we should consider the fact that it falls in the alchemical section of the *Turba*, which focuses on the color of metal and its transformation. I find this reference to color extremely interesting: it is closely connected to the problem of motion in Xenophanes' "astronephology," where, for instance, a certain internal motion explains luminescence.[77] If—as I am inclined to believe—Xenophanes' soul is simply a principle of life, especially of beings like breathing animals, I wonder whether, on this point, Xenophanes may be linked to Alcmaeon's idea of motion as the essence of the soul.[78] Thus, just as different kinds of motion, either steady and internal (like the moon, sun, stars) or sudden, short-lived, and forced by wind (such as lightning or shooting stars), produce light and color, so too is the soul made of a kind of steady, internal motion, ultimately traceable to the God who "swings (i.e. moves) everything"—πάντα κραδαίνει. In this regard, the *Turba*'s text above could really have preserved something originally Xenophanean in postulating a link between life and color, i.e., between (*lato sensu*) "biological" phenomena and their epiphenomenal "qualities."

The other passage of the *Turba* recorded in Strobel and Wöhrle's edition, Xen 305, contains *sermo* 14.[79] Here, Xenophanes (if the allusion actually refers to him) is indicated with the name Arsuberes.[80] His speech appears in the alchemical section of the work, which discusses sulfur and moisture, both held together by a similar element. Here, we find a new and (for our purposes) more relevant reference to the soul. The crowd asks Arsuberes what moisture is, and Arsuberes gives the following answer:

---

[77] 22 A 39 DK (= Xen 97 SW).
[78] 24 A 12 [I] DK (= Alk 3 Wöhrle) and A 12 [IV] DK (= Alk 57 Wöhrle).
[79] *Turba phil.* 74–78 Lacaze (pp. 405–411) = 123.9–124.22 Ruska.
[80] See Strobel and Wöhrle 2018:314n1.

cum uenenum corpus penetrat, inuariabili ipsum colore colorat, et <u>nunquam dimittit corpus animam, quae compar sibi est, a se separari</u>. De quo inuidi dixerunt quod persequente fugienti obuiante ab eis fuga aufertur et ueritas sequitur; et quod natura suum cepit comparem ut inimicum et se inuicem continuerunt, eo quod ex sulfure sulfuri mixto pretiosissimus fit color qui non uariatur nec ab igne fugit quando anima corporis intima infertur ac corpus continet et colorat.[81]

When poison penetrates the body, it colors it with an invariable color, and <u>the body never allows the soul, which is its partner, to separate from it</u>. On which the envious said that, when the pursuer meets with the fugitive, the escape is removed by them and the truth follows; and that nature (i.e., the body) has taken as its partner (i.e., the soul) what had to be its enemy and they have joined one another, since from sulfur mixed with sulfur derives a precious color, which does not change or escape from fire when the soul enters the intimacy of the body and contains (i.e., keeps fixed) and gives color to the body.[82]

As we can see, in this passage of the *Turba*, soul and body are linked not through the concept of a soul that "feels" according to the perceptions of the body, but through a body that shares its own "chemical-biological" structure with the soul. Thus, although it is a late and very problematic piece of evidence,[83] *sermo* 14 of the *Turba* not only does not contradict, but in many ways confirms my argument thus far: viz., that Xenophanes' *psyche* does not resemble an *anima patiens* in any way and, further, that it also bears no resemblance to an *anima cogitans*.

---

[81] *Turba phil.* 78.1–3 Lacaze: cf. Riccardiana (**R**) + MS of Prague (**Q**), p. 123 Lacaze.

[82] The translation is mine.

[83] The text deals with transformation of ignoble metals into noble ones (color → moisture → purple).

V. RETROSPECT

A systematic analysis of the entire *Corpus Xenophaneum* shows that Xenophanes' psychology essentially remains anchored to the archaic vision of a *psyche* as the center of vegetative functions, rather than as an *autonomous* source of perception and principle of knowledge. As mentioned above, this view is attested (although with a few exceptions) particularly in the *Iliad*. This does not mean, however, that Xenophanes blindly accepted the concept of *psyche* chiefly employed by archaic Greek epic. Like all of his contemporaries, he himself, by his own admission, learned everything from Homer,[84] but he also had the courage to criticize the poet for the aspects of Homeric culture he considered unacceptable, particularly in the theological field.[85] Thus, despite the weight of Homeric heritage, Xenophanes also had to develop his own psychology, consistent with the basic principles of his thought, and to adapt the archaic conception of the soul to his *physiologia*, which we cannot consider—as Aristotle claimed—mere *theologia*. For Xenophanes, the soul's dependence on the physical elements (earth and water) did not make it the "identity card" of the individual (living or not), but merely an essential part of a constant, circular physical process, whose functioning is completely detached from the spheres of religion and ethics.

FRIEDRICH-SCHILLER-UNIVERSITÄT JENA,
INSTITUT FÜR ALTERTUMSWISSENSCHAFTEN

WORKS CITED

Alt, Karin. 1973. "Zum Satz des Anaximenes über die Seele: Untersuchungen von Aetios ΠΕΡΙ ΑΡΧΩΝ." *Hermes* 101:129–164.

Bartoš, Hynek, and Colin Guthrie King, eds. 2020. *Heat, Pneuma, and Soul in Ancient Philosophy and Science*. Cambridge.

Betegh, Gábor. 2013. "On the Physical Aspect of Heraclitus' Psychology: With New Appendices." In *Doctrine and Doxography: Studies on*

---

[84] 21 B 10 DK (= Xen 71 SW).
[85] 21 B 11–12 DK (= Xen 87, 81 SW).

Heraclitus and Pythagoras, ed. David Sider and Dirk Obbink, Sozomena 14, 225–261. Berlin and Boston. Revised version of "On the Physical Aspect of Heraclitus' Psychology," *Phronesis* 52 (2017): 3–32.

———. 2020. "Thinking with Empedocles: Aristotle on the Soul as *Harmonia*." *Oxford Studies in Ancient Philosophy* 59:1–44.

Böhme, Joachim. 1929. *Die Seele und das Ich im homerischen Epos: Mit einem Anhang; Vergleich mit dem Glauben der Primitiven.* Leipzig and Berlin.

Bremmer, Jan N. 1983. *The Early Greek Concept of the Soul.* Princeton.

Cherniss, Harold F. 1976. *Aristotle's Criticism of Presocratic Philosophy.* New York (orig. pub. Baltimore, 1935).

Deichgräber, Karl. 1938. "Xenophanes ΠΕΡΙ ΦΥΣΕΩΣ." *Rheinisches Museum für Philologie*, n.s., 87:1–31.

Diels, Hermann. 1879. *Doxographi Graeci.* Berlin.

Edmonds, Radcliffe G., III. 2014. "A Lively Afterlife and Beyond: The Soul in Plato, Homer, and the Orphica." *Études platoniciennes* 11. http://doi.org/10.4000/etudesplatoniciennes.507.

Ernout, Alfred, and Antoine Meillet. 2001. *Dictionnaire étymologique de la langue latine: Histoire des mots.* Reprint of 4th rev. ed., rev. Jacques André, 1959. Paris (orig. pub. Paris, 1932).

Forster, Edward S., and David J. Furley, trans. 1955. *Aristotle: On Sophistical Refutations; On Coming-To-Be and Passing Away; On the Cosmos.* Loeb Classical Library 400. Cambridge, MA, and London.

Fränkel, Hermann. 1993. *Dichtung und Philosophie des frühen Griechentums: Eine Geschichte der griechischen Epik, Lyrik und Prosa bis zur Mitte des fünften Jahrhunderts.* 4th ed. Munich (orig. pub. New York, 1951).

Frede, Dorothea, and Burkhard Reis, eds. 2009. *Body and Soul in Ancient Philosophy.* Berlin and New York.

Gomperz, Theodor. 1922. *Griechische Denker: Eine Geschichte der antiken Philosophie.* Vol. 1. 4th ed. Berlin and Leipzig (orig. pub. Leipzig, 1896).

Graham, Daniel W. 2013. "The Theology of Nature in the Ionian Tradition." *Rhizomata* 1, no. 2:194–216.

Hett, Walter S., trans. 1957. *Aristotle: On the Soul; Parva naturalia; On Breath.* Rev. ed. Loeb Classical Library 288. Cambridge, MA (orig. pub. London and Cambridge, MA, 1936).

Hicks, Robert D., trans. 1970–1972. *Diogenes Laertius: Lives of Eminent Philosophers.* 2 vols. Reprint. Loeb Classical Library 184–185. Cambridge, MA, and London (orig. pub. Cambridge, MA, and London, 1925).

Holwerda, Douwe. 1993. "Textkritisches und Exegetisches zur pseudo-Aristotelischen Schrift Περὶ τοῦ κόσμου." *Mnemosyne*, n.s., 46, no. 1:46–55.

Huffman, Carl. 2009. "The Pythagorean Conception of the Soul from Pythagoras to Philolaus." In Frede and Reis 2009, 21–43.

Inwood, Brad. 2009. "Empedocles and *Metempsychôsis*: The Critique of Diogenes of Oenoanda." In Frede and Reis 2009, 71–86.

Lacaze, Grégoire. 2018. *Turba Philosophorum: Congrès pythagoricien sur l'art d'Hermès; Édition critique, traduction et présentation.* Philosophia Antiqua 150. Leiden and Boston.

Laks, André. 2018. "How Preplatonic Worlds Became Ensouled." *Oxford Studies in Ancient Philosphy* 55:1–34.

Laks, André, and Glenn W. Most, eds. and trans. 2016. *Early Greek Philosophy.* 9 vols. Loeb Classical Library 524–532. Cambridge, MA, and London.

Lesher, James H. 1992. *Xenophanes of Colophon. Fragments.* Phoenix Suppl. 30 / Presocratics 4. Toronto, Buffalo, and London.

Lloyd, Geoffrey E. R. 1966. *Polarity and Analogy: Two Types of Argumentation in Early Greek Thought.* Cambridge.

Long, Anthony A. 2009. "Heraclitus on Measure and the Explicit Emergence of Rationality." In Frede and Reis 2009, 87–109.

Mansfeld, Jaap. 2018a. "Alcmaeon and Plato on Soul." In Mansfeld 2018d, 251–261. Previously published in *Études platoniciennes* 11 (2014). http://doi.org/10.4000/etudesplatoniciennes.508.

———. 2018b. "Anaximenes' Soul." In Mansfeld 2018d, 167–176. English translation of "De ziel van Anaximenes," *Nederlands theologisch Tijdschrift* 70, no. 3 (2016): 187–194.

————. 2018c. "Heraclitus on Soul and Super-Soul: With an Afterthought on the Afterlife." In Mansfeld 2018d, 218–250. Previously published in *Rhizomata* 3 (2015): 62–93.

————. 2018d. *Studies in Early Greek Philosophy: A Collection of Papers and One Review.* Philosophia Antiqua 151. Leiden and Boston.

Mansfeld, Jaap, and David T. Runia. 2020. *Aëtiana V: The Method and Intellectual Context of a Doxographer.* Vol. 5, *An Edition of the Reconstructed Text of the Placita with a Commentary and a Collection of Related Texts.* 4 parts. Philosophia Antiqua 153. Leiden and Boston.

Mourelatos, Alexander P. D. 2020. "All the Texts for Xenophanes of Colophon: Critical Discussion of Benedikt Strobel & Georg Wöhrle (Elvira Wakelnig & Christian Vassallo, Collaborators), Xenophanes von Kolophon, Traditio Praesocratica 3 (Berlin and Boston: De Gruyter, 2018)." *Rhizomata* 8, no. 1:132–147.

Osborne, Catherine. 1987. *Rethinking Early Greek Philosophy: Hippolytus of Rome and the Presocratics.* Ithaca, NY.

Primavesi, Oliver. 2012. "Aristotle, *Metaphysics* A: A New Critical Edition with Introduction." In *Aristotle's Metaphysics Alpha: Symposium Aristotelicum,* ed. Carlos Steel, 385–516. Oxford.

Reale, Giovanni, and Abraham P. Bos. 1995. *Il trattato Sul cosmo per Alessandro attribuito ad Aristotele: Monografia introduttiva, testo greco con traduzione a fronte, commentario, bibliografia ragionata e indici.* 2nd ed. Temi metafisici e problemi del pensiero antico 42. Milan (orig. pub. Naples, 1974).

Rechenauer, Georg. 2009. "Demokrits Seelenmodell und die Prinzipien der atomistischen Physik." In Frede and Reis 2009, 111–142.

Rohde, Erwin. 1903. *Psyche: Seelencult und Unsterblichkeitsglaube der Griechen.* 2 vols. 3rd ed. Tübingen and Leipzig (orig. pub. Freiburg im Breisgau and Leipzig, 1894).

Sassi, Maria Michela. 2020. *Gli inizi della filosofia: In Grecia; Nuova edizione rivista e con una nuova postfazione.* 2nd ed. Turin (orig. pub. Turin, 2009).

Schäfer, Christian. 1996. *Xenophanes von Kolophon: Ein Vorsokratiker zwischen Mythos und Philosophie.* Beiträge zur Altertumskunde 77. Stuttgart and Leipzig.

———. 2009. "Das Pythagorasfragment des Xenophanes und die Frage nach der Kritik der Metempsychosenlehre." In Frede and Reis 2009, 45–69.

Schirren, Thomas. 2013. "Xenophanes." In *Die Philosophie der Antike*, ed. Dieter Bremer, Hellmut Flashar, and Georg Rechenauer, vol. 1, *Frühgriechische Philosophie*, 2 parts, 339–374. Basel.

Schofield, Malcolm. 1991. "Heraclitus' Theory of the Soul and Its Antecedents." In *Psychology*, ed. Stephen Everson, Companions to Ancient Thought 2, 13–34. Cambridge.

Snell, Bruno. 2011. *Die Entdeckung des Geistes: Studien zur Entstehung des europäischen Denkens bei den Griechen.* 9th ed. Göttingen (orig. pub. Hamburg, 1947).

Strobel, Benedikt, and Georg Wöhrle. 2018. *Xenophanes von Kolophon.* In collaboration with Elvira Wakelnig and with contributions by Christian Vassallo. Traditio Praesocratica 3. Berlin and Boston.

Tor, Shaul. 2020. "Parmenides on the Soul." In Bartoš and King 2020, 61–79.

Trépanier, Simon. 2020. "The Spirit in the Flesh: Empedocles on Embodied Soul." In Bartoš and King 2020, 80–105.

Untersteiner, Mario. 2008. *Senofane: Testimonianze e frammenti.* Reprint. Milan (orig. pub. Florence, 1956).

van der Eijk, Philip J. 2000–2001. *Diocles of Carystus: A Collection of the Fragments with Translation and Commentary.* Vol. 1, *Text and Translation.* Vol. 2, *Commentary.* Studies in Ancient Medicine 22–23. Leiden, Boston, and Cologne.

Vassallo, Christian. 2020. "Is the *Logos* a Kind of *World Soul*? On the Relationship between Cosmology and Psychology in Heraclitus." In *World Soul - Anima Mundi: On the Origins and Fortunes of a Fundamental Idea*, ed. Christoph Helmig, Topics in Ancient Philosophy 8, 27–59. Berlin and New York.

Vitali, Renzo. 2000. *Senofane di Colofone e la scuola eleatica.* Cesena.

Zhmud, Leonid. 2012. *Pythagoras and the Early Pythagoreans.* Oxford.

———. 2016. "Pythagoras' Northern Connections: Zalmoxis, Abaris, Aristeas." *Classical Quarterly* 66, no. 2:446–462.

MAKING A MARTYR

DEMOSTHENES AND EUPHRAEUS OF OREUS
(*THIRD PHILIPPIC* 59–62)

Guy Westwood

I. THE OREUS NARRATIVE

IN THE *THIRD PHILIPPIC*,[1] a version of a speech Demosthenes made in an Assembly debate probably in the spring of 341 BC,[2] the orator includes a brief but lively narrative (9.59–62) of Philip II of Macedon's takeover of the Euboean city of Oreus,[3] an event of the previous year and one which he expects his audience to be aware of (9.55).[4] The starring role in the narrative is played by a citizen of Oreus called Euphraeus, who is depicted by Demosthenes as a noble-spirited champion of his fellow citizens' freedom. Both the passage and Euphraeus's resistance end with the latter's suicide after his imprisonment by the dominant pro-Macedonian faction prior to their betrayal of the city to Philip's forces. Picking up on a similar sequence earlier in the speech (9.11–12), the passage is shaped by Demosthenes to serve as the climactic

I am very grateful to Chris Pelling and the late Peter Rhodes for reading early drafts of this article, to Andrew Lintott and William Mack for advice on particular points, and to *HSCP*'s readers for their comments.

[1] Texts: Dilts 1997, 2002, and 2005 are used for Demosthenes and Aeschines throughout. Translations of the *Third Philippic* (Dem. 9) are from Trevett 2011 and of Aeschines from Carey 2000. Other translation sources are given in the notes; unattributed translations are mine.

[2] Dating: Dion. Hal. *Amm.* 1.10 (to 342/1); Cawkwell 1978:52; Sealey 1993:181; Worthington 2013:220.

[3] By the 340s BC the city's primary name: Reber, Hansen, and Ducrey 2004:656–658. In some of the evidence used below, its name is Histiaea/Hestiaea.

[4] Dating the takeovers of Olynthus, Eretria, and Oreus: Brunt 1969:252–253; Cawkwell 1978:66–67; Griffith 1979:546–547; Picard 1979:249; Sealey 1993:141–143, 175, 177; Herrman 2019:255.

final example in a chronologically organized series of three "takeover sequences" from the recent past, the takeover in each case being enabled by Philip's local stooges. First, in 348, Olynthus falls (9.56); then Eretria, in 343–342 (9.57–58, a longer passage); and soon after it is Oreus's turn (in the longest passage of the three, 9.59–62):[5]

> (59) καὶ τί δεῖ τὰ πολλὰ λέγειν; ἀλλ' ἐν Ὠρεῷ Φιλιστίδης μὲν ἔπραττε Φιλίππῳ καὶ Μένιππος καὶ Σωκράτης καὶ Θόας καὶ Ἀγαπαῖος, οἵπερ νῦν ἔχουσι τὴν πόλιν (καὶ ταῦτ' ᾔδεσαν ἅπαντες), Εὐφραῖος δέ τις ἄνθρωπος καὶ παρ' ἡμῖν ποτ' ἐνθάδ' οἰκήσας, ὅπως ἐλεύθεροι καὶ μηδενὸς δοῦλοι ἔσονται. (60) οὗτος τὰ μὲν ἄλλ' ὡς ὑβρίζετο καὶ προὐπηλακίζετο ὑπὸ τοῦ δήμου, πόλλ' ἂν εἴη λέγειν· ἐνιαυτῷ δὲ πρότερον τῆς ἁλώσεως ἐνέδειξεν ὡς προδότην τὸν Φιλιστίδην καὶ τοὺς μετ' αὐτοῦ, αἰσθόμενος ἃ πράττουσιν. συστραφέντες δ' ἄνθρωποι πολλοὶ καὶ χορηγὸν ἔχοντες Φίλιππον καὶ πρυτανευόμενοι ἀπάγουσι τὸν Εὐφραῖον εἰς τὸ δεσμωτήριον, ὡς συνταράττοντα τὴν πόλιν. (61) ὁρῶν δὲ ταῦθ' ὁ δῆμος ὁ τῶν Ὠρειτῶν, ἀντὶ τοῦ τῷ μὲν βοηθεῖν, τοὺς δ' ἀποτυμπανίσαι, τοῖς μὲν οὐκ ὠργίζετο, τὸν δ' ἐπιτήδειον ταῦτα παθεῖν ἔφη καὶ ἐπέχαιρεν. μετὰ ταῦθ' οἱ μὲν ἐπ' ἐξουσίας ὁπόσης ἠβούλοντ' ἔπραττον ὅπως ἡ πόλις ληφθήσεται, καὶ κατεσκευάζοντο τὴν πρᾶξιν· τῶν δὲ πολλῶν εἴ τις αἴσθοιτο, ἐσίγα καὶ κατεπέπληκτο, τὸν Εὐφραῖον οἷ' ἔπαθεν μεμνημένοι. οὕτω δ' ἀθλίως διέκειντο, ὥστε οὐ πρότερον ἐτόλμησεν οὐδεὶς τοιούτου κακοῦ προσιόντος ῥῆξαι φωνήν, πρὶν διασκευασάμενοι πρὸς τὰ τείχη προσήεσαν οἱ πολέμιοι· τηνικαῦτα δ' οἱ μὲν ἠμύνοντο, οἱ δὲ προὐδίδοσαν. (62) τῆς πόλεως δ' οὕτως ἁλούσης αἰσχρῶς καὶ κακῶς οἱ μὲν ἄρχουσι καὶ τυραννοῦσι, τοὺς τότε σῴζοντας ἑαυτοὺς καὶ τὸν Εὐφραῖον ἑτοίμους ὁτιοῦν ποιεῖν ὄντας τοὺς μὲν ἐκβαλόντες, τοὺς δ' ἀποκτείναντες, ὁ δ' Εὐφραῖος ἐκεῖνος ἀπέσφαξεν ἑαυτόν,

---

[5] On the style of this sequence: Mader 2005:31–32 with n48; Wooten 2008:161–162. Other chronologically organized evocations of the gradual creep of Philip's influence in Demosthenes' Assembly speeches: Dem. 1.9, 12; 2.6–7; 4.34–35.

ἔργῳ μαρτυρήσας ὅτι καὶ δικαίως καὶ καθαρῶς ὑπὲρ τῶν
πολιτῶν ἀνθειστήκει Φιλίππῳ.

(59) What need is there to speak at length? At Oreus
Philistides, Menippus, Socrates, Thoas, and Agapaeus acted
for Philip; these men now possess the city, as everyone
knew they would, but a man named Euphraeus, who once
lived here among us, acted to try to ensure that they would
be free and slaves to nobody. (60) This man—and much
could be said about the other ways in which he was insulted
and treated with contempt by the people—in the year
before the city fell charged Philistides and his supporters
with treason, since he saw what they were up to. But
many men banded together, with Philip as paymaster
and controller, and took Euphraeus off to prison, claiming
that he was throwing the city into disorder. (61) When
they saw this, the people of Oreus, instead of helping the
one and cudgeling the others to death, did not get angry
with them, but said that Euphraeus deserved his suffering,
and were glad about it. Later one party began to act with
perfect freedom to ensure that the city would be seized,
and started to arrange the deed; and any member of the
majority who noticed what was happening kept silent and
was intimidated, recalling what kinds of things Euphraeus
had suffered. They were in such a wretched condition that
no one dared speak out, as such an evil drew near, until
their enemies had equipped themselves and approached
the city walls. At that point some resisted, but others
turned traitor. (62) After the city was captured in this
shameful and evil way, the one group has been ruling it as
tyrants, after exiling some and killing others of the men
who at that time had been prepared to protect them and to
do all manner of harm to Euphraeus, while the admirable
Euphraeus killed himself, thereby demonstrating that he

had resisted Philip, acting with justice and honesty, on behalf of his fellow citizens.

The series of takeover sequences that this passage rounds off, placed close to the end of the *Third Philippic* as it is, serves to crystallize Demosthenes' concerns about how Athens should respond to the threat of Philip as articulated throughout the speech so far, and to alert listeners to the risk that Athens will be the next captured city in the series unless it takes action. This risk is communicated explicitly in the passage that follows (9.63–69), where Demosthenes sets out the reasons why the politicians working for Philip in each city have succeeded, and why they must not be allowed to succeed now. This message has greater impact for being built up to obliquely: Demosthenes has skillfully kept his audience engaged by getting them to trace the pattern for themselves across the trio of "takeover sequences." Also essential is his construction of Oreus, in particular, as a parallel Athens.[6] Euphraeus is fashioned not only as an antitype to his powerful local opponents (and Philip) but also as a mirror for Demosthenes himself.[7] The passage is a fervent appeal to the Athenian audience not to allow Macedonian influence in Athens (as embodied in those politicians Demosthenes identifies as Philip's supporters, who thus parallel Philistides and his associates in Oreus) to continue deceiving the Athenian *demos* about Philip's ultimate goals. It is also an appeal to the audience not to allow their disinterested, "true" advisers to end up failing as Euphraeus had, even though he had seen what was coming the previous year and had taken action (9.60). These "true" advisers, of course, are Demosthenes himself (whose ability to foresee events accurately is a key aspect of his political self-fashioning in his Assembly speeches and elsewhere) and (though only by implication) his political allies.[8]

---

[6] See in particular Herrman 2020:143–146.

[7] Mader 2007a:174–176; Mader 2007b:352–353.

[8] Demosthenes' rhetoric of foresight: Mader 2005:31–32; Mader 2007b. Allies: Dem. 9.72 (cf. 9.6, 14).

In *On the Chersonese*, delivered by Demosthenes shortly before the *Third Philippic* in early 341,[9] Oreus features as only one of several states Philip has taken over by deceit and infiltration, and its three appearances are all brief: it is mentioned on its own at 8.18 as a recent acquisition by Philip; it appears (but not by name) in a point about Philip's strategic establishment of tyrannies in Euboea, where Demosthenes imagines other Greek states criticizing Athens's failure to act (yet) in these cases (8.35–37, cf. 66); and it is featured again at 8.59 in a rapid-fire trio with Pherae and Olynthus. The coverage of Oreus's fall in our passage of the *Third Philippic* is on a different scale, reflecting this speech's more thoroughgoing interrogation of the whole phenomenon of Philip's expansionist activity.[10] It stands out in its trio of examples (and in Demosthenes' Assembly corpus as a whole) for its length and its vivid narrative qualities and has something in common with narrative set pieces in Demosthenes' lawcourt speeches like the famous "news from Elatea" sequence in *On the Crown* (18.169–173). Its paradigmatic impact is increased by its chronological placement, as the most recent of the three takeovers listed.[11] This positioning—as well as the detail that Euphraeus had once lived in Athens (59)—helps signal to the audience that this is the example which is most immediately relevant to their situation. The episode therefore offers a useful means of examining the scope and ambitions of his selection and crafting of his paradigmatic or illustrative material more generally. The Athenian orators' illustrations and examples are often (and productively) discussed in terms of their persuasive intersection with wider popular understandings of the events or persons being featured,[12] but the reconstruction I propose here serves to highlight how the orator could also deploy primarily personal knowledge, packaged in a sufficiently accessible and compelling—if also misleading—way that it could

---

[9] Dating: Dion. Hal. *Amm.* 1.10 (to 342/1); Brunt 1969:253; Cawkwell 1978:52; Worthington 2013:216.

[10] Herrman 2020:140.

[11] This is marked by τουτοισὶ in 9.12: Herrman 2019:214. On paradigmatic recency: Maltagliati 2020.

[12] See, e.g., Clarke 2008:245–303; Steinbock 2013; Grethlein 2014; Kostopoulos 2019; Barbato 2020.

perform the same functions in the argument as versions of more widely known and recognizable material. Demosthenes' fashioning of the Euphraeus example (as I reconstruct it) suggests very great creative latitude for the orator, in this case probably facilitated by patchy Athenian popular knowledge of the precise circumstances of Oreus's fall. The choice of Euphraeus as a projected *alter ego* was not at all obvious: as we shall see, he was a deeply compromised figure to present to an Athenian audience as a democratic paragon and martyr to liberty. This article therefore seeks to identify possible reasons for Demosthenes' decision.

First, I assess the likely levels of Demosthenic distortion at work in the passage (sections II–III) and then suggest (section IV) that Demosthenes' compositional decision-making in it is shaped not only by immediate rhetorical exigencies but also (possibly) by bias arising from personal connections between Demosthenes himself, Euphraeus, the city of Oreus, and Demosthenes' political opponents. I conclude (section V) that Demosthenes' decision to use Euphraeus (and Oreus) constituted a challenge to those opponents and invited contestation—something which, in this relatively brief period of his real political prominence, Demosthenes was actively courting. As our text of the *Third Philippic* is likely to be the product of postperformance revision,[13] I also suggest that broader literary aims—including self-fashioning for posterity—are at work as well. First, I review Euphraeus's historical profile beyond the *Third Philippic*.[14]

II. THE TRADITION ABOUT EUPHRAEUS

In Athenaeus, two references to the *Historical Notes* by the second-century BC historian Carystius of Pergamum[15] tell us why Euphraeus

---

[13] Sealey 1993:233–235; Wooten 2008:167–173; Herrman 2019:20–26, 34–36. Trevett 1996:428–429 and 2011:154–155 see the speech as an unrevised draft. It is just conceivable that 9.59–62 did not appear (or appear in this form) in the "live" speech; if so, the dynamics I trace must have been shaped solely with subsequent readers in mind.

[14] Key modern treatments are Trampedach 1994:93–97, Natoli 2004:32–40, and Wareh 2012:165–175.

[15] *FHG* IV 356–357, FF 1–2, from Ath. 11.506e–f and 508d–e. Doubt about his anecdotes' value: Jacoby 1919:2255, lines 42–44; Brunt 1993:292n29. Treated as a serious historian: Natoli 2004:23–24, 32–33.

had "once lived in Athens": he was a pupil of Plato, who had subsequently sent him to the Macedonian court to advise the young king Perdiccas III.[16] (This transaction is the setting for the pseudo-Platonic *Fifth Letter*,[17] where Euphraeus's main commission is framed as helping Perdiccas investigate monarchy's special qualities as a constitution-type—how to practice kingship in a theoretically aware way, in effect.[18]) Although it is unclear how much time Euphraeus spent at Pella, it was apparently long enough to alienate Perdiccas's nobles: in one of Athenaeus's two references to Carystius, we hear not only of Euphraeus's vicious (διάβολος) personality but also of his baleful influence, which apparently became so great that he "acted like a king himself" and "organized life within the king's inner circle so pedantically that it was impossible to have a meal with them, unless you understood geometry and philosophy."[19] Although the regular *topoi* of attacks on Platonists are visible here, and reflect the priorities of this whole section of Athenaeus,[20] there is no particular reason to dismiss the substance of what Athenaeus and Carystius transmit, even if the details and inflection can be questioned.[21] The passage ends with Athenaeus's speaker reporting that Euphraeus's influence led to his execution by Parmenion in Oreus "when Philip seized power (Φιλίππου τὴν ἀρχὴν παραλαβόντος)" (11.508e). There is no suicide here, as there is in Demosthenes, and there is no clear way of telling whose version is

---

[16] Ath. 11.506e–f. Euphraeus is also linked to Plato in Harp. s.v. *Euphraios*.

[17] Most scholars think the *Fifth Letter* inauthentic, but see Harward 1932:183–184; Scholz 1998:112–113n139. Isnardi Parente 1970:42–43 and 1979:258n33 and 285 suggests that it is an Academy exercise from the period after Euphraeus's death; cf. Wareh 2012:168n87.

[18] [Pl.] *Ep*. 5.321e–322a; Trampedach 1994:93–96.

[19] Ath. 11.508d–e. Translation: Olson 2009 (and below).

[20] Wörle 1981:116; Trampedach 1994:93–97.

[21] As Natoli 2004:23–24, 32–35 argues; cf. also Griffith 1979:206–208 (with caution), Hatzopoulos 2011:62; Lane Fox 2011a:264. Müller 2016:230–232, with further bibliography at 394nn124 and 128, is skeptical about both references to Carystius. Some caution is justified given the appearance of geometry—part of the stereotype of Academic activity promoted by Plato's detractors: Brunt 1993:292, 318 with n74, 320; Sonnabend 1996:53–54 and n87; Roisman 2010:163. However, Natoli 2004:34n74 offers a constructive skeptical rationalization. Carney 2019:79–82, at 81 mentions the possible involvement of Eurydice, Perdiccas's mother, in the court's intellectual activities.

right.[22] The looseness with chronology (i.e., either Athenaeus's or Carystius's failure to note the seventeen-year gap between Philip's accession and Euphraeus's death) also invites caution.[23]

Athenaeus's other reference to Carystius tells us that Euphraeus resolved a quarrel between Perdiccas and his younger brother Philip by persuading Perdiccas to grant Philip a tract of land which the latter used to support a military force. Philip then used this force to secure the throne for himself in 359 after Perdiccas's death.[24] Although Athenaeus's speaker expresses uncertainty about this story, its implications are worth noting because they illustrate the highly ambiguous character of our evidence for Euphraeus's activities in general. Putting the two pieces of Carystius together yields a curious scenario where Euphraeus apparently resolved the quarrel in Philip's favor and then Philip responded years later by allowing him to be executed in Oreus *because of* his earlier influence.[25] However, coherent reconstructions are possible. A simple one, and one which harmonizes with Demosthenes, is that Philip may have felt by 342 that Euphraeus's recent anti-Macedonian activity canceled out his good service some two decades earlier. Another possible reconstruction arises from a closer look at one of Carystius's sources: he plausibly identifies an allusion to the land grant in a passage from a letter of Speusippus, Plato's nephew and successor as head of the Academy. Whether or not this letter is the very *Letter to Philip* by Speusippus that we possess[26]—it

---

[22] Most scholars favor Demosthenes: Cawkwell 1963:203; Bertelli 1976:285 (though cf. Wareh 2012:172–173); Griffith 1979:518n1, 546–547n3; Isnardi Parente 1979:285n70; Brunt 1993:292; Trampedach 1994:96–97. Wörle 1981:119 favors Carystius. Herrman 2019:255 notes that the two accounts are reconcilable.

[23] Athenaeus's telescoping may be the problem: Wareh 2012:173 (but cf. 167n86).

[24] Ath. 11.506e–f. For interpretation, see note 29 below.

[25] Clarified by ὅθεν (Ath. 11.508e). As Trampedach 1994:97 notes, Philip may have wished to gratify Parmenion (a good candidate for a key court figure whom Euphraeus might have alienated).

[26] Since Bickermann and Sykutris 1928, Speusippus's *Letter to Philip* has normally been regarded as authentic: Isnardi Parente 1980:391–402; Natoli 2004:23–31 (whose translation I use); Wareh 2012:162–195. Frede 2015:27–40 was inclined to reject it; Bertelli 1977 (building on 1976) rejected Speusippean authorship but still saw the *Letter* as a near-contemporary Academy document.

could well be,[27] as our *Letter* not only has a parallel section but immediately afterward alludes to differences between Perdiccas and Philip[28]—the aim of this passage was transparently to remind Philip of Plato's role (via Euphraeus, directly or indirectly) in the original establishment of his power; Speusippus was responding to reports that Philip was now either badmouthing Plato (Carystius's version) or listening to such criticisms (the version in Speusippus's extant *Letter*). An appeal to Philip made by an Academic author might naturally misrepresent as a favor to Philip something that Euphraeus may actually have intended at the time as a way of protecting Perdiccas (or as a pragmatic solution which would keep both brothers happy and/or safeguard some key territory).[29] This consideration would apply whether or not the letter known to Carystius or his source was a letter genuinely composed by Speusippus in 343 or 342[30]—the setting assumed by the *Letter to Philip* and reflected, for example, in its tactful refusal to name Euphraeus, as someone hostile to Philip by 343[31]—or was instead a piece of later writing intended to evoke such a context. The upshot is that we cannot be sure whether or not Philip would have regarded Euphraeus as an enemy before the latter began his anti-Macedonian activity in Oreus. Consequently, we have no clear way of telling why Euphraeus might have left the Macedonian court whenever he did (clearly before 343), or indeed whether he did so of his own volition or under positive[32] or negative compulsion.[33]

---

[27] Griffith 1979:207; Natoli 2004:148. Note the doubts expressed by Frede 2015:31, 33, 38 and Bertelli 1977:76–83; but on the latter's case, again, see Wareh 2012:165–178.

[28] Speusippus *Letter of Philip* 12: "as if Plato had not laid the basis for your rule (τὴν ἀρχὴν τῆς ἀρχῆς ... κατασκευάσαντος) during the reign of Perdiccas and had not always been most concerned should anything uncivilized and unbrotherly occur at court."

[29] Attempts to rationalize the politics of the land grant: Griffith 1979:206–208; Hammond 1979:188; Trampedach 1994:94–95; Hatzopoulos 1996:178–179; Sonnabend 1996:55–56; Scholz 1998:114 and n145; Natoli 2004:35–37, 149–150; Wareh 2012:170. For skepticism about it: Müller 2016:230–231 (with 394n124).

[30] For this date: Bickermann and Sykutris 1928:29–37; Natoli 2004:17, 64–66. Against: Bertelli 1976, especially 287.

[31] Isnardi Parente 1980:397–398; Brunt 1993:292; Natoli 2004:172; Wareh 2012:167.

[32] E.g., a commission by Philip to build pro-Macedonian sentiment in Oreus.

[33] The default assumption is perhaps that of Cawkwell 1963:203: that Euphraeus returned "disillusioned and out of favor," perhaps on Perdiccas's death and Philip's

In order to turn Euphraeus into his own mirror, therefore, Demosthenes had to present as impeccably civically minded a former mentor/counselor of an autocrat (possibly two autocrats) and former member of the Academy—aspects which would have jeopardized his compelling illustration if revealed to the audience. Demosthenes could not, in this context, afford to be thought to possess—or at least had to avoid stating or suggesting—admiration for, or close connection with, people who were (or had been) linked to despots or the elite training and networking experience provided by the Academy. The kind of slurs which orators level at pupils of Isocrates,[34] and instances like Aeschines' negative characterization of Socrates in *Against Timarchus* (1.173–175),[35] make clear that as far as public discourse went any such associations had to be played down or at least carefully packaged.[36] Before I suggest why Demosthenes might have gone to this trouble when there were presumably other less compromised public figures in Oreus who could be singled out for praise, other aspects of Demosthenes' strategy in *Third Philippic* 59–62 need to be examined, in particular his construction of Oreus as a traditionally democratic *polis* like Athens.

III. MAKING THE MIRROR: EUPHRAEUS'S OREUS AND DEMOSTHENES' ATHENS

The mutual reflectivity of Athens and Oreus and Demosthenes and Euphraeus is carefully built up. It seems very likely (not least from a parallel phrase in Demosthenes' late 350s lawcourt speech *Against Aristocrates*) that the reference in our passage to Euphraeus's sojourn in

---

accession; cf. Griffith 1979:206; Wörle 1981:118; Natoli 2004:40. He may have stayed later, though—there are intriguing hints of Platonic influence during Philip's reign: Hatzopoulos 1996:158–160. By 349/8, the climate at court had apparently changed in a way Euphraeus would surely have found unpalatable: see Dem. 2.17–19, supported by Theopompus, a disagreeable presence at Pella by 343 or 342 (Speusippus *Letter* 12–13): *FGrH* 115 FF 162, 224, 225b; cf. 236.

[34] See, e.g., Dem. 35.15, 40–41; also [Dem.] 52.14.

[35] See Fisher 2001:319–323.

[36] Ober 1989:170–173. Note the derogatory oratorical use of σοφιστής ("sophist"): e.g., Lys. 33.3; Dem. 18.276; 19.246; 29.13; Aeschin. 1.125; 2.112; 3.16, 202. See Haake 2009:120–131 and 2020:72–74 on the Academy's "politically dubious and socially exclusive" (73) public image; Isnardi Parente 1970:42 notes the specific risk for Demosthenes.

Athens (παρ' ἡμῖν) is designed to imply that this was where Euphraeus picked up his uncompromising approach to civic freedom.[37] Meanwhile, the shortsighted, slow-moving, and easily led *demos* of Oreus clearly resembles (in particular in its lethargy) the Athenians of both the *Third Philippic* itself and Demosthenes' other Assembly speeches,[38] who are unwilling to act until it is too late. The legal terms used of the procedures instituted by Euphraeus against Philistides and of the summary arrest of Euphraeus by his "gang" of opponents (an Athenian oratorical *topos* itself[39]) would also inevitably recall the Athenian equivalents for an Athenian audience (regardless of whether the same terms were in fact used in Oreus).[40] Meanwhile ἀποτυμπανίσαι (perhaps "beat to death"[41]) denotes a grisly fate Demosthenes wishes elsewhere, in similar terms, on Philip's Athenian supporters.[42]

However, these efforts to construct a familiar-looking "parallel Athens" drastically simplify a complex picture. Demosthenes' version does not guarantee that Euphraeus had in any sense attained a leading position in any formal political movement, democratic or otherwise, or any anti-Macedonian group (in the way that Demosthenes himself had by now), or indeed that he was even a regular political leader at all; we are left to make these assumptions about his political activities by the contrast with Philistides and the others (59) and by the very

---

[37] Dem. 9.59. In *Against Aristocrates*, the Lampsacenes Thersagoras and Execestus kill the despotic Philiscus because they "took a view on tyrants very similar to our own" (παραπλήσια τοῖς παρ' ἡμῖν γνόντες περὶ τῶν τυράννων, Dem. 23.142). They are also introduced in a similar way to Euphraeus: ἐν δὴ Λαμψάκῳ τινὲς ἄνθρωποι γίγνονται δύο· Θερσαγόρας ὄνομ' αὐτῶν θατέρῳ, τῷ δὲ Ἐξήκεστος, "now in Lampsacus there were two men: Thersagoras was the name of one of them, and the other's was Execestus"; cf. 9.59: Εὐφραῖος δέ τις ἄνθρωπος, "but a man named Euphraeus ..." In each case this comes immediately before the connection with Athens is made.

[38] Dem. 1.8; 2.22–24; 3.35; 4.8–12, 17, 35–37; 5.2; 6.3, 27; 8.12, 49; 9.75; 10.6–7, 20, 30, 49; 13.20; 14.15.

[39] E.g., Aeschin. 2.178; Dem. 18.322.

[40] The procedures are *endeixis* and *apagoge* (60). The Athenian atmosphere of 9.60 is reinforced by the metaphors χορηγὸν ἔχοντες Φίλιππον and πρυτανευόμενοι ("with Philip as paymaster and controller"): Herrman 2019:253–254; Herrman 2020:143–145; also Mader 2005:32n49 (on συνταράττοντα).

[41] In detail: Cirio 2015.

[42] Dem. 8.61; 19.137.

fact that he seems to be set up as a mirror for Demosthenes.[43] All that is actually asserted in the passage is that Euphraeus was a principled opponent of Philistides and his associates, was motivated by the will to keep Oreus free, and was not listened to by the *demos*, either at an undefined earlier stage ("much could be said about the other ways in which he was insulted and treated with contempt by the people," 60) or when Philistides and his faction moved against him. This depiction of Euphraeus assists Demosthenes' own characterization of himself as a lone, critical outsider voice to whom the *demos* will not listen (but a voice repeatedly validated by events nonetheless).[44] This was an especially useful self-image to cultivate given that he had by 341 attained a leading position, had gained plenty of support both from fellow politicians and from the wider *demos,* and would have been finding it increasingly difficult to present himself as a talented outsider.[45] Constructing a Euphraeus who has been "repeatedly" abused over a long period of time—as Demosthenes claims to know ("much could be said")—encourages audience members to see in the Demosthenes of 341 the Demosthenes of the *Olynthiacs*—i.e., of the early 340s and earlier: a vigorous external critic, uncompromised by "establishment" associations. But this image of Euphraeus also cannot help suggesting that the *demos* of Oreus might have had other reasons to reject him whether he was a regular politician or not. The non-Demosthenic evidence for Euphraeus's career readily supplies a possible one: an Academy-trained intellectual who had spent time at the Macedonian court might well be suspect in a democracy, even that of his home city. The question of where his true loyalties now lay would have been a reasonable and valid one for his fellow citizens by 343; there had been prominent examples in other states in the past two decades of the involvement of Plato's pupils either in establishing

[43] Trampedach 1994:97; Wareh 2012:173–174.

[44] See especially Dem. 5.4–9, 11–12; cf. 14.24 and 15.6. Self-construction in opposition to an imagined political establishment more broadly: e.g., 3.12–13, 22, 27–32; 4.1, 44; 13.12–14, 20, 31; 15.33–34.

[45] He still places himself outside the imagined main political group: Dem. 8.33–34, 68; 9.19.

autocratic regimes or in murdering rulers and thus indirectly ushering in periods of instability or disunity.[46]

Even assuming that Euphraeus could count as a regular political leader, we are hardly obliged to follow Demosthenes as far as believing that he was the *only* prominent individual opposing Philistides and his associates, just as these future "tyrants"[47] (as Demosthenes terms them) should hardly be thought of as the only pro-Macedonian (and/or anti-Athenian) politicians at Oreus either.[48] The existence of some sort of anti-Philistides grouping beyond Euphraeus (and perhaps separate from him) is suggested by the general exile and execution of opponents once Philistides' regime came to power (τοὺς μὲν ἐκβαλόντες, τοὺς δ' ἀποκτείναντες, 62) and indicated even more clearly by the fact that the internal political troubles in Oreus can be characterized as being on the scale of *stasis* earlier in the *Third Philippic* (12):[49] the implication of that passage is that opposition to Philistides and his group was more widespread and larger-scale. Moreover, *IG* II/III³ 1, 398 gives us the names of some newly appointed Athenian *proxenoi*, probably from Oreus,[50] and if this inscription is correctly dated to about 348 (or else the 350s),[51] these men (Ampheritus, Heracleodorus, and a third individual) are plausible candidates for membership of a pro-Athenian (and/or anti-Macedonian) group in Oreus, assuming they were still

[46] Isnardi Parente 1979:289–299; Trampedach 1994:79–92, 111–124. Note Clearchus of Heraclea Pontica, murdered by Chion, another former pupil of Plato, in 353 or 352; Dion's and Callippus's successive coups in Syracuse (mid-350s); and Python and Heracleides' murder of the Thracian linchpin king Cotys in 360.

[47] For Demosthenes' tendentious labeling here: Harris 1995:116; Herrman 2019:219.

[48] Clarke 2021:125, 144.

[49] This instance is partly focalized by Philip, but the echoing of νοσοῦσι ("sick") in νοσοῦντας at 9.50 (where there is no such focalization) makes it clear that Demosthenes is framing Oreus as a state where *stasis* had struck. The designation of civic division as a νόσος or νόσημα is familiar from elsewhere in Demosthenes (9.39; 18.45; 19.259, 262): Herrman 2019:112–113, 214. See Brock 2013:69–76 and Das 2019 for background.

[50] Knoepfler 1995:326; Knoepfler 2016:145; note, however, Landucci 2013:244n53.

[51] Dreher 1995:193–197 prefers ca. 348, as does Lambert 2006:129 with n50, who also accepts it (with a question mark) in *IG* II/III³ 1.2. After arguing for ca. 375 in 1995, Knoepfler 2016:141–155 (especially 150–155) now prefers a 350s date, specifically ca. 357. He accepts that a 348 date is possible but doubts a late 340s date (for which see Landucci 2013:246).

on the political scene in the later 340s. Heracleodorus looks especially plausible if he is the same as (or related to) the Heracleodorus mentioned by Aristotle as pivotal in overthrowing an oligarchic regime in Oreus sometime earlier in the century.[52] Euphraeus's stance, whether pro-Athenian (as Demosthenes implies) and/or anti-Macedonian, or simply proindependence (on which more below), should in theory have been shared by others, whether formally associated with Euphraeus or not. Demosthenes' strategic motivations in 9.59–62 sufficiently explain the absence of other anti-Philistides voices here, though: earlier in the speech, he could safely hint at a more substantial opposition, but here he aims to heighten the dramatic qualities of the passage by concentrating on a single figure who can function as his own personal mirror.

The existence by the late 340s of broad pro-Macedonian (and/or anti-Athenian) and pro-Athenian (and/or anti-Macedonian) political groups—both of which will have included democratic politicians—is clearly plausible for northwest Euboean Oreus, which had historical associations with Athens but was geographically much closer to the Macedonian sphere of influence than the other major Euboean cities.[53] Debates about its international affiliations must have been a staple of fourth-century Oreus's political life; in the previous decade, *stasis* in the Euboean cities between pro-Athenian and pro-Theban groups seems to have played a role in the Theban invasion of the island and the subsequent Athenian expedition which promptly drove them out (357).[54] But, as well as polarized groups, Oreus's political spectrum in the late 340s probably included politicians who advocated a judicious balance in foreign policy—that is, retaining as far as possible the friendship of both

[52] Arist. *Pol.* 1303a18–20. Picard 1979:239–240, Knoepfler 1995:326, 2016:144–145, 154–155, Dreher 1995:194, 196, Lambert 2006:129n51, and Lintott 2018:73 are all happy to entertain this identification.

[53] Associations with Athens: Reber, Hansen, and Ducrey 2004:656–657. Geography: the Athenian envoys used it as a jumping-off point for the north on the first two embassies to Philip in 346 (Dem. 19.155, 163; Aeschin. 2.89), suggesting that this was normal; see Griffith 1979:549; Ryder 2000:76. An Oreus in the wrong hands could be seen (as in Dem. 8.36) as a threat to Sciathus (a key Athenian military base in the mid-fourth century: cf. Dem. 4.32); Clarke 2021:145. Oreus's strategic importance: Picard 1979:234; Stylianou 1998:279.

[54] Diod. Sic. 16.7.2; Aeschin. 3.85.

Athens and Macedon. In Demosthenes' passage, though, it is the *demos* that is happy with the status quo; any politicians who champion it (or occupy pragmatic, moderate policy stances more broadly) are invisible—either ignored or tacitly lumped in either with those whose failure to see what was coming led them to mock and sideline Euphraeus, or with the pro-Philip plotters—because what Demosthenes needs is to create a firmly binary image of corrupt agents of Philip versus the lone freedom fighter. His distortion also probably extends to the dynamics of the wider Euboean political scene; for example, he may well be exaggerating the extent of Philip's influence in Oreus, at least in the early stages of the situation described.[55] Moreover, the internal politics of Oreus in the late 340s also need to be viewed as responsive to the wider tension between the efforts on the part of Callias of Chalcis to build a Euboean League under Chalcidian (i.e., his own) headship—something he was pursuing in concert with Demosthenes certainly by early 341, Aeschines claims—and proindependence movements in individual Euboean cities.[56] So a range of politicians—not just Philistides and his associates—may, for example, have argued publicly to be allowed to seek Philip's support as a way of deterring Callias, winning a broad base of popular endorsement for this balancing act. Once Demosthenes' compelling narrative of group delusion is confronted with considerations of this type, it becomes much harder to see where Euphraeus might actually have fit in his city's political spectrum in 343.[57]

[55] Philip's influence in Euboea in the late 340s: Brunt 1969:252, 262–263; Cawkwell 1963:200–205; Cawkwell 1978, especially 50–55; Tritle 1993:237–238. For the earlier 340s: Griffith 1979:318–319 and n2; Landucci 2013:234–237.

[56] For Aeschines' claims: Aeschin. 3.85–105, especially 91–105. This passage may well fuse together a number of chronologically disparate elements to serve Aeschines' line of attack, and dating Callias's and Demosthenes' diplomatic activities has therefore proved difficult: Sealey 1993:262–264; Teegarden 2014:59–60n9. Broad scholarly consensus (which I follow) places all or most of the events of Aeschin. 3.91–105 in 342/1: Brunt 1969:255–260; Griffith 1979:545–551; Picard 1979:245–251; Knoepfler 1995:347n144 and 351–359; Landucci 2013:239–247. My main point is not affected, though, if the alternative 343/2 date is right, for which see Cawkwell 1963:210–213; Cawkwell 1978:55–67; Sealey 1993:263–264.

[57] He may even have been pro-Callias: by spring 341 Demosthenes viewed Callias as a friend to Athenian interests (Griffith 1979:547–549; Knoepfler 1995:347, 353), so he might have wished to represent a pro-Callias politician as a champion of autonomy, whatever the reality.

Demosthenes' suppression of any political middle ground in Oreus reflects his wider view of the attitude Athens and other Greek states should adopt toward Philip and his supporters in the late 340s and is a familiar feature of his Assembly speeches of that period: his fellow Athenian politicians' range of attitudes toward Philip is typically reduced to a similarly stark polarization, with much nuance deliberately suppressed.[58] Moreover, at *Third Philippic* 61 Demosthenes depicts the terrified condition of the ordinary people of Oreus in terms which recall, and may rework, the passage where Thucydides depicts fear taking hold among the Athenian *demos* and its leaders in 411, during the takeover of the state by the Four Hundred: nobody is sure who among them is secretly supporting the oligarchs, and most stay silent (8.66.3–5).[59] If so, Demosthenes radically simplifies the complex Thucydidean picture. Instead, he gives his audience a strictly dichotomized environment where the people stay silent because they already know who their new masters are due to Euphraeus's very public arrest:

> τῶν δὲ πολλῶν εἴ τις αἴσθοιτο, ἐσίγα καὶ κατεπέπληκτο,
> τὸν Εὐφραῖον οἷ' ἔπαθεν μεμνημένοι.

Demosthenes 9.61

> ... and any member of the majority who noticed what was happening kept silent and was intimidated, recalling what kinds of things Euphraeus had suffered.

> ἀντέλεγέ τε οὐδεὶς ἔτι τῶν ἄλλων, δεδιὼς καὶ ὁρῶν πολὺ
> τὸ ξυνεστηκός· εἰ δέ τις καὶ ἀντείποι, εὐθὺς ἐκ τρόπου
> τινὸς ἐπιτηδείου ἐτεθνήκει, ... ἀλλ' ἡσυχίαν εἶχεν ὁ δῆμος

---

[58] See, e.g., Dem. 9.2, 6, 14, 37–40, 53–68 (especially 64); 10.4, 19, 55–60, 63, 66, 68–70, 75–76; also 6.28–36. *On the Chersonese* begins by alluding to the possibility of genuine alternative viewpoints but gradually merges their holders with those represented as Philip's supporters: see 8.1, 4–10, 18, 23, 27 (clarified at 29), 32 (clarified at 56–58), giving way to starker polarization: 8.20, 40, 52–53, 56–58, 61, 64, 66–67, 68–72, 76. On this technique: Herrman 2020:139–140. Aeschines pithily targets it at 2.8.

[59] On Thucydides' influence on Demosthenes in general: Canfora 1992:15–25; Yunis 1996:240–241 and n7, 256–257, 268–277; Mader 2007a; Gotteland 2010.

καὶ κατάπληξιν τοιαύτην ὥστε κέρδος ὁ μὴ πάσχων τι
βίαιον, εἰ καὶ σιγῴη, ἐνόμιζεν.

Thucydides 8.66.2

Nobody else now spoke against them, out of fear and also
seeing the size of the conspiracy. If someone did speak
out, he was immediately killed in some suitable way, ... but
the people kept quiet, and were so terrified that individuals thought it a positive gain not to suffer some form of
violence, even if they stayed silent.[60]

Demosthenes reinforces this dichotomy by careful polarization of the
identity of key groups in the passage, so that no clear intermediate
alternatives to "hero" or "villain" can emerge: a chain of pronouns
(τῷ μὲν ... τοὺς δ' ...; τοῖς μὲν ... τὸν δ' ...; οἱ μὲν ... τῶν δὲ ...; οἱ
μὲν ... οἱ δὲ ...; οἱ μὲν ... τοὺς ... [τοὺς μὲν ... τοὺς δ' ...], ὁ δ' ...) guides
the audience through the narrative in a way that encourages easy and
intuitive application of positive or negative labels to those involved.
For example, when the Macedonians advance to besiege Oreus,
Demosthenes does not tell us which people seek to defend the city
(οἱ μὲν ἠμύνοντο); while Philistides and his group are clearly meant by
οἱ δὲ προὐδίδοσαν ("others turned traitor"), there is also the possibility
that the enormity of the crisis forced others to advocate surrender on
purely pragmatic grounds too. But Demosthenes does not want us to
think of that; for his purposes, the important thing is that we keep in
mind that Euphraeus has been the only citizen of Oreus fully alert to
the threat (and powerless to act in person), a sole spiritual defender of
the city against a consortium of villains within and without. Likewise,
in 9.62, Demosthenes does not tell us exactly who is killed or exiled by
the new regime: they are described as τοὺς τότε σῴζοντας ἑαυτοὺς καὶ
τὸν Εὐφραῖον ἑτοίμους ὁτιοῦν ποιεῖν ὄντας ("the men who at that time
had been prepared to protect them and to do all manner of harm to
Euphraeus"). Are these (some of) the gloating *demos* of 9.61? It seems so,
whether we take ἑαυτοὺς ("them") to refer to Philistides and his group
or to the members of the *demos* who were taken in by their assurances

---

[60] Text: Stuart Jones 1963.

that they could carry on living a quiet life (cf. 9.64), an alternative sense for σῴζοντας.[61] But were large numbers of the *demos* killed or exiled? Their leaders must be the ones primarily referred to here; but the sentence is not over, and Demosthenes does not give us time to realize that we have had no clear previous indication in the passage of what role the *demos*'s leaders played in the public ridiculing and removal of Euphraeus, as opposed to (unspecified) members of the *demos* in general. The headline message that emerges is that Euphraeus himself (like Demosthenes) was the only "true" democratically minded political leader in Oreus, regardless of whether the *demos* would have thought of him as one of their leaders or not. The whole passage, then, can be read as an exercise in reflecting the basic outline of Oreus's internal circumstances in 343 and 342 without filling in any of the participants' real motivations and so risking distraction from the binary focus on Euphraeus versus the group around Philistides.

A final casualty of Demosthenes' polarization technique is the likely complexity of Oreus's own constitutional profile in the period covered by recent memory. The city was clearly a democracy until 342 and again after 341 (and still in 330),[62] but the preceding decades indicate some turbulence.[63] We hear of a tyranny under Neogenes in ca. 380–378 (ended by the citizens, rallied by Sparta)[64] and also of an oligarchy which had to be dismantled (and *politeia* and democracy introduced) by Heracleodorus, traditionally in 377/6 when Oreus revolted from Sparta with Theban assistance;[65] it shortly afterward joined the Second Athenian League.[66] It had attached itself to the Thebans by 370 (if not

[61] Most favor the first alternative: e.g., Sandys 1900:235–236; Trevett 2011:173; Herrman 2019:255. The second I owe to one of *HSCP*'s readers. For a third: Canfora 1992:104–105.

[62] Aeschin. 3.103. For the liberation in 341, see note 124 below.

[63] Gehrke 1985:73–75; Reber, Hansen, and Ducrey 2004:657; Clarke 2021:157.

[64] Diod. Sic. 15.30.3–4; Bertoli 2013:199–202.

[65] Arist. *Pol.* 1303a18–20. The revolt of 377/6: Xen. *Hell.* 5.4.56–57. For 377/6 (or just after) as the traditional date: Knoepfler 1995:330–331 with n87; Knoepfler 2016:151; Lambert 2006:129n51. Gehrke 1985:74 and n5 prefers ca. 395; cf. Reber, Hansen, and Ducrey 2004:657. Lintott 2018:73–74 sees Heracleodorus's activity either in the 370s or post-357.

[66] Oreus joins the Athenian League (ca. 375): Knoepfler 1995:324; Rhodes and Osborne 2003: no. 22, line 114, with page 103; Reber, Hansen, and Ducrey 2004:657; Bertoli 2013:204. Occhipinti 2020:145–149 prefers 377.

earlier, around 377/6)[67] and contributed to their Mantinea campaign in 362.[68] After Athens's expedition to Euboea in 357 to counter Thebes's invasion of the island, Oreus was probably obliged to re-ally with Athens as other Euboean cities did,[69] and there may well have been constitutional repercussions. Finally, somewhere in the second half of the fifth century or the first half of the fourth must belong the otherwise unattested *dynasteia* involving Charigenes, the father of the Gnosidemus mentioned by Aeschines in *Against Ctesiphon* as a contact of Demosthenes (Γνωσίδημον τὸν Χαριγένους υἱὸν τοῦ δυναστεύσαντός ποτε ἐν Ὠρεῷ, "Gnosidemus son of Charigenes, who once had power in Oreus," 3.103).[70] So it seems likely that, to construct an Oreus which can parallel the Athenian ideal in its "traditional" commitment to democracy, Demosthenes has again simplified a complex picture; as with the broader political situation in Oreus itself, this was a picture whose complexity he was probably well aware of.[71] If his audience knew something about Oreus's fall (9.55), some of them at least would have known whether it was a democracy or not, and roughly what kind of democracy it was, especially if we consider the exposure of many Athenian citizens to Euboean affairs through service in the campaigns of 357 and 348. Demosthenes' simplification was therefore a risky strategy.

[67] Histiaea/Oreus and Thebes made an alliance sometime in the 370s: Aravantinos and Papazarkadas 2012:244–250; they favor ca. 377/6, as does Knoepfler 2016:129–130 and n22. If so, it must have been short-lived: Knoepfler 2013:473. Strabo gives Philistides a tyranny after Leuctra (10.1.3), but this is likely to be either incorrect or loosely phrased: Moggi 1976:352.

[68] Xen. *Hell.* 6.5.23.

[69] *IG* II² 124, line 16 (Athenian alliance with Carystus, 357/6 BC); Bertoli 2013:214–218; Landucci 2013:230–234; Occhipinti 2020. *IG* II/III³ 1, 399 (decree of Hegesippus on Euboean affairs) has been traditionally associated with *IG* II² 124 (cf. Occhipinti 2020:149–151), but is now generally dated to the 340s: Dreher 1995:167–173 and 196–197 (preferring 348, as does Lambert in *IG* II/III³ 1.2); Rhodes and Osborne 2003: no. 69; Knoepfler 2016:132–138, 150 (preferring ca. 343). Laursen 2019 argues for 341.

[70] Berve 1967:674 lists Charigenes as a tyrant, but if he had been, Aeschines' rhetorical aims in this passage would probably have prompted him to say so. The unspecific δυναστεύσαντος suggests that the truth was less exciting: Charigenes could have been part of a narrow oligarchy, for example (cf. Thuc. 3.62.3).

[71] Certainly so if his link with Gnosidemus (Aeschin. 3.103) went back to the previous year; note also his visits to Oreus in 346.

IV. DEMOSTHENES' MOTIVATIONS

Given the obstacles which Demosthenes had to overcome, then, two questions emerge. First: what motivated him to elaborate the Oreus passage in the detail he did, rather than the examples of Olynthus and Eretria? It is true that the Macedonian takeover of Oreus was the most recent of the three, and expanding the third element in a sequence of three makes good rhetorical sense, but the scale and nature of the elaboration invite us to seek other reasons as well. Second: why does Demosthenes develop as compromised a figure as Euphraeus into a personal mirror? In this section, I suggest a reason for each (subsections IV.1 and IV.2, the latter falling into two parts). Neither is meant to exclude other possibilities, and they could well have played a mutually productive role in Demosthenes' compositional approach. Both are necessarily speculative given the nature of the evidence. First, depicting the breakdown of democratic government in Oreus at the hands of the men identified as Philip's local supporters may be a means for Demosthenes to launch a particularized attack on one of his main pro-Macedonian opponents—Aeschines—while also identifying him and other opponents via the much more generalized, oblique modes of reference which our evidence suggests were normal enough for formal speeches in the Assembly. Second, although it cannot be proved, it is quite possible that Demosthenes encountered Euphraeus directly, or at least knew those who had, during the latter's sojourn in Athens and when the young (and intellectually impressionable) future orator seems to have been moving in the right circles. The mirroring we see in the *Third Philippic* then looks like an appropriate response to a situation where Demosthenes wanted to pay tribute to Euphraeus but was required by the context of performance to avoid giving the impression that he had close personal connections, especially personal connections of an intellectual nature, with him or with the Academy. Hence, as we saw earlier, Demosthenes' careful finessing of Euphraeus's reasons for being in Athens. I now look at these possible motivations in turn.

IV.1. WHY OREUS?

My first suggestion, then, is that Demosthenes' elaboration of the Oreus narrative as such relates to Oreus's connections with Athenian politics and politicians. Demosthenes had, by the time of Oreus's capture by the Macedonians, visited the city on at least two occasions, both in 346, while on two Athenian embassies to Philip.[72] The envoys halted at Oreus for some time on the second of these (Aeschin. 2.89). It was probably on one of these visits that Demosthenes spent time at the house of Anaxinus, a man with connections to the Macedonian royal family.[73] Aeschines was on both embassies too, and in 343 he was able to claim that Demosthenes had represented Aeschines' activities in Oreus as purely self-interested ("[Demosthenes] has told you that ... I ... sat at Oreus with my fellow envoys arranging to get posts as foreign representatives [*proxenoi*]," 2.89). Demosthenes does not in fact mention *proxenia* awards in our text of *On the False Embassy*, but a passage of *On the Crown* (of 330) indicates that Aeschines was certainly a *proxenos* of Oreus (and Eretria) by 341.[74] It is therefore highly likely that during their visits in 346, especially the lengthy second visit, Demosthenes, Aeschines, and their fellow envoys met some of Oreus's leading figures and learned about others.[75] It is equally likely that in 346 these leading men included some of those involved in the 343–342 episode covered in the *Third Philippic*: Philistides and his associates, and possibly Euphraeus himself if he had returned from Pella by then. The *proxenia* award to Aeschines makes it likely that he in particular

[72] Dem. 19.163 (first); 19.155 (second).

[73] Schäfer 1886:494n1; Worthington 2013:229. In *Against Ctesiphon* (3.223–224), Aeschines accuses Demosthenes of arresting Anaxinus as a spy (and torturing him) while the latter was in Athens on Macedonian court business (late 340s?); cf. Demosthenes' response (18.137).

[74] Dem. 18.82 with Hennig 1997:355–356n2 and Yunis 2001:156. The structure of Dem. 18.81–82 interestingly recalls that of *Third Philippic* 65–66 and 68. I assume a spring-to-summer 341 date (when the Athenian-led expeditions were already in prospect) because Demosthenes describes the public attitude to the Euboean envoys as hostile, and because he uses the temporal marker τότε ("at that time"), which points back to his references to these expeditions at 18.79–80.

[75] As Knoepfler 1995:343 notes, Aeschines probably met his informant Cleochares of Chalcis on this same journey (2.120).

would have had to deal with prominent politicians like Philistides: the award presumably needed a vote of the *demos* as it did in Athens, and even the *Third Philippic* would suggest that it was influential individuals like Philistides who could help secure that.[76] Indeed, we find Demosthenes claiming in *On the Crown* that Aeschines gave lodging in Athens to envoys from Philistides and from Cleitarchus, the Philip-backed "tyrant" of Eretria (presumably later in 341)—a misleadingly and maliciously spun statement rather than a baseless one, as it was Aeschines' duty as *proxenos* to host envoys from these states.[77]

These suggested connections in turn support the idea that Demosthenes' extended description, in the *Third Philippic*, of the breakdown of the democracy and capitulation to Philip in Oreus is intended to strengthen the parallel between Oreus in 343 and 342 and Athens in the present, by encouraging audience members to align the pro-Philip element in each of the two cities and so draw the inference that Aeschines and other pro-Macedonians have the potential to be just as dangerous as Philistides and his group, something the next sections of the speech would clarify. This mode of indirect suggestion would suit a speech for the Assembly, a context where speakers often refer to political opponents without naming them: indeed, there is only one instance in Demosthenes' Assembly speeches where an opponent is named (and singled out for special attack: 10.70–74). The other six surviving classical Athenian Assembly speech-texts avoid names too,[78] and the wider evidence tends to confirm this as a more general habit, especially in the case of formal expressions of opinion or policy delivered from the *bēma* (like the speeches we possess).[79] The

---

[76] For background: Mack 2015:92–104.

[77] Dem. 18.81–82; see note 74 above.

[78] Unnamed opponents: Lys. 28.9; 34.5; [Dem.] 7.45; 17.23–24; Andoc. 2.2–5; 3.1.

[79] Tuplin 1998:302–303n24. Naming in formal speeches from the *bēma*: e.g., Thuc. 3.44.3, 47.1, 5 (all Diodotus); Xen. *Hell.* 1.7.17–18, 26 (in special trial-like circumstances); Dem. 19.14 (though note τοιούτους τινὰς there—verisimilitude may not be Demosthenes' aim). In Thuc. 6.16.1 and 6.17.1 Alcibiades names Nicias as a way of countering references Nicias had previously made to him *without* using his name (6.12.2–13.1). The evidence we have for the less formal, faster-moving parts of Assembly meetings (direct debate, reaction, heckling) supports the common-sense assumption that names would appear more often in those parts: e.g., Aeschin. 1.110–111; Dem. 13.12 (hypothetical); 18.143; 19.46.

nonnaming therefore looks like a common strategy, and one that would often make sense rhetorically; consistently failing to name opponents whom the audience could nonetheless identify (or try to identify) would serve to discredit and diminish those opponents' point of view and in context could help communicate messages (in a variety of tones) about their moral character, policy aims, and qualifications for giving political advice at all. The *Third Philippic* itself is full of warnings to the audience to be on their guard against Philip's local supporters (no names given), who are usually implied to include those opposing Demosthenes.[80] Importantly for us, though, oblique and generalized modes of Assembly reference could also act as vehicles for pinpointed personal attack or comment.[81] In his *Second Philippic* of 344/3, for example, Demosthenes references a joke made at his expense in the Assembly in 346 by "others" (6.29–30). We know from elsewhere that the joke came from Philocrates,[82] but here he is not named, in keeping with Demosthenes' aim to condemn as a collective those politicians who had enthusiastically promoted peace with Philip.

In *Third Philippic* 59–62, therefore, Demosthenes may be rhetorically harnessing the audience's knowledge of Aeschines' position as a *proxenos* of two Euboean cities—something brought to public attention in the recent Embassy trial of 343, but perhaps reasonably well known anyway[83]—to suggest to the Athenian *demos* the sinister potential relevance of a situation which at first sight has nothing directly to do with them. Demosthenes' decision to elaborate as his climactic example the loss of freedom and subjugation to Philip of one of the very cities where Aeschines holds a *proxenia* might serve to imply that Aeschines was either an inadequate *proxenos*—in (apparently) not using his influence to encourage more resistance to Philip in Oreus—or a treacherous one (which consequently hints at his potential for subverting his native Athens in a similar way), or both. In sowing doubt about Aeschines' efficacy and/or integrity as a *proxenos*, Demosthenes would be striking

---

[80] See the instances in note 58 above.

[81] See e.g., Thuc. 4.27.5; 6.12.2 (above); Aeschin. 1.110; 2.52; Dem. 2.28–29; 4.24; 5.10; 6.28–36.

[82] Dem. 19.46 (in a lawcourt context, where names are typically used freely).

[83] Public knowledge of *proxeniai*: Trevett 1999:185; Mack 2015:115n98.

at his rival's political identity and good faith as a whole, in a way which supported the passage's wider implication that in someone like Aeschines the Athenian audience should see a Philistides-in-waiting. The first sentence shows us both sides in Oreus taking action (ἔπραττε, 59)—Philistides and his associates working to turn the city over to Philip, and Euphraeus working to keep it free: what action, if any, was Aeschines taking?

It is interesting, then, that when attacking Demosthenes in *Against Ctesiphon*, in the Crown trial of 330, Aeschines says nothing at all about any efforts he may have undertaken as a *proxenos* (whether in Athens or beyond) to keep Oreus and Eretria independent and democratic in the late 340s or to argue for their liberation in 341 (and nor do we hear about any anywhere else). At no stage does he say which politicians in Oreus (if any) he favored. Given his exhaustive focus on the events of that decade in this speech, we should probably conclude that any interventions he did make (if he did) had been less than impressive and/or ultimately unsuccessful, or were upstaged by those of Demosthenes. Instead, Aeschines spends considerable time criticizing Demosthenes' political network building in Euboea with Callias and Taurosthenes of Chalcis at the end of the 340s (3.85–105). In particular, he accuses Demosthenes of profiting from the proposal of an Assembly decree in these men's interest, for which service Demosthenes allegedly charged Chalcis, Eretria, and Oreus a talent each (3.103–105).[84] Aeschines capitalizes rhetorically on the fact that his audience would see him as possessing special knowledge about Oreus derived from his *proxenia*, presenting it as a city with uncomplicated democratic credentials (δημοκρατουμένων τῶν Ὠρειτῶν καὶ πάντα πραττόντων μετὰ ψηφίσματος, "Oreus is a democracy and conducts all its business through public decrees," 3.103). Aiming for an illusion of stability, he simplifies the city's variegated recent constitutional profile even more than Demosthenes had in the *Third Philippic*: by 330, when Aeschines was speaking, Oreus certainly was a democracy again (if under Macedonian hegemony), and it had also been one at the time

---

[84] Rational explanations in the case of Oreus: Schäfer 1886:491–492; Bertoli 2013:212.

Aeschines is referring to, probably 341 or soon after.[85] But he allows no room here for the palpable, very recent counterexample: the regime run by Philistides and his associates in 342–341. Aeschines then has the court clerk read the decree by which the *demos* of Oreus arranged the payment for Demosthenes (105). He also does everything he can to indicate that the contacts through whom Demosthenes supposedly secured his money were all dubious, antidemocratic figures: Callias in Chalcis, Cleitarchus in Eretria,[86] and in Oreus, as we saw above, Gnosidemus, son of the "once-powerful" Charigenes.

This sequence is clearly (among other things) a way of hitting back at Demosthenes' constant allegations in the 340s (and echoed in *On the Crown*) that Philip was systematically subjugating the mainland Greek states with the help of an international network of traitors who, like Aeschines, were men of influence in their individual cities;[87] but it can also be read as a response to the specific insinuations of *Third Philippic* 59–62 (and perhaps other speeches) against Aeschines himself—and a dynamic, adversarial response where a more defensive one was possible. Aeschines still wishes, in *Against Ctesiphon,* to frame responses to several topics which had surfaced in Demosthenes' prosecution in the Embassy trial of 343,[88] so there need be no difficulty imagining him also responding to attacks made by Demosthenes in 341, even ones made in an oblique way, and especially ones articulated via memorable set pieces like Demosthenes' Oreus passage. Indeed, Aeschines is indirectly targeted in several of Demosthenes' Assembly speeches from the later 340s,[89] and he clearly judged the Crown trial and his prosecution speech against Ctesiphon, with its avowedly broad focus on

[85] See note 56 above.

[86] On numerous scholars' dating (note 56 above), Cleitarchus had already been deposed. If so, Aeschines' error could well be deliberate; he could be confident that listeners would not recall the sequence of events clearly eleven years on. See for similar instances Tritle 1993:232–234.

[87] Examples from other Assembly speeches: Dem. 8.40; 10.4–5; from lawcourt speeches: 18.45–49, 61, 294–296; 19.259–267, 295. This rhetoric is echoed by Hyperides in *Against Diondas* 21 Horváth, with Horváth 2014:155–156, 173–176.

[88] Especially the discussion of the Peace of Philocrates (Aeschin. 3.58–75).

[89] See the instances in notes 58 and 81 above.

Demosthenes' career from its beginning (3.54–57), a good opportunity to make a definitive and holistic counterattack.

Aeschines' emphasis on Oreus's democratic credentials (103) seems specifically geared to recapturing rhetorical control of his right to talk authoritatively about Oreus as a *proxenos*—a right (in my reading) usurped and targeted obliquely by Demosthenes in the *Third Philippic* (and perhaps elsewhere)—and if so it synergizes well with his attacks on Demosthenes' status as a *proxenos* of Thebes in this speech.[90] Although he does not mention Demosthenes' Theban *proxenia* as such (presumably because there was no need), he uses his opponent's close connection with Thebes later to attack what he represents as Demosthenes' privileging of Theban over Athenian interests before Chaeronea (e.g., 3.141–147) and his subsequent alleged failure to support the revolt of Thebes properly (3.156, 239–240), leading to the city's destruction by Alexander in 335. Aeschines also focuses plaintive attention on the catastrophic (if, he says, self-inflicted) fate of Athens's "neighbor city" (3.133), followed up later with a lavish passage of multileveled *ekphrasis* which encourages his audience to visualize the plight of the Thebans, young and old (3.156–157)—all ultimately Demosthenes' fault, he claims. Oratorical competition may be in the air here too: *Against Ctesiphon* 156–157 echoes, and may respond to, Demosthenes' similar, and similarly compelling, description in *On the False Embassy* in 343 of the grim reality of the fate of the defeated and destitute Phocians in 346 (19.64–66)—all Aeschines' fault, he claims.[91] Given this kind of context, it makes sense to read Aeschines' passage about Oreus in *Against Ctesiphon* as another clever piece of table turning, responding both to Demosthenes' "takeover rhetoric" in general and to the *Third Philippic* in particular.

Oreus, therefore, may have had a specific kind of rhetorical potential for Demosthenes as well as general potential for mirroring Athens as a good democratic state. In this it was a safer rhetorical option

---

[90] Demosthenes had held this since at least 343: Aeschin. 2.141, 143 with Trevett 1999, especially 185–186; Steinbock 2013:153, 268–271; Mack 2015:114–115.

[91] On both these passages: Theon *Progymnasmata* 63, lines 3–13 Patillon; Webb 2009a:114–115, 152–153; Webb 2009b:141–144; O'Connell 2017:128–136 (with 222n40); Westwood 2023:159–166.

than Eretria, which also had Aeschines as a *proxenos*. Eretria notoriously failed to maintain democratic regimes for long in the mid-fourth century,[92] and Demosthenes' audience, especially those who had performed military service at the time, would remember its recent period of tyranny under Plutarchus, supported in 348 by an Athenian expedition, with disastrous consequences.[93] Accordingly, Demosthenes is open about how brief Eretria's recent democratic interlude was when he covers it just before the Oreus passage (57–58).

IV.2. WHY EUPHRAEUS?

Even if Oreus's value for Demosthenes is accepted, we still need to ask why he does so much with the unpromising Euphraeus. As noted above, there was latitude here because of the lapse of time since Euphraeus's period in Athens (where he might not in any case have resided for very long): a safe figure, perhaps, to use in front of an Athenian Assembly audience whose chances of remembering him or his Platonic connections would probably be low. That said, nothing obliged Demosthenes to use him, and it would only take one knowledgeable opponent to subvert the illustration by telling the Assembly audience what the allegedly admirable Euphraeus had "really" been like, but Demosthenes goes ahead and uses him anyway. He is committed to this portrayal. I now offer two connected, and tentative, suggested reasons why: first, that Demosthenes may have been in the right circles at the right time to become aware of, or come into contact with, Euphraeus himself when he was in Athens in the 360s, and therefore to have a personal reason to select him for elaboration here in the *Third Philippic*; and, second, that aspects of Demosthenes' portrayal of Euphraeus's fate align suggestively with aspects of Plato's portrayal of Socrates' ill-fated engagement with Athenian political life, inviting the idea that Demosthenes (perhaps with subsequent readers in mind, but also in order to frame the content in a more emotive and compelling way

---

[92] Teegarden 2014:66–67.
[93] In detail: Tritle 1988:76–89. Demosthenes opposed the expedition: Dem. 5.5.

for listeners) may be deliberately shaping the narrative to provide this Academy "alumnus" with an Academy-themed (even heroized) exit.[94]

A tenacious tradition in antiquity identified Demosthenes as a pupil or student of Plato.[95] That is now normally rejected.[96] Although the Academy clearly fostered a distinctive group identity, modern scholarship tends to present personal connection with it as something that could take a variety of forms and be experienced in a variety of ways (at least by those of a certain social status), pushing against the exclusive view encouraged by ancient sources whose tendency is to systematize.[97] So some degree of exposure to the Academy and its members is plausible for the young Demosthenes,[98] and made likelier by various pieces of circumstantial evidence. The mid-350s certainly find him associated with the family and friends of one of Athens's most renowned generals, Chabrias—a relative of Plato's, according to Philochorus.[99] Demosthenes spoke on behalf of Chabrias's son Ctesippus in *Against Leptines* in 355/4, stating their connection in the proem (20.1)[100] and eulogizing the recently deceased Chabrias in a lengthy passage which dominates the center of the speech (20.75–87)[101]—and the young Ctesippus's guardian was Phocion,[102] the major contemporary political figure most likely to have had close links to the Academy.[103] Plutarch

[94] Perhaps especially necessary if Euphraeus was in fact executed: see note 22 above. Euphraeus's suicide (as presented by Demosthenes) seems to satisfy the conditions specified by Plato's Athenian in Pl. *Leg.* 9.873c.

[95] Pernot 2006:239–248.

[96] Pernot 2006:21–60; see also the scholars in the first of his three lists (27–28).

[97] Like the list of Plato's pupils at Diog. Laert. 3.46–47. On Academy access: Lynch 1972:57–58, 61; Brunt 1993:284–285; Dillon 2003:2–13; Haake 2009; Haake 2020:74; see also Aristocles F 2 Chiesara with Chiesara 2001:70.

[98] As Pernot 2006:39 admits, and this is maintained by the scholars in his second list (28–29).

[99] Philochorus *FGrH* 328 F 223. This information is deemed reliable by Jacoby 1954:483, Düring 1957:256–258, and Gigon 1962:51, but doubted by Trampedach 1994:135–136. Plutarch instead mentions Academy influence on Chabrias (*Mor.* 1126c): Wörle 1981:55–56.

[100] Kremmydas 2012:178 (though contrast Canevaro 2016:181–183); cf. Din. 1.111.

[101] Westwood 2020:105–111.

[102] Plut. *Phoc.* 7.3–4.

[103] Plut. *Phoc.* 4.2, 14.7; *Mor.* 1126c; Wörle 1981:56–63; Tritle 1988:50–53, 141–145; Trampedach 1994:136–138, 145; Sonnabend 1996:94–95.

even carries the improbable detail that Demosthenes was courting Chabrias's widow.[104] Demosthenes plausibly had contact with this group of people earlier too, though. In 366/5, when he reached majority and started gaining public notice by prosecuting his very well-connected guardians, Euphraeus was probably still in Athens (as Perdiccas only became king, at least in his own right, in 365).[105] The year 366/5 also saw Chabrias and the leading political orator Callistratus prosecuted for Athens's loss of Oropus to Thebes. Their trials cast a long shadow over politics and the intellectual world:[106] Diogenes Laertius even (implausibly) puts Plato on Chabrias's defense team,[107] while Plutarch claims that Callistratus's speech in his own defense drew the young Demosthenes to oratory as a career.[108] What is certainly the case is that Demosthenes' speeches of the 350s and later display regard, sometimes high regard, for both Chabrias and Callistratus,[109] and barely concealed animus against their chief accuser in 366/5, Leodamas;[110] and as late as the mid-340s he was still emphasizing the harshness of the attack on Chabrias by Leodamas's coaccuser Philostratus.[111]

It seems likely, then, that the young Demosthenes either moved in the right circles to come into contact with Euphraeus personally, or admired or had dealings with those with the relevant connections, making it probable in turn that he would become aware of Euphraeus. He may even simply have heard him speak and been impressed.[112] If so, this awareness would supply a good reason on its own both for

[104] Plut. *Dem.* 15.3; Kremmydas 2012:179; Canevaro 2016:182.

[105] Dating Euphraeus's departure: Sonnabend 1996:48–49 (365/4); Haake 2007:33 (second half of the 360s). Perdiccas's accession in 365, at eighteen: Diod. Sic. 15.77.5; Hammond 1979:185–186. Carney 2019:37–41 makes him king from 368/7 under Ptolemy's regency; cf. Roisman 2010:162.

[106] Arist. *Rhet.* 1364a18–23; 1411b6–10; Hansen 1975:92–93 (no. 83); Sealey 1993:86–88; Hochschulz 2007:151–160.

[107] Diog. Laert. 3.23–24.

[108] Plut. *Dem.* 5.1–5.

[109] Chabrias (beyond *Against Leptines*, though note 20.133): Dem. 4.24; 21.64; 23.171 (pointedly defending Chabrias). 19.287 is less generous. Chabrias's celebrity: Dem. 13.22; 23.198; 24.180. Callistratus: Dem. 18.219; 19.297; 24.135.

[110] Dem. 20.146–147; Kremmydas 2012:425–427; Canevaro 2016:34, 409–411.

[111] Dem. 21.64.

[112] Egermann 1952:146n87; cf. Pernot 2006:38–39.

his decision to heroize Euphraeus in spite of the risk and for his disinclination to specify the reason for Euphraeus's sojourn in Athens in *Third Philippic* 59—i.e., that he knew exactly what it was but preferred to avoid implying close personal connections with Plato's Academy in an Assembly speech aimed at a popular audience. Furthermore, as suggested above, he may have met Euphraeus in Oreus on one or both of his visits there on the embassies to Philip in 346.

My second suggestion—also tentative—is that there may be signs that Demosthenes is shaping his version of the events that led up to the imprisonment and suicide of Euphraeus in such a way as to recall themes and events relevant to the trial, imprisonment, and execution of Socrates in the Platonic tradition. We need not assume that Demosthenes had read specific Platonic texts in order to be able to claim that he was able to reflect the tradition in the general ways I suggest here. Nor does it seem likely that he was trying to map Euphraeus's death onto Socrates' in a thoroughgoing way: a suicide is not an execution (although Demosthenes' wording does bridge the gap),[113] and the issue is complicated by the fact that Demosthenes' version of it differs from Carystius's (where Euphraeus is executed). But the prison setting (i.e., the death of a principled intellectual while under confinement for a crime he did not commit) may be suggestive in itself.[114] Moreover, there are clear general resemblances between some of Plato's depictions of Socrates' attitude to, and relationship with, the question of good statesmanship (for example, in the *Gorgias*, but also in the *Apology*) and Demosthenes' portrayal of his own principled

---

[113] Dem. 9.62: ἀποσφάττω (lit. "cut [someone's] throat") occurs in a number of contexts where formal execution is in point: e.g., Thuc. 7.86.2; Lys. 13.78; also [Dem.] 59.103 (though the two different uses there demonstrate the term's range).

[114] It is also interesting that Demosthenes uses καθαρῶς (lit. "cleanly," "purely") of Euphraeus's resistance to Philip. Euphraeus's nonviolence toward others (Herrman 2019:256, cf. 242) may well be the primary referent (and probably would be for the Assembly audience), but in Plato's *Phaedo* καθαρός and its cognates help articulate the conditions under which the voluntary separation of soul and body by suicide might be deemed rational for the philosopher (i.e., after personal purification): see *Phaedo* 66d–67d (eight instances of καθαρός-cognates); cf. 61c–62e, with Warren 2001:104–105. Cognates of καθαρός appear only twice in Demosthenes' Assembly speeches (here and in an explanation of homicide law at 9.44).

civic contributions, especially in his Assembly speeches and in *On the Crown*.[115] These resemblances might be relevant here too, given that Demosthenes is constructing Euphraeus as a clear political analogue for himself, and presenting Euphraeus's suicide as "a practical proof of the honesty and disinterested patriotism of his opposition to Philip" (62). It therefore seems possible that Demosthenes fashioned the Euphraeus passage not only as a nightmare version of what he himself and his political associates might suffer should their opponents succeed, but also as a way of giving a former pupil of Plato (and possibly someone he knew personally) an exit from public life attended by fitting echoes of the fate of the Academy's intellectual hero.

Any three-way parallel between Demosthenes' Euphraeus, Plato's Socrates, and Demosthenes himself would hinge on the way that each is depicted taking a solitary, principled stand, powered by superior insight, against threats to the civic order: in Demosthenes, against Philip's supporters in Oreus and Athens; in Plato, against the *demos*'s bad decision-making in the mid-400s.[116] Each man is attacked for his efforts by a *demos* that does not understand the benefits he is trying to confer and that listens to wrongheaded or malevolent opposing voices.[117] Possible echoes emerge most clearly in the similar descriptions of a critical event in each case: in Euphraeus's case, his attempt to prosecute Philistides and his associates, followed by his removal from the political scene (behind which lurks the possibility that the same fate will befall Demosthenes); in Socrates' case, his public objection to the proposed collective trial of the Athenian generals accused of abandoning survivors after the sea battle of Arginusae in 406. This objection mattered because Socrates was on the Council, and his tribe in prytany, at the time of this decision; two (possibly all three) of Xenophon's versions even have Socrates serving as that day's chairman

---

[115] Yunis 1996:153–161, 276–277; Hunter 2012:114–116.

[116] Particularly bad because it would be followed by defeat in the Peloponnesian War and by the coming of the Thirty (alluded to by Socrates at Pl. *Grg.* 457b–c and followed up at 460d).

[117] Dem. 9.61 for Euphraeus; Pl. *Ap.* 32b for Socrates; see also the "trial of the doctor" theme in *Gorgias*: 464d–e and 521e–522c (directly after Socrates' self-description as Athens's only true living statesman: 521d).

of the *prytaneis* and refusing to put the proposal to the vote, not just refusing to support it.[118] In both Demosthenes and Plato, this event is determinative for the circumstances of the hero's death: Euphraeus will kill himself while still in prison (it is implied), and in Plato's *Apology* Socrates brings up the stance he took in 406 at his trial in 399 as proof of his consistent prioritization of just courses of action over expedient ones—something he admits makes him vulnerable in court now (32a).

There are also similarities in how Demosthenes and Plato describe the critical event happening: just as Euphraeus is hauled off to prison with the blessing of a gloating and vocal *demos* when his principled attempt to indict Philistides and the others rebounds on him (60–61), Socrates in the *Apology* recalls how the *demos* loudly supported his opponents when they threatened to impeach him and haul him off for refusing to join the consensus in the Arginusae affair (32b). In Plato's *Gorgias*, Socrates alludes to that occasion in a context where his own voluntary detachment from public life is foregrounded;[119] this is something which his interlocutor Callicles later sees as leaving him vulnerable to "being seized and taken away to prison, unjustly accused of some crime" (486a–b)[120] and to subsequent execution due to not knowing how to conduct a good self-defense in court—a clear foreshadowing of Socrates' trial and death (made even more explicit later in the dialogue: 521b–522e). As with *Apology* 32a, and Socrates' fearless prioritizing of the just course, these moments in the *Gorgias* are framed by a dialogue-wide discussion of what constitutes a good statesman, and here Socrates' provocative claim that he himself is in fact Athens's only true living statesman (521d), despite his studied detachment from politics, finds a loose echo in the language of Demosthenes' own rhetorical self-presentation in his Assembly speeches and in *On the Crown* not only as a true statesman *par excellence*, but also as the only speaker in Athens whose policy has been proved

---

[118] Pl. *Ap.* 32b–c; Xen. *Hell.* 1.7.15; *Mem.* 1.1.18, 4.4.2.

[119] Pl. *Grg.* 473e–474a; there may also be an allusion in 516d–e (a similar intervention which succeeded).

[120] Translation: Waterfield 1994.

consistently right;[121] this is all even more explicit in the case of Euphraeus in the *Third Philippic*, who really does stand absolutely alone. Another prominent common aspect here is the clear stand taken by Euphraeus and Demosthenes himself (in the Oreus passage and what immediately follows it) and by Socrates in the *Gorgias* against politicians who merely satisfy the desires of the *demos* without considering their spiritual, moral, and cultural welfare.[122]

The resemblances I have sketched here suggest that Demosthenes may have found aspects of the Platonic tradition about Socrates' political engagements and fate an appropriate thematic template for his Oreus parable if he had a personal reason to concentrate on Euphraeus in particular (rather than somebody else). None of the resemblances I have highlighted requires us to assume any serious level of personal ideological commitment to Plato or Plato's Socrates, or of exposure to Platonic texts, on Demosthenes' part—only a meaningful level of awareness of the Academy's traditions about Socrates' actions in 406 and their relevance to his trial in 399, combined with a personal motivation to compose an appropriate send-off for Euphraeus. Demosthenes may also have had a specific rhetorical motivation, though, as I now suggest.

V. CONCLUSION

From the points made in sections II–III above, *Third Philippic* 59–62 emerges as a sequence which is very likely to offer a misleading, even a very misleading, picture of Euphraeus himself, of his supposed political role, of the nature of the political alignments prevailing at Oreus in 343 and 342, and of where he belongs within those alignments. Demosthenes may even have finessed the manner of Euphraeus's death; his Euphraeus chooses his own way out rather than waiting to be executed by Parmenion. All this is done in the service of Demosthenes' self-construction and his construction of Athens. He manufactures

---

[121] Dem. 5.5; 14.24; 15.6; *Ep.* 2.8; cf. the triumphant 18.173; also 19.302.

[122] See, e.g., Pl. *Grg.* 503b–c, 515c–517c, 518e–519d. Demosthenes had already explored the same concerns at length, and in terms intriguingly similar to those of Plato's Socrates, in the *Third Olynthiac* (349/8): 3.21–36; Yunis 1996:265–268.

an arresting mirror for his own struggle, aimed at making his fellow
citizens appreciate the danger both of Philip and of his "agents" in
Athens and recognize Demosthenes himself as the true statesman who
can resolve the situation if they will only listen to him. In section IV
above, I identified two possible reasons why he might have gone to the
trouble of creating the tissue of virtuosic misrepresentation that we
see in this passage. Each reason may reflect a particular mix of literary
and strategic motives and address two types of audience member
to differing extents: both members of the live audience who heard
something like this speech in 341, and readers studying the text in its
revised and disseminated form later.

The choice of Oreus itself enables Euphraeus's opponents and
Demosthenes' own to be brought into alignment: Aeschines, a *proxenos*
of Oreus, has his own specialist territory invaded and occupied; perhaps
significantly, he hits back in *Against Ctesiphon*. Although readers would
have leisure to extract more meaning from Demosthenes' choice,
the allusive attack on Aeschines can also be seen as participating
in a strategic tendency toward oblique attack common in formal
Assembly speeches, and therefore discernible for listeners too (as
other such instances elsewhere in the *Third Philippic* and in other
Demosthenic Assembly speeches help to show). Meanwhile, if we
entertain the possibility that Demosthenes is casting Euphraeus,
"alumnus" of the Academy, in a quasi-Socratic role (in ways we find
reflected in Platonic presentations of Socrates) we can see that this
would allow him to reach two audiences. Any Socratic "packaging"
allows Demosthenes to generate for *all* Assembly audience members
a vivid and pathetic set piece which stands out in its context. But for
similarly equipped listeners, and especially for subsequent readers—
who would interpret the Euphraeus passage at leisure and beyond the
Assembly context—the cluster might communicate the impression
that Demosthenes and Euphraeus not only shared political ideals but
also belonged in the same tradition as a figure who had by now been
fashioned by Plato, Xenophon, and the Academy as an unstintingly
moral operator in public contexts and thus a viable loose parallel for
Demosthenes. In revising the *Third Philippic* and perhaps others of his
Assembly speeches from the 340s for readers at all, Demosthenes was

in the business of building his own legacy as not only the guiding voice but also the moral powerhouse of the Athenian resistance to Philip—the heroic figure we see in *On the Crown*—and for the purpose of communicating this to posterity (rather than for the immediate purpose of persuading an Assembly audience suspicious of overeducated elite politicians), reflections of appropriate aspects of an already lively tradition about Socrates would help to mark his speech-texts as complex, lasting intellectual contributions rather than simply a series of practical exercises in statesmanship, aimed at career justification and with limited wider cultural significance. This would remain true regardless of whether Demosthenes' Assembly speeches were disseminated in his lifetime, or of who disseminated them.

What Demosthenes gives his audience(s) is a parallel Athens, a home from home: Euphraeus both is and is not Demosthenes; the Athenian *demos* both is and is not the *demos* of its former cleruchy, Oreus. It is essential that the sequel Demosthenes and all his listeners (and implied listeners) want for Athens is not the same as the sequel which Oreus suffered; Euphraeus and Oreus are an awful warning, but not yet a reality (9.65, 70). So the gap between Oreus and Athens is critical: in that gap, Demosthenes confides that the Athenians will be able to act against Macedonian encroachment and thereby sustains a key thread of projected optimism which runs right through the "Philippic" part of the Assembly corpus.[123] The compositional choices that he makes in the Oreus narrative enable him to communicate forcibly that Athens stands at a crossroads: it can follow its current course, listen to its pro-Macedonian politicians, and eventually (cf. 9.67) become the latest in the chain of examples of Philip's conquests—a new Oreus—or it can follow Demosthenes' advice and take action to break that chain. The Athenians would choose the latter, voting in the summer of 341 first for an expedition to liberate Oreus, with Chalcidian assistance, and then for a second to liberate Eretria.[124] Both expeditions were

---

[123] Dem. 1.10, 24; 2.9–10, 20, 31; 4.2, 45; 8.47; 9.4–5; 10.23, 31.

[124] The expeditions to Oreus and Eretria: Diod. Sic. 16.74.1; Philochorus *FGrH* 328 FF 159, 160; Charax *FGrH* 103 F 19; schol. *ad* Aeschin. 3.85 (184 Dilts); schol. *ad* Aeschin. 3.103 (222 Dilts); Sealey 1993:261–262; Harding 2006:104–108 (for Philochorus); Teegarden 2014:58–59; Liddel 2020:557–565.

successful, and Philistides and Cleitarchus were killed. All this came too late for Euphraeus, but not for Demosthenes, who proposed the decrees that launched the expeditions[125] and was crowned in Athens for these and other foreign-policy efforts in late 341 or early 340.[126] The policy direction to which the *Third Philippic* belongs was bearing fruit and bringing Demosthenes success, and that is important for making conclusions about the Euphraeus passage, in the following sense.

In all the speeches for public contexts which have him as a center of interest, whether as the adviser giving the advice or as a litigant in the trial at hand (and even in some speeches where neither of these is the case), Demosthenes shows a keen interest in persuasive but often discreet presentation of personal models from the Athenian past, from Solon to very recent times—figures who will reflect positively on him and negatively on his opponents.[127] Demosthenes' compelling variation on that habit in *Third Philippic* 59–62, here applied to another state's very recent past, provides good evidence of the versatility and functional potential of sustained paradigmatic narratives as compositional elements and argumentative devices. If the suggestions I made in section IV are entertained, then what we see is Demosthenes using an example whose full significance can only really be grasped within specific contextual parameters (of his own intellectual formation and compositional intentions, or of his ongoing rivalry with Aeschines) to fulfill two aims whose field of application is much wider: first, to shape his public articulation of his views on issues which matter for Athens as a whole; and, second, to give the starring role in that articulation to this personal material, rather than to material likely to be more familiar to audience members (listeners and readers alike). The likely unfamiliarity of Euphraeus to the Athenian audience makes this possible in the first place, but, as noted above, any of Demosthenes' opponents could intervene and "remind" listeners of Euphraeus's "true" nature. Demosthenes deliberately took on a

---

[125] Dem. 18.79, 87; Plut. *Dem.* 17.1; Liddel 2020:559–561.

[126] Dem. 18.83–87; Liddel 2020:565–568. The honors in Oreus misrepresented by Aeschines (3.103) were probably contemporary.

[127] In more detail: Westwood 2020.

compromised individual and a problematic model for Athens itself because the rhetorical opportunities outweighed the potential costs. Both Euphraeus and Oreus offered him creative latitude and possibilities but also staked out a competitive arena for Demosthenes as political orator, a chance to be seen mounting an impressive resistance to any contestation of his chosen examples by opponents that might occur either in this debate or later, perhaps in a public trial. This dynamic mutual contestation of examples by opponents had been a key feature of Demosthenes' and Aeschines' clash in the Embassy trial of 343 and would be so again in 330 when they opposed one another in the Crown trial.[128] Demosthenes' appetite for such contestation fits with other aspects of his rhetoric in the late 340s. By the time of the *Third Philippic*, he was politically in the ascendant, challenging political rivals to do their worst; in the *Second Philippic* and *On the Chersonese*, he had challenged and threatened the politicians he claimed were working in Philip's interest.[129] It is therefore possible to read Demosthenes' Euphraeus passage not only as an astutely crafted means to three ends—reflecting Demosthenes' own virtues, commemorating Euphraeus's "martyrdom," and warning the Athenians—but also as a rhetorical gauntlet thrown down to his rivals.

UNIVERSITY OF OXFORD

WORKS CITED

Aravantinos, Vassilios, and Nikolaos Papazarkadas. 2012. "Ἡγεμονία: A New Treaty from Classical Thebes." *Chiron* 42:239–254.

Barbato, Matteo. 2020. *The Ideology of Democratic Athens: Institutions, Orators and the Mythical Past.* Edinburgh.

Bearzot, Cinzia, and Franca Landucci, eds. 2013. *Tra mare e continente: L'isola d'Eubea.* Milan.

Bertelli, Lucio. 1976. "L'epistola di Speusippo a Filippo: Un problema di cronologia." *Atti della Accademia delle Scienze di Torino* 110:275–300.

---

[128] On contestation in these trials: Hesk 2012:217–226; Westwood 2020:223–327.

[129] Especially Dem. 6.29–36 and 8.52–67.

————. 1977. "La lettera di Speusippo a Filippo: Il problema dell'autenticità." *Atti della Accademia delle Scienze di Torino* 111:75–111.

Bertoli, Marcello. 2013. "L'Eubea nella prima metà del IV secolo a.c. tra aspirazione alla libertà e dipendenza da Atene." In Bearzot and Landucci 2013, 191–223.

Berve, Helmut. 1967. *Die Tyrannis bei den Griechen.* Vol 2. Munich.

Bickermann, Elias J., and Johannes Sykutris. 1928. *Speusipps Brief an König Philipp: Text, Übersetzung, Untersuchungen.* Leipzig.

Brock, Roger. 2013. *Greek Political Imagery from Homer to Aristotle.* London.

Brunt, Peter A. 1969. "Euboea in the Time of Philip II." *Classical Quarterly,* n.s., 19, no. 2:245–265.

————. 1993. *Studies in Greek History and Thought.* Oxford.

Canevaro, Mirko. 2016. *Demostene. Contro Leptine: Introduzione, traduzione e commento storico.* Berlin.

Canfora, Luciano. 1992. *Demostene. Terza Filippica.* Palermo.

Carey, Chris. 2000. *Aeschines.* Austin.

Carney, Elizabeth D. 2019. *Eurydice and the Birth of Macedonian Power.* Oxford.

Cawkwell, George L. 1963. "Demosthenes' Policy after the Peace of Philocrates. II." *Classical Quarterly,* n.s., 13, no. 1:200–213.

————. 1978. "Euboea in the Late 340's." *Phoenix* 32, no. 1:42–67.

Chiesara, Maria L. 2001. *Aristocles of Messene: Testimonia and fragments.* Oxford.

Cirio, Amalia M. 2015. "L'ἀποτυμπανισμός e una singolare pluralità di interpretazioni." *Seminari romani di cultura greca* 4:187–212.

Clarke, Katherine. 2008. *Making Time for the Past: Local History and the Polis.* Oxford.

Clarke, Stephen. 2021. *Greek Orators.* Vol. 7, *Demosthenes 8, On the Chersonese.* Liverpool.

Das, Allison E. 2019. "Health, Harm, and the Civic Body: Medical Language in the Speeches of Demosthenes." *Greek, Roman, and Byzantine Studies* 59, no. 3:340–367.

Dillon, John M. 2003. *The Heirs of Plato: A Study of the Old Academy (347–274 BC).* Oxford.

Dilts, Mervin R. 1997. *Aeschinis Orationes.* Stuttgart.

————. 2002. *Demosthenis Orationes.* Vol. 1. Oxford.

————. 2005. *Demosthenis Orationes*. Vol. 2. Oxford.

Dreher, Martin. 1995. *Hegemon und Symmachoi: Untersuchungen zum zweiten athenischen Seebund*. Berlin.

Düring, Ingemar. 1957. *Aristotle in the Ancient Biographical Tradition*. Gothenburg.

Egermann, Franz. 1952. *Vom attischen Menschenbild*. Munich.

Fisher, Nick. 2001. *Aeschines. Against Timarchos*. Oxford.

Frede, Michael. 2015. "Part I." In *The Pseudo-Platonic Seventh Letter*, ed. Dominic Scott, 3-67. Oxford.

Gehrke, Hans-Joachim. 1985. *Stasis: Untersuchungen zu den inneren Kriegen in den griechischen Staaten des 5. und 4. Jahrhunderts v. Chr.* Munich.

Gigon, Olof. 1962. *Vita Aristotelis Marciana*. Berlin.

Gotteland, Sophie. 2010. "Conseiller et persuader: Quelques échos thucydidéens dans les *Harangues* de Démosthène." In *Ombres de Thucydide*, ed. Valérie Fromentin, Sophie Gotteland, and Pascal Payen, 35–50. Bordeaux.

Grethlein, Jonas. 2014. "The Value of the Past Challenged: Myth and Ancient History in the Attic Orators." In *Valuing the Past in the Greco-Roman World*, ed. James Ker and Christoph Pieper, 326–354. Leiden.

Griffith, Guy T. 1979. "Part II: The Reign of Philip the Second." In Hammond and Griffith 1979, 203-698.

Haake, Matthias. 2007. *Der Philosoph in der Stadt: Untersuchungen zur öffentlichen Rede über Philosophen und Philosophie in den hellenistischen Poleis*. Munich.

————. 2009. "'Doing Philosophy': Soziales Kapital versus politischer Mißkredit?" In *Rollenbilder in der athenischen Demokratie: Medien, Gruppen, Räume im politischen und sozialen System*, ed. Christian Mann, Matthias Haake, and Ralf von den Hoff, 113–145. Wiesbaden.

————. 2020. "The Academy in Athenian Politics and Society: Between Disintegration and Integration: The First Eighty Years (387/6–306/5)." In *Plato's Academy: Its Workings and Its History*, ed. Paul Kalligas, Chloe Balla, Effie Baziotopoulou-Valavani, and Vassilis Karasmanis, 65–88. Cambridge.

Hammond, Nicholas G. L. 1979. "Part I: The Development of the Macedonian State and the Struggle for Survival." In Hammond and Griffith 1979, 3-202. Oxford.

Hammond, Nicholas G. L., and Guy T. Griffith. 1979. *A History of Macedonia*. Vol. 2, *550-336 B.C.* Oxford.

Hansen, Mogens H. 1975. *Eisangelia: The Sovereignty of the People's Court in Athens in the Fourth Century B.C. and the Impeachment of Generals and Politicians.* Odense.

Harding, Phillip. 2006. *Didymos. On Demosthenes.* Oxford.

Harris, Edward M. 1995. *Aeschines and Athenian Politics.* New York.

Harward, John. 1932. *The Platonic Epistles.* Cambridge.

Hatzopoulos, Miltiades. 1996. *Macedonian Institutions under the Kings.* Vol. 1. Paris.

——. 2011. "Macedonians and Other Greeks." In Lane Fox 2011b, 51–78.

Hennig, Dieter. 1997. "Die Beherbergung von 'Staatsgästen' in der hellenistischen Polis." *Chiron* 27:355–368.

Herrman, Judson. 2019. *Demosthenes. Selected Political Speeches.* Cambridge.

——. 2020. "Seeing Others as Athenians in Demosthenes' Third *Philippic*." In *The Making of Identities in Athenian Oratory*, ed. Jakub Filonik, Brenda Griffith-Williams, and Janek Kucharski, 137–149. London.

Hesk, Jon. 2012. "Common Knowledge and the Contestation of History in Some Fourth-Century Athenian Trials." In *Greek Notions of the Past in the Archaic and Classical Eras: History without Historians*, ed. John Marincola, Lloyd Llewellyn-Jones, and Calum Maciver, 207–226. Edinburgh.

Hochschulz, Barbara. 2007. *Kallistratos von Aphidnai: Untersuchungen zu seiner politischen Biographie.* Munich.

Horváth, László. 2014. *Der Neue Hypereides. Textedition, Studien und Erläuterungen.* Berlin.

Hunter, Richard L. 2012. *Plato and the Traditions of Ancient Literature: The Silent Stream.* Cambridge.

Isnardi Parente, Margherita. 1970. *Filosofia e politica nelle Lettere di Platone.* Naples.

————. 1979. *Studi sull'Accademia platonica antica.* Florence.

————. 1980. *Speusippo. Frammenti.* Naples.

Jacoby, Felix. 1919. "Karystios." In *Paulys Realencyclopädie der classischen Altertumswissenschaft: Zehnter Band (Jugurtha-Katochos),* ed. W. Kroll, 2254–2255. Stuttgart.

————. 1954. *Die Fragmente der griechischen Historiker: III. Geschichte von Staedten und Voelkern (Horographie und Ethnographie), B (Supplement); A Commentary on the Ancient Historians of Athens (Nos. 323a–334).* Vol. 2, *Notes, Addenda, Corrigenda, Index.* Leiden.

Knoepfler, Denis. 1995. "Une paix de cent ans et un conflit en permanence: Étude sur les relations diplomatiques d'Athènes avec Érétrie et les autres cités de l'Eubée au IVe siècle av. J.-C." In *Les relations internationales: Actes du Colloque de Strasbourg, 15–17 juin 1993,* ed. Edmond Frézouls and Anne Jacquemin, 309–364. Paris.

————. 2013. "Bulletin Épigraphique: Béotie-Eubée." *Revue des Études Grecques* 126, no. 2:462–500.

————. 2016. "'Pour qube demeurent la *philia* et la *symmachia* entre Athènes et les Eubéens' (*IG* II^2 149 = *IG* II^3 1, 2, 398, une inscription attique à réconsiderer)." In *La symmachia comme pratique du droit international dans le monde grec: D'Homère à l'époque hellénistique,* ed. Jean-Christophe Couvenhes, 125–160. Besançon.

Kostopoulos, Katharina. 2019. *Die Vergangenheit vor Augen: Erinnerungsräume bei den attischen Rednern.* Stuttgart.

Kremmydas, Christos. 2012. *Commentary on Demosthenes Against Leptines: With Introduction, Text, and Translation.* Oxford.

Lambert, Stephen D. 2006. "Athenian State Laws and Decrees, 352/1–322/1: III Decrees Honouring Foreigners. A. Citizenship, Proxeny and Euergesy." *Zeitschrift für Papyrologie und Epigraphik* 158:115–158.

Landucci, Franca. 2013. "L'Eubea nella politica macedone." In Bearzot and Landucci 2013, 227–256.

Lane Fox, Robin J. 2011a. "The 360's." In Lane Fox 2011b, 257–269.

————. 2011b. *Brill's Companion to Ancient Macedon: Studies in the Archaeology and History of Macedon, 650 BC-300 AD.* Leiden.

Laursen, Simon. 2019. "*IG* II^3 399: Context and Date." *Zeitschrift für Papyrologie und Epigraphik* 212:102–108.

Liddel, Peter P. 2020. *Decrees of Fourth-Century Athens (403/2-322/1 BC)*. Vol. 1, *The Literary Evidence*. Cambridge.

Lintott, Andrew W. 2018. *Aristotle's Political Philosophy in its Historical Context: A New Translation and Commentary on Politics Books 5 and 6*. London.

Lynch, John P. 1972. *Aristotle's School: A Study of a Greek Educational Institution*. Berkeley.

Mack, William J. 2015. *Proxeny and Polis: Institutional Networks in the Ancient Greek World*. Oxford.

Mader, Gottfried. 2005. "*Pax Duello Mixta*: Demosthenes and the Rhetoric of War and Peace." *Classical Journal* 101, no. 1:11–35.

———. 2007a. "Dramatizing *Didaxis*: Aspects of Demosthenes' 'Periclean' Project." *Classical Philology* 102, no. 2:155–179.

———. 2007b. "Foresight, Hindsight, and the Rhetoric of Self-Fashioning in Demosthenes' Philippic Cycle." *Rhetorica* 25, no. 4:339–360.

Maltagliati, Giulia. 2020. "Persuasion through Proximity (and Distance) in the Attic Orators' Historical Examples." *Greek, Roman, and Byzantine Studies* 60:68–97.

Moggi, Mauro. 1976. *I sinecismi interstatali greci: I. Dalle origini al 338 a.C.* Pisa.

Müller, Sabine. 2016. *Die Argeaden: Geschichte Makedoniens bis zum Zeitalter Alexanders des Grossen*. Paderborn.

Natoli, Anthony F. 2004. *The Letter of Speusippus to Philip II: Introduction, Text, Translation and Commentary; With an Appendix on the Thirty-First Socratic Letter Attributed to Plato*. Stuttgart.

Ober, Josiah. 1989. *Mass and Elite in Democratic Athens: Rhetoric, Ideology, and the Power of the People*. Princeton.

Occhipinti, Egidia. 2020. "The Treaty of Alliance between Athens and Carystus: Supplements for Lines 2–3 and 4–6 and Further Historical Considerations." *Ancient History Bulletin* 34:138–154.

O'Connell, Peter A. 2017. *The Rhetoric of Seeing in Attic Forensic Oratory*. Austin.

Olson, S. Douglas. 2009. *Athenaeus. The Learned Banqueters*. Vol. 5, *Books 10.420e–11*. Cambridge, MA.

Pernot, Laurent. 2006. *L'Ombre du Tigre: Recherches sur la réception de Démosthène*. Naples.

Picard, Olivier. 1979. *Chalcis et la Confédération eubéenne: Étude de numismatique et d'histoire, IVe-Ier siècle*. Paris.

Reber, Karl, Mogens H. Hansen, and Pierre Ducrey. 2004. "Euboea." In *An Inventory of Archaic and Classical Poleis*, ed. Mogens H. Hansen and Thomas H. Nielsen, 643–663. Oxford.

Rhodes, Peter J., and Robin G. Osborne. 2003. *Greek Historical Inscriptions, 404-323 BC*. Oxford.

Roisman, Joseph. 2010. "Classical Macedonia to Perdiccas III." In *A Companion to Ancient Macedonia*, ed. Joseph Roisman and Ian Worthington, 145–165. Malden, MA.

Ryder, Timothy T. B. 2000. "Demosthenes and Philip II." In *Demosthenes: Statesman and Orator*, ed. Ian Worthington, 45–89. London.

Sandys, John E. 1900. *Demosthenes. On the Peace, Second Philippic, On the Chersonesus, Third Philippic*. London.

Schäfer, Arnold. 1886. *Demosthenes und seine Zeit*. Vol. 2. 2nd ed. Leipzig.

Scholz, Peter. 1998. *Der Philosoph und die Politik: Die Ausbildung der philosophischen Lebensform und die Entwicklung des Verhältnisses von Philosophie und Politik im 4. und 3. Jh. v. Chr*. Stuttgart.

Sealey, Raphael. 1993. *Demosthenes and His Time: A Study in Defeat*. Oxford.

Sonnabend, Holger. 1996. *Die Freundschaften der Gelehrten und die zwischenstaatlichen Politik im klassischen und hellenistischen Griechenland*. Hildesheim.

Steinbock, Bernd. 2013. *Social Memory in Athenian Public Discourse: Uses and Meanings of the Past*. Ann Arbor.

Stuart Jones, Henry. 1963. *Thucydidis Historiae*. Vol. 2. 2nd ed. Rev. J. E. Powell. Oxford.

Stylianou, P. J. 1998. *A Historical Commentary on Diodorus Siculus Book 15*. Oxford.

Teegarden, David A. 2014. *Death to Tyrants! Ancient Greek Democracy and the Struggle against Tyranny*. Princeton.

Trampedach, Kai. 1994. *Platon, die Akademie, und die zeitgenössische Politik*. Stuttgart.

Trevett, Jeremy. 1996. "Did Demosthenes Publish His Deliberative Speeches?" *Hermes* 124, no. 4:425–441.

———. 1999. "Demosthenes and Thebes." *Historia* 48, no. 2:184–202.

———. 2011. *Demosthenes. Speeches 1–17.* Austin.

Tritle, Lawrence A. 1988. *Phocion the Good.* London.

———. 1993. "Philip, Athens, and Euboea." In *Alpha to Omega: Studies in Honor of George John Szemler on his Sixty-Fifth Birthday,* ed. William J. Cherf, 227–238. Chicago.

Tuplin, Christopher J. 1998. "Demosthenes' *Olynthiacs* and the Character of the Demegoric Corpus." *Historia* 47, no. 3:276–320.

Wareh, Tarik. 2012. *The Theory and Practice of Life: Isocrates and the Philosophers.* Cambridge, MA.

Warren, James. 2001. "Socratic Suicide." *Journal of Hellenic Studies* 121:91–106.

Waterfield, Robin. 1994. *Plato. Gorgias.* Oxford.

Webb, Ruth. 2009a. *Ekphrasis, Imagination and Persuasion in Ancient Rhetorical Theory and Practice.* London.

———. 2009b. "Eschine et le passé athénien: Narration, imagination et construction de la mémoire." *Cahiers des études anciennes* 46:129–147.

Westwood, Guy. 2020. *The Rhetoric of the Past in Demosthenes and Aeschines: Oratory, History, and Politics in Classical Athens.* Oxford.

———. 2023. "Imagining Justice in the Athenian Lawcourt: Aeschines and Others." In *The Imagination of the Mind in Classical Athens: Forms of Thought,* ed. Emily Clifford and Xavier Buxton, 151–172. London.

Wooten, Cecil W. 2008. *A Commentary on Demosthenes' Philippic I: With Rhetorical Analyses of Philippics II and III.* Oxford.

Wörle, Andrea. 1981. *Die politische Tätigkeit der Schüler Platons.* Lauterburg.

Worthington, Ian. 2013. *Demosthenes of Athens and the Fall of Classical Greece.* Oxford.

Yunis, Harvey. 1996. *Taming Democracy: Models of Political Rhetoric in Classical Athens.* New York.

———. 2001. *Demosthenes. On the Crown.* Cambridge.

TRUST AND PERSUASION

TESTIMONY IN [PLATO] *DEMODOCUS*

PETER OSORIO

I. WHAT IS *DEMODOCUS* ABOUT?

D*EMODOCUS* [*DEM.*] IS one of the surviving spurious dialogues in the so-called Appendix that travels in Plato's manuscripts.[1] Like other *spuria* in the Appendix it was recognized in antiquity not to have been written by Plato,[2] and modern commentators have disagreed about its authorship. Because of its dialectical (or eristic) elements and minimal dramaturgy, twentieth-century scholars frequently assigned it to the Megarian school of the fourth century BCE.[3] More recently, Carl Werner Müller and Francesco Aronadio have argued that it was written in the Academy in two periods.

Demodocus stands out from other works in the Appendix and the Platonic *corpus* for containing four distinct parts (*Dem.* I–IV), each of

This paper was given to the proseminar of the Collaborative Specialization in Ancient & Medieval Philosophy at the University of Toronto in September 2021, and I owe James Allen thanks for the offer to give it. For their comments, questions, or later discussion, I thank James Allen, Rachel Barney, George Boys-Stones, Jessica Gelber, Lloyd Gerson, Samuel Meister, Christian Pfeiffer, Alexander Stopfgeshoff, and, above all, Máté Veres and Matthew Watton. I am also grateful to *HSCP*'s editors and reader for their help; to Marta Heckel, Ian Hensley, Freya Möbus, and John Proios, who heard and improved an earlier version; and to Kathleen Garland, whom I consulted from the start.

[1] Appearing in Parisinus graecus 1807 (A), Vaticanus graecus 1 (O), Vindobonensis 21 (Y), and Parisinus 3009 (Z), as well as the less important Laurentianus 80.17 (L) and Vaticanus graecus 1029.B (V): see Souilhé 1930:42. I note where I do not follow Burnet's text of *Demodocus* and other works in the Platonic corpus; for other authors I cite the editions used in the bibliography. Translations are mine.

[2] Diogenes Laërtius 3.62; *Prolegomena to Platonic Philosophy* 26.2–4 (Westerink et al. 1990).

[3] Souilhé 1930:40–41; Shorey 1933:441; Isnardi 1954.

Peter Osorio

which has its own narrative setting and centers on a different problem.
In view of some differences between the first part and the other three,
Müller and Aronadio date *Dem.* I to the Old Academy (Xenocrates to
Polemo, ca. 350–260 BCE) and *Dem.* II–IV to the skeptical Academy.[4] A
perceived disunity of *Demodocus*'s parts has licensed breaking up the
text in this way, and its piecemeal nature is also partly responsible
for the often dismissive comments made of it.[5] Souilhé called its parts
"médiocres et sophistiques dissertations," Guthrie an "unimportant
Sophistic [exercise] in paradox," and Dillon "dismal."[6] We ought not
to dismiss the *Demodocus*, as these derisions partly rest on an assumed
incoherence of the work and a failure to see the consistent conceptual questions the dialogue raises. Its episodic structure and aporetic
framing might still leave us wanting more, but we should not condemn
it for lacking conceptual focus.

I start with a summary of the forms and arguments of the four
parts and note where commentators begin to go wrong in grasping
what *Demodocus* is about. Besides the punctuated settings of its parts,
the *Demodocus* also differs from other Platonic and spurious dialogues

---

[4]   Müller 1975:127; Aronadio 2008:65. While Müller 1975:271 favors post-Arcesilean
authorship for *Dem.* II–IV (latter half of the third century to second century BCE; cf.
Heidel 1896:15), Aronadio 2008:81, 83 (see also Aronadio 2009:236) argues for authorship
under Arcesilaus's scholarchy (268/7–240/1 BCE). Oświecimski 1978 unconvincingly
traces *Demodocus* back to Plato himself, on the grounds that it is comprised of lecture
notes written up by his students.
[5]   Souilhé 1930:37: "Il comprend quatre pièces dont les sujets n'ont entre eux aucun
rapport"; Müller 1975:39n1: "Nun haben 'Demodokos II–III–IV' in der Tat keine Einzeltitel
und ihrer jetziger Sammeltitel ist sinnlos"; Müller 1975:107n1: "[*Dem.* II–IV] mit der Rede
[viz., *Dem.* I] nichts zu tun haben"; Guthrie 1978:397: "[*Demodocus*] has four unrelated
themes ..."; Oświecimski 1978:32: "... *Demodocus* contains really four, thematically not
interconnected, dialogues"; Hutchinson 1997: "What has come down to us under the
title *Demodocus* seems to be a combination of two separate works ..."; Aronadio 2008:64
(though cf. Aronadio 2009:225): "Certo è che lo spirito che informa lo scritto [sc. *Dem.*
I] ... è concettualmente distante dalle sfumature scettiche che la filosofia platonica
assunse con Arcesilao"; Aronadio 2008:81: "a differenza dal *Demodoco* I, la conduzione
della stringate argomentazioni [of *Dem.* II–IV] non ripropone tipici motivi concettuali
socratico-platonici, ma è interamente giocata sul sovvertimento eristico delle tesi in
discussion e del buon senso."
[6]   Souilhé 1930:37; Guthrie 1978:397; Dillon 2010; cf. Brisson 2014:14 on *Dem.* II–IV: "...
des pastiches de mauvaise qualité de dialogues platoniciens."

in that its central characters are anonymous.[7] The exception is Demodocus, to whom *Dem.* I is delivered in response to his request that the speaker give advice in the assembly. Demodocus himself, however, never speaks. Since Demodocus appears in the *Theages* as an elite Athenian seeking from Socrates an education for his son, we can surmise that Demodocus's request concerns the Athenian assembly.[8] As Müller has shown, the speaker delivers a symbuleutic speech explaining why he will not give advice in the assembly.[9] First, he outlines three puzzles about the normative presumptions of deliberative procedures (380a1–382a8), such that he is at a loss as to how the assembly is able to take advice effectively (382a8–b7). His three puzzles are: why does the assembly *meet* to get advice from others (380a5–381a3)? Why are its speakers willing and even *eager* to give advice (381a4–c4)? And why does the assembly *vote* after getting advice (381c5–382a8)? In the shorter, second half of his speech, he argues against the propriety of giving advice in the absence of knowledge (382b7–e5).

In *Dem.* II, a narrator reports that he was witness to a debate between two peers (ἑταῖροι) arguing on either side of whether a judge ought to listen to both accuser and defendant before deciding a case. The first speaker raises three arguments for his position that judgments will be more just and correct if judges hear both sides (383a5–7): by *analogy* to gold and the purple dye of the murex snail, λόγοι, due to their potential value, ought to be evaluated comparatively (383a7–b2); by the *authority* of the lawgiver, who believed that cases will be decided more justly and better if judges first listen to the accuser and the accused, given that he allotted time to each party and instituted the oath for judges to hear both sides (383b2–5); and by the *consensus* of most people, since the hexameter "Don't judge a case until you hear the speech of both" (μηδὲ δίκην δικάσῃς, πρὶν ἀμφοῖν μῦθον ἀκούσῃς,

---

[7] While the questioner is never named in *Sisyphus*, Sisyphus is named; in *De virtute* and *De iusto* Socrates is named. By contrast, in *Demodocus* no speakers are ever named.

[8] Demodocus is also mentioned at Plato *Apology* 33e. Assemblies other than that of Athens appear in the Appendix (see *Sisyphus* 387c on Pharsalus) and in the Platonic corpus (see [Plato] *Alcibiades* I.116d on Peparethus).

[9] Müller 1975:116.

Hesiod, Fr. 338 [Merkelbach and West 1967])[10] would not have become so popular unless it were truly said (383b5–c3).[11] The second speaker first argues that whatever can be known by hearing a true and a false speech can be known from hearing only one speaker (383c5–d5).[12] Then, he argues in an eristic (and self-defeating) way to the stronger conclusion that it is useless to listen to whoever speaks second, since whatever can be known by hearing two speeches can be known from the *first* speaker (383d6–384a5).[13] The narrator says that he was not able to judge the dispute, although others in the audience sided with the first speaker, and asks the reader or otherwise unknown addressee what they think and if they are able to contribute anything to the debate (384a6–b5).

---

[10] I discuss the relation of *Dem.* II with Plutarch *De Stoicorum repugnantiis* 8.1034E–F in section IV.

[11] The argument type is familiar from rhetoric (Quintilian *Institutio* 5.11.41), as are the previous considerations of the wisdom of the lawgiver (Lysias 1.32–33; Aeschines 3.6; Cicero *Lucullus* 146; see also Gagarin 2020) and of the analogy of the judge to an assayer of precious metal (Aristotle *Rhetoric* 1.15.7).

[12] There are three versions of this argument, according to whether one could not *truly believe/know* (γνῶναι) that one speech is true or false but could know whether two speeches are true or false (383c5–7), whether one could not *learn* (μαθεῖν; διδαχθῆναι) from one true speech but could learn from one true and one false speech (383c7–d2), or whether a true speaker could not *make evident* (ἐμφανίσαι) that his speech is true but a true speaker and a false speaker could make evident that one speech is true (383d2–5). The three versions might differ in what cognitive state the audience can gain from speakers (γνῶναι vs. μαθεῖν vs. ἐμφανίσαι), but each verb used can refer to coming to know or to making knowable. More important is that each offers a different relation between speaker and hearer: either the hearer can/cannot know *on their own* (γνῶναι), or the hearer can/cannot know *from the speaker* (μαθεῖν; διδαχθῆναι), or the speaker can/cannot make something known *to a hearer* (ἐμφανίσαι). The latter two relations require that the single person from whom something might be known or made knowable is saying what is true, while the first relation allows for something to be known from a single speaker even if that person is saying what is false. Therefore, the latter two versions of the argument only support that it is superfluous to have heard both speakers, not that it is useless to listen to the second speaker.

[13] There are two versions of this argument, both of which wrongly infer that each speaker makes evident the same thing. The first, positive version (383d6–e10) illicitly moves from both speakers making something evident (383d8–e2) to each of them making it evident (383e5–7); the second, negative version (384a1–5) illicitly moves from the denial that both do not make something evident (384a2–3) to the affirmation that each of the two make it evident (384a3–4).

Dem. III is the most threadbare in its framing, with a narrator reporting a dispute between two parties and the narration concluding without any address to the reader. Someone objected to another for not trusting him and lending him money, and the one criticized defended himself. Then, someone standing by examines the objector (384b8–e6). After this examiner refutes the initial objector, another interlocutor takes the objector's place. The examiner reduces this second interlocutor also to *aporia* (384e6–385c1). Against the objector's complaint that the man who was reluctant to trust him made an error, the examiner argues that the objector made an error in not persuading the reluctant man to lend money (384b8–d2) and that the reluctant man did not make an error (384d2–e6).[14] The objector's substitute asserts that we are right to blame others if we judge that we are owed a benefit but do not get it (385a1–4) and that we also blame others who wrong us in order that in the future they and their friends treat us right (385b1–3; cf. Plato *Protagoras* 324b). The examiner gets this new interlocutor to agree to the (Platonic[15]) condition that if we know what a person is capable of then we cannot fail to speak persuasively to them.[16] If we failed to persuade (and so failed to speak finely), then we lacked knowledge of what that person was capable of (385b5–6: "But then he does not seem to you to

[14] This attitude finds a parallel at Plato *Phaedrus* 272a8–b2: ἀλλ' ὅτι ἂν αὐτῶν τις ἐλλείπῃ λέγων ἢ διδάσκων ἢ γράφων, φῇ δὲ τέχνῃ λέγειν, ὁ μὴ πειθόμενος κρατεῖ ("... but if anyone falls short of these [sc. knowledge conditions on speaking finely] in speaking or teaching or writing but claims to speak with art, one acts better by not being persuaded").

[15] Plato *Phaedrus* 271c10–272b2; a similar reasoning can be applied to the examiner's refutation of the initial objector: if we converse with others as one ought (i.e., with knowledge), then we will never make an error. Accordingly, I do not find the examiner's arguments as eristic or non-Socratic/non-Platonic as other commentators describe them (see Isnardi 1954:427–428; Müller 1975:264, 268).

[16] "If he is not capable [of giving the benefit], how then did he judge finely, judging that he [ought to do] what he is incapable of. But if he is capable, how did he not persuade such a person as this, or how in saying such things did he speak finely?" (385a6–b1). The last question gives the premise that if one judges rightly about their audience then one will speak finely (and so persuasively) to them. While this only gets us as far as judging finely as a sufficient condition for persuasion, it may imply that being persuasive requires knowing one's audience (in particular, their character types); cf. the similar reasoning of Isnardi 1954:428: "l'aporia, a mio parere, si spiega solo tenendo conto di certa concezione astratta della verità come pura evidenza logica, che di per sé deve necessariamente convincere."

have judged rightly?"). Likewise, our blame won't get others to treat us better in the future if we aren't speaking or judging rightly (385b6-7).

Finally, in *Dem.* IV a narrator tells how a questioner examined someone who was accusing another of naivety for *quickly* trusting persons met by *chance* (ταχέως καὶ τοῖς τυχοῦσιν ἀνθρώποις ... πιστεύοι). The accuser's position, as he explains himself, is that (i) it is reasonable (εἰκός) to trust fellow citizens and family but (ii) very foolish to trust those whom you neither know nor have heard speak before, especially if you are aware that most people are boastful and conniving (ἀλαζόνες καὶ πονηροί) (385c3-d1). In his refutation, the examiner seeks to clarify the grounds of the accusation that it is an error to quickly trust persons met by chance. The accuser explains that it is an error to trust persons met by *chance*, because they may not be saying what is *true* (385d1-e4), and that it is an error to trust such persons *quickly*, because one ought to first *investigate* (σκέψασθαι) whether what they are saying is true (385e4-386a3). The examiner persuades the accuser that family members and acquaintances may also say what is untrustworthy, such that (i) and (ii) no longer seem compatible (386a3-b2). Since the truth or falsity of what is said does not track the divide of whether the speaker is a friend or stranger (386b2-c1), the accuser agrees that it is persuasive (πιθανόν) that one instead ought to treat what friends and strangers say alike (386c2-3).[17] The narrator steps back in to report that after hearing this conversation he puzzled over whether one ought to trust friends and acquaintances or those who are trustworthy and know what they are talking about (τοῖς πιστοῖς καὶ τοῖς εἰδόσι περὶ ὧν λέγουσιν), and he asks the reader or unknown addressee what he thinks about this question (386c4-7).

With a summary of these four scenes in hand, we can now see where past judgments of *Demodocus* go wrong. As I mentioned above

---

[17] The persuasive conclusion is paradoxically stated as οὐκοῦν καὶ τοῖς λέγουσιν αὐτὰ ὁμοίως πιστευτέον λέγουσιν αὐτά ("So, then, we must trust even those [viz., strangers] who say them [viz., trustworthy or untrustworthy things] in the same way as those [friends] who say them [viz., trustworthy or untrustworthy things]?"). By eliminating the importance of the distinction between friends and strangers as it pertains to the evaluation of testimony, both are referred to as τοῖς λέγουσιν αὐτά, where the neuter pronoun picks up πιστὰ ἤ ἄπιστα from the previous question.

(see note 5), scholars have not grasped any thematic unity in the dialogue. Part of the problem is that they often mistake the topic of *Dem.* I to be deliberation (βουλεύεσθαι).[18] Earlier critics have even thought that *Sisyphus* and *Demodocus* share a single authorship on the grounds that *Sisyphus* is also about deliberation. Indeed, *Sisyphus*'s subtitle is ἤ περὶ τοῦ βουλεύεσθαι.[19] *Demodocus*'s subtitle, however, is ἤ περὶ τοῦ συμβουλεύεσθαι, and I will discuss in the next section the important differences between deliberation and consultation (συμβουλεύεσθαι). For now, it is enough to say that consultation, or taking advice, involves accepting what another says, whereas deliberation need not involve hearing from others when deciding what to do. When *Dem.* I is seen as a refutation of the utility of deliberation, the relation it bears to *Dem.* II–IV, which report debates about trusting others, becomes shadowy. The connection is then further muddied by *Dem.* I's unique formal characteristics, featuring the only named character and lacking a functional interlocutor.[20] Some take the divorce between *Dem.* I and *Dem.* II–IV to be so great as to indicate that *Dem.* II–IV were acephalous dialogues without titles and only happened to be later appended to *Dem.* I.[21]

---

[18] Souilhé 1930:37; Shorey 1933:441; Isnardi 1954:425; Guthrie 1978:397. The other parts are sometimes also summarized in ways that are misleading, e.g., by Heidel 1896:23: "... the third [part], a quibble on the ambiguity of the term ἁμαρτάνειν ..."

[19] E.g., Hermann 1839:415; Hirzel 1895:341; Heidel 1896:15; cf. Isnardi 1954. Müller 1975:126 lists others of this view but affirms it lacks adequate grounds. For *Sisyphus*'s arguments about deliberation, see Fine 2021.

[20] Aronadio 2008:83 takes *Dem.* II–IV as unified only by narrative structure and argumentative technique. Sometimes it is remarked that *Dem.* I and II form a group, each critiquing a different democratic institution (Isnardi 1954:425–427), although in his discussion of *Dem.* I Müller 1975 points out that its arguments apply to any political scheme of consultation (e.g., advisors to tyrants or kings).

[21] Müller 1975:39 conjectures that *Dem.* II–IV were attached to *Dem.* I as late as the fifth and sixth centuries CE, even though Stobaeus, who seems to have written in the fifth century CE, quotes a section of *Dem.* II and attributes it to "Plato in *Demodocus*" (*Anthology* 4.5.64). Oświecimski 1978:32: "... because of either their shortness of the lack or loss of their own titles [*Dem.* II–IV] appeared in our manuscripts under the same title *Demodocus*, which in fact belonged but to the first of them"; Hutchinson 1997: "The trilogy [sc. of *Dem.* II–IV] may have been among the Platonic works said in antiquity to be 'without a head' ... At some point a scribe seems to have attached the trilogy to the end of *Demodocus* I by accident, which caused all subsequent copies to have the expanded

My contention is that the four episodes of *Demodocus*, individually and jointly, explore a single methodological problem concerning interpersonal belief and testimony under the competing slogans of πιστεύειν ('to trust') and πείθεσθαι ('to be persuaded').[22] One of the core controversies in social epistemology is whether, according to nonreductionists, testimony itself provides *sui generis* justification, or whether, *per* reductionists, justification for testimonial-based beliefs must be gained elsewhere, such as from justified beliefs of the speaker's competency and sincerity.[23] Which view you take has implications for how testimony ought to be used for acquiring knowledge. Nonreductionists incline to think that we are entitled to accept testimony by default, whereas reductionists think that one ought to have evidence for accepting testimony. The *Demodocus* assumes rather than argues for a reductionist view of testimony, and this assumption guides its investigation into the related problem of what the appropriate rules are for testimony's use. If I am right, we make much better sense of the unity of the *Demodocus* by attending to its two slogans—trust and persuasion—and we can stop treating it as either an eristic showpiece or a mere school exercise.[24] Even if it is a teaching text, it is not simply to be used to train students to diagnose arguments and identify sophisms; it also causes the reader to consider the conditions under which it is appropriate to trust and what we ought to do with testimony when those conditions are not met. For new students in a philosophical school, this is a problem that must be addressed early on: ought we to begin studying with philosophers by trusting them, with the expectation that we will learn later why

format"; Brisson 2014:12: "Ceux dont il est dit qu'ils sont dépourvus de titre pourraient être en réalité les trois dernières sections du *Démodocos*, ainsi que le *Sur le juste* et le *Sur la vertu*, qu'il ne mentionne nulle part ailleurs."

[22] By "testimony" I mean the spoken or written words of other persons rather than to a witness's report of past events given as evidence in forensic speeches (sc. μαρτυρία). *Demodocus* is interested in how to treat the λόγοι we receive from others.

[23] Reductionist papers: Hume 1748/1993 ["On Miracles"]; Fricker 1994; Fricker 2006; antireductionist works: Reid 1764/1983 [Ch. 6.24 of *Inquiry*]; Coady 1992; Graham 2006; Zagzebski 2012.

[24] For *Demodocus* II–IV as school texts, see Aronadio 2008:83.

what they say is true, or should we start with a critical attitude that conditions our belief on understanding why a given doctrine is true?

II. CONSULTATION AND TWO VIEWS OF TESTIMONY

Before I defend my view, it will be helpful to distinguish deliberation from consultation in ancient assemblies. By doing so, we will also see that already by the fourth century BCE there were conflicting attitudes about the process of giving and taking advice in the assembly that are set in opposition in *Demodocus* I. Men admitted to an assembly meeting could speak about a resolution up for discussion, and all present voted, whether by raising hands or casting ballots.[25] The division of labor between speaking and judging is reflected in how members of the assembly are described in symbuleutic speeches and related contexts.[26] Daniela Cammack has recently shown that in their role as audience and judge assemblygoers are consistently called "deliberators" (βουλευόμενοι), while as speakers and advice givers they are "consultants" (σύμβουλοι).[27] Of course, whoever speaks also votes, but by choosing to speak a consultant is committing himself to a course of action before hearing any other speeches. Consultants are therefore literally prejudiced, by having eliminated the possibility that they might be persuaded by others about what the best course of action is. Speakers were not expected to be open to changing their mind and to vote against the course of action they prescribed.[28] Consultants, then,

---

[25] See Hansen 1991:141–149 for an overview of the deliberative process of the popular assembly in Athens. The distinction between deliberators and consultants is not unique to democratic deliberative bodies: kings and advisors presume the same dynamic, and oligarchic assemblies differ from democratic ones only in their barriers of entry.

[26] E.g., [Plato] *Alcibiades* I.106c5–9: εἰ οὖν μέλλοντός σου ἰέναι ἐπὶ τὸ βῆμα λαβόμενος ἐροίμην· "Ὦ Ἀλκιβιάδη, ἐπειδὴ περὶ τίνος Ἀθηναῖοι διανοοῦνται βουλεύεσθαι, ἀνίστασαι συμβουλεύσων; ἆρ' ἐπειδὴ περὶ ὧν σὺ ἐπίστασαι βέλτιον ἢ οὗτοι;" τί ἂν ἀποκρίναιο; ("What would you answer if I asked when you were about to go up to the speaker's platform, 'Alcibiades, since you stand up to give advice, about what matter do the Athenians intend to deliberate? Surely it's about what you know better than they?'").

[27] Cammack 2020:509–511 (e.g., Lysias 6.54; Aeschines 2.49; Demosthenes 4.1, 5.3, 15.1); cf. Ober 1989:317–318. The distinction is as early as Herodotus (8.101; 3.156; 5.124; 7.10), see Cammack 2020:508.

[28] Cammack 2020:516.

do not deliberate with others in the assembly before voting. Contrast this division of labor with the conversations more familiar from Plato. In a friendly dialectical exchange, interlocutors typically offer reasons for or against a view, and no party forecloses the possibility of being persuaded to change an initial position. When such dialectical exchange is used for deliberation, interlocutors are "co-deliberators" (κοινῇ βουλευόμενοι).[29] Unlike the deliberators in the assembly who listen but do not speak, co-deliberators speak and listen to each other before deciding what to do.

Demodocus I pinpoints the following tension in the assembly's method of deliberation by consultation. On the one hand, consultants ought to be knowledgeable about what they advise. By committing themselves to a course of action before hearing others, they presume that there is no need to deliberate and are unshakably convinced about the correctness of their advice. Those taking counsel, meanwhile, benefit from listening to their consultants and are expected to take their advice. Thus, Demosthenes can praise the many for keeping silent in the assembly, and Aristotle notes that we bring in consultants when we distrust ourselves to judge important matters.[30] On the other hand, deliberators ought to assemble on the condition that they lack knowledge about what to do. By discussing the problem with each other, co-deliberators can inquire into and settle on the best course of action. Thucydides' Pericles famously praises the Athenians for collectively deciding the city's affairs by weighing arguments, and Demosthenes sets out as a precept for assemblygoers not to be prejudiced before voting but to "investigate [contrary opinions] by patiently listening to everything."[31] Given these two norms, one can

---

[29] Plato *Gorgias* 487c; *Meno* 91a1; *Critias* 119d4, 120e8–d1; *Laws* 6.784b5; [Plato] *Theages* 125a6.

[30] Demosthenes 18.308: ἔστι γάρ, ἔστιν ἡσυχία δικαία καὶ συμφέρουσα τῇ πόλει, ἣν οἱ πολλοὶ τῶν πολιτῶν ὑμεῖς ἁπλῶς ἄγετε; Aristotle *Nicomachean Ethics* 3.3.1112b10-11: συμβούλους δὲ παραλαμβάνομεν εἰς τὰ μεγάλα, ἀπιστοῦντες ἡμῖν αὐτοῖς ὡς οὐχ ἱκανοῖς διαγνῶναι.

[31] Thucydides 2.40.2: ἔνι τε τοῖς αὐτοῖς οἰκείων ἅμα καὶ πολιτικῶν ἐπιμέλεια, καὶ ἑτέροις πρὸς ἔργα τετραμμένοις τὰ πολιτικὰ μὴ ἐνδεῶς γνῶναι· μόνοι γὰρ τόν τε μηδὲν τῶνδε μετέχοντα οὐκ ἀπράγμονα, ἀλλ' ἀχρεῖον νομίζομεν, καὶ αὐτοὶ ἤτοι κρίνομέν γε ἢ ἐνθυμούμεθα ὀρθῶς τὰ πράγματα, οὐ τοὺς λόγους τοῖς ἔργοις βλάβην ἡγούμενοι, ἀλλὰ

deliberate in roughly one of two ways. In consultation, one listens (but does not speak) to a consultant who knows, either trusting them or (ideally) learning *from them* what is the best course of action. In co-deliberation, one listens and speaks to others who lack knowledge. By exchanging views, co-deliberators (ideally) learn or at least settle *on their own* what is the best course of action. By allowing only a few speakers but making everyone listen, the assembly combines consultation and co-deliberation. This combination is not an easy one, for two reasons. The first is that consultants are drawn from the same pool as co-deliberators, but the epistemic obligations on consultants and co-deliberators diverge: consultants ought to have knowledge, whereas it is permissible or even expected that co-deliberators be ignorant. Second, different mechanisms facilitate consultation or co-deliberation: a gathering of up to six thousand persons around a *bēma* is suitable for consultation, but it is a singularly bad arrangement for co-deliberation. The problem is captured by the ambiguity in the stem συμβουλευ-, which could cover the sense of co-deliberation but in practice indicates consultation, leaving phrases like "deliberate in common" (κοινῇ βουλεύεσθαι) to refer to co-deliberation (see note 29).

These problems can be mitigated by a disjunctive mixture of consultation and co-deliberation. As Socrates notes in the *Protagoras*,

μὴ προδιδαχθῆναι μᾶλλον λόγῳ πρότερον ἢ ἐπὶ ἃ δεῖ ἔργῳ ἐλθεῖν ("The same men care simultaneously both for their own and the city's business, and others who are devoted to their work do not have inadequate knowledge of public affairs. For we alone believe that one who does not participate in this is not apolitical but useless, and we ourselves at least judge, if not propose, matters rightly, on the grounds that we take as an obstacle to actions not arguments but to approach what must be done without having earlier been taught by argument"); Demosthenes *Exordia* 18: μὴ πάντα, ὡς ἕκαστος ἔχει γνώμης ὑμῶν περὶ τῶν παρόντων, ὀρθῶς ἐγνωκέναι πεπείσθω, ἀλλ᾽ ἐὰν παρὰ ταῦτά τι συμβαίνῃ λέγεσθαι, σκοπείτω πάνθ᾽ ὑπομείνας ἀκοῦσαι, εἶτ᾽ ἂν ὀρθῶς εἰρῆσθαί τι δοκῇ, χρήσθω. οὐ γὰρ ἧττον ὑμέτερον ἔσται τῶν χρησαμένων τὸ κατορθωθὲν <ἢ> τοῦ πρὸς ὑμᾶς εἰπόντος. ἡ μὲν οὖν ἀρχὴ τοῦ σκοπεῖν ὀρθῶς ἐστιν μὴ βεβουλεῦσθαι πρὶν ἐξ ὧν δεῖ βουλεύσασθαι ἀκοῦσαι ("Don't be convinced that every opinion each of you has about these matters is rightly known, but if something happens to be said contrary to these opinions, investigate it by patiently listening to everything. Then, if something seems to have been said rightly, accept it. For what is successful belongs to you who accepted it no less than to the one who spoke to you. Thus, the first step to a proper investigation is not to have come to a decision before hearing that on the basis of which you ought to make your decision").

when the resolution up for discussion is a technical matter, assemblygoers' prior beliefs of who the relevant professionals are allow for an easy selection of consultants, and the assembly works on the model of consultation (319b5–c8).[32] But when the resolution concerns matters of justice, there is no professional class of bureaucrats to consult, whether because the bureaucrat's science has yet to be invented, because there is no such science (319d6–7), or because all citizens partially share in knowledge of justice (322e2–323c2). In these cases, the assembly reverts to a model of co-deliberation, in which speakers, regardless of profession, are welcome to speak (319c8–d6). This disjunctive solution, however, creates superfluities in the assembly's practices. When in the consultative mode, the rules that allow multiple speakers and the process of voting become *pro forma*, whereas in the mode of co-deliberation the manner in which speakers confidently commit themselves to their views is merely performative. The conclusion of *Dem.* 1's methodological critique of the assembly says this succinctly:

ἢ πῶς οὐκ ἐναντιοῦται ἡ σύνοδος ὑμῶν ταῖς ψήφοις καὶ αἱ ψῆφοι τῇ τῶν συμβουλευόντων ὑμῖν προθυμίᾳ; ἡ μὲν γὰρ σύνοδός ἐστιν ὑμῶν ὡς οὐχ ἱκανῶν ἀλλὰ συμβούλων

---

[32] Plato *Protagoras* 319b5–c8 (cf. 322d5–e2; Plato *Gorgias* 455b2–c3): ὁρῶ οὖν, ὅταν συλλεγῶμεν εἰς τὴν ἐκκλησίαν, ἐπειδὰν μὲν περὶ οἰκοδομίας τι δέῃ πρᾶξαι τὴν πόλιν, τοὺς οἰκοδόμους μεταπεμπομένους συμβούλους περὶ τῶν οἰκοδομημάτων, ὅταν δὲ περὶ ναυπηγίας, τοὺς ναυπηγούς, καὶ τἆλλα πάντα οὕτως, ὅσα ἡγοῦνται μαθητά τε καὶ διδακτὰ εἶναι· ἐὰν δέ τις ἄλλος ἐπιχειρῇ αὐτοῖς συμβουλεύειν ὃν ἐκεῖνοι μὴ οἴονται δημιουργὸν εἶναι, κἂν πάνυ καλὸς ᾖ καὶ πλούσιος καὶ τῶν γενναίων, οὐδέν τι μᾶλλον ἀποδέχονται, ἀλλὰ καταγελῶσι καὶ θορυβοῦσιν, ἕως ἂν ἢ αὐτὸς ἀποστῇ ὁ ἐπιχειρῶν λέγειν καταθορυβηθείς, ἢ οἱ τοξόται αὐτὸν ἀφελκύσωσιν ἢ ἐξάρωνται κελευόντων τῶν πρυτάνεων. περὶ μὲν οὖν ὧν οἴονται ἐν τέχνῃ εἶναι, οὕτω διαπράττονται ("When we gather in the assembly, I see that, if the city needs to do something involving architecture, architects are summoned as consultants about buildings; but if the matter involves shipbuilding, shipwrights are summoned, and similarly for every other matter thought to be learned and taught. Further, if anyone whom they do not consider to be a craftsman tries to give them counsel, even if he is very fine, wealthy, and noble, they still do not receive him but ridicule him and shout him down, until either the one trying to speak stands down due to the heckling or the armed guards drag him away or remove him at the bidding of the presiding officers. This is what they do if the matter concerns something they consider to belong to a craft").

δεομένων, αἱ δὲ ψῆφοι φέρονται ὡς οὐ συμβούλων
δεομένων ἀλλὰ καὶ κρίνειν καὶ συμβουλεύειν δυναμένων.
Καὶ ἡ μὲν προθυμία τῶν συμβουλευόντων ὑμῖν ὡς
εἰδότων ἐστίν, αἱ δὲ παρ' ὑμῶν ψῆφοι ὡς οὐκ εἰδότων τῶν
συμβουλευόντων φέρονται.

382a8–b7

Or, how is it not that your coming together is opposed
by your voting and your voting is opposed by the willingness[33] of your consultants? You come together on the
grounds that you are not sufficient [to judge] but need
consultants, but your votes are given on the grounds that
you do not need consultants but are able to judge and to
give advice. And while the willingness of your consultants
is grounded by their knowing, you give your votes on the
grounds that the consultants do not know.

The deliberators' voting (ψῆφοι) can be understood on the model
either of consultation or co-deliberation, but on each model voting
conflicts with other procedural norms. If auditors in an assembly vote
to express their judgment of what speech gave the best advice, then
they act like epistemic peers of consultants, experts fit to judge advice;
but their meeting (σύνοδος) to hear from others presumed they lacked
knowledge and thus were seeking the advice of consultants. Voting, as
judgment, is ill-suited to having deliberators meet with consultants. By
contrast, if auditors recognize that they lack knowledge and vote not
to judge presumed experts but to form a fair consensus from their own
differing opinions, then they act as co-deliberators with their fellow
speakers; but the prejudicial commitment of speakers (προθυμία) is
grounded by the supposition that they are expert consultants. Voting,
as a political agreement that may be epistemically imperfect, is now

---

[33] An alternate reading is that deliberators' voting is opposed by *their own* eagerness
for consultants, where προθυμίᾳ takes τῶν συμβουλευόντων as an objective rather than
subjective genitive. But the preceding discussion of the willingness *of* the consultants
to speak (381a4–c4) makes the sense here clear. The argument uses each of the three
preceding topics: the meeting of deliberators *qua* listeners, the confidence of consultants
qua speakers, and the voting of deliberators *qua* judges.

dysfunctional insofar as it follows speeches by those who excused themselves from deliberating with their peers.

The upshot of this critique is that we are offered a clear division of ways of treating advice, although rather than speak further of "advice" I will refer broadly to testimony (see note 22). The first use of testimony is suitable for consultation, where an auditor accepts testimony without weighing it against opposing reasons or inspecting the reasons that support it. Evaluating a consultant's testimony in this way is dispensable, since consultation presupposes that the consultant has knowledge and the consultee doesn't. I'll refer to this as the *trust* use of testimony.

> *Trust*: an auditor is entitled to accept testimony without examining it, on the supposition that its speaker is trustworthy.

The second use of testimony, then, is suitable for co-deliberation and opposed by its pair. This *trial* use of testimony does not presuppose that speakers have knowledge, and so their testimony is not entitled to unexamined acceptance. Instead, auditors who wish to use their co-deliberators' testimony in their inquiry ought to examine the reasons for and against its truth.

> *Trial*: an auditor is entitled to accept testimony only if upon examination it satisfied some criterion for acceptance (e.g., it seems persuasive).

To return to my contention, I'm arguing that *Demodocus* sets out an examination of the *trust* and *trial* uses of testimony. *Dem.* I does this by a critique of the assembly, where the uses of testimony are conflated. By critiquing the assembly, *Dem.* I sets the stage for subsequent discussion of each use. These later discussions refer to the two uses of testimony by the associated verbs of πιστεύειν and πείθεσθαι. Since πείθεσθαι in its middle sense commonly refers to trust just as well as πιστεύειν, I will show along the way that *Demodocus* uses the verbs consistently to refer to two distinct uses of testimony, such that πείθεσθαι should always be understood as 'to be persuaded' rather than 'to obey' or 'to trust'.

III. TRUST AND TRIAL IN *DEMODOCUS*

Besides helping to delineate two uses of testimony by pointing to the opposing presuppositions of the assembly's procedures, *Dem.* I also sketches a view of what ideal consultation might look like and how it differs from ordinary consultation. The speaker, in the second part of his speech (382b7–e5), argues against the propriety of giving advice. He contrasts consultation as it occurs with its best-case scenario. In actual cases of consultation, where neither consultants nor consultees know whether their advice will lead to an intended, good outcome, the Athenians "lose trust (ἀπιστεῖν) and often change their minds about whatever advice they took and about whatever they voted."[34] The speaker then compares the consultation of οἱ ἀγαθοί:[35]

> ἴσασι γὰρ καὶ περὶ ὧν συμβουλεύουσιν ποῖά τ' ἐστίν, καὶ <u>τοῖς πεισθεῖσιν αὐτοῖς</u> ὅτι βεβαίως ὑπάρξει[36] ὧν ἕνεκα συμβουλεύουσιν, καὶ ὅτι οὔτε αὐτοῖς οὔτε <u>τοῖς πεισθεῖσιν αὐτοῖς</u> πώποτε μεταμελήσει.
>
> 382d5–e1 [emphasis added]

> For [the good] know both of what kind are the things about which they give advice and that, *for those persuaded by them*, that for the sake of which they give advice will be securely attained, as well as that neither they nor *those persuaded by them* will ever change their mind.

That ordinary consultees come to distrust (ἀπιστεῖν) their consultants implies that they previously trusted them. When it comes to ideal consultants with knowledge, however, the speaker refers not to trust but to persuasion. Those advised by ideal consultants are twice called

---

[34] *Dem.* I.382d3–4: … ἀπιστεῖν καὶ μεταμέλεσθαι πολλάκις αὐτοῖς καὶ περὶ ὧν ἂν συμβουλεύσωνται καὶ περὶ ὧν ἂν ψηφίσωνται.

[35] *Pace* Müller 1975:123–126, the contrast between the good and ordinary consultants is not derived from any ultimate difference in the objects of their cognitive attitudes (sc. stable entities opposed to fluid non-entities) but solely from the strength or weakness of their attitudes (sc. knowledge opposed to ignorance).

[36] I accept the emendation of Barnes 1997 ad loc.

"the ones persuaded by them [viz., the consultants]."[37] A few moments earlier, in the critique of the voting procedure in the assembly, the speaker had further described the hypothetical consultant with knowledge:

> οὐδ' αὖ τοῦτό γε ἐρεῖ εἷς ὢν ὁ συμβουλεύων ὑμῖν οὗτος ὑμᾶς διδάξειν ἃ πρακτέον ὑμῖν ἐστιν, καὶ κρίνειν τοὺς κακῶς καὶ μὴ συμβουλεύοντας ὑμῖν, οὕτως ἐν ὀλίγῳ χρόνῳ καὶ ὄντας τοσούτους.

382a2–5

> This one giving you advice [viz., with knowledge] will not say this, that he will teach you—in so little time and so many of you—how to see what you must do and how to judge who gives advice badly or not.

Consultants with knowledge, it seems, would teach (or transmit knowledge) but for the short duration of and large number of auditors in assembly meetings.[38] So ideal consultants are associated with teaching and persuading, while ordinary consultants expect their audiences merely to trust their advice.[39]

The contrast is Platonic. Socrates in *Theaetetus* 201 argues that court speakers are at best able to persuade judges to form true beliefs, but that they cannot teach or transmit knowledge, due to the water clock as well as the unique grasp eyewitnesses have of what they witnessed.[40] The parallel is imperfect, since in *Theaetetus* Socrates contrasts teaching with mere persuasion (cf. *Gorgias* 458e7–59a1), while the speaker of *Dem.* I contrasts teaching and persuasion with trust. Still, the views

[37] The aorist passive participle πεισθεῖσιν makes it clear that πειθ- here is not used in its middle sense of trust or obey.

[38] Athenian assembly meetings (with a quorum of up to six thousand) lasted a few hours, so deliberation for a single resolution could not have accommodated more than a few brief speeches (Hansen 1991:136–137).

[39] Curiously, the speaker alludes to but rules out the epistemic democrat's argument that scaling up the number of co-deliberators produces better advice than can be given by deliberators individually (381e3–8; cf. Aristotle *Politics* 3.11.1281b). Perhaps he precludes discussion of this argument to limit the scope of his objections.

[40] Plato *Theaetetus* 201a7–c7.

of Socrates and the speaker of *Dem.* I look compatible. Even without time constraints, the court speaker at best persuades others to accept true beliefs about what can only be known through autopsy.[41] It may have been left unstated by Socrates that an even worse outcome would be if judges were to merely trust court speakers, due to time constraints on speeches. Meanwhile, without time constraints and perhaps in a more intimate venue, the assembly speaker ideally teaches others to know what to do. Perhaps since there is no comparable privileging of autopsy in the domain of deliberating about prospective actions, there is no prior reason why the ideal assembly speaker cannot teach. Thus, while the ideal court speaker merely persuades and does not teach, the ideal assembly speaker teaches and persuades.[42] In hurried court trials and assembly meetings, audiences are motivated simply to trust certain speakers on the basis of appearances and reputation rather than by weighing offered reasons (cf. *Gorgias* 454d1–455a7).

On the view emerging from *Dem.* I, ideal consultation is peculiar. It does not entail the *trust* use of testimony and instead it is associated with persuasion. At the same time, it does not involve the *trial* use of testimony familiar to co-deliberators, because audiences learning from speakers with knowledge are not evaluating comparative testimonies. Ideal consultation, then, offers a picture of how to combine the procedures of consultation and co-deliberation in a way that would not create the superfluities of the assembly. Ideal consultants persuade and offer reasons for believing their testimony, such that they also teach, yet they are not questioned or made to defend themselves against rival, ignorant speakers. Thus, *Dem.* I contains a positive, if only hypothetical, account of advice giving, which continues to rely on the competing notions of trust and persuasion.

Before we hear the arguments in the debate over whether one ought to hear both accuser and defendant before judging a case, *Dem.* II opens with the narrator quoting the first speaker's charge against his peer:

---

[41] On the difficulty of why knowledge gained from autopsy could not be transmitted by testimony, see the discussion in Barnes 1980.

[42] Socrates has such a view of what a court speaker ought to do at Plato *Apology* 35b9–c2. Teaching and persuasion are not in conflict also at Plato *Laches* 181d6; *Protagoras* 352e5–6; *Gorgias* 453d7–454a5; *Laws* 10.885d2.

Peter Osorio

Παρεγενόμην δ' ἀνθρώπῳ τινὶ νουθετοῦντι ἑαυτοῦ
ἑταῖρον, διότι ἐπίστευεν τῷ κατηγοροῦντι οὐκ ἀκούσας
τοῦ ἀπολογουμένου ἀλλὰ μόνου τοῦ κατηγοροῦντος.
ἔλεγεν οὖν ὡς δεινὸν πρᾶγμα ποιοῖ καταγιγνώσκων τοῦ
ἀνθρώπου, οὔτε αὐτὸς παραγενόμενος οὔτε τῶν φίλων
ἀκούσας παραγενομένων, οἷς εἰκὸς ἦν αὐτὸν λέγουσιν
πιστεύειν· οὐδ' αὖ ἀμφοτέρων ἀκούσας, οὕτως προπετῶς
ἐπίστευσε τῷ κατηγοροῦντι.

382e6–383a3

I was witness[43] to a man rebuking his friend because he
trusted the accuser after hearing not the defendant but
only the accuser. He said that he did a terrible thing by
condemning the man, since he was neither himself a
witness nor did he hear from the defendant's friends who
were witnesses and whose testimony it was reasonable to
trust. Since he had not listened to both, he rashly trusted
the accuser.

The first speaker charges his friend with rashly trusting the accuser,
and, in a quite explicit reference to *Dem.* I, he concludes by advising
(συμβουλεύω) him not to rashly praise or blame others.[44] (This advice
about praise and blame also anticipates *Dem.* III.) His friend's rashness
consists in not hearing the defendant and the defendant's witnesses
before forming a judgment. On the surface, the first speaker seems
to accept a version of the *trial* use of testimony, where acceptance is
conditioned on something like an examination of opposing arguments.
One can object against this surface reading that he might accept a
mitigated *trust* under certain conditions (viz., when the defendant is

---

[43] In Athenian forensic oratory, testimony formulae use εἰδέναι for accidental
witnesses and παρεῖναι / παραγενέσθαι for witnesses summoned to oversee a business
exchange or striking of a contract (Thür 2005:153). The speaker's invocation of the latter
formula implies that he was overseeing the debate in the capacity of a judge, confirmed by
his concluding remark that he could not judge the debate (384a6–7: κρίνειν οὐχ οἷός τ' ἦν).

[44] *Dem.* II.383c3–5: συμβουλεύω οὖν σοι, ἔφη, τοῦ λοιποῦ μὴ προπετῶς οὕτως τοὺς
ἀνθρώπους μήτε μέμφεσθαι μήτ' ἐπαινεῖν ("'So, I advise you,' he said, 'from here on out to
not so rashly praise and blame people'").

this person, or when the accuser is *that* person). After all, he says it is reasonable to trust the defendant's witnesses, so it may be that he does not reject all *trust* uses of testimony. Against this objection, however, the first speaker seems only to be reiterating one of the defendant's own arguments (which his friend failed to take into consideration), by using the εἰκός-argument form that is familiar from forensic speeches. His point, then, is methodological rather than substantive. The rebuke is that the friend failed to consider the defendant's testimonies, not that the friend, in fact, ought to have trusted the defendant's witnesses. Furthermore, the first speaker's opening argument is that λόγοι are correctly judged (κατὰ τρόπον κρῖναι) when they are compared against each other (παραβαλλομένους). This argument accords well with *trial* uses of testimony, where the criterion of acceptance often presumes an examination of opposing reasons.[45] Even if the friend critically listened to the accuser, his examination is incomplete unless he hears the defendant. Finally, note that this argument places emphasis on the λόγοι themselves, rather than on who says them. Throughout *Demodocus*, the objects of πιστεύειν are people, whereas the objects of πείθεσθαι are propositions and what gets said. While there is nothing extraordinary about this, the argument draws attention to it. The narrator emphasizes again the importance of the λόγοι themselves in his concluding narration, where he asks the reader if they have something to contribute to the debate (εἰ οὖν τι ἔχεις συμβάλλεσθαι). The βαλ- root, present also in παραβαλλομένους, signifies the *exchange* of reasons implied by the *trial* use of testimony.

---

[45] Compare how this argument also appears at Lucian *Hermotimus* 30, a passage that contains further similarities to the other arguments of the first speaker of *Dem.* II (sc. appeal to lawgivers and the use of the dual ἀμφοῖν, recalling the pseudo-Hesiodic maxim): οἱ δέ γε νομοθέται, ὦ Λυκῖνε, οὐχ οὕτω προστάττουσι τοῖς δικασταῖς ποιεῖν οὐδὲ τοῦ ἑτέρου μὲν ἀκούειν, τὸν δὲ ἕτερον οὐκ ἐᾶν λέγειν ὑπὲρ ἑαυτοῦ ἃ οἴεται ξυμφέρειν, ἀλλ᾿ ὁμοίως ἀμφοῖν ἀκροᾶσθαι, ὡς ῥᾷον ἀντεξετάζοντες τοὺς λόγους εὑρίσκοιεν τἀληθῆ τε καὶ ψευδῆ ... ([Plato, Pythagoras, and Aristotle are the imagined speakers] "Lycinus, the lawgivers, no less, do not order judges to act in this way, to hear one litigant but not to allow the other to say on his own behalf what he thinks aids his case, but they order judges to hear both alike, so that by cross-examining the speeches we discover what is true and false ...").

What about the friend who speaks second? Does he, contrary to the first speaker, endorse a *trust* view of testimony? In his arguments he doesn't deny that he, in fact, trusted the accuser. Instead, he attacks the view that by listening to both sides one can come to know something that could not have more easily been known by listening to a single speaker. Throughout, he assumes the possibility of learning, or coming to know, from another (see note 12). So, while he does not use the language of πιστεύειν or πείθεσθαι, he assumes the ground of the *trust* view, that an auditor's trust is warranted by a speaker's knowledge. It is also telling that his arguments ignore the possibility of learning from speakers who do *not* have knowledge, which is what the *trial* use assumes. The debate of *Dem.* II, then, fits squarely within the *trust-trial* opposition.

The contrast between *trust* and *trial* is even starker in *Dem.* III, where the examiner turns his interlocutor's complaint about trust into a problem about persuasion. To review, the examiner's first interlocutor objects to another for not trusting him and lending him money. The examiner questions if the objector's obligation to persuade was not greater than the other's obligation to trust.[46] His later reasoning makes clear that he is arguing not that there exist *mutual* obligations of trust and persuasion but that there is only an obligation to persuade.[47] This obligation is related to the speaker's view that those who judge finely about their audiences will always succeed in persuading them (385a6–b1; see notes 15–16). It is presupposed that finely judging speakers intend to persuade when seeking to influence the action of

---

[46] *Dem.* III.384b8–c2: ἄλλος δέ τις τῶν παρόντων ἠρώτησε τὸν ἐγκαλοῦντα πότερον ὁ μὲν μὴ πιστεύσας αὐτῷ μηδὲ χρήσας ἥμαρτεν· σὺ δ', ἔφη, οὐ πείσας σοι χρῆσαι οὐχ ἡμάρτηκας; ("But another one who was present asked the one objecting [to not being lent money] if the man who neither trusted him nor lent him money made an error, 'but you,' he said, 'despite not having persuaded him to lend you money, have not made an error?'").

[47] *Dem.* III.384d3–e1: ἀλλ' ἐκεῖνος πῶς οὐχ ἥμαρτεν, ὁ μὴ πιστεύσας μοι; — Ἆρ' οὖν, ἔφη, εἰ προσωμίλησας αὐτῷ ὡς προσήκει, οὐκ ἂν ἥμαρτες οὐδέν; — Οὐ γὰρ δή. — Νῦν ἄρα οὐχ ὡς προσήκει αὐτῷ προσωμίλησας. — Φαίνομαι, εἰπεῖν. — Εἰ οὖν ὡς μὴ προσήκει ὁμιλοῦντός σου μὴ ἐπείσθη, πῶς ἂν δικαίως ἐγκαλοίης ἐκείνῳ; — Οὐκ ἔχω εἰπεῖν ("... but how did he, as he didn't trust me, not make an error? — Had you conversed with him as one ought, wouldn't you have made no error? — I would not. — As it is, then, you didn't converse with him as one ought. — It appears so. — So if he wasn't persuaded when you spoke as one ought not, how could you justly object to him? — I cannot say").

others. The connection between fine judgment and speaking finely recalls ideal consultation in *Dem.* I, where the wise person is said to persuade and teach his audience. The parallel to *Dem.* I is made explicit by the examiner's use of the phrase "those not persuaded by them" (τοῖς μὲν μὴ πεισθεῖσιν αὐτοῖς) to refer to audiences who do not trust people like the examiner's frustrated interlocutor.[48] Recall that the speaker of *Dem.* I referred to those who listen to wise persons as "those persuaded by them" (τοῖς πεισθεῖσιν αὐτοῖς). If we therefore borrow premises from the *trust* and *trial* views familiar from *Dem.* I, the examiner has an argument for why there is no obligation to trust speakers:

1. Trust and being persuaded (by being given reasons) are exclusive ways of accepting testimony [*Dem.* I on *trust* in consultation and *trial* in co-deliberation].

2. It is rational to trust a speaker only if the speaker is knowledgeable [*Dem.* I on *trust* in consultation].

3. But knowledgeable speakers only persuade others to accept their testimony [*Dem.* I on ideal consultation and *Dem.* III on knowledgeable speakers].

4. So, there are no knowledgeable speakers to trust [follows from 1, 3].

5. So, trusting a speaker is never rational [follows from 2, 4].

Dem. III thus raises a consideration against *trust* that complements the pro-*trial* arguments of *Dem.* II: knowledgeable persons do not allow themselves to be trusted.

Finally, in *Dem.* IV we find another line of attack against *trust*, leading toward the view that there are no qualities other than having knowledge that suffice to make a speaker trustworthy and that having knowledge is not reliably correlated with other qualities. To repeat the examiner's refutation, he argues that, if we are

---

[48] *Dem.* III.384e6–385a1 [emphasis added]: Τί οὖν ποτε οἱ ἄνθρωποι, ἔφη, τοιαῦτα ἐγκαλοῦσιν πρὸς ἀλλήλους, καὶ τοῖς μὲν μὴ πεισθεῖσιν αὐτοῖς ὅτι οὐκ ἐπείσθησαν μέμφονται, αὐτοῖς δέ, ὅτι οὐκ ἔπεισαν, οὐδ' ὁτιοῦν ἐγκαλοῦσιν; ("Why do people make these kinds of objections to one another and blame *those who aren't persuaded by them* for not having been persuaded, but they make no objection whatsoever to themselves for not having persuaded?").

obliged to make a trial (σκέψασθαι) of whether what strangers say is true before accepting it (as his interlocutor, who objected to one who quickly trusts chance persons, holds), then we ought to also test what our friends and acquaintances say, since they may also say what is untrustworthy (386a9: ἄπιστα). The interlocutor had two reasons for not trusting strangers: that most people are boastful (ἀλαζόνες), such that they exaggerate the truth, and conniving (πονηροί), such that they conceal it.[49] The interlocutor's reasons for doubt thus target a speaker's *sincerity*, and the examiner never questions that these qualities are indeed reasons for doubt. But since the examiner still argues that family and friends (386a6-7: οἰκείων καὶ συνήθων), whose moral character (ἦθος) we know, may say what is untrustworthy, he seems to have in mind another class of reasons for doubt. These reasons, I suggest, relate to a speaker's *competency*. While being a friend eliminates doubt about one's sincerity, it does not mitigate doubt about their competency. The narrator confirms this line of thought in his concluding remarks, where he appears to gloss "the trustworthy" as "those who know" (386c5: τοῖς πιστοῖς καὶ τοῖς εἰδόσι περὶ ὧν λέγουσιν). Although he does not go through a list of other candidates, we can easily imagine the examiner doubting other qualities that, while possibly creating a reputation for sincerity, do not eliminate doubts about whether a speaker has knowledge (e.g., being old, wealthy, popular, or powerful). The trend of the examiner's refutation is to move toward a *trial* view of testimony, by dissolving distinctions among speakers that are irrelevant to examining whether a speaker has knowledge. His conclusion refers to both family and strangers as merely "speakers" (see note 17):

> Οὐκοῦν καὶ τοῖς λέγουσιν αὐτὰ ὁμοίως πιστευτέον
> λέγουσιν αὐτά;
> Πιθανόν, εἶπεν.

386c2-3

---

[49] At least, this is my attempt at distinguishing the two. The first reason is also found at Cicero *Lucullus* 115 (... *qui sibi persuaserint scire se solos omnia* ...) and the second at Lucian *Hermotimus* 75. I discuss *Demodocus*'s relation to these sources in section IV.

"So, then, we must trust even those [strangers] who say
them [viz., trustworthy or untrustworthy things] as much
as those [friends] who say them [viz., trustworthy or
untrustworthy things]?" "That's persuasive," he said.

The conclusion that we ought to trust two parties similarly does not
entail we ought to trust them both. While left unexpressed, the take-
away is that we ought to trust neither.[50] Finally, the interlocutor's
agreement that the inference is "persuasive" signals his shift from *trust*
to *trial*, from trusting certain speakers given *who* they are to examining
whether *what* they say is persuasive.

IV. *DEMODOCUS* AND THE SKEPTICAL ACADEMY

The *Demodocus* is a coherent philosophical dialogue. More than that,
it is the only ancient Greek philosophical text I know of dedicated to
themes in social epistemology and testimony. For that reason alone it
merits our attention in the history of philosophy, but it is also of more
local interest to students of the Platonic tradition. I end with a discussion of the dialogue's Hellenistic dating and consider the impact this
has on our understanding of the skeptical Academy.

There is no reason to conclude that its last three parts were incorporated by chance into *Dem.* I because they lacked independent titles.
There is also less reason than is usually thought for attributing it to
the hand of two authors in two periods of the Academy. The mainstay
of this view has been the dialogue's perceived conceptual disunity.
I have argued, in support of single authorship, that this appearance is deceptive, and that there are philological grounds for dating
Demodocus as a whole to the Hellenistic period. Earlier commentators[51]

---

[50] Cf. Lucian *Hermotimus* 29: ὥστε ἢ πᾶσι πιστεύειν χρή, ὅπερ γελοιότατον, ἢ ἀπιστεῖν
ὁμοίως ("So, then, either we ought to trust them all, which is most ridiculous, or distrust
them evenly").

[51] Heidel 1896:23 identified the markers of *Dem.* I, while Müller 1975:271 those of
Dem. II. Though he disagrees with Heidel's dating, Müller does not address Heidel's
identifications. Granted, not all of Heidel's Hellenistic markers are useful: e.g., Heidel may
have thought adverbial accusative ἀρχὴν (I.381d4) is a Hellenistic Ionicism (see Genesis
41.21 in the Septuagint; cf. Herodotus 1.9, 2.28, 8.132), but it occurs elsewhere in Plato
and the Platonic corpus (Plato *Gorgias* 478c; [Plato] *Epistle* 7.344a).

identified Ionicisms and other peculiarities of Hellenistic prose that run through *Dem.* I and II: impersonal συμπίπτειν (I.382d3),[52] οἴδατε for ἴστε (I.381e4),[53] λοιπόν as an inferential adverb (II.383e5),[54] and πρῶτος for πρότερος (II.384a7).[55] Since these stylistic markers appear in *Dem.* II no less frequently than in *Dem.* I, Müller and Aronadio's hypothesis that *Dem.* I was written in an earlier period than the subsequent parts loses further ground.[56] And there are much better reasons for crediting *Demodocus* to an author of the skeptical, later Hellenistic Academy than to someone from Polemo's earlier Hellenistic one.

John Glucker and Francesco Aronadio have discussed the parallel between *Dem.* II and Plutarch's anecdote of Zeno's debate with an anonymous interlocutor about whether one ought to listen to both sides of a case (*De Stoicorum repugnantiis* 8.1034E–F).[57] The similarities are striking.[58] First, in each source the first speaker, who defends hearing

---

[52] Common in Herodotus (1.139, 5.35, 8.15, 8.132), although not without precedent in fifth-century Athenian authors (Thucydides 1.49, 4.68) or the fourth century (*SIG* [= Dittenberger 1915–1924] 306.7).

[53] Other early uses of this particular form (cf. οἴδαμεν, Herodotus 2.17) occur in the Septuagint (Genesis 31.6, 44.15; Exodus 23.9; Deuteronomy 13.3, et al.), a pseudonymous letter of Diogenes of Sinope (*Epistle* 28.2 [Hercher 1873]), Diodorus Siculus (21.13.1), and Philo of Alexandria (*On the Special Laws* 2.96; *Questions on Exodus* 2.2).

[54] Cf. Polybius 1.15.11. Related is the Hellenistic progressive sense of adverbial λοιπόν (cf. *PSI* [= *Papiri greci e latini*] IV 340.18). For discussion, see Blomqvist 1969:100–102; Müller 1975:271; for further Hellenistic *comparanda* (e.g., in Polybius, Alciphron, and Philodemus), see Sophocles 1887 s.v. and Blomqvist 1969:100–102.

[55] See Thackeray 1909:183–184 on the phenomenon in the Septuagint.

[56] There remain other reasons to attribute dual authorship to the work (with only the second, later author of *Dem.* II–IV belonging to the skeptical Academy): *Dem.* I does not seem to foreclose the possibility of knowledge—though this does not rule out skeptical authorship, and I have emphasized that *Dem.* III–IV also conceive of knowledgeable speakers—and it seems to draw from Plato more than the other parts. (I thank Marta Heckel for pushing me to account for this option.) If the hypothesis of dual authorship is right, I point out that the second author was a fine reader of *Dem.* I, who saw what was of interest about it and developed it further. The second author would also be a fine author: by adding to *Dem.* I three independent scenes, he avoids the problem of leaving a noticeable seam where he added new material—the seam is now merely one of three structural breaks in the dialogue.

[57] Glucker 1988; Aronadio 2009. The parallel was first remarked upon by Müller 1975:270.

[58] Aronadio 2009:233–234 compares the arguments against hearing both sides, which I pass over here.

both sides, quotes the maxim Cicero calls "pseudo-Hesiodic":[59] "Don't judge a case until you hear the speech of both."[60] Second, both Zeno and the second speaker of *Dem.* II argue dialectically, restricting themselves to advancing premises only through questions.[61] This dialectical questioning is typical of Demodocus: the speaker of *Dem.* I and both examiners of *Dem.* III–IV also avoid assertions by asking for premises. Against the earlier position of Weische, that Zeno was criticizing the methods of Arcesilaus, Glucker stresses that Zeno is ironically indulging in Megarian dialectical questioning.[62] However, Arcesilaus learned from Diodorus (Diogenes Laërtius 4.33; Sextus *Pyrrhonian Outlines* 1.234, Numenius fr. 25 [Des Places]), so Glucker's Megarian genealogy of Zeno's argument only lends further credence to Weische and his supporters.[63] Zeno ostentatiously imitated dialecticians because he was poking fun at Arcesilaus. Are we to suppose, then, that the first speaker of *Dem.* II is Arcesilaus and the second Zeno? No, for two reasons. First, because the first speaker asserts his premises, whereas Arcesilaus restricts himself to playing the questioner (Cicero *De finibus* 2.2). Second—to jump ahead a bit—the anonymity of speakers in *Demodocus* is deliberate. While Plutarch is drawing from the same anecdote of a dispute between Zeno and Arcesilaus or some student of his, we are not supposed to know who's speaking in *Demodocus*. Thus, the author seems not to have in

---

[59] Cicero *Letters to Atticus* 7.18.4: ψευδησιόδειον. The verse (referenced at Aristophanes *Wasps* 725–726; Euripides *Andromache* 957–958; *Heraclidae* 179–180) is also claimed by pseudo-Phocylides (87) and attributed to Democritus (*Mantissa proverbiorum* 2.6) as well as to Sisyphus or Pittheus by Theophrastus (Schwartz 1891:39)—Fortenbaugh 2011:318–319 doesn't realize the Euripides scholiast doesn't give the entire line, just as Cicero refers to it simply as "μηδὲ δίκην." In light of the various attributions, the speaker of *Dem.* II.383b6 is right to say simply it is ὑπὸ τῶν πολλῶν λεγόμενον (383b6).

[60] *Dem.* II.383c1; Plutarch *De Stoicorum repugnantiis* 1034E.

[61] Glucker 1988:482–486 notes that Plutarch paraphrases Zeno's argument (in a series of asserted premises) but ends by saying Zeno "asked for this argument" (τοῦτον δὲ τὸν λόγον ἐρωτήσας).

[62] Weische 1961:77–78; Glucker 1988:488: "The anecdote as we have it is no piece of philosophical doctrine, taken out of one of Zeno's serious books, but an amusing χρεία, in which Zeno is reported by someone else as refuting an adversary who thinks he is 'too clever by half,' and he does this by using precisely that sort of Megaric dialectic which he spent much of his time refuting."

[63] Ioppolo 1986:43n67; Gourinat 2000:85; Aronadio 2009. The suggestion of Alesse 2000:125 that Zeno learned his argument from *Demodocus* itself strikes me as dubious.

mind a particular cast of characters that readers can reconstruct. As for what this implies for the dating of *Dem.* II, we have a *terminus post quem* of Arcesilaus's skeptical turn. If *Dem.* I should not be separated from the rest of the dialogue on either stylistic or philosophical grounds, then no part of *Demodocus* dates to Polemo's scholarchate.

A few other circumstances indicate that *Demodocus* shares the epistemological perspective of the skeptical Academy:

1. The narrators of *Dem.* II and IV express puzzlement (II.384a6, IV.386c4: ἠπόρουν), but not of the more familiar kind that comes from being refuted. It is an *aporia* from hearing arguments on either side by others. The narrator of *Dem.* II reveals he suspended judgment (II.384a6–7: κρίνειν οὐχ οἷός τ᾽ ἦν), while the narrator of *Dem.* IV suggests his puzzlement was due to competing considerations (IV.386c4–6: πότερον ... ἤ).[64]

2. The first speakers of *Dem.* II and IV view making judgments before inquiring or hearing an opposing argument to be rash: II.383a3 (προπετῶς ἐπίστευεν); II.383c4–5 (προπετῶς ... μέμφεσθαι); IV.385c2–3 (ταχέως ... πιστεύοι); IV.385e7–8 (πρὸ τοῦ σκέψασθαι ταχέως πιστεύων). This view recalls how the Academy turns the Stoics' injunction not to assent rashly against them (Cicero *Lucullus* 133; cf. Sextus *Pyrrhonian Outlines* 2.37): Cicero *Lucullus* 120 (*temere*), 128, 130 (*inconsideratius*); Sextus *Pyrrhonian Outlines* 1.212, 2.17.[65]

On their own, these points do not allow us to narrow the dating any further. These details cannot be associated with Arcesilaus in particular, or with Carneades alone, or with any of their particular students. It might be of help that the debate of *Dem.* IV ends with the response that trusting different speakers equally is πιθανόν. Is this an allusion to Carneades' criterion of action and of inquiry? Perhaps, but given *Demodocus*'s larger concerns, there seems to be more sense in seeing the

[64] Additionally, the speaker of *Dem.* I explains his *aporia* by setting up two clear oppositions (I.382a8: ἐναντιοῦται) between σύνοδος v. ψῆφοι and ψῆφοι v. προθυμία.

[65] Aronadio 2009:232. It also recalls skeptics calling dogmatists arrogant: Cicero *Lucullus* 115 (*adrogantes*); Sextus *Pyrrhonian Outlines* 1.90 (φίλαυτοί τινες), *Against Mathematicians* 7.314 (φιλαύτως). For discussion of *temeritas* in Cicero, see Lévy 2018.

interlocutor's final response as showing that he is now working under the *trial* view of testimony by invoking its slogan of persuasion.[66]

There are implications to attributing *Demodocus* to the thought of skeptical Academics that have not been noted before. Now that we have a better sense of what is philosophically interesting about the dialogue, we can see that it also belongs to a body of evidence about the skeptical Academy's philosophy of education and attitudes toward authority.[67] Their educational practices were intended to counter the prejudicial effect of authority on two fronts. First, they sought to limit the effect of their own authority on others' judgments. They did this not only by preferring the role of questioner when engaged in dialectical exchange but also by concealing their evaluative responses when hearing others argue.[68] The later Academic Favorinus is known to have done the latter in his dialogues. Galen says several times that Favorinus's policy was to "leave the judgment of arguments on either side to his students" (ἐπιτρέπει τὴν κρίσιν τῶν εἰς ἑκάτερα ἐπιχειρουμένων τοῖς μαθηταῖς).[69] *Demodocus* offers a picture of how exactly Favorinus may have done this in his dialogues, for the narrators of *Dem.* II and IV ask the reader/addressee what they think about the questions raised in their stories (II.384b1–5; IV.386c6–7: περὶ τούτων οὖν πῶς σὺ νομίζεις;).[70]

---

[66] Alternatively, the author may be aiming to recall not a particular Academic but Plato himself (*Gorgias* 486a2–3; *Symposium* 223a8; *Statesman* 287e1; *Critias* 110d5; *Laws* 3.677a7, 7.791b2). Of course, these considerations are compatible with authorship under Carneadean influence: Carneades' criterion was no doubt influenced by reading Plato and concerns about the proper evaluation of arguments.

[67] For discussion, see Brittain and Osorio 2021a; Brittain and Osorio 2021b. There are also traces of this view for the earliest period of the Academy (e.g., Plato *Phaedo* 91b8–c5; *Phaedrus* 270c3–7, 275b3–c2; *Republic* 10.595c3; *Symposium* 201c8–9; Aristotle *Nicomachean Ethics* 1.6.1096a16).

[68] Since we don't know, by design, which speakers in *Demodocus* may be Academics, we cannot say whether *Demodocus* also depicts Academics adhering to the former practice of always playing the questioner.

[69] Galen *De optima doctrina* 3.2; cf. 3.4; 5.2; 5.4.

[70] If in his dialogues Favorinus narrated conversations he represents himself as having been a witness to—as seems likely given that we know that in *Against Epictetus* Favorinus's slave Oenisemus argues with Epictetus (Galen *De optima doctrina* 1.2)—then the parallel to *Demodocus* II and IV is strengthened. It also follows that (at least some of) Favorinus's dialogues would follow the Aristotelian model that Cicero uses in his late dialogues (Cicero *Letters to Atticus* 4.16.2; 13.19.4).

Second, skeptical Academics sought to block the influence of authorities outside the Academy. To this end they developed a series of arguments against reasons for believing someone is trustworthy (πιστός), which are variously preserved in Cicero's *Academica*, Sextus, and Lucian's *Hermotimus* (or *On Sects*).[71] The reasons for trust controverted by these sources include one's virtuous appearance (Lucian *Hermotimus* 18–20), old age (Sextus *Against Mathematicians* 7.321–323), work ethic (Sextus *Against Mathematicians* 7.324), intelligence (Sextus *Pyrrhonian Outlines* 2.39–42; M 7.325–326), and various kinds of corroborating testimony that the individual in question is trustworthy (e.g., Augustine *Contra academicos* 3.15; Sextus *Pyrrhonian Outlines* 1.89, 2.38, 2.43–44; *Against Mathematicians* 7.328–334; Lucian *Hermotimus* 16–17, 47–50). It is sufficient here to say that these arguments against authority question whether the supposed reasons for trust successfully indicate who is competently speaking the truth, and I've discussed above how the examiner of *Dem.* IV turns his interlocutor from thinking about his reasons in favor of a speaker's sincerity (viz., that a speaker is familiar or known to us) to reasons for doubting a speaker's competency (viz., that a speaker lacks knowledge).[72] *Demodocus* thus prompts the reader to search for knowledge as a sufficient criterion to separate the trustworthy (πιστοί) from the untrustworthy (ἄπιστοι). As we often find expressed in Cicero (*Lucullus* 7–9; *De finibus* 2.1–3; *De natura deorum* 1.10–13; *De divinatione* 1.7, 2.8; *De fato* 1), the dialogue suggests that this search is on better footing if we attend to arguments irrespective of the authority of their speakers.[73]

---

[71] Cicero *Lucullus* passim (including Augustine *Contra academicos* 3.15); Sextus *Pyrrhonian Outlines* 1.87–91, 2.22–47; *Against Mathematicians* 7.314–342; Lucian *Hermotimus* 16–20, 27–33, 47–50. The evidence of Cicero implies that at least some of these arguments predate Aenesidemus and are Academic in origin.

[72] Lucian *Hermotimus* 29–32, incidentally, argues against the fact that Hermotimus is Lycinus's friend as a reason to trust him (30: ἐξαρκέσει μοι ἂν εἴπω ὅτι Ἑρμοτίμῳ ἐπείσθην φίλῳ ἀνδρί;), which falls in line with the sincerity-based reasons for trust of the interlocutor in *Dem.* IV. Like the examiner of *Dem.* IV, Lycinus's arguments question Hermotimus's competency, conceding that he is sincere.

[73] One might think that only Philonian, mitigated skeptics were concerned with matters of authority in philosophical education (Brittain 2001; Tarrant 2018), but there are no independent grounds for dating *Demodocus* to Philo's middle period or later. In

I conclude, then, by insisting that we can make sense of the anonymity of *Demodocus*'s speakers in the light of its philosophical aims. Previous readers have often assumed that certain characters (viz., the speaker of *Dem.* I, the second disputant of *Dem.* II, and the examiners of *Dem.* III and IV) are Socrates, on the model of *sōkratikoi logoi* in the pseudo-Platonica.[74] But while Socrates' interlocutors are left unnamed in *De iusto* and *De virtute*, and Sisyphus's interlocutor is never called Socrates in *Sisyphus*, *Demodocus* is the only spurious dialogue in which *every* speaker is anonymous, and the only named character, Demodocus, *never* speaks. We are certainly made to question whether Socrates is the speaker of *Demodocus* I and elsewhere, but the dialogue makes a point of setting the question aside. Since none of us know, who is speaking does not matter.

UNIVERSITY OF TORONTO

WORKS CITED

Alesse, Francesca. 2000. *La Stoa e la tradizione socratica*. Naples.

Aronadio, Francesco. 2008. *Dialoghi spuri di Platone*. Turin.

———. 2009. "Tracce di una polemica fra Accademici e Stoici: [Platone] *Demodoc.* 382 e-384 b e Plut., *De Stoic. Rep.* 1034 e." In *Gli antichi e noi: Scritti in onore di Antonio Mario Battegazzore*, ed. Walter Lapini, Luciano Malusa, and Letterio Mauro, 225–237. Genova.

Barnes, Jonathan. 1980. "Socrates and the Jury: Paradoxes in Plato's Distinction between Knowledge and True Belief (Response)." *Proceedings of the Aristotelian Society* 54:193–206.

———. 1997. "Demodocus." In Cooper 1997, 1699–1706.

Blomqvist, Jerker. 1969. *Greek Particles in Hellenistic Prose*. Lund.

Brisson, Luc, ed. 2014. *Écrits attribués à Platon*. Paris.

Brittain, Charles. 2001. *Philo of Larissa: The Last of the Academic Sceptics*. Oxford.

other words, to attribute *Demodocus* to a Philonian skeptic begs the question about which Academics were concerned about the place of authority in dialectical inquiry.

[74] Müller 1975:39n1, 266–268; Brisson 2014:16; Joyal 2019. Oświecimski 1978 is exceptional in that he also tries (but fails) to make sense of the anonymity in the pseudo-Platonica.

Brittain, Charles, and Peter Osorio. 2021a. "The Ciceronian Dialogue."
    In *The Cambridge Companion to Cicero's Philosophy*, ed. Jed W. Atkins
    and Thomas Bénatouïl, 25–42. Cambridge.

———. 2021b. "Philo of Larissa." *Stanford Encyclopedia of Philosophy*.
    https://plato.stanford.edu/entries/philo-larissa/.

Burnet, John. 1900–1907. *Platonis opera*. 5 vols. Oxford.

Butcher, Samuel H. 1903. *Demosthenis orationes*. Vol. 1. Oxford.

Bywater, Ingram. 1894. *Aristotelis Ethica Nicomachea*. Oxford.

Cammack, Daniela. 2020. "Deliberation in Ancient Greek Assemblies."
    Classical Philology 115, no. 3:486–522.

Coady, Cecil A. J. 1992. *Testimony: A Philosophical Study*. Oxford.

Cooper, John M., ed. 1997. *Plato: Complete Works*. Indianapolis.

Dillon, John. 2010. Review of *Dialoghi spuri di Platone*, by Francesco
    Aronadio. *Bryn Mawr Classical Review*. https://bmcr.brynmawr.
    edu/2010/2010.03.05/.

Dittenberger, Wilhelm, ed. 1915–1924. *Sylloge Inscriptionum Graecarum*.
    4 vols. 3rd ed. Leipzig.

Fine, Gail. 2021. "Meno's Paradox and the *Sisyphus*." In *Essays in Ancient
    Epistemology*, ed. Gail Fine, 189–217. Oxford.

Fortenbaugh, William W., ed. 2011. *Theophrastus of Eresus, Commentary
    6.1: Sources on Ethics (with Contributions on the Arabic Material by
    Dimitri Gutas)*. Leiden.

Fricker, Elizabeth. 1994. "Against Gullibility." In *Knowing from Words:
    Western and Indian Philosophical Analysis of Understanding and
    Testimony*, ed. Bimal Krishna Matilal and Arindam Chakrabarti,
    125–161. Dordrecht.

———. 2006. "Second-Hand Knowledge." *Philosophy and Phenomenological
    Research* 73, no 3:592–618.

Gagarin, Michael. 2020. "Storytelling about the Lawgiver in the Athe-
    nian Orators." *Cahiers des études anciennes* 57:33–44.

Glucker, John. 1988. "Πρὸς τὸν εἰπόντα—Sources and Credibility of *De
    Stoicorum Repugnantiis* 8." *Illinois Classical Studies* 13, no. 2:473–489.

Gourinat, Jean-Baptiste. 2000. *La dialectique des stoïciens*. Paris.

Graham, Peter. 2006. "Liberal Fundamentalism and Its Rivals." In *The
    Epistemology of Testimony*, ed. Jennifer Lackey and Ernest Sosa,
    93–115. Oxford.

Guthrie, William K. C. 1978. *A History of Greek Philosophy*. Vol. 5, *The Later Plato and the Academy*. Cambridge.

Hansen, Mogens Herman. 1991. *The Athenian Democracy in the Age of Demosthenes: Structure, Principles, and Ideology*. Oxford.

Heidel, William A. 1896. *Pseudo-Platonica*. PhD diss., University of Chicago. Baltimore.

Hercher, Rudolf. 1873. *Epistolographi Graeci*. Paris.

Hermann, Karl F. 1839. *Geschichte und System der platonischen Philosophie*. Vol. 1, *Die historisch-kritische Grundlegung*. Heidelberg.

Hirzel, Rudolf. 1895. *Der Dialog: Ein literarhistorischer Versuch*. Vol. 1. Leipzig.

Hume, David. 1748/1993. *An Enquiry Concerning Human Understanding; A Letter from a Gentleman to His Friend in Edinburgh; Hume's Abstract of a Treatise of Human Nature*. Ed. Eric Steinberg. 2nd ed. Indianapolis.

Hutchinson, Douglas S. 1997. "Demodocus." In Cooper 1997, 1699.

Ioppolo, Anna Maria. 1986. *Opinione e scienza: Il dibattito tra Stoici e Accademici nel III e nel II secolo a. C.* Naples.

Isnardi, Margherita. 1954. "Sugli apocrifi platonici *Demodoco* e *Sisifo*." *La parola del passato* 9:425–431.

Joyal, Mark. 2019. "What Is Socratic about the Pseudo-Platonica?" In *Brill's Companion to the Reception of Socrates*, ed. Christopher Moore, 211–236. Leiden.

Kilburn, K. 1959. *Lucian*. Vol. 6. Cambridge, MA.

Lévy, Carlos. 2018. "De la rhétorique à la philosophie: le rôle de la *temeritas* dans la pensée et l'œuvre de Cicéron." In *Philosophie in Rom - Römische Philosophie? Kultur-, literatur- und philosophiegeschichtliche Perspektiven*, ed. Gernot Michael Müller and Fosca Mariani Zini, 285–303. Berlin.

Merkelbach, Reinhold, and Martin L. West. 1967. *Fragmenta Hesiodea*. Oxford.

Müller, Carl Werner. 1975. *Die Kurzdialoge der Appendix Platonica: Philologische Beiträge zur nachplatonischen Sokratik*. Munich.

Mutschmann, Hermann. 1912–1914. *Sexti Empirici opera*. 2 vols. Leipzig.

Ober, Josiah. 1989. *Mass and Elite in Democratic Athens: Rhetoric, Ideology, and the Power of the People*. Princeton.

Oświecimski, Stefan. 1978. "The Enigmatic Character of Some of Plato's Apocrypha." *Eos* 66:31–40.

Papiri greci e latini. 1917. Vol. 4. Firenze.

Places, Édouard des. 1973. *Numénius. Fragments.* Paris.

Plasberg, Otto. 1922. *M. Tulli Ciceronis scripta quae manserunt omnia.* Vol. 42, *Academicorum reliquae cum Lucullo.* Leipzig.

Pohlenz, Max, and Rolf Westman. 1959. *Plutarchi Moralia.* Vol. 6.2. Leipzig.

Reid, Thomas. 1764/1983. *Inquiry and Essays.* Ed. Ronald E. Beanblossom and Keith Lehrer. Indianapolis.

Rennie, William. 1931. *Demosthenis orationes.* Vol. 3. Oxford.

Rusten, Jeffrey S. 1989. *Thucydides. The Peloponnesian War Book II.* Cambridge.

Schwartz, Eduard. 1891. *Scholia in Euripidem.* Vol. 2, *Scholia in Hippolytum, Medeam, Alcestin, Andromacham, Rhesum, Troades.* Berlin.

Shorey, Paul. 1933. *What Plato Said.* Chicago.

Sophocles, Evangelinus A. 1887. *Greek Lexicon of the Roman and Byzantine Periods (from B.C. 146 to A.D. 1100).* New York.

Souilhé, Joseph. 1930. *Platon. Œuvres complètes.* Vol. 13.3, *Dialogues apocryphes.* Paris.

Tarrant, Harold. 2018. "Philo of Larissa." In *Skepticism: From Antiquity to the Present*, ed. Diego E. Machuca and Baron Reed, 81–92. London.

Thackeray, Henry St. John. 1909. *A Grammar of the Old Testament in Greek: According to the Septuagint.* Cambridge.

Thür, Gerhard. 2005. "The Role of the Witness in Athenian Law." In *The Cambridge Companion to Ancient Greek Law*, ed. Michael Gagarin and David Cohen, 146–169. Cambridge.

Weische, Alfons. 1961. *Cicero und die neue Akademie.* Münster.

Westerink, Leendert G., Jean Trouillard, and Alain P. Segonds. 1990. *Prolégomènes à la philosophie de Platon.* Paris.

Zagzebski, Linda Trinkaus. 2012. *Epistemic Authority: A Theory of Trust, Authority, and Autonomy in Belief.* Oxford.

NEAR EASTERN POETICS IN CALLIMACHUS'S
HYMN TO APOLLO

JAMES J. CLAUSS AND SCOTT B. NOEGEL

εἰδυῖαι φαλιὸν ταῦρον ἰηλεμίσαι
"(Egyptian) women who know how to
mourn the bull with a white patch."
Callimachus *Aetia* 54.16 Harder[1]

I. INTRODUCTION

IN RECENT YEARS, scholars of Hellenistic poetry have begun to find evidence for multicultural poetics represented by multivalent subjects and themes that speak to both Greek and Egyptian audiences.[2] As Susan Stephens so eloquently put it: "Our inability to see an Egyptian allusion in their works results not from their failure to make such allusions, but from our own lack of familiarity with their frames of reference."[3] In the present contribution, we offer additional evidence for these poetics by focusing on Callimachus's *Hymn to Apollo* and examining it in the light of Near Eastern texts, especially Egyptian and biblical poetry. Although we could have chosen texts from elsewhere in the Near East, we focus on these texts because Alexandria had sizable

---

[1] The reference is to the Apis bull associated with Epaphus, the son of Io, thus underscoring the close connection between Egypt and Greece for which we argue in this paper.

[2] See Selden 1998; Stephens 1998, 2002, 2003, 2015; Noegel 2004; Clauss 2019. Secondary literature on the Alexandrian propensity for esoteric mythological and literary allusions is voluminous and too well known to warrant even a judicious selection. Cameron 1995 argued that the Alexandrians had sought a broader audience than was once supposed. His arguments counter the notion that their poetry was read only by fellow scholars. Moreover, we argue for an audience that also possesses the ability to see beyond the cultural confines of the poem under consideration.

[3] Stephens 2003:6.

and literate Egyptian and Jewish populations. It strikes us that Egyptian and biblical sources would have been more available to him, the latter likely through early Greek translations. In fact, some of the evidence below strongly supports previous arguments that Callimachus indeed had access to the Septuagint or a prototype.[4]

We divide our treatment into three sections. In the first, we examine the poet's use of polysemy and paronomasia in the light of Near Eastern usage. In the second, we turn to the poem's use of parallelism, a widespread structural feature of ancient Near Eastern poetry. Our third section focuses on multivalent mythological references in the hymn that can be read in the light of ancient Egyptian religious traditions. Together these features imbue the hymn with a Near Eastern atmosphere suited to the new pharaohs, whose insinuation of themselves in Egyptian culture and religion as international rulers is manifest in Alexandria and throughout Egypt.

II. POLYSEMY AND PARONOMASIA IN THE *HYMN TO APOLLO*

In what follows, we set aside the oft-used terms "wordplay," "pun," "alliteration," and the like, in favor of a more exact vocabulary found

---

[4] Fraser argues that Callimachus's *Ep.* 55, in which a lamp speaks the words "Hesperos, how you have fallen," borrows from the Septuagint of Isa 14:12: "O Ben-Shahar, how you are fallen from heaven!" (1972: vol. 1, 584–585). He states: "I find it hard to believe that a resemblance at so many points can be dismissed as a series of coincidences and am prepared to accept that Call(imachus) at some point, in his life, read a Greek version of Isaiah ..." (1972: vol. 2, 1000). Theocritus too appears to have known a Greek translation of the biblical Song of Songs (Fraser 1972: vol 2, 1002n255). Franz Dornseiff long ago contended that the Song of Songs and Callimachus (*Hymns* and *Aetia*) both drew from Egyptian poetry (1936), a view accepted by the biblical scholars Robert and Tournay 1963:378–380. Agatharchides later also evinces a knowledge of the Septuagint, especially the text of Ecclesiastes, in his work on the Red Sea (Fraser 1972: vol. 1, 517, vol. 2, 784). Copies of the Septuagint and commentaries on it appear to have been housed in the library in the Serapeum, possibly dated to the third century BCE (Fraser 1972: vol. 1, 323–324, 330). While we feel that the Letter of Aristeas is somewhat apocryphal, we note the authoritative comment of Emanuel Tov 2001:136: "According to the generally accepted explanation of the testimony of the Epistle of Aristeas, the translation of the Torah was carried out in Egypt in the third century BCE. This assumption is compatible with the early date of several papyrus and leather fragments of the Torah from Qumran and Egypt, some of which have been ascribed to the middle or end of the second century BCE."

in the most recent and exhaustive treatment on the topic.[5] Therefore, we distinguish two broad categories into which we may place many different devices: *polysemy* and *paronomasia*. The former includes at least fourteen different devices of meaning, whereas the latter involves at least twelve different devices of sound.[6] Polysemy involves *multiple meanings* and/or readings of a word or sign in a *single* context. To demonstrate, we turn to an Egyptian love poem:

> My sister is more potent than all medicines. Greater she is
>   to me than the compendium.
> My wḏꜣ.t is her entering from outside.
> Seeing her then is health. She opens her eyes,
>   rejuvenating my body.
>
> P. Chester Beatty I 4,10-5,1

Here the polyseme is wḏꜣ.t. It can mean "amulet" or "healing." As "amulet," it looks back to the "medicines" and the "compendium," a collection of magical recipes. As "healing" it looks ahead to "health"

---

[5] We have placed the terms "wordplay," "pun," and "alliteration" in quotation marks to draw attention to their problematic nature. Indeed, it is our contention that the terms "wordplay" and "pun" are too vague to be useful. Sometimes one finds them used interchangeably, while elsewhere they appear to be distinct. Some have applied them to devices of sound, while others use them for devices of meaning. Moreover, for some writing systems, such as ancient Egyptian and Akkadian, the "word" is not the primary operative linguistic unit but rather the sign. Further, in the great majority of contexts in which we find these devices, there is little that is "playful." On the contrary, these devices have serious functions, and in many cases, this function is performative. We also refrain from using the term "alliteration," as we see it not as *a tool or type* of paronomasia but rather the *sonic effect* of many different devices. Thus, we adopt the approach and taxonomy of devices found in Noegel 2021. The book is open access and available freely for download from the Society of Biblical Literature.

[6] The fourteen devices of polysemy include: contronymic polysemy, *double entendre*, antanaclasis, unidirectional polysemy, multidirectional polysemy, double polysemy, bilingual polysemy, polysemy clusters, numerical polysemy, isopsephy, noṭariqon, acrostics (also telestichs and menostichs), transposition, and amphiboly. The twelve paronomastic devices are homoeopropheron, homoioteleuton, anastrophe, epanastrophe, parasonance, homonymic paronomasia, numerical paronomasia, bilingual paronomasia, anagrammatic paronomasia, hendiadic paronomasia, rhyme, and geminate parallelism and clustering. For definitions, see Noegel 2021. Only the devices that we discuss appear in the glossary of terms at the end of this article.

and the rejuvenation of the body. Moreover, in the hieroglyphic script, *wḏȝ.t* is written as 𓂀 (the Eye of Horus). It therefore not only embodies a magical amulet, but it also visually conveys the act of seeing, which anticipates "seeing her then is health" and the opening of her eyes.

Paronomasia operates *across* word divisions and involves a *dissimilarity in meaning*. An excellent demonstration appears in the same text, which the poet divides into seven stanzas, each of which he numbers and immediately follows with paronomasia upon that number. Thus, the "fourth (*fdw.t*) full stanza" begins "My mind flees (*ifd*) me quickly" and concludes "O my mind, don't you flee (*ifd*)!" (2,9, 3,4). Here the verb *ifd* (pronounced *yefed*) "flee" paronomastically starts and ends the *fdw.t* (pronounced *fedu*) "fourth" stanza.[7]

Many (but not all) cases of polysemy are effective on a purely visual register, whereas all cases of paronomasia (in a consonantal writing system) are effective both aurally and visually. If accomplished in a writing system not restricted to consonants (such as Egyptian), some cases of paronomasia may not operate simultaneously on aural and visual registers.

While cases of polysemy and paronomasia have long been observed in Greek literature, there has been little effort to organize the phenomena by type. In addition, little comparative work has been done, even though these same devices appear in earlier texts from the ancient Near East.[8] One of the present writers has examined the works of Callimachus, in particular the *Hymn to Zeus* and the *Aetia*, for cases of appellative paronomasia that offer etiologies, and has seen in the clustering of these devices a reflection of Egyptian practice.[9] While such etiological treatments are attested in earlier periods, they were of minor literary interest until the Hellenistic period.[10] Conversely,

---

[7] The final *t* was not pronounced. This is a case of numerical paronomasia. See Noegel 2021:266–270.

[8] Noegel 2021 has shown that at least eleven different devices of polysemy and paronomasia attested in Greek literature appear earlier in Near Eastern texts.

[9] Clauss 2019. Appellative paronomasia draws upon the name of a god, person, place, or thing. It is not a type of paronomasia but rather one of its functions (Noegel 2021:97–110).

[10] Selden 1998:320. Williams 1978:3 has called this the poet's "aetiological *style*." Emphasis added. See also Codrignani 1958.

the use of polysemy and paronomasia for etiological purposes is widely attested in the Near East, especially in Egyptian and biblical texts.[11] Similarly, while scholars have observed cases of polysemy in Callimachus's works before, some of them appear to be of Near Eastern vintage. For example, in the *Hymn to Demeter* one finds the line: "Feed our cattle (βόας), bring forth μᾶλα, bring forth corn (στάχυν), bring the harvest, and nourish peace" (136–137). As Selden has shown, the term μᾶλα can designate "sheep and goats" (which faces back to βόας "cattle") as well as "fruit" (which faces forward to στάχυν "corn").[12] What has gone unnoticed is that this form of polysemy has long been known by scholars of the Near East as "Janus parallelism," or by its more recent sobriquet "multidirectional polysemy," because each of its meanings faces related terms in opposite directions.[13] It is most widely attested in the Hebrew Bible, but it also occurs in Akkadian, Ugaritic, and Egyptian texts, like the Egyptian love poem cited above. The same can be said for all other types of polysemy in Callimachus's poems, such as amphiboly,[14] which is especially at home in Egyptian texts.[15]

With these observations in mind, we now turn to a detailed examination of the evidence for polysemy and paronomasia in the *Hymn to Apollo*. We begin with cases of polysemy. We shall proceed in order of their appearance in the hymn and categorize them by type.

II.1. Polysemy

The *Hymn to Apollo* contains at least seven cases of polysemy.

---

[11] Noegel 2021:97–113. Compare the following case of appellative paronomasia in a letter sent by the high priests of the Isis-Hathor temple in Aphroditopolis to Apollonius in 275 BCE. The letter requests funds for the burial of the sacred cow worshipped as the manifestation of the goddess Isis-Hathor. Its concluding wish reads: "may she (the goddess) grant you favor (ἐπαφροδισίαν) in the eyes of the king," with the word for "favor" here suggesting the name "Aphrodite." See Tait 1980:194. We thank Susan Stevens for the reference. While the Greek is a reflex of the Egyptian word ḥs.t "favor," often used in letter formulae like this one, it strikes us that the author of the Greek letter would have recognized the paronomasia in Egyptian that occurs in the present context between ḥs.t "favor" and ḥs.t "Hesis," the cow identified with Isis.

[12] Selden 1998:379.

[13] Noegel 2021:175–181.

[14] Selden 1998:377–378, 386.

[15] Noegel 2021:233–239.

HYMN 2.9–11

ὡπόλλων οὐ παντὶ φαείνεται, ἀλλ' ὅ τις ἐσθλός·
ὅς μιν ἴδῃ, μέγας οὗτος, ὃς οὐκ ἴδε, λιτὸς ἐκεῖνος·
ὀψόμεθ', ὦ Ἑκάεργε, καὶ ἐσσόμεθ' οὔποτε λιτοί.

Apollo does not φαείνεται everyone, but upon whoever is good.
Whoever sees him, this man is great, whoever does not
    see him, he is of no account.
We shall see you, O Hekaergos, and we shall never be of no
    account.[16]

Concerning the meaning of the verb φαείνεται, Stephens remarks:
"'Shine' is appropriate for Apollo, but the following ἴδῃ also requires
that 'appear' be implicit."[17] Thus, in one word, Apollo both "shines upon"
and "appears to." What is of interest to us here is that this form of polysemy is known to scholars of the Near East as unidirectional polysemy.
Unlike the "Janus parallelism" in the Hymn to Demeter, the polyseme
here in both of its meanings faces other lexemes in the same direction.
As "shine" it faces forward to the name Ἑκάεργε, whose meaning (literally "Far-worker") suggests that Apollo's sunrays give life from afar.[18] As
"appear" φαείνεται looks ahead to the three references to "seeing."

HYMN 2.16–19

ἠγασάμην τοὺς παῖδας, ἐπεὶ χέλυς οὐκέτ' ἀεργός.
εὐφημεῖτ' ἀΐοντες ἐπ' Ἀπόλλωνος ἀοιδῇ.
εὐφημεῖ καὶ πόντος, ὅτε κλείουσιν ἀοιδοί
ἢ κίθαριν ἢ τόξα, Λυκωρέος ἔντεα Φοίβου.

I do admire the boys, seeing as the χέλυς is no longer idle.
Be silent while you listen to the song for Apollo.
The sea too is silent when the singers celebrate
either the cithara or the bow, the implements of
    Lycoreian Apollo.

[16] Our translations follow those of Stephens 2015, with periodic minor variations.
[17] Stephens 2015:84, cf. Montanari, s.v. B2.
[18] Stephens 2015:84.

Well known is the polysemous use of χέλυς for both "lyre" and "tortoise shell," the material used to make the lyre's music box.[19] Here again we have a case of unidirectional polysemy. As "lyre" χέλυς looks ahead to the "song for Apollo," "singers," and "cithara" in lines 17–19. As "tortoise shell" the χέλυς anticipates the "sea," which ironically unlike the χέλυς is now silent.

HYMN 2.17, 22–24

εὐφημεῖτ᾽ ἀίοντες ἐπ᾽ Ἀπόλλωνος ἀοιδῇ ...

. . . .

καὶ μὲν ὁ δακρυόεις ται ἄλγεα πέτρος,
ὅστις ἐνὶ Φρυγίῃ διερὸς λίθος ἐστήρικται,
μάρμαρον ἀντὶ γυναικὸς ὀιζυρόν τι χανούσης.

Be silent while you listen to the song for Apollo ...

. . . .

And the weeping rock postpones its grief,
the moist stone that is fixed in Phrygia,
a marble rock in place of a woman uttering some lament.

Selden describes these lines as an example of amphiboly, the employment of an ambiguous morphology or grammatical structure for polysemous effect. His observation is worth citing in full.[20]

> From the general call to silence, it is clear that the middle ἀναβάλλεται should mean 'defer,' as it does at *Iliad* 2.436. In the *Odyssey*, however, the form has the opposite significance, 'to begin' or 'strike up,' in particular a song, and, as an ironic countersense, it would be equally appropriate for Niobe here to renew her afflictions (ἀναβάλλεται ἄλγεα) at the sound of a paean to the god who had slaughtered her young. The adjective διερός, used to describe the rock itself, likewise has a double valence in this passage. From Hesiod on, the word normally means 'wet,' though for the two occurrences

[19] Williams 1978:28; Stephens 2015:85.
[20] Selden 1998:378.

of the term in Homer this sense is clearly inappropriate: διερὸς βροτός and διερῷ ποδί. Aristarchus subsequently conjectured that to Homer the word meant 'living,' and this meaning for the term is also found in the lexicographers. Callimachus' διερὸς λίθος, which clearly rewrites the Homeric phrase διερὸς βροτός, combines the senses of 'wet' and 'living,' both apposite to the double nature of weeping rock and transfigured woman.

In the study of Near Eastern literary devices, this example is considered a case of double polysemy, since each successive verse contains a polyseme. In line 22 it is ἀναβάλλεται, and in line 23 it is διερός. Double polysemy abounds in the Hebrew Bible but also appears in some Egyptian texts.[21]

HYMN 2.18-21

εὐφημεῖ καὶ πόντος, ὅτε κλείουσιν ἀοιδοί
ἢ κίθαριν ἢ τόξα, Λυκωρέος ἔντεα Φοίβου.
οὐδὲ Θέτις Ἀχιλῆα κινύρεται αἴλινα μήτηρ,
ὁππόθ' ἰὴ παιῆον ἰὴ παιῆον ἀκούσῃ.

The sea too is silent when the singers celebrate,
either the cithara or the bow, the implements of
      Lycoreian Apollo.
Nor does Thetis, his mother, mourn for Achilles,
whenever she hears ἰὴ παιῆον ἰὴ παιῆον.

The repeated cry ἰὴ παιῆον ἰὴ παιῆον is a particularly clever case of double polysemy. The word ἰὴ suggests both "voice, cry" (ἰά) and "arrows" (ἰά), both fitting here. The word παιῆον suggests a "paean," of course, which would go with the notion of uttering or voicing, but also a "physician" or "healer" (παιῆον), which Apollo also was. Moreover, these polysemes also constitute a case of multidirectional polysemy, again a device at home in ancient Near Eastern poetry. As "arrow," ἰὴ looks back to the τόξα in line 19. As "voice, cry" it looks ahead to

---

[21] Noegel 2021:181–185.

the reference to mourning and the weeping rock (22). Moreover, as Stephens observes, one also could interpret ἰὴ with Clearchus of Soli (fr. 64) and derive it from ἵε, παῖ ("shoot, boy") the encouraging words said by Leto to Apollo to strike the Python.[22] The polysemous cry is repeated in condensed form as ἰὴ ἰὴ in line 25 and as ἰὴ ἰὴ παιῆον in line 97. In both places the ambiguity remains, but the reference to a golden bow in line 99 tilts the interpretation considerably. We last hear ἰὴ ἰὴ παιῆον in line 103, where it is followed immediately by ἵει βέλος, which, as Stephens also notes, suggests that the cry was ἵει, παῖ, ἰόν.[23]

HYMN 2.26–27

ὃς μάχεται μακάρεσσιν, ἐμῷ βασιλῆι μάχοιτο:
ὅστις ἐμῷ βασιλῆι, καὶ Ἀπόλλωνι μάχοιτο.

Whoever fights with the Blessed Ones, let him fight with
    my king.
Whoever fights with my king, let him fight with Apollo.

This polysemy is truly amphiboly. As Selden notes:[24]

The irresolution hinges on the syntactic ambiguity of καί, which can be alternatively the copula or an adverbial emphatic. Does Callimachus mean to distinguish the king from Apollo ('Who fights with the king would also [καί] fight with the god'), or does he intend to conflate the two ('Who would fight with the king actually [καί] fights with Apollo')?

The amphiboly allows us to consider the relationship between the king and Apollo in both Greek and Egyptian terms, the latter as a fusion of the king with the sun god—a topic to which we will return below. While amphiboly does occur in biblical texts, it is attested more widely in Egyptian texts.[25]

---

[22] Stephens 2015:97.
[23] Stephens 2015:97.
[24] Selden 1998:385.
[25] Noegel 2021:233–239.

HYMN 2.95

> ... μνωόμενος προτέρης ἁρπακτύος.

> ... remembering the earlier rape.

In this brief clause, which also functions as a case of allusive paronomasia (see below), the word μνωόμενος is polysemous. As Frederick Williams aptly notes, it means both "remember, be mindful of" and "woo":[26]

> In this context, after the mention of the nymph, the latter significance might have been expected, but the following genitive shows that the former is intended; however, there is a further twist, since what Apollo remembers is his wooing.

From the perspective of ancient Near Eastern devices, we may classify it more precisely both as a double entendre, because its intended meaning differs from its allusive, more scandalous one, and also as a case of unidirectional polysemy, since both of its meanings face forward to the rape.[27]

HYMN 2.110

> Δηοῖ δ' οὐκ ἀπὸ παντὸς ὕδωρ φορέουσι μέλισσαι.

> Not from any sources do bees carry water to Demeter.

Williams has commented on the polysemous nature of the word μέλισσαι as meaning "priestesses," "bees," and "poets":[28]

> there are three strands in the lines on the bees: first, the naturalistic, in which 'bees are bees'; secondly, the religious, in which the insects are visualized as Demeter's devotees, with a possible allusion to her human priestesses; and thirdly, the common metaphor of poets as 'bees'.

---

[26] Williams 1978:81.
[27] Noegel 2021:159–164, 171–175.
[28] Williams 1978:93.

More recently, Stephens has shown how the bee denotes the hiero-glyphic Egyptian sign 𓆤 read as *bi.t*, meaning "king of Lower Egypt."[29] Thus, the bee resonates also with an Egyptian audience. Selden characterizes this as a "bilingual pun."[30] However, we cannot label it as such. While the Egyptian word *bi.t* can mean "bee" or "King of Lower Egypt," depending on the context, μέλισσαι cannot be read as anything but "bees" (however used) and sounds nothing like the Egyptian title.[31] More aptly, it is an iconographic reference that alludes to the hiero-glyphic sign. Nevertheless, we have included it in our collection since it has been suggested as a form of polysemy.

HYMN 2.113

χαῖρε, ἄναξ· ὁ δὲ Μῶμος, ἵν' ὁ Φθόνος, ἔνθα νέοιτο.

Hail, Lord. But Blame, let him νέοιτο where Envy is.

In a poem that exploits the cultural ambiguity of its subjects and themes, the polysemousness of the last word is perhaps fitting. Typically νέοιτο is derived from νέομαι "go," the usual transla-tion. However, one also may derive it from νέω meaning "swim." While clearly "go" is the primary sense here, in the previous eight lines Callimachus makes wide metaphoric use of water imagery in his metaliterary conclusion anticipating potential critics. In that brief section we hear πόντος, ποταμοῖο, ῥόος, ὕδατι, ὕδωρ, πίδακος, and λιβάς. The three bodies of water brought into contrast—the sea, Assyrian river, and drops from pure springs—represent three different poetic models, as Stephens explains:[32]

> ... pure drops of water equate to small, perfect poems,
> which are better than the seas or the Assyrian river. The
> river seems to equate with longer poems that necessarily
> have flaws because of their vastness, just as the river

[29] Stephens 2015:68.

[30] Selden 1998:383.

[31] For this to be a case of bilingual polysemy the word μέλισσαι would need to mean something in Egyptian. On bilingual polysemy and paronomasia in ancient Near Eastern texts (both of which are notably absent in Egyptian!), see Noegel 2021:185–195, 270–273.

[32] Stephens 2015:73.

carries impurities upon it surface. The third body of water in the comparisons is the sea, which Phthonos proposes as his preferred poetic model, even though the sea had previously silenced itself before hymns to Apollo (18).

Though the exact identity of Blame and Envy remains a matter of debate, their roles as stand-ins for critics seem clear enough. The parting shot, then, would appear a bit stronger than merely having the two occupy the same space. Rather, Callimachus suggests that they should attempt to swim the large (and considerably more dangerous) "bodies of water" that represent their own preferences.[33] The type of device employed here is again unidirectional polysemy.

The seven accepted cases of polysemy studied here are of the following types: amphiboly, double polysemy, multidirectional polysemy, and unidirectional polysemy. One of the cases of unidirectional polysemy also constitutes a *double entendre*. Thus, every type of polysemy employed by Callimachus appears first in Near Eastern poetry. Each type has analogues in both Egyptian and biblical texts, though amphiboly is more frequent in the former, and double polysemy in the latter.

II.2. PARONOMASIA

In this section we examine numerous cases and types of paronomasia. Before doing so, it is important to note that ancient Egyptian and Hebrew record no vowels, and so one can register cases of paronomasia in those languages only by way of consonants.[34] However, since Greek records vowels, studies on paronomasia also take them into

---

[33] While the verb νέω is used primarily in the active voice, the nautical context, together with its availability as a middle voice in the future, allow for the possibility of appealing to the sense of motion in water. Clauss 1985 long ago argued that, in the first poem of his second book of satires, Horace was looking at the end of *Hymn* 2, specifically in the image of Augustus kicking a poet whose words are ill timed and inept, focusing on the princeps's ear (*Sat.* 2.1.16-20). Just prior to this, Horace's lawyer, Trebatius, suggests as a cure for insomnia—the reason why Horace says he must write verse—swimming another large river, the Tiber (*Sat.* 2.1.7-9). It is possible, then, that the Roman poet caught the polysemy latent in νέοιτο.

[34] The vowel system for ancient Hebrew was added to the text in medieval times by the Masoretes. The Masoretes represent a particular interpretive tradition of vocalization.

account, though pedantically speaking, the repetition of vowel sounds constitutes assonance. Here we note both instances of paronomasia and assonance whenever present. Since many of our examples focus on the names Apollo or Cyrene, we treat both as separate cases at the end of this section.

HYMN 2.1–2

Οἷον ὁ τὠπόλλωνος ἐσείσατο δάφνινος ὅρπηξ,
οἷα δ' ὅλον τὸ μέλαθρον·³⁵ ἑκάς ἑκὰς ὅστις ἀλιτρός.

How Apollo's laurel branch shakes!
How the whole edifice shakes! Begone, begone, whoever
        is sinful!

The opening phrase that includes Apollo's name (Οἷον ὁ τὠπόλλωνος) echoes at the beginning of the second line (οἷα δ' ὅλον). In addition to the repetition of οἷος, we find a phonetic inversion between τὠ ... όλλων and ὅλον τὸ.³⁶ While this may seem far from significant, even accidental, the second line in turn initiates a false etymology of the god's epithet, Ἑκάεργος (11), that certainly leads us to expect paronomasia as a significant feature of the poem. The adverb ἑκάς (literally "far away") instructs all who are sinful (ἀλιτρός) to remove themselves from the temple. Apollo, the narrator tells us, does not shine upon (or appear to) everyone (φαείνεται, 9), in particular those who are λιτός ("of no account," 10). The narrator then urges the boys to play the lyre and dance, which they do, for which reason the instrument is termed active: οὐκέτ' ἀεργός (16). Thus ends the first section of the hymn, just before the call for ritual silence. ἑκάς and ἀεργός appear, a notion signaled by φαείνεται, to explain the term Ἑκάεργος; that is, the combination implies that, at the god's appearance, those who are not fully engaged in his worship with music should stay far

---

³⁵ τὸ μέλαθρον (roof beam for the whole temple) sits in the same metrical *sedes* as τὰ θύρετρα (doors of the temple) in the following verse (καὶ δή που τὰ θύρετρα καλῷ ποδὶ Φοῖβος ἀράσσει), both at the main caesura following the third trochee; the paronomasia appears purposeful.

³⁶ Stephens 2015:89 suggests that the phrases "produce a sound effect that links Apollo and 'whole.'"

away from his shrine, suggesting that the name means something like "away from here you who are unwilling/unable to participate!"[37] The banished sinner (ἀλιτρός) appears to be equated with a person of no account (λιτός) because both are denied access to the god, an equation supported by the phonetic similarity. While the traditional meaning of the word is "the one who works from afar" (cf. EM 319.51), a reference to Apollo's role as archer described later in the hymn, its suggestive reinterpretation here suits the context: wicked people of no account and those who fail to sing in honor of the god must stay away.

HYMN 2.3–5

> καὶ δή που τὰ θύρετρα καλῷ ποδὶ Φοῖβος ἀράσσει·
> οὐχ ὁράᾳς; ἐπένευσεν ὁ Δήλιος ἡδύ τι φοῖνιξ
> ἐξαπίνης, ὁ δὲ κύκνος ἐν ἠέρι καλὸν ἀείδει.

> It surely must be Apollo kicking at the doors with his fair foot.
> Do you not see? The Delian palm gently nodded its head,
> of a sudden, and the swan sings beautifully in the air.

As Williams noted, the adjective Δήλιος prompts us to expect Apollo as the Delian referred to, but in place of Φοῖβος, named in the previous line, we read φοῖνιξ, the famous palm next to which Apollo was born.[38] The similar opening syllables and ending sibilants create an association between the two words.[39] Moreover, like Aratus when he wants his readers to see his acrostics,[40] Callimachus invites the audience to have a look, οὐχ ὁράᾳς, which echoes the sound of the verb at the end of the previous line, ἀράσσει, in the same way that the φοῖνιξ echoes Φοῖβος, two clear cases of homoeopropheron.[41] Additionally, the first

---

[37] The term also anticipates the etymology of ἰὴ ἰὴ παιῆον in lines 97–104, where Apollo demonstrates his skill in shooting the bow: ἐκηβολίην (99).

[38] Williams 1978:9.

[39] ἐξ-απίνης appears to invert the sound of the preceding φοῖν-ιξ inasmuch as πίν and φοῖν possess initial labials followed by i-vocalization with terminal nasal. Stephens 2015:83 also calls attention to the fact that φοι- prompts the expectation of Φοῖβος. The poet is clearly manipulating sound in these verses.

[40] E.g., σκέπτεο prior to his celebrated ΛΕΠΤΗ acrostic, *Phaenomena* 778-787.

[41] In biblical texts, writers often invite their audiences to listen closely to consider a text's devices (Noegel 2021:28).

line imagines the presence of Apollo at the shaking of the laurel branch: ἐσείσατο δάφνινος ὄρπηξ. Later in the hymn we learn that Apollo honored Cyrene with great blessings, "mindful of (or wooing) his earlier carrying off" (μνωόμενος προτέρης ἁρπακτύος, 2.95). With this and such traditional rape stories in mind, δάφνινος ὄρπηξ might suggest by way of appellative paronomasia δάφνινος ἅρπαξ, alluding to the aition that explains why laurel became associated with Apollo in the first place. Notable also is the fact that the phrase ἐσείσατο δάφνινος ὄρπηξ is reechoed by ἐπένευσεν ὁ Δήλιος ἡδύ τι φοῖνιξ in sound, shape, and sense. Thus, both the laurel and palm tree, plants intimately linked with Apollo's major cult sites at Delphi and Delos, involve subtle parono-masia in a manner similar to the god's name. Binding the passage further is additional paronomasia between φοῖνιξ, ἐπένευσεν, and ἐξαπίνης. Finally, while Δήλιος φοῖνιξ must refer to the palm tree in this context, given the presence of another bird in the following sentence (κύκνος), there exists the possibility of a clever allusion to the mythic benu bird of Egypt, known in Greek as the φοῖνιξ (cf. Hdt. 2.73).

HYMN 2.17–31

In the next section of the hymn, the narrator calls for ritual silence in preparation for the coming song to be performed in honor of the god, which begins at line 32. As noted by Williams, the call for shouting ἰή (25), the use of the epithet Λυκωρέος that alludes to Delphi, and the etiology of the phrase ἰὴ ἰὴ παιῆον (97–104) demonstrate that the coming song will be a paean.[42] In fact, Callimachus underscores the

---

[42] Williams 1978:30, s.v. Λυκωρέος, who also adduces Ap. Rhod. *Argon.* 4.1490 as an intertext without suggesting any possible relevance apart from noting the important fact that "the use of Φοῖβος qualified by another adjective is most unusual." In the *Argonautica*, Caphaurus is identified as the grandson of "Lycoreian Phoebus" and Minos's daughter Acacallis, who was banished by her father to Libya because she became preg-nant by Apollo; for the full story involving the death of the Argonaut Canthus, see *Argonautica* 4.1485–1501. Since Callimachus will provide an account of the Greek settle-ment of Cyrene later in the hymn, this story of Greek presence in Libya, prior even to the Argonautic sojourn, is pertinent to the theme of colonization central to the hymn. Unfortunately, we do not know who is imitating whom. Callimachus included the town Lycoreia in the *Aetia*, but all we have is mention of this fact; see Harder 2012: vol. 2, 498–499.

importance of this song by noting what and who are silent as it is performed: the sea (which reappears at the end of the hymn in a meta-poetic context), Thetis, and Niobe. Additionally, related words for singing and song are mentioned five times within this short section: ἀοιδῇ (17), ἀοιδοί (18), ἀείδει (28), ἀείσει (30), and ἀείδοι (31), as well as elsewhere in the hymn (5, 43, 44, 104, and 106). The importance of song in general is made clear in the hymn's epilogue where Apollo defines the best sort of song through water imagery (105–112); on its associa-tion with ἀεί, see below.[43]

The silence of the sea represents an instance of the so-called pathetic fallacy, more often associated with pastoral verse, whereby nature responds to remarkable human or divine phenomena.[44] In this case Callimachus notes that the ocean maintains silence when-ever singers perform their celebration of Apollo's kithara and bow. As such, the sea responds not only to the god's epiphany but also to songs sung in honor of the manifesting divinity. Like the gods them-selves, music exerts a powerful control not only over nature (not surprising in a poem that concludes with imagery about the nature of the finest poetry) but also two celebrated women, one divine and the other mortal, who ceased weeping over, and despite the loss of, their children at the sound of ἰὴ παιῆον ἰὴ παιῆον (21). In the case of Thetis, the line describing the cessation of her mourning for Achilles demonstrates epanastrophe: οὐδὲ Θέτις Ἀχιλῆα κινύρεται αἴλινα μήτηρ (20).[45] As Williams noted, the juxtaposition of κινύρεται αἴλινα alludes to and even generates the sound of wailing so common in Greek, the

---

[43] Calame 1993:50–51 notes how multiple instances of ἀείδω/ἀοιδός/ἀοιδή under-score "the musical isotopy centered on the song theme" and create a more intimate connection to the hymn's celebrated epilogue. Because we are focused on Egyptian and biblical Hebrew stylistics, we will not fully engage the metapoetic dimension of the poem's conclusion but touch upon relevant points as they emerge.

[44] E.g., Dick 1968. Williams 1978:29 provides other examples of nature's response to divine epiphanies.

[45] In the study of ancient Near Eastern texts, the term epanastrophe applies also to syllables that end one line and appear at the start of the next line. See Noegel 2021:254–256.

source of several etiological stories: αἰαῖ.[46] Moreover, etymologies of the name Achilles associate the first part of his name with "grief," ἄχος, that would be expressed as αἰαῖ.[47] Additional paronomasia and assonance between Ἀχιλῆα and αἴλινα underscore the connection. Note in particular the assonance between the vowels α and ι (α also starts both words), abetted by repetition of the λ. The sequence -ῆα and αἴ are near aural palindromes. Such allusive and appellative functions of paronomasia are well attested in ancient Near Eastern texts.[48]

HYMN 2.22–24

Niobe, who is not specifically named, refrains from grief over the deaths of her fourteen children, which she continues to express even in metamorphosis:

καὶ μὲν ὁ δακρυόεις ἀναβάλλεται ἄλγεα πέτρος,
ὅστις ἐνὶ Φρυγίῃ διερὸς[49] λίθος ἐστήρικται,
μάρμαρον ἀντὶ γυναικὸς ὀϊζυρόν τι χανούσης.

And the weeping rock postpones its grief, the moist stone
that is fixed in Phrygia, a marble rock in place of a woman
uttering some lament.

What links the sea, Thetis, and Niobe is that all three refer to bodies of water. The sea is obvious; Thetis as a Nereid is a sea goddess;[50] Niobe's tears in metamorphosis have become a fountain atop Mt. Sipylus. Additionally, both women lost children killed by Apollo's arrows.[51]

---

[46] Williams 1978:32. One of those stories involves the death of Apollo's lover Hyacinthus, whose petals in his metamorphosed resurrection as the hyacinth bear the letters AIAI; for references to the various versions, see Gantz 1993:94. Stephens 2015:86 notes that αἴλινα was derived from the phrase αἶ Λίνον, adducing Aeschylus *Agamemnon* 121.

[47] On Achilles' name and its association with ἄχος, see Nagy 1979:69–83.

[48] Noegel 2021:97–110.

[49] Williams 1978:33 notes the juxtaposition of φρυγίῃ (alluding to φρύγιος, suggesting "dry") and διερός, which here means "wet."

[50] Noted by Williams 1978:31. In fact, Burkert 1992:92–93 argues that Thetis represents a transformation of the name Tethys, the wife of Oceanus, while West 1997:147 connects Tethys with Tiamat, the Mesopotamian primordial goddess Sea.

[51] Williams 1978:31 notes both points.

These connections prompt two observations. We are told that Thetis and Niobe cease grieving at the sound of ἰὴ παιῆον. We learn near the end of the hymn that the ritual cry ἰὴ παιῆον arose at the time when Apollo killed the serpent Pytho, deriving from the shout of locals ἵει, ἵει, παῖ, ἰόν, whose etymology Callimachus makes clear by appending the phrase ἵει βέλος to ἰὴ παιῆον (103).[52] Knowing this etymology, one might wonder if the women stop grieving because of the beauty of the music or rather from shock at the reminder of how their children died: "shoot the arrow, boy!" The connection is certainly unsettling. Secondly, all three bodies of water anticipate the contrast between literary styles featured at the end of the hymn, represented as the sea, the Assyrian river, and a pure stream, and not without irony in that the goddess is listed in the same order as the large polluted river while Niobe, a distant mountain stream, is effectively associated with the positive image of the pure fountain. In describing Niobe's postponement of her grief, Callimachus uses the phrase ἀναβάλλεται ἄλγεα (22). As noted above, the middle of ἀναβάλλω in Homer is followed by the infinitive ἀείδειν with the meaning "begin." In essence, the paronomastic and paradoxical phrase (cf. Φρυγίη διερὸς) underscores the poet's point that the onset of singing simultaneously initiates the cessation of grief.

HYMN 2.28–31

> Τὸν χορὸν ὠπόλλων, ὅ τι οἱ κατὰ θυμὸν ἀείδει,
> τιμήσει. δύναται γάρ, ἐπεὶ Διὶ δεξιὸς ἧσται.
> Οὐδ’ ὁ χορὸς τὸν Φοῖβον ἐφ’ ἓν μόνον ἦμαρ ἀείσει,
> ἔστι γὰρ εὔυμνος. τίς ἂν οὐ ῥέα Φοῖβον ἀείδοι;

> The chorus that sings what is pleasing to his heart, Apollo
> will honor. He is able to do this because he sits at the right
> 　　　hand of Zeus.
> Nor will the chorus hymn Phoebus for one day only,
> Since he is a copious subject for song. Who would not
> 　　　readily sing of Apollo?

---

[52] As Williams 1978:85 noted.

The last four lines of this section include three forms of the verb ἀείδω. The beginning of the "paean" that immediately follows, describing Apollo's appearance and his areas of expertise (32–46), continues the thematic and phonetic resonance of this verb that is linked with the god's bow and his immortal beauty and youth. The bow carries the rare term ἄεμμα (το τ' ἄεμμα τὸ Λύκτιον, 33);[53] Apollo is described as ἀεὶ καλὸς καὶ ἀεὶ νέος (36); and he is the divine patron of poet (ἀοιδόν) and song (ἀοιδή, 43–44). Callimachus employed the same ἀεί- ἀείδω association in the adjoining *Hymn to Zeus*, subtly linking both father and son by way of assonantal homoeopropheron.[54] The god's golden clothing and accoutrements (χρύσεα ... χρύσεα ... πολύχρυσος, 32–34), given their association with "imperishability," further support the quality of immortality.[55] We suspect that the cluster of words with the diphthong ει as the second or third syllable also echoes the combination of singing and eternity: θηλείαις ... παρειαῖς (37), ἔθειραι (39), πανάκειαν, ἐκεῖναι (40). Bolstering the assonance is that παρειαῖς, ἔθειραι, and ἐκεῖναι each conclude their respective colons.

To these we add the homoeopropheron created by the repetition of four dentals in the words in 29: τιμήσει, δύναται, Διὶ, and δεξιὸς, noted first by Williams as "alliteration."[56] The device is well attested in Egyptian and biblical texts, where it lends cohesiveness to a text and often encourages one to form meaningful relationships between the words involved.[57] Paronomasia and assonance also occur between ἓν μόνον and εὔυμνος (30–31). Note especially the anagrammatically repeated consonants μ and ν and the repeated

---

[53] That Lyctos is a Cretan town might connect with the Cretan association of Lycoreian Apollo as seen in Apollonius's use of the epithet; see above note 42.

[54] See Clauss 2019:75–78 plus references. Similar to *Hymn* 1.91-93, *Hymn* 2.104–106 concludes with multiple instances of the verb and noun for singing and song. At line 29, Callimachus states that Apollo is powerful because he sits at the right hand of Zeus. Fantuzzi 2011:450–451 made the attractive observation that the *Hymn to Apollo* would have been located to the right of the *Hymn to Zeus*. Another connection between the hymns is a focus on the gods' patronage of human activity: *Hymn* 1.70-80 = *Hymn* 2.32–64. Both hymns also include unnamed references to the poet's kings: *Hymn* 1.84-90 = *Hymn* 2.26–27.

[55] Verdenius *apud* Williams 1978:39.

[56] Williams 1978:37.

[57] Noegel 2021:241–248.

vowels ε and o. In Near Eastern contexts, such examples represent anagrammatic paronomasia, a device in which two or more roots contain the same consonants but in a different order. There also appears to be another specious etymology: Apollo's hair does not drip common grease (λίπος) but rather πανάκειαν ("the essence of healing," Stephens), by which everything becomes unharmed, ἀκήρια πάντ᾽ ἐγένοντο (41).[58] Thus we might add ἀκήρια to the phonetic cluster. Indeed, as Williams records, πανάκειαν also is paronomastic with ἀκήρια πάντα.[59] See especially the repeated κ and παν sequence, as well as the repetition of the α vowel. The relationship of <u>παν</u>άκειαν to <u>πάν</u>τα is one of homoeopropheron.

HYMN 2.42

τέχνῃ δ᾽ ἀμφιλαφὴς οὔτις τόσον ὅσσον Ἀπόλλων.

No one has as many skills as Apollo.

Especially paronomastic and assonantal in this line is the expression τόσον ὅσσον, attested elsewhere in Greek literature (e.g., Iliad 17.410). Here the consonants σ and ν, plus the vowel o, repeat in immediate succession. This phrase is followed soon thereafter with τόξον (44). As a somewhat frozen expression, τόσον ὅσσον is akin to cases of hendiadic paronomasia found in Near Eastern texts, such as ꜥḏ wḏꜣ "safe (and) sound" in Egyptian and petaꜥ pitʾom "suddenly" in biblical Hebrew.[60] Assisting the paronomasia of τόσον ὅσσον here is the σ concluding ἀμφιλαφὴς, the vowel o in οὔ, and the τ and σ in τις.

HYMN 2.60–64

Ἄρτεμις ἀγρώσσουσα καρήατα συνεχὲς αἰγῶν
Κυνθιάδων φορέεσκεν, ὁ δ᾽ ἔπλεκε βωμὸν Ἀπόλλων,
δείματο μὲν κεράεσσιν ἐδέθλια, πῆξε δὲ βωμόν
ἐκ κεράων, κεραοὺς δὲ πέριξ ὑπεβάλλετο τοίχους.
ὧδ᾽ ἔμαθεν τὰ πρῶτα θεμείλια Φοῖβος ἐγείρειν.

---

[58] Noted by Stephens 2003:89.
[59] Williams 1978:44.
[60] Noegel 2021:280–282.

Hunting continually, Artemis brought him the heads of
     Cynthian goats,
and Apollo wove an altar;
he constructed the foundations with horns, and fitted the altar
from horns, and he built up walls of horn around it.
In this way Phoebus first learned to raise foundations.

Here homoeopropheron connects the καρήατα ("heads") of the
Cynthian goats with their κεράεσσιν (... κεράων ... κεραούς), "horns,"
the very items Apollo used to construct the altar. While the Delian altar
of horn was famous in antiquity (the main tourist attraction of the site,
as Williams notes), the repetition of the sound κερα- and its association with καρήατα seems purposeful.[61] One is reminded of Penelope's
description of the two gates from which dreams come: one of ivory
and the other of horn (Od. 19.560–569). Those dreams issuing from the
gate of horn are true because the noun κέρας recalls the verb κραίνω
"fulfill." The four-year-old god's ability to fulfill his first remarkable
feat—the construction of an altar from seemingly impossible, or at least
improbable, material—underscores his precociousness.[62] Moreover, the
homoeopropheron anticipates the founding of Κυρήνη and Sparta's
cult epithet associated with his worship in the Libyan city: Καρνεῖος
(71, 72, 80, 87).

II.2.1. Appellative Paronomasia on the Name Apollo

As explained above, appellative paronomasia occurs first on Apollo's
epithet Ἑκάεργος in the opening section. The device continues in the
rest of the hymn. We first encounter sound fragments of Apollo's name
in the words πυλάων (6) and μολπήν (8). At lines 34–35, Ἀπόλλων is
described as πολύχρυσος and πουλυκτέανος. In lines 38–39, we also
happen upon λείβουσιν and λίπος Ἀπόλλωνος, which finds additional

---

[61] Williams 1978:59–61.
[62] On the Egyptian Horus, with whom Apollo was associated, as architect and builder,
see Selden 1998:392–405, and below pages 182–190.

homoeopropheron with ἀποστάζουσιν.[63] The poet's focus on echoes of the god's name continues in the next section, where Apollo abounds in skills, with no one possessing as many as the god (τέχνῃ δ' ἀμφιλαφὴς οὔτις τόσον ὅσσον Ἀπόλλων, 42); while there is no paronomasia on his name in this phrase, Apollo's association with having many things (here, skills) and his oversight of mortals with many possessions reverberates in subsequent sections. Apollo increases (τελέθοι πλέον) herd animals at 50–54. Those who found cities (ἑσπόμενοι πόλιας ... ἀεὶ πολίεσσι, 55–56) look to Apollo for assistance; these words occur within four lines that contain the name Φοῖβος (55–58) and the vocalic sounds before and after πολ evoke the god's name. We hear πόληι again shortly thereafter (77). The placement of Φοῖβος immediately after ἄνθρωποι, thus creating epanastrophe, further strengthens the use of meaningful syllables. Many people call Apollo by many names because he has many names: ὤπολλον, πολλοί σε Βοηδρόμιον καλέουσι, / πολλοὶ δὲ Κλάριον, πάντῃ δέ τοι οὔνομα πουλύ (69–70). Many are the bulls who fall on their haunches during sacrifice in honor of Apollo (ᾗ ἔνι πολλοὶ / ὑστάτιον πίπτουσιν ἐπ' ἰσχίον, ὦ ἄνα, ταῦροι, 78–79).[64] Apollo is also often sought in prayer, πολύλλιτε (80). We add that three contiguous sections of the poem, in ascending lengths (tricolon crescendo), begin with the name Phoebus but in different cases, making this an instance of polyptoton, a multiplicity of the god's name: Φοῖβον (47), Φοίβῳ (55), and Φοῖβος (65). Such devices contribute to the preponderance of p-sounds in this passage that Williams notes.[65]

In addition to forms of πολύς, Callimachus associates the adjective ἄλλος with his name. At line 93 we read οὐ κείνου χορὸν εἶδε θεώτερον ἄλλον Ἀπόλλων, and in 95–96 οὐδὲ μὲν αὐτοὶ / Βαττιάδαι Φοίβοιο πλέον θεὸν ἄλλον ἔτισαν. This is followed by πόλει (94) and πλέον, again with ἄλλον (96). The appellative paronomasia is enhanced by the

---

[63] This instance stands out because the operative words are framed by terms referring to the god's hair, one of his identifying features and the source of πανάκεια, which is the subject of an ensuing homoeopropheron discussed above.

[64] Note the clausula ἐν δὲ πόλη in the preceding line. Are we to hear the name Apollo in both phrases, ἐν δὲ πόλη and ᾗ ἔνι πολλοί? The Suda interestingly preserves the phrase ὁ ἀνάταυρα πέσων (the one falling backward, glossed as παλιμβάλης). Might this be reflected paronomastically in the phrase πίπτουσιν ... ἄνα, ταῦροι?

[65] Williams 1978:56.

tight parallelism between the phrases. The association of ἄλλος with the god's name is even more pronounced in the penultimate section of the hymn, containing the etiology of the ritual response ἰὴ ἰὴ παιῆον at the time Apollo killed the Delphian serpent Pytho with his arrows (101–103):

τὸν μὲν σὺ κατήναρες ἄλλον ἐπ' ἄλλῳ
βάλλων ὠκὺν ὀϊστόν, ἐπηΰτησε δὲ λαός,
"ἰὴ ἰὴ παιῆον, ἵει βέλος ..."

You slew him, shooting one swift arrow
after another, and the people cried:
"hie, hie paiêon, shoot your arrow ..."

The phrase elegantly links the god's name with the numerous arrows that he shot when he killed the monstrous snake and recalls the etymology for Apollo cited by Plato (Cra. 405c): Ἀειβάλλων.[66] While Callimachus suggests that the god's name evinces abundance, the concluding metapoetic coda introduces an irony with this association. Phthonos scorns the poet who does not sing as much as the sea, a return to, but also a reversal of, the image of the silent sea found earlier in the hymn (18). Rejecting poetic plenitude as a model, Apollo rebukes Phthonos, kicking him with his foot, a negative image of his knocking on the door of his temple with his "fair foot" (καλῷ ποδί, 3) at the beginning of the hymn, with poetological and metrical implications as noted by Stephens (105–112):[67]

ὁ Φθόνος Ἀπόλλωνος ἐπ' οὔατα λάθριος εἶπεν·
"οὐκ ἄγαμαι τὸν ἀοιδὸν ὃς οὐδ' ὅσα πόντος ἀείδει."
Τὸν Φθόνον ὡπόλλων ποδί τ' ἤλασεν ὧδέ τ' ἔειπεν·
"Ἀσσυρίου ποταμοῖο μέγας ῥόος, ἀλλὰ τὰ πολλά
λύματα γῆς καὶ πολλὸν ἐφ' ὕδατι συρφετὸν ἕλκει.
Δηοῖ δ' οὐκ ἀπὸ παντὸς ὕδωρ φορέουσι μέλισσαι,
ἀλλ' ἥτις καθαρή τε καὶ ἀχράαντος ἀνέρπει
πίδακος ἐξ ἱερῆς ὀλίγη λιβὰς ἄκρον ἄωτον."

---

[66] Mentioned by Williams 1978:84.
[67] Stephens 2015:83.

Envy spoke secretly into Phoebus' ear:
"I do not admire the singer who does not even sing as
     much as the sea."
Apollo pushed Envy off with his foot and spoke the following:
"The flow of the Assyrian river is vast, but it draws
along much refuse from the land and much garbage on its
     waters.
Not from any sources do bees carry water to Demeter,
but from what comes up pure and undefiled
     from a holy fountain, a small drop, the choicest of waters."

In short, poems whose claim to excellence resides in size do not guarantee quality but rather risk carrying along much dross like the Assyrian river.[68] Small and elegant bodies of water, similar to pure springs, are the appropriate metaphor. As such, while Apollo is associated with much wealth, many skills, many sacrifices, and many arrows (πολύς, ἄλλος), when it comes to poetry, the alpha that begins his name becomes privative. A-pollo does not approve of <u>ἀλλὰ τὰ πολλά</u> / λύματα γῆς καὶ <u>πολλὸν</u> ἐφ' ὕδατι συρφετὸν.

We find other resonances of the god's name embedded in the phonetic texture of the hymn. The narrator asks the bolts of the door to open spontaneously at the arrival of the god (6–8):

αὐτοὶ νῦν κατοχῆες ἀνακλίνασθε πυλάων,
αὐταὶ δὲ κληῖδες· ὁ γὰρ θεὸς οὐκέτι μακρήν·
οἱ δὲ νέοι μολπήν τε καὶ ἐς χορὸν ἐντύνασθε.

Now, you door-fastenings, open of your own accord,
and you bolts! The god is no longer far away.
Young men, make ready for the song and the dance.

The sound of the god's name is echoed both in ἀνακλίνασθ-<u>ε πυλάων</u> and νέ-<u>οι μολπήν</u>. As seen above, Niobe is said to delay her grief when

---

[68] Stephens 2015:98 offers the attractive suggestion that lines 109-110 contain an acrostic that spells out the name of Antimachus's poem Λυ-Δη (Lyde), which Callimachus famously despised (fr. 398 Pf.). Acrostics are also a widespread feature of ancient Near Eastern poetry, though they are far rarer in Egyptian literature than in the Hebrew Bible. See Noegel 2021:218–229.

hearing Apollo's song, the paean: ἀναβάλλεται ἄλγεα. With the name Apollo a constant theme, ἀν-αβάλλε-ται potentially becomes operative. In the section describing Apollo's patronage of those founding cities, Callimachus associates this activity with the fact that the god fashioned an altar and its peribolos wall out of horn (60–63):

> Ἄρτεμις ἀγρώσσουσα καρήατα συνεχὲς αἰγῶν
> Κυνθιάδων φορέεσκεν, ὁ δ᾽ ἔπλεκε βωμὸν Ἀπόλλων.
> δείματο μὲν κεράεσσιν ἐδέθλια, πῆξε δὲ βωμόν
> ἐκ κεράων, κεραοὺς δὲ πέριξ ὑπεβάλλετο τοίχους.[69]

> Hunting continually, Artemis brought him the heads of
>   Cynthian goats
> and Apollo wove an altar;
> he constructed the foundations with horns, and fitted the altar
> from horns, and he built up walls of horn around it.

ὑπ-εβάλλε-το, similar to ἀν-αβάλλε-ται, appears to reecho the sound of the god's name at a significant moment: the building of his fabled altar when he was only four years old (τετραέτης, 58). The hymn concludes with the god's signature feat: the killing of Pytho, followed by the metaliterary epilogue. Callimachus describes this as a display of his archery: ἦμος ἐκηβολίην χρυσέων ἐπεδείκνυσο τόξων. Given the paronomasia involving Ἑκάεργος at the beginning of the hymn and the numerous reflections of the god's name, the related ἐκηβολίην might here be heard as ἐκ-ηβολί-ην.[70]

---

[69] Callimachus's description of Apollo as weaving the altar (ὑφαίνει [57] and ἔπλεκε [61]) appears to evoke the well-known metaphor for poetical composition, which underscores the numerous terms for singing and anticipates the metapoetic epilogue, as noted by Stephens 2015:91. The central issues raised by this oft-discussed section pertain to controversies regarding literary tastes, a topic unrelated to our main point and far too broad to include in this contribution.

[70] As Williams 1978:49–50 and Stephens 2015:90 both observe, the name Admetus ("unbroken") is "semantically equivalent" (Williams) to ἠϊθέου ("unmarried youth"). Callimachus's coinage ζευγίτιδας of the previous line must also be included within this verbal sophistication, as ζεύγνυμι, ζεῦγος, and related words can refer to marriage.

II.2.2. Appellative Paronomasia on the Name Cyrene

The third and longest element of the tricolon fronted by different forms of the name Phoebus features the founding of Cyrene and the celebration of the Carneia festival. Considering the clusters of similar sounding words to underscore points in the hymn, which, as mentioned, are a feature of ancient Near Eastern poetry, we find the collocation of κ-ρ noteworthy—each of them constituting homoeopropheron. Apollo in the form of a raven (κόραξ, 66) leads the colonists to the site that would become Κυρήνη (73, 94), the name of the woman he raped (μνωόμενος προτέρης ἁρπακτύος, 95)—i.e., Cyrene, who is only referred to only by way of her patronymic (the "daughter of Hypseus," Ὑψηίς, 92). This constitutes a case of paronomasia in the service of allusion, a function also found in Egyptian and biblical texts.[71] The priamel on the names of Apollo, which includes appellative paronomasia on the adjective πολύς, ends in his title Καρνεῖος (69–71), a term repeated at 72, 80, and in the form Καρνειάδες at 87. The god points out the celebration of the Carneia to Cyrene "standing upon horned Myrtussa" (στὰς ἐπὶ Μυρτούσσης κερατώδεος, 91). Additional paronomasia and assonance also occur between καλέουσι and Κλάριον (homoeopropheron) and between Κλάριον and Καρνεῖον (69–71). Some ancients (cf. Stephanus Byzantinus, cited by Williams[72]) derived the name of the city from the local fountain Κύρη, mentioned at 88, as well as Cyrene. More evidence of appellative paronomasia.

While scholars have noted much paronomasia in Greek literature in general, beginning with Homer and Hesiod, it was a fundamental feature of ancient Near Eastern literature, especially in creating etiologies or inferring etymological connections. The *Hymn to Zeus*, which sat immediately before the *Hymn to Apollo*, reveals a similar intensity in appellative paronomasia, with a focus on the immortality of song (ἀεί and forms of the nouns and verbs for singing, ἀει- and ἀοι-), as does the *Aetia*.[73] The former also involved the theme of kingship, present in the second hymn as well, both pertaining to unnamed kings.

---

[71] Noegel 2021:91–110.
[72] Williams 1978:77.
[73] As argued by Clauss 2019:79–93.

In terms of the specific paronomastic devices employed, the hymn offers many instances of at least three, mostly of homoeopropheron, though Callimachus also creates epanastrophe and anagrammatic paronomasia. Most are employed for appellative purposes that draw connections between words or suggest etiologies and/or etymologies. Others are exploited for allusive purposes. All this was an essential component of Egyptian and Hebrew poetry and would have created a perfect blend of native and Greek narrative texture, giving us the opportunity, as it were, to *hear* double.

III. PARALLELISM IN THE *HYMN TO APOLLO*

Parallelism (also called "parallelismus membrorum") is arguably the most fundamental aspect of Near Eastern poetry. It is everywhere present in Levantine poetry, such as the epics from Ugarit and the psalms, prophecies, laments, and songs of the Hebrew Bible. It is also found earlier but with less frequency in Akkadian and Egyptian poetry.[74] Adele Berlin defines parallelism as "the repetition of the same or related semantic content and/or grammatical structure in consecutive lines or verses."[75] This repetition can occur over two or three lines and, more rarely, over more.

A staple feature of parallelism is the use of word pairs, i.e., words that recur frequently in parallelism.[76] Thus, if the A-line contains "subdued," the B-line employs "repressed"; if the A-line uses "arms," the B-line might have "legs" and so on. Some are culturally specific, such as "water" and "milk," common beverages of hospitality in ancient nomadic culture, and "eternity" and "foreverness," two different conceptions of time in Egyptian thought. Scholars have identified more than a thousand word pairs (both verbs and nouns), many of which are shared across languages (e.g., Ugaritic, Phoenician, and Hebrew), evidence that they were transmitted over many centuries in

[74] Firchow 1953; Donald 1966; Foster 1977, 1980; Kugel 1981, 1984; Assmann 1982; Segert 1983; Watson 1984/1986:114–159, 1985, 1989; Berlin 1985, 1992; Streck 2007; Jay 2010; Abbott 2011.

[75] Berlin 1985:155.

[76] Avishur 1984.

learned circles.[77] Often these word pairs assist the creation of polysemy by providing synonyms for each of the polyseme's meanings in adjacent lines. We demonstrate parallelism and word pairs below by way of several examples from Egyptian and biblical poems. Since we are interested only in illustrating the device, we dispense with the literary contexts. However, we italicize the words that serve as pairs. First, the Egyptian examples.

1. *Tale of Sinuhe* R 6–7

> The god *ascended* to his *horizon* ...
>> he *flew up* to the *sky*.
> *United* with the *solar disk*
>> the body of the god *merged* with *the one who made him*.

2. *Great Hymn to Aten*, col. 6

> Who *makes seed* grow in *women*,
>> who *creates people* from *sperm*.

3. *Instructions of Amenemhet*, 3,1–3,2

> I *subdued lions*,
>> I *captured crocodiles*.
> I *repressed* those of *Wawat*,
>> I *captured* the *Mediai*.

4. *Tale of Sinuhe*, B 26–27

> Thereupon he gave me *water*,
>> he boiled *milk* for me.[78]

5. *Tale of Sinuhe*, B 212

> May they (the gods) give to you *eternity* without *its limits*,
>> *foreverness* without *its end*.

[77] The study of parallelism and word pairs is far more advanced in biblical, Ugaritic, and Akkadian poetry than in Egyptian poetry. Nevertheless, the nouns and verbs that serve as word pairs and give parallelism its structure are fairly obvious in context. Still, much work needs to be done in Egyptology along the lines of Foster 1977, 1980, and Jay 2010.

[78] Cf. the use of the same word pair in the biblical account of Jael and Sisera: *mayim šāʾal ḥālāb nātānāh*, "he asked for water, she gave him milk" (Judg 5:25).

6. *Tale of Sinuhe*, B 167

> Let my body become *young.*
> > For now that *old age* has descended.

7. *Tale of Sinuhe*, B 169–170

> My *arms* have become weak.
> > My *legs*, they no longer follow the will.

8. *Tale of Sinuhe*, B 234

> The *water* of the *river*, it is *drunk* at *your desire.*
> > The *air* in the sky is *breathed* when *you say* (so).

9. *Great Hymn to Aten*, col. 12

> When you have *dawned,* they *live,*
> > when you *set,* they *die.*

10. *Love Poem*, P. Chester Beatty, 2,10–3,1

> It (my heart) does not let me *don* a *garment,*
> > I cannot *put on* a *cloak.*
> I cannot *apply kohl* to my eyes,
> > I cannot *anoint* myself.

11. *Tale of Sinuhe*, B 234

> *My eldest son in charge* of *my tribe,*
> > *my tribe* and all my things *in his hand.*

12. *Prayer to Ra-Horakthy*, 10, 3–4

> My *heart rejoices,*
> > my *bosom exults.*
> Hear my prayers,
> > my *supplications* every *day,*
> > my *hymns* by *night.*

13. *Debate Between a Man and His Ba*, 134-136

> Death is in my sight today,
> > like the *fragrance* of *lotuses,*
> > like *sitting* on the brink of *intoxication.*

14. *Tale of Sinuhe*, B 183–184

> You *did not curse* that your words should be *opposed*.
>> You *did not speak against* the council of nobles that
>> your phrases should be *opposed*.

These examples demonstrate a few of the many types of parallelism, some of which can occur together in a single passage. Most of them illustrate *synonymous parallelism*, since their B-lines essentially echo or mirror their A-lines. To this type belong the following parallels: ascended/flew up, united/merged (no. 1), makes grow/creates, seed/sperm, women/people (no. 2), subdued/captured, lions/crocodiles, repressed/captured, Wawat/Mediai (no. 3) eternity/foreverness (no. 5), arms/legs (no. 7), don/put on, garment/cloak, apply kohl/anoint (no. 10), heart/bosom, rejoices/exults, supplications/hymns (no. 12). *Antithetic parallelism*, which employs opposites, is represented by young/old age (no. 6), and water/air, river/sky (no. 8), dawned/set, live/die (no. 9), and day/night (no. 12). One passage (no. 11) demonstrates *chiastic parallelism*, since syntactically the phrase (my tribe/my tribe) and expressions (eldest son in charge/in his hand) are reversed in each line. Two examples illustrate *forked parallelism* (nos. 12-13). This occurs when an A-line offers an initial thought and is followed by a couplet, in which each line begins identically but expands in different ways upon the A-line. Examples 8, 9, 10, 12, 13, and 14 display *grammatical parallelism*, because the verbal conjugations and syntax of the A- and B-lines are equivalent.

The types of parallelism from the Hebrew Bible are more varied, but again, can overlap in a single passage. A representative selection includes:

1. Ps 29:3–5

> The *voice* of *Yahweh* is over the *waters*,
>> the *God of glory thunders*, Yahweh, over the *mighty waters*.
> The voice of Yahweh is *power*,
>> the voice of Yahweh is *majesty*.
> The voice of Yahweh *breaks* cedars,
>> Yahweh *shatters* the cedars of Lebanon.

2. Ps 73:25

> Whom have I in *heaven* but you?
>> And there is nothing upon the *earth* that I desire
>>> except you.

3. Isa 1:4

> Ah, *nation of sin*!
>> A *people* heavy with *iniquity*!
> The *seed* of *evildoers*!
>> *Children* who are *corrupters*!

4. Isa 59:9

> We *wait* for *light*,
>> but behold *obscurity*;
> For *brightness*,
>> but we *walk* in *darkness*.

5. Ps 1:6

> For Yahweh knows the way of the *righteous*,
>> but the way of the *ungodly* shall perish.

6. Prov 10:1

> The son of a *wise man* brings *joy* to his *father*,
>> a *fool's* son is the *grief* of his *mother*.

7. Prov 10:12

> *Hatred* stirs up strife,
>> but *love* covers all sins.

8. Jer 4:5

> *Proclaim* in *Judah*,
>> and in *Jerusalem declare*!

9. Josh 10:13

> The *sun* stood *still*, *stay* did the *moon*.

10. Ezek 6:11

> *Clap* your *hand*, and *stomp* your *foot*.

11. Judg 5:12

> *Awake, awake,* Deborah!
>> *Awake, awake,* chant a song!

12. Ps 29:1–2

> *Give unto Yahweh,* O you *mighty,*
>> *give unto Yahweh, glory and strength.*
> Ascribe to *Yahweh* the glory of His name,
>> bow down to *Yahweh, majestic in holiness.*

13. Ps 1:2

> For the *teaching* of *Yahweh* is his delight,
>> and he *studies* that *teaching* day and night.

14. Gen 49:27

> Benjamin is a *ravening wolf;*
>> in the *morning* he *devours* (the) *prey,*
>> and in the *evening* he divides the *spoil.*

15. Psalm 103:10

> Not according to our *sins* did he *deal with* us,
>> and not according to our *transgressions* did he *require* us.

In this corpus too *synonymous parallelism* predominates. Thus, we find voice/thunders, Yahweh/God of glory, waters/mighty waters, power/majesty, breaks/shatters, cedars/cedars of Lebanon (no. 1), heaven/earth (no. 2), nation/people, sin/iniquity, seed/children, evildoers/corrupters (no. 3), and sins/transgressions, deal with/require (no. 15). *Antithetic parallelism* appears in four of the examples: wait/walk, light/obscurity, brightness/darkness (no. 4), righteous/ungodly (no. 5), wise man/fool, joy/grief, father/mother (no. 6), and hatred/love (no. 7). The prophecy from Jeremiah (no. 8) demonstrates *chiastic parallelism,* since syntactically the verbs (proclaim/declare) and proper nouns (Judah/Jerusalem) are reversed in the second line. The passages from

Joshua and Ezekiel (nos. 9–10) are cases of *internal parallelism* in which the device is achieved within a single verse. The song from Judges and the next Psalm (nos. 11–12) illustrate *staircase parallelism*. This often involves verbatim repetition in successive lines. The two following passages from the Psalms (nos. 12–13) evidence *synthetic parallelism* (also called *formal parallelism*), in which the thought put forward in the A-line is completed or enlarged in the B-line. Psalm 29 (no. 12) is also an example of *climatic parallelism*, which combines synonymous, staircase, and synthetic parallelism. The passage from Genesis (no. 14) demonstrates *forked parallelism*. The final psalm (no. 15) constitutes *grammatical parallelism*, because the verbal conjugations and syntax of both colons are identical.

Callimachus employs several types of parallelism in the *Hymn to Apollo*.

HYMN 2.1–2

> Οἷον ὁ τὠπόλλωνος ἐσείσατο δάφνινος ὅρπηξ,
> οἷα δ' ὅλον τὸ μέλαθρον· ἑκὰς ἑκὰς ὅστις ἀλιτρός.

> How Apollo's *laurel branch shakes*! How the whole
> *edifice shakes*! *Begone, begone*, whoever is sinful!

Synonymous parallelism is achieved by placing the trembling laurel in line A and the trembling of the temple edifice in line B. Antithetic parallelism counterposes Apollo's implicit arrival in the A-line with the sinner departing in the B-line. Moreover, the ὅρπηξ and the μέλαθρον also constitute a parallel, since the former denotes "a laurel sapling growing in the *temenos*, like the palm of 4 ..."[79]

HYMN 2.4–5

> οὐχ ὁράᾳς; ἐπένευσεν ὁ Δήλιος ἡδύ τι φοῖνιξ
> ἐξαπίνης, ὁ δὲ κύκνος ἐν ἠέρι καλὸν ἀείδει.

> Do you not see? The Delian *palm gently nodded* its *head*,
> of a sudden, and the *swan sings* beautifully in the air.

---

[79] Williams 1978:16.

Callimachus employs synonymous parallelism here in having the palm nod in the A-line, while the swan sings in the B-line—both actions are positive affirmations of Apollo's presence. In addition, the paronomastic allusion to the φοῖνιξ bird discussed above offers an allusive parallel to the swan.

HYMN 2.6–7

αὐτοὶ νῦν κατοχῆες ἀνακλίνασθε πυλάων,
αὐταὶ δὲ κληῖδες· ὁ γὰρ θεὸς οὐκέτι μακρήν·

Now, you *door-fastenings, open* of your own accord,
and you *bolts!* The god is *no longer far away.*

Synonymous parallelism occurs in this passage by way of the door-fastenings in the A-line and bolts in the B-line. Also parallel is the opening of the door by itself in A, signaling Apollo's approach, which finds a match in the god being no longer far away in B.

HYMN 2.9–11

ὡπόλλων οὐ παντὶ φαείνεται, ἀλλ' ὅ τις ἐσθλός·
ὅς μιν ἴδῃ, μέγας οὗτος, ὃς οὐκ ἴδε, λιτὸς ἐκεῖνος·
ὀψόμεθ', ὦ Ἑκάεργε, καὶ ἐσσόμεθ' οὔποτε λιτοί.

Apollo does not *shine* upon everyone, but upon *whoever is good.*
Whoever *sees* him, *this man is great*; whoever does not *see*
    him, *he is of no account.*
We *shall* see you, O Hekaergos, and we shall never be *of no
    account.*

This tricolon is bound by several cases of parallelism. The first is φαείνεται (A), which in its meaning "appear" (discussed above) parallels the references to "seeing" in lines B and C. Internal antithetic parallelism exists between the one "who is good" in A, as well as the man who is "great" in B1, with those who are "of no account" in B2 and C. The latter also constitutes staircase parallelism. It is noteworthy that internal parallelism has been identified in biblical poetry but not in Egyptian poetry.

HYMN 2.12–15

> μήτε σιωπηλήν κίθαριν μήτ' ἄψοφον ἴχνος
> τοῦ Φοίβου τοὺς παῖδας ἔχειν ἐπιδημήσαντος,
> εἰ τελέειν μέλλουσι γάμον πολιήν τε κερεῖσθαι,
> ἑστήξειν δὲ τὸ τεῖχος ἐπ' ἀρχαίοισι θεμέθλοις.

> The young men should not keep the *cithara silent* or
> the *dance* step *noiseless* when Apollo is present,
> if they are going to *celebrate a marriage*, or live long
> enough to *dedicate a lock* of gray hair,
> and if the *city* is to remain firm upon its *ancestral*
> foundations.

These four lines exhibit several cases of parallelism. As elements of music, the "cithara" in A finds a parallel with "dance" in B. Also parallel are "silent" (A) and "noiseless" (B). Since ἐπιδημήσαντος in B (here translated as "present") is often used to mean "'to be in town' specifically for a religious festival,"[80] it perfectly matches the celebration of marriage and dedication of the lock in line C. Moreover, the prayer for longevity expressed in dedicating a gray lock in the C-line parallels the hope that the city will remain firm for future generations in line D. There also may be a subtle parallel between the gray lock (πολιήν) in C and the foundations in D, which Callimachus labels as "ancestral" (ἀρχαίοισι), literally "old." Similarly subtle is Callimachus's use of πολιήν for "gray lock" in C, as it suggests the πόλις "city," and thus anticipates the foundation of Cyrene later while providing a fitting parallel for τεῖχος "city walls," a synecdoche for the entire city.

HYMN 2.16–19

> ἠγασάμην τοὺς παῖδας, ἐπεὶ χέλυς οὐκέτ' ἀεργός.
> εὐφημεῖτ' ἀΐοντες ἐπ' Ἀπόλλωνος ἀοιδῇ.
> εὐφημεῖ καὶ πόντος, ὅτε κλείουσιν ἀοιδοὶ
> ἢ κίθαριν ἢ τόξα, Λυκωρέος ἔντεα Φοίβου.

---

[80] Williams 1978:25.

I do admire the boys, seeing as the *tortoise shell* is *no longer idle*.
Be *silent* while you listen to the *song* for Apollo.
The sea too is *silent* when the *singers* celebrate
either the *cithara* or the bow, the implements of Lycoreian
Phoebus.

This passage exhibits several types of parallelism. The first three lines display forked parallelism. We have indented two lines of the translation to make this structure more obvious. Note how the second and third lines start with a form of the verb εὐφημέω. Connecting the first line to the second and third are the tortoise shell (i.e., lyre), which parallels song and singers in the next two lines, and the words "no longer idle," which form an antonymic match for the repeated verb for "be silent." In the last two lines, synonymous parallelism binds the singer (18) to the cithara (19). The buildup that we find in 17–19 also makes this a form of staircase parallelism. Though forked parallelism occurs in Egyptian and Hebrew, it is far more widely attested in the former. Staircase parallelism is a staple feature in biblical poems but has not been observed in Egyptian poetry.

HYMN 2.25–27

ἰὴ ἰὴ φθέγγεσθε· κακὸν μακάρεσσιν ἐρίζειν.
ὃς μάχεται μακάρεσσιν, ἐμῷ βασιλῆι μάχοιτο·
ὅστις ἐμῷ βασιλῆι, καὶ Ἀπόλλωνι μάχοιτο.

Give the ritual cry *hie, hie!* It is a bad thing to *quarrel* with
the *Blessed Ones*.
Whoever *fights* with the *Blessed Ones*, let him *fight* with my *king*.
Whoever *fights* with my *king*, let him *fight* with *Apollo*.

We have examined this passage above for its use of amphiboly. Here we note the presence of several cases of verbatim parallelism. Note that μακάρεσσιν appears in A and B, βασιλῆι in B and C, and μάχοιτο also in B and C. These lines constitute staircase parallelism, again a feature at home in biblical poetry but not Egyptian poems. The parallel between "quarrel" and "fight" in A and B illustrates synonymous parallelism.

HYMN 2.28–31

> τὸν χορὸν ὡπόλλων, ὅ τι οἱ κατὰ θυμὸν ἀείδει
> τιμήσει· δύναται γάρ, ἐπεὶ Διὶ δεξιὸς ἧσται,
> οὐδ' ὁ χορὸς τὸν Φοῖβον ἐφ' ἓν μόνον ἦμαρ ἀείσει,
> ἔστι γὰρ εὔυμνος· τίς ἄν οὐ ῥέα Φοῖβον ἀείδοι;

The chorus that sings what is pleasing to his *heart, Apollo*
will *honor*.
He is able to do this because he sits at the *right hand of Zeus*.
Nor will the *chorus hymn Phoebus* for one day only,
since he is a copious subject for *song*. Who would not
readily *sing* of *Phoebus*?

In this passage, each line parallels the names of gods: Apollo (A), Zeus (B), Phoebus (C), and Phoebus (D). In addition, the reference to honor beginning B, but ostensibly ending the A-line in sense, parallels the sitting at the right hand, which marked an honored position. Paralleling the C line's "chorus hymn" is "song" and "sing" in line D. All are cases of synonymous parallelism.

HYMN 2.32–35

> χρύσεα τὠπόλλωνι τό τ' ἐνδυτὸν ἥ τ' ἐπιπορπὶς
> ἥ τε λύρη τό τ' ἄεμμα τὸ Λύκτιον ἥ τε φαρέτρη,
> χρύσεα καὶ τὰ πέδιλα· πολύχρυσος γὰρ Ἀπόλλων.
> καὶ δὲ πουλυκτέανος· Πυθῶνί κε τεκμήραιο.

Apollo's *garment* is golden, and his *cloak* fastening,
and his *lyre*, and his Lyctian *bow and quiver*
his sandals too are *golden*; Apollo is *rich in gold*
and *rich in flocks*. You would find proof of this in Pytho.

Three cases of internal parallelism appear in this passage. Thus "garment" (A1) parallels "cloak" (A2), "lyre" (B1) parallels "bow and quiver" (B2), and "golden" (C1) matches "rich in gold" (C3). Synonymous parallelism continues in the passage with "rich in gold" (C), which the poet follows with "rich in flocks (literally rich in possessions)" (D). It is possible that "Pytho" in D also parallels "rich in gold" (C), as Pytho was famed for the richness of its treasury. Finally, we note that lines C and D also form a chiastic parallelism. Again, internal parallelism appears in biblical poetry but has not been identified in Egyptian poems.

HYMN 2.38–41

αἱ δὲ κόμαι θυόεντα πέδῳ λείβουσιν ἔλαια·
οὐ λίπος Ἀπόλλωνος ἀποστάζουσιν ἔθειραι,
ἀλλ᾽ αὐτὴν πανάκειαν· ἐν ἄστεϊ δ᾽ ᾧ κεν ἐκεῖναι
πρῶκες ἔραζε πέσωσιν ἀκήρια πάντ᾽ ἐγένοντο.

His *hair drips* fragrant *oils* upon the ground.
Apollo's *hair* does not *drip* the *oils of fat*,
but the essence of *healing*. And in whatever town those
drops might fall to the ground, everything is *free from harm*.

Synonymous parallelism occurs between κόμαι ("hair") (A) and ἔθειραι ("hair") (B), ἔλαια ("oil") (A) and λίπος ("fat") (B), and between λείβουσιν ("drip") (A) and ἀποστάζουσιν ("drip") (B). Chiastic parallelism obtains by way of πανάκειαν ("healing") (C) and ἀκήρια ("free from harm") (D).

HYMNS 2.43–46

κεῖνος ὀϊστευτὴν ἔλαχ᾽ ἀνέρα, κεῖνος ἀοιδὸν
(Φοίβῳ γὰρ καὶ τόξον ἐπιτρέπεται καὶ ἀοιδή),
κείνου δὲ θριαὶ καὶ μάντιες· ἐκ δέ νυ Φοίβου
ἰητροὶ δεδάασιν ἀνάβλησιν θανάτοιο.

That one has received the *archer* as his lot, and the *singer*
(for to Apollo is entrusted the *bow* and *song*),
and his are *diviners* and *prophets*. And from Phoebus
doctors have learned the postponement of death.

In this passage "archer" (A) parallels "bow" (B) and "singer" (A) goes with "song" (B). Similarly, the "diviners" and "prophets" in C, who were sought to ascertain the divine will, find a parallel in "doctors" in D as another profession. Each is a case of synonymous parallelism. The anaphoric quasi-polyptoton involving κεῖνος thus brings these four lines together: Apollo is in charge of not only music and archery but also prophecy and even cures for death![81]

HYMN 2.50–54

ῥεῖά κε βουβόσιον τελέθοι πλέον, οὐδέ κεν αἶγες
δεύοιντο βρεφέων ἐπιμηλάδες, ᾗσιν Ἀπόλλων
βοσκομένησʼ ὀφθαλμὸν ἐπήγαγεν· οὐδʼ ἀγάλακτες
οἴιες οὐδʼ ἄκυθοι, πᾶσαι δέ κεν εἶεν ὕπαρνοι,
ἡ δέ κε μουνοτόκος διδυμητόκος αἶψα γένοιτο.

Effortlessly would the *herd increase*, and the *nanny goats*
pastured with the *sheep* would *not lack young*, if Apollo
cast his eye upon them while they were grazing. The *ewes*
would *not lack milk, nor*
were they barren, but all would *have lambs beneath them*.
And whoever was the *mother* of one *offspring* would soon
produce *twins*.

The synonymous parallelisms in this passage build upon the theme of Apollo as provider of fertility. All five of the lines reference animals: "herd" and "nanny goat" (A), "sheep" (B), "ewes" (C), "lambs" (D), and "offspring" and "twins" (E). Each of the lines also refers to the flocks' productivity: "increase" (A), "not lack young" (B), "not lack milk" (C), "not barren" (D), and again, "offspring" and "twins" (E). In addition, the mention of each animal having "lambs beneath them" in the D-line naturally parallels the "mother" in the E-line.

HYMN 55–59

Φοίβῳ δʼ ἑσπόμενοι πόλιας διεμετρήσαντο
ἄνθρωποι· Φοῖβος γὰρ ἀεὶ πολίεσσι φιληδεῖ
κτιζομένησʼ, αὐτὸς δὲ θεμείλια Φοῖβος ὑφαίνει.
τετραέτης τὰ πρῶτα θεμείλια Φοῖβος ἔπηξε
καλῇ ἐν Ὀρτυγίῃ περιηγέος ἐγγύθι λίμνης.

---

[81] Is it possible that the ἰὴ of ἰητροί (D) calls to mind ἰὴ ἰὴ φθέγγεσθε above and ἰὴ ἰὴ Καρνεῖε πολύλλιτε (80) and ἰὴ ἰὴ παιῆον below (97)?

> Men *lay out the foundations of cities* following Phoebus.
> For Phoebus always takes pleasure in *cities being built*,
> and Phoebus himself *weaves together foundations*.
> Phoebus was four years old when he first *fitted together foundations*
> in fair Ortygia near the round lake.

Synonymous parallelism informs this passage as well. Note how the A-line's πόλιας διεμετρήσαντο ("lay out the foundations of cities") is followed in lines B through C with πολίεσσι/κτιζομένησ' ("cities being built"). The C-line builds upon these parallels with θεμείλια ("foundations") and ὑφαίνει ("weaves together"). In turn, the D-line concludes with θεμείλια ("foundations") and ἔπηξε ("fitted together"). One also wonders whether the use of τετραέτης in line 58 provides a numerical equivalent for the fourfold mention of Phoebus in this passage. Such numerical allusions are well attested devices in Egyptian and biblical poetry.[82]

HYMN 2.60–64

> Ἄρτεμις ἀγρώσσουσα καρήατα συνεχὲς αἰγῶν
> Κυνθιάδων φορέεσκεν, ὁ δ' ἔπλεκε βωμὸν Ἀπόλλων,
> δείματο μὲν κεράεσσιν ἐδέθλια, πῆξε δὲ βωμόν
> ἐκ κεράων, κεραοὺς δὲ πέριξ ὑπεβάλλετο τοίχους.
> ὦδ' ἔμαθεν τὰ πρῶτα θεμείλια Φοῖβος ἐγείρειν.

> Hunting continually, Artemis brought him the *heads* of Cynthian goats,
> and Apollo *wove* an *altar*;
> he *constructed* the *foundations* with *horns*, and *fitted* the *altar* from *horns*, and he *built up walls* of *horn* around it.
> In this way Phoebus first learned to raise *foundations*.

Here the καρήατα ("heads") of the goats (A) parallel βωμόν ("altar") (B), i.e., the place on which they are to be offered. In B, ἔπλεκε ("wove") parallels δείματο ("constructed") and πῆξε ("fitted") in line C. βωμόν

---

82 Noegel 2021:207–210, 266–270.

("altar") (B) parallels βωμόν and ἐδέθλια ("foundations," literally "shrines") in the C-line. Line D then parallels the previous line's δείματο and πῆξε with ὑπεβάλλετο ("built up") and ἐδέθλια with τοίχους ("walls") and twice repeats the "horns" of line C. All the cases here illustrate synonymous parallelism except for the repetition of horns, which constitutes staircase parallelism. The latter appears in biblical poetry but has not been found in Egyptian poems.

HYMN 2.69–71

> ὤπολλον, πολλοί σε Βοηδρόμιον καλέουσι,
> πολλοὶ δὲ Κλάριον, πάντη δέ τοι οὔνομα πουλύ·
> αὐτὰρ ἐγὼ Καρνεῖον· ἐμοὶ πατρώιον οὕτω.

> O Apollo, many call you *Boedromios,*
> Many *Clarius,* and indeed everywhere many a name is yours.
> But I call you *Carneius,* for thus is my ancestral custom.

This priamel also constitutes staircase parallelism that is based on three successive names associated with Apollo: Boedromios, Clarius, and Carneius. The device concludes by characterizing the calling of Apollo's names as an ancestral custom. The parallelism involving names is similar to the first biblical example cited above (Ps 29:3–5), in which "Yahweh" parallels his epithet "the God of glory."[83]

The hymn contains at least eight different types of parallelism: synonymous, antithetic, chiastic, internal, forked, staircase, synonymous, and verbatim, with synonymous parallelism being by far the most frequently employed. It is worth emphasizing that internal and staircase parallelism are features unknown to Egyptian poetry but occur often in the Hebrew Bible.

After this point in the poem, Callimachus no longer employs parallelism. What follows is the narrative of the foundation of Cyrene that moves, slightly but decidedly, from the divine to the human plane and features the movement from Sparta to Thera to Cyrene and the local celebrations of the god. Moreover, the focus is on Greek colonization and its establishment of a Hellenic cult in Libya. Evocation of

---

[83] See also Num 24:4, where El parallels Shaddai.

the cult of Apollo in Delphi brings us back to Greece proper. All this is Hellenocentric. Based on the sudden disappearance of parallelism, it almost feels as if Callimachus, wittingly or unwittingly, moved away from a Near Eastern mode of composition as he entered a fully Hellenic context.

IV. THE *HYMN TO APOLLO* IN THE LIGHT OF ANCIENT EGYPTIAN RELIGIOUS TRADITIONS

Scholars of Hellenistic poetry have come to acknowledge Callimachus's use of subjects and themes that multivalently speak to both Greek and Egyptian textual and iconographic religious traditions. Most prominent among them are the identification of Apollo with Horus and the depictions of the Ptolemaic kings as the sun god, both of which were facilitated by the spread of the cult of Harpokrates (Egyptian *ḥr pꜣ ḫrd* "Horus the child").[84] Stephens's observation that the "bee" alludes to the Egyptian hieroglyphic sign 𓆤 meaning "king of Lower Egypt" is another example of the phenomenon.[85] Selden too has made a strong case for connecting the hymn's references to Apollo as the founder of cities to Egyptian traditions that cast Horus as the architect of palaces and temples.[86] We also have seen above that the ambiguity of *Hymn* 2.26–27 allows Callimachus's audience to conflate the Ptolemaic king and Apollo, and thus, identify him as Ra incarnate. In an Egyptian context, such a fusion is reflected in the name *ḥr-rꜥ* "Horus-Ra."[87] To this growing body of evidence we add the following observations.

HYMN 2.9

> ὠπόλλων οὐ παντὶ φαείνεται, ἀλλ' ὅτις ἐσθλός·
>
> Apollo does not φαείνεται upon everyone, but upon
> whoever is good.

---

[84] As Selden 1998:392 notes: "... the surviving artifacts suggest that his cult provided a strategic link between the Greek and Egyptian populations of the empire, particularly vis-à-vis the crown, and one of the purposes of Callimachus' *Hymn* was surely to help articulate that connection."

[85] Stephens 2015:68.

[86] Selden 1998:393.

[87] Leitz 2002–2003: vol. 5, 271.

We have seen already that the verb φαείνεται means both "shine upon" and "appear to" and that both work in the immediate context. What has not been observed is that both meanings also apply perfectly to the Egyptian sun god and pharaoh. In fact, both the appearance and illumination of Ra and the pharaoh can be expressed in a single word *ḫʿ*, usually translated "appear in glory," and written with the hieroglyph of the rising sun (⌂). Since the Egyptian king was understood as the sun god made flesh, texts that describe him use language that draws on solar imagery. Thus, Amenhotep III is *nṯr nfr mity rʿ sḥḏ tꜣ.wy mi ꜣḫ.ty nb st.wt m ḥr mi itn ḫᶜᶜ.w n=f nb.wt*, "The good god, likeness of Ra, who illuminates the Two Lands like the One-of-the-Horizon, Lord of Rays in the face (of whom) like the sun disk, everyone rejoices."[88] Seti I is the *šw n rḫy.t* ("Sun of the common people").[89] Ramesses II is described as *qꜣ rn pḥ.n=f ḥr mi rʿ* ("lofty of name, he has reached heaven like Ra").[90] Elsewhere he is *rʿ n tꜣ sḥḏ n=sn itn ṯhn n rḫy.t ʿnḫ=sn m mꜣꜣ st.wt=f* ("Ra of the land who illuminates them, gleaming sun disk of the common people who live by seeing his rays").[91] Pharaoh Merneptah is said to be *rʿ n kmt itn psḏ.t pḏ.wt* ("Ra of Egypt, sun disk of the Nine Bows [i.e., Egypt's traditional enemies]").[92] Indeed, one of the commonest epithets for the pharaoh is that of *sꜣ rʿ* "son of Ra" who *wbn m ꜣḫ.t* "rises on the horizon." Therefore, Callimachus's use of a verb that combines Apollo's appearance with his illumination is also fitting from an Egyptian perspective. Moreover, the verb goes well with the repeated use of the epithet φοῖβος (seventeen times), which recalls the divine sun as *ḥr-ḫʿ* "Horus the Shining/Appearing One."[93]

HYMN. 2.32–35

χρύσεα τὠπόλλωνι τό τ' ἐνδυτὸν ἥ τ' ἐπιπορπίς
ἥ τε λύρη τό τ' ἄεμμα τὸ Λύκτιον ἥ τε φαρέτρη,

[88] Sethe 1906–1909:1670, lines 7–8.
[89] Kitchen 1968–1990: vol. 1, 240, line 14.
[90] Kitchen 1968–1990: vol. 2, 236, lines 10–12.
[91] Kitchen 1968–1990: vol. 2, 236, line 2.
[92] Kitchen 1968–1990: vol. 4, 89, line 8.
[93] Leitz 2002–2003: vol. 5, 278. See also Horus's epithets: *ḥr-ʿꜣ-iꜣḫw* "Horus Great in Luminosity" and *ḥr-wpš* "Horus the Luminous One" (Leitz 2002–2003: vol. 5, 247, 249).

χρύσεα καὶ τὰ πέδιλα· πολύχρυσος γὰρ Ἀπόλλων
καὶ πουλυκτέανος·

Apollo's garment is golden, and his cloak fastening,
and his lyre, and his Lyctian bow and quiver.
His sandals too are golden; Apollo is rich in gold
and rich in flocks.

Of interest here is the identification of the light-giving Apollo as bedecked in gold. No less than three times in this brief passage we hear some form of χρυσός. Stephens suggests that the gold

> marks Apollo as the sun god, which in turn accounts for his beneficence to flocks in the following lines, but the statues were often painted with gold, and here the drape, pin, bow, quiver, lyre, and sandals are all objects that might easily have been gilded.[94]

From an Egyptian perspective, gods are consistently described as having gold skin, but it is Horus who is known as the *nbw* ("Golden One").[95] Ra-Horakhty also is called the *nbw-mꜣꜥ-ḥꜥw=f* ("One Whose Limbs are Gold") and the *wnb-ḥr-bꜣ=f-m-ḥrt-hrw* ("Golden One Who Soars in the Sky Daily").[96] So closely was Horus tied to gold that pharaohs possessed a *rn n nbw* "name of gold" also known as a "Gold Horus" name, because it was written with the Horus falcon standing atop the hieroglyph for gold (🦅).[97]

Of additional interest in this passage is Apollo's expertise with the bow (also in line 44). While this image certainly fits within Greek tradition, an Egyptian might have just as easily thought of Horus, who is sometimes depicted on healing cippi as he wages war with a bow and arrow against the serpent Apep (more on Apep below).[98] Pharaoh

---

[94] Stephens 2015:88.
[95] Leitz 2002–2003: vol. 4, 178.
[96] Leitz 2002–2003: vol. 4, 179, 185.
[97] Schenkel 1977.
[98] Ritner and Scalf 2019:199, figs. 18–19. The cippi contain magical spells against Apep. For images and descriptions of the cippi, see Allen 2005:51, 53.

too, as Horus incarnate, is frequently depicted on temple reliefs as a master archer.[99] Moreover, line 11 gives Apollo the epithet Ἑκάεργε ("One Who Acts from Afar"), about which Stephens states:[100]

> Ancient commentators derive Apollo's epithet, Ἑκάεργε ("Far-worker"), either from his prowess as an archer, shooting arrows from afar (ἑκάς), or to the fact that as the sun god his life-giving rays work from afar. Callimachus exploits both meanings as the hymn continues: Apollo is the god of abundant nature (47–54) and the slayer of the Delphic Pytho with his arrows (97–104).

What makes Ἑκάεργε especially potent in this context, despite the primary association of the epithet with Apollo from Homer on, is that it also is a Pythagorean term meaning "nine."[101] In Egyptian, the word for this number (*psḏ.t*) denotes several things beyond just the cardinal. First, *psḏ.t* can refer to the "Nine Bows," which is a literary and artistic trope that refers to pharaoh's traditional enemies on all sides. One writes *psḏ.t* with the bow sign (⌒), sometimes with nine of them, a fitting image for the archer Apollo.[102] By extension, the "Nine Bows" express the cosmological reach of pharaoh's power in all directions. Hence, his title inscribed at the temple of Horus at Edfu: *ḥry-tp pḏ. wt-psḏ.t-m-ȝḫ.t*, "Head of the Nine Bows of the Horizon."[103]

However, *psḏ.t* also can refer to the Ennead, the group of nine primordial deities who emanated from the sole creator and self-created Atum. These gods were responsible for the creation of the universe and included Osiris and Isis, the parents of Horus.[104] This sense of Ἑκάεργε is also reflected in the Pythagorean conception of the number nine:

---

[99] Wilkinson 1991.

[100] Stephens 2015:84.

[101] Waterfield 1988:106–107 translates Iamblichus *Theol. Ar.* 78 with the rather puzzling definition: it is called Ἑκάεργε "because it prevents the voluntary progress of number." We thank John Dillon, whom we consulted on Iamblichus. He also referred us to Waterfield's translation.

[102] Also read as *pḏ.wt-psḏ.t* ("Nine Bows").

[103] Leitz 2002–2003: vol. 5, 393.

[104] Leitz 2002–2003: vol. 3, 133–163.

"At any rate, as regards the word, it is probably a riddling reference to affinity and equivalence, in the sense that it is called 'ennead' as if it were the 'henad' of everything within it, by derivation from 'one.'"[105] Indeed, according to the Pythagoreans "... it is by no means possible for there to subsist any number beyond the nine elementary numbers. Hence they called it 'Oceanus' and 'horizon,' because it encompasses both of these locations and has them within itself."[106] Compare this with the reference to the *psḏ.t ꜣḫt.yt* ("Ennead of the Horizon") on a wall at the temple of Dendara.[107]

Finally, the word *psḏ.t* can mean "illumination," especially in reference to Horus.[108] Though not written with the bow determinative(s), it is suggested by way of homophony with *psḏ.t* "nine." It appears as an epithet for the "Eye of Horus" in Greco-Roman times: *psḏ.t-m-wḫꜣ*, "that which shines in the dark."[109] Both "illumination" and the "bows" come together in a Hymn to Amun-Re, in which the faithful says of the god: *psd-m-dwꜣ.w shḏ.n=k sn-wri* ("brighter in the morning, you lit the great ocean").[110] Thus, Callimachus's reference to Apollo as Ἑκάεργε works on multiple Greek and Egyptian levels.

HYMN 2.36

καὶ μὲν ἀεὶ καλὸς καὶ ἀεὶ νέος·

And indeed he is ever fair and ever young.

The twofold description of Apollo is equally applicable to Horus, who is also beautiful and forever young. Regarding the former, we may cite his epithets *ḥr-nfr* ("Horus the Beautiful"),[111] *ḥr-nfr-n-psḏ.t* ("Beautiful Horus of the Nine [i.e., Ennead]"),[112] *ḥr-nfr-n-nbw* ("Beautiful Horus of Gold"),[113]

---

[105] Waterfield 1988:105.

[106] Waterfield 1988:105.

[107] Leitz 2002–2003: vol. 3, 136.

[108] Leitz 2002–2003: vol. 3, 118.

[109] Leitz 2002–2003: vol. 3, 130.

[110] Papyrus Chester Beatty IV (= Papyrus BM EA 10684), Recto: 10,11.

[111] Leitz 2002–2003: vol. 5, 264–265.

[112] Leitz 2002–2003: vol. 5, 265.

[113] Leitz 2002–2003: vol. 5, 265.

and *ḥr-nfr-n-nbwt* ("Beautiful Horus, the Golden").[114] Regarding the god's perpetual youth, we note the following: *ḥr-rnpy* ("Horus the Young") and the epithet *rnpy-ḏt* ("Young of Eternity").[115]

HYMN 2.50–52

ῥεῖά κε βουβόσιον τελέθοι πλέον, οὐδέ κεν αἶγες
δεύοιντο βρεφέων ἐπιμηλάδες, ᾗσιν Ἀπόλλων
βοσκομένῃσ' ὀφθαλμὸν ἐπήγαγεν·

Effortlessly would the herd increase, and the nanny goats pastured with the sheep would not lack young, if Apollo cast his eye upon them while they were grazing.

Two features in this passage speak to both Greek and Egyptian religious traditions. The first is the description of Apollo in the role of a shepherd. Certainly, one may cite Homeric references to the sun (Helios) as a herdsman.[116] Yet, this trope also works well from an Egyptian perspective, for gods and pharaohs alike are called the shepherds of their people. The *Admonitions of Ipuwer* (12:1) refer to Ra as *mni.w pw n bw nb* ("the shepherd of everyone"). Therefore, humankind are the "cattle of God."[117] A temple inscription of Seti I at Kanais calls the king the *mni.w nfr* ("good shepherd") (Text A:2). It is this tradition that informs the iconographic depictions of pharaoh holding the shepherd's crook. Ra also is called the *mni.w mry.ty* ("loving shepherd")[118] and the *mni.w ʿ3* ("great shepherd"),[119] and at the temple of Edfu Horus is described as *mni.w sšm ḥḥw s3wty* ("shepherd, guardian who leads millions").[120] A

---

[114] Leitz 2002–2003: vol. 5, 265.

[115] Leitz 2002–2003: vol. 5, 272 for the former and Leitz 2002–2003: vol. 6, 684–685 for the latter. Elsewhere he is the *ḥrd* "Child" (Leitz 2002–2003: vol. 6, 49) and *rnpy* "Young" (Leitz 2002–2003: vol. 6, 682–683). See similarly *rʿ-ḥr-p3-ḥrd* "Ra-Horus the Child" (Leitz 2002–2003: vol. 6, 635).

[116] Williams 1978:53.

[117] Helck 1977:1222.

[118] P. Chester Beatty IV, recto, 12,4; Leitz 2002–2003: vol. 3, 297.

[119] P. Chester Beatty IV, recto, 11,12–14; Leitz 2002–2003: vol. 3, 297.

[120] The inscription appears on the first register on the west wall. See Kurth 2004:127, line 74, verses 16–17.

papyrus from the Graeco-Roman era grants Ra-Horakhty the epithet *mni.w nfr nṯr.w rmṯ*, "the good shepherd of gods and humankind."[121] The second multicultural feature in this passage is the reference to Apollo's eye (ὀφθαλμόν) that bestows fertility upon the herds. Though one can cite several passages in Greek literature that identify the sun as an eye,[122] Egyptian texts also are replete with reference to the Eye of Ra and the Eye of Horus. The former is identified with the sun disk, often flanked by wings and a uraeus (𓈖𓇳𓏏), and as such, it is one of the most ubiquitous iconographic images in temple architecture. In religious texts, the Eye often acts independently as one of several goddesses and thus as a female extension of Ra's power. One of these was Hathor, a goddess of love, music, sex, and fertility, often depicted in bovine or partially bovine form.

The Eye of Horus was identified with the moon and healing.[123] In amuletic form, it was known as *wḏꜣ.t* (𓂀), and it was widely used in offerings and rituals for protection and healing.[124] It also was embedded between mummy wrappings as a technology to assist the entrance of the dead into the afterlife. Harpokrates also appears in numerous magical cippi keeping noxious animals at bay. The accompanying inscriptions function to heal snakebites and other ailments. Therefore, Callimachus's reference to Apollo's single eye (instead of "eyes") and its role as guarantor of fertility and healing also fits an Egyptian context.

HYMN 2.100–101

Πυθώ τοι κατιόντι συνήντετο δαιμόνιος θήρ,
αἰνὸς ὄφις.

When you were going down to Pytho a demonic beast met you,
a dire serpent.

---

[121] P. Berlin 3031; Leitz 2002–2003: vol. 3, 297.

[122] Williams 1978:53.

[123] On the rich textual materials relating to Horus, see Broze 1996; Meltzer 2001:119–122. See also Horus's epithet: *sḥd-tꜣ.wy-m-ir.ty=fy*, "Who illuminates the Two Lands with his eyes" (Leitz 2002–2003: vol. 5, 278).

[124] Westendorf 1980:48–51.

Finally, we note that in Egyptian cosmology Ra sailed in his solar boat through the heavens during the day and switched boats to continue his journey through the underworld at night.[125] During the eleventh hour, a giant serpent named Apep (Egyptian ꜥꜣpp, Greek Ἄποφις/Ἀπύφις) threatened the sun god's safe passage, thus putting the entire cosmos at risk. The sun god then pierced Apep, which allowed the boat to continue, permitting the new day to occur at sunrise.[126]

Bolstering the reading of the serpent as Apep is the word ὄφις, which provides a paronomastic reference to Ἄποφις.[127] In Egyptian texts, Apep embodies isf.t "chaos, evil, unrighteousness," the very opposite of mꜣꜥ.t "order, good, righteousness," the cosmic force by which the universe functioned smoothly and kings kept their thrones.[128] Apep's role as an agent of chaos is encapsulated by his epithet "He (who) overthrows."[129] Supporting the reading of the serpent as Apep are the words used to describe the serpent: δαιμόνιος "possessing god-like powers" and αἰνὸς "dread, horrible." In Egyptian texts, Apep is wꜣy "ill-minded," of ḫd ḏw "evil character," ḏw ḏw "most evil," the ḫrwyt "enemy" and sbi "rebel" of Ra.[130] He is filled with nšni "rage" and is a terror to behold.[131] He is "fierce-faced," his four lethal fangs cause dread, and his eye projects evil and spits fire.[132] His appearance is so frightening that

---

[125] Assmann 1995; Hornung and Badawy 1975:350–352.

[126] In the Egyptian textual and iconographic record, the weapon is sometimes a harpoon, but also can be a spear or knife. In the Hymn to Apollo (103), the weapon is called a βέλος, which is translated as "arrow" to fit the context of the bow. However, a βέλος can denote many different projectiles: a dart, sword, axe, even a rock or lightning.

[127] The Septuagint, another product of Ptolemaic Alexandria, also renders the primordial serpent of chaos in Isa 27:1 with ὄφις and δράκων. In the account of the Egyptian magicians (Exod 7:9) we similarly find δράκων for the serpent that came from Moses's staff, though in Exod 4:3 the same serpent is called ὄφις. Though a relatively common word, one wonders here too whether ὄφις was chosen for its closeness to Ἄποφις/Ἀπύφις. This would fit well the Ptolemaic flavor of the Septuagint. See, e.g., Görg 1978. For the Greek translation of the Egyptian word, see Ritner 1993:212n980.

[128] Morenz 2004; Teeter 1997.

[129] i.e., whn=f. Spell 160. They are variant readings of the same passage. See de Buck 1938:379.

[130] Faulkner 1933:76, 89.

[131] Spell 1094. De Buck 1961:376b.

[132] Faulkner 1938:52 translates as "fierce-faced," though the text appears to read ḥꜣw-ḥr, literally "excessive of face." On the other hand, the presence of the pustule

when Ra and his divine hypostases encounter him, their fear paralyzes them and forces Seth to employ magic against him.[133] In short, Apep is a permanent threat to the order of creation.[134] Moreover, the serpent that Apollo killed was a chthonic and primordial creature. Apep too was a primordial monster and his battle with the sun god occurred in the underworld (Egyptian *dwꜣt*). Apollo's killing of Pytho, very Greek in all earlier accounts, takes on an Egyptian potential because of the hymn's geographical, religious, and political context. Like the Greek basileus who is also Pharaoh, the snake is both Pytho and Apep.[135]

V. CONCLUSION

Callimachus's adeptness for weaving Egyptian topics and themes into his poems is by now well known. However, the research presented here suggests that Callimachus went far beyond topic and themes and employed specific devices and structures, in particular, various types of polysemy, paronomasia, and parallelism that were fundamental to Near Eastern poetry.[136] We may see the poet's use of such "Egyptianisms," with Selden, as an act of cultural negotiation, if not reappropriation: "What the *Hymn to Apollo* suggests, then, is that Greek myth supports—or can be

---

determinative (G Aa2) perhaps suggests the reading (w)ḥꜣw-ḥr "sickening of face." See Faulkner 1933:89 (32:16). The description of Apep's fangs reads: *ir ḥfꜣ ꜣꜥ n ꜣꜥpp wnn=f dšr.t r ḏr=f ḥf.t ḥḏ iw ibḥ.wt 4 m r=f psḥw=f s mt=f ḥr-ꜥ*, "As for the great serpent Apep, it is red in its entirety, his belly is white, it has four fangs in its mouth. If he bites a man, he dies" (Brooklyn Papyrus, No. 47.218.48 + 85). See Sauneron 1989. The fangs identify Apep as a cobra. See Bickel 2007. On the serpent's eye, see Spell 414. De Buck 1954:247c refers to the fire-spitting eye (*ir.t wt.t*) of Apep.

[133] Spell 160. De Buck 1938:379.

[134] Hornung and Badawy 1975:351.

[135] Additional evidence that such a double reading was possible comes from Apollonius who offers a similar treatment of the hydra as Apep in his *Argonautika*. See Noegel 2004. It is reasonable to think that both Callimachus and Apollonius were aware of the multivalent possibilities of giant serpent imagery.

[136] Given the complexities of ancient Egyptian and the changes that occur over its three-thousand-year history, those interested in learning the language do best to find a formal setting in a university. Nevertheless, some progress can be made by starting with Middle Egyptian and consulting the following works: Gardiner 1988; Faulkner 1988; Allen 2014a, 2014b; and Junge 2005.

made to support—the Egyptian ideology of kingship, which Callimachus accordingly domesticates for a Greek constituency."[137] Nevertheless, our research also shows that some of these features appear only in biblical poetry. This means that Egyptian religious traditions could not have been his only foreign sources, which likely included some early form of the Septuagint.[138] If this is the case, then what might Callimachus's use of these features mean since they have little to do with Egyptian kingship? Is he merely demonstrating his erudition? Or might he have employed these features as a form of "style-switching," in the same way that biblical stories set in Egypt refer to Egyptian practices and beliefs and employ themes and plot lines found in Egyptian texts? Indeed, we have seen how Callimachus ceased creating parallelisms when his poem turned to Cyrene. Alternatively, might these features represent the sort of blending of traditions that one finds slightly later in the *Greek Magical Papyri* (*PGM*), in which we find Egyptian, Greek, and Jewish divine names and textual references combined in new and highly syncretistic ways?[139] Be that as it may, we hope that we have established that Callimachus incorporated ancient Near Eastern literary modes of expression into his *Hymn to Apollo* in a way that reflects multicultural Alexandria and serves the Ptolemaic project of cultural assimilation.[140]

UNIVERSITY OF WASHINGTON

---

[137] Selden 1998:402. In many ways, this mirrors the sort of reworking of Jewish traditions by Jews writing in Alexandria. See Gruen 1998.

[138] Ironically, Egyptian solar imagery would have a similar impact on the Israelite written and iconographic record. See Stähli 1985; Tigay 1986:95; Taylor 1993; Wiggins 1996; Klingbeil 1999; Shnider 2006, 2016; Lauber 2006; Koch 2012; Whitley 2015; Noegel (forthcoming).

[139] Some of these texts show an awareness of the same Greek traditions found in our hymn. Just to cite a couple examples, in *PGM* I 297–298, and elsewhere, we hear: Ἄναξ Ἀπόλλων ἐλθὲ σὺν Παιήονι. The same hymn refers to the ritual use of his laurel branch. In *PGM* VI 25–26, we find: (φοῖβε) Ἀπόλλον Λητοΐδη ἑκάεργε. See Preisendanz 1928–1931: vol. 1, 14, 198. Though the *PGM* texts come from a slightly later period, it might prove informative to study them for evidence of parallelism.

[140] Many have noted too Callimachus's knowledge of ancient Lydian disputation texts as evidenced in his *Iambi* 4.6–8: "Once upon a time the ancient Lydians say the laurel had a quarrel with the olive on Timolus." Cited in Jiménez 2017:132. For bibliography in support of this view, see Kerkhecker 1999:86n15.

GLOSSARY OF TERMS

Though most of the terms employed in this study are clearly of Greco-Roman origin, they are more often utilized nowadays in studies of ancient Near Eastern literature because of the prevalence of the phenomena that they describe. So, we offer this glossary for the convenience of readers unfamiliar with this scholarship. It is not exhaustive but includes only those terms employed above.

Anaphora is the repetition of a word or phrase at the beginning of successive clauses.

Paronomasia operates *across* word divisions and involves a *dissimilarity in meaning.*

Allusive Paronomasia occurs when a text evokes a word, text, or tradition that does not occur in the present context.

Appellative Paronomasia reflects on the name of a god, person, place, or thing.

Anagrammatic Paronomasia involves the employment of the same consonants as another word but in a different sequence.

Epanastrophe occurs when the author repeats the final syllable of one word or line in the first syllable of the next.

Hendiadic Paronomasia is a paronomastic idiom that combines two words to convey a single idea or action.

Homoeopropheron is a type of paronomasia that employs the repetition of the initial sounds of words.

Polysemy involves *multiple meanings* and/or readings of a word or sign in a *single* context.

Amphiboly (also called "Amphibology") is the employment of an ambiguous morphology or grammatical structure for polysemous effect.

Double entendre is a form of polysemy that employs an idiom or other figure of speech that may be understood in two ways. The first is straightforward and innocuous, whereas the second is usually risqué.

Double Polysemy exploits two words in successive verses, each of which projects multiple meanings.

Multidirectional Polysemy occurs when a single word has two meanings, one of which faces back to a previous line, while the other faces forward to one that follows.

Unidirectional Polysemy employs a polyseme that produces two meanings, both of which face a single direction, either back to a previous line or ahead to one that follows.

Polyptoton is the repetition of a word in a different case, inflection, or voice in the same sentence.

Parallelism (also called "Parallelismus Membrorum") involves the repetition of the same or related semantic information and/or grammatical structures in successive lines or verses. This repetition can occur over two or three lines, and more rarely over more.

Antithetic Parallelism occurs when successive lines are opposite in meaning.

Chiastic Parallelism occurs when the parallels in successive lines appear are reversed (chiastic) order.

Climatic Parallelism combines Synonymous, Staircase, and Synthetic Parallelism.

Forked Parallelism occurs when an A-line offers an initial thought and is followed by a couplet, in which each line begins identically but expands in different ways upon the A-line.

Grammatical Parallelism occurs when the verbal conjugations and syntax of the A- and B-lines are equivalent.

Internal Parallelism occurs when the parallel is achieved within a single verse.

Staircase Parallelism creates a steplike pattern in which some elements from the A-line are repeated in the B-line and others are added to expand the thought.

Synonymous Parallelism occurs when the A-line essentially echoes or mirrors the B-line.

Synthetic Parallelism (called "Formal Parallelism") occurs when the B-line expands or completes the contents found in the A-line.

Verbatim Parallelism involves verbatim repetition in successive lines.

Word pairs are a staple feature of parallelism. The words that constitute pairs are set by convention and can be verbs or nouns. Many word pairs are shared among Northwest Semitic languages.

WORKS CITED

Abbott, Richard. 2011. "Forked Parallelism in Egyptian, Ugaritic and Hebrew Poetry." *Tyndale Bulletin* 62, no. 1:41–64.

Acosta-Hughes, Benjamin, Luigi Lehnus, and Susan A. Stephens, eds. 2011. *Brill's Companion to Callimachus.* Leiden.

Allen, James P. 2005. *The Art of Medicine in Ancient Egypt.* New York.

———. 2014a. *Middle Egyptian: An Introduction to the Language and Culture of Hieroglyphs.* 3rd ed. Cambridge.

———. 2014b. *Middle Egyptian Literature: Eight Literary Works of the Middle Kingdom.* Cambridge.

Assmann, Jan. 1982. "Parallelismus membrorum." *Lexikon der Ägyptologie* 4:900–910.

———. 1995. *Egyptian Solar Religion in the New Kingdom: Re, Amun and the Crisis of Polytheism.* Trans. Anthony Alcock. London.

Avishur, Yitshak. 1984. *Stylistic Studies of Word-Pairs in Biblical and Ancient Semitic Literatures.* Alter Orient und Altes Testament 210. Kevelaer.

Berlin, Adele. 1985. *The Dynamics of Biblical Parallelism.* Bloomington, IN.

———. 1992. "Parallelism." In *The Anchor Yale Bible Dictionary*, vol. 5, ed. D. N. Freedman, 154–162. New York.

Bickel, Susanne. 2007. "Apophis." In *Iconography of Deities and Demons in the Ancient Near East.* Electronic prepublication. https://www.religionswissenschaft.uzh.ch/idd/prepublications/e_idd_apophis.pdf.

Broze, Michèle. 1996. *Les aventures d'Horus et Seth dans le Papyrus Chester Beatty I: Mythe et roman en Égypte ancienne.* Leuven.

Buck, Adriaan de. 1938. *The Egyptian Coffin Texts.* Vol. 2, *Texts of Spells 76-163.* Oriental Institute Publications 49. Chicago.

————. 1954. *The Egyptian Coffin Texts*. Vol. 5, *Texts of Spells 355–471*. Oriental Institute Publications 73. Chicago.

————. 1961. *The Egyptian Coffin Texts*. Vol. 7, *Texts of Spells 787–1185*. Oriental Institute Publications 87. Chicago.

Burkert, Walter. 1992. *The Orientalizing Revolution: Near Eastern Influence on Greek Culture in the Early Archaic Age*. Cambridge, MA.

Calame, Claude. 1993. "Legendary Narration and Poetic Procedure in Callimachus' *Hymn to Apollo*." In *Callimachus*, Hellenistica Groningana 1, ed. M. Annette Harder, Remco F. Regtuit, and Gerry C. Wakker, 37–55. Groningen.

Cameron, Alan. 1995. *Callimachus and His Critics*. Princeton.

Clauss, James J. 1985. "Allusion and Structure in Horace *Satire* 2.1: The Callimachean Response." *TAPA* 115:197–206.

————. 2019. "The Near Eastern Background of Aetiological Wordplay in Callimachus." In *Callimachus Revisited: New Perspectives in Callimachean Scholarship*, Hellenistica Gronigana 24, ed. Jacqueline J. H. Klooster, M. Annette Harder, Remco F. Regtuit, and Gerry C. Wakker, 65–96. Leuven.

Codrignani, Giancarla. 1958. "L''aition' nella poesia greca prima di Callimaco." *Convivium* 26, no. 5:527–545.

Dick, Bernard F. 1968. "Ancient Pastoral and the Pathetic Fallacy." *Comparative Literature* 20, no. 1:27–44.

Donald, Trevor. 1966. *Parallelism in Akkadian, Hebrew, and Ugaritic*. PhD diss., University of Manchester.

Dornseiff, Franz. 1936. "Ägyptische Liebeslieder, Hoheslied, Sappho, Theokrit." *Zeitschrift der Deutschen Morgenländischen Gesellschaft* 90, no. 3/4:589–601.

Fantuzzi, Marco. 2011. "Speaking with Authority: Polyphony in Callimachus' Hymns." In *Brill's Companion to Callimachus*, ed. Benjamin Acosta-Hughes, Luigi Lehnus, and Susan A. Stephens, 429–453. Leiden.

Faulkner, Raymond O. 1933. *The Papyrus Bremner-Rhind (British Museum No. 10188)*. Bibliotheca Aegyptiaca 3. Bruxelles.

————. 1938. "The Bremner-Rhind Papyrus: IV." *Journal of Egyptian Archaeology* 24:41–53.

————. 1988. *A Concise Dictionary of Middle Egyptian*. Reprint. Oxford.

Firchow, Otto. 1953. *Grundzüge der Stilistik in den Altägyptischen Pyramidentexten. Untersuchungen zur ägyptischen Stilistik 2.* Berlin.

Foster, John L. 1977. *Thought Couplets and Clause Sequences in a Literary Text: The Maxims of Ptah-hotep.* Toronto.

———. 1980. "Sinuhe: The Ancient Egyptian Genre of Narrative Verse." *Journal of Near Eastern Studies* 39, no. 2:89–117.

Fraser, Peter M. 1972. *Ptolemaic Alexandria.* 3 vols. Oxford.

Gantz, Timothy. 1993. *Early Greek Myth: A Guide to Literary and Artistic Sources.* Baltimore, MD.

Gardiner, Alan. 1988. *Egyptian Grammar: Being an Introduction to the Study of Hieroglyphs.* 3rd ed. Oxford.

Görg, Manfred. 1978. "Ptolemäische Theologie in der Septuaginta." In *Das ptolemäische Ägypten: Akten des internationalen Symposions 17–29 September 1976 in Berlin,* ed. Herwig Maehler and Volker M. Strocka, 177–185. Mainz.

Gruen, Erich S. 1998. *Heritage and Hellenism: The Reinvention of Jewish Tradition.* Berkeley, CA.

Harder, M. Annette. 2012. *Callimachus. Aetia: Introduction, Text, Translation and Commentary.* 2 vols. Oxford.

Helck, Wolfgang. 1977. "Hirt." *Lexikon der Ägyptologie* 2:1222.

Hornung, Erik, and Alexander Badawy. 1975. "Apophis." *Lexikon der Ägyptologie* 1:350–352.

Jay, Jacqueline E. 2010. "Parallelism in the Correspondence between Senwosret I and Sinuhe." *Studien zur Altägyptischen Kultur* 39:165–189.

Jiménez, Enrique. 2017. *The Babylonian Disputation Poems: With Editions of the Series of the Poplar, Palm and Vine, the Series of the Spider, and the Story of the Poor, Forlorn Wren.* Culture and History of the Ancient Near East 87. Leiden.

Junge, Friedrich. 2005. *Late Egyptian Grammar: An Introduction.* Trans. David Warburton. 2nd Eng. ed. Oxford.

Kerkhecker, Arnd. 1999. *Callimachus' Book of Iambi.* Oxford.

Kitchen, Kenneth A. 1968–1990. *Ramesside Inscriptions: Historical and Biographical.* 8 vols. Oxford.

Klingbeil, Martin. 1999. *Yahweh Fighting from Heaven: God as Warrior and as God of Heaven in the Hebrew Psalter and Ancient Near Eastern Iconography*. Orbis Biblicus et Orientalis 169. Göttingen.

Koch, Ido. 2012. "The 'Chariots of the Sun' (2 Kings 23:11)." *Semitica* 54:211–219.

Kugel, James L. 1981. *The Idea of Biblical Poetry: Parallelism and Its History*. New Haven, CT.

———. 1984. "Some Thoughts on Future Research into Biblical Style: Addenda to the Idea of Biblical Poetry." *Journal for the Study of the Old Testament* 9, no. 28:107–117.

Kurth, Dieter. 2004. *Edfou VII, Die Inschriften des Tempels von Edfu, Abteilung I. Übersetzungen, Band 2*. Wiesbaden.

Lauber, Stephan. 2006. *"Euch aber wird aufgehen die Sonne der Gerechtigkeit" (vgl. Mal 3,20): Eine Exegese von Mal 3,13–21*. Arbeiten zu Text und Sprache im Alten Testament 78. St. Ottilien.

Leitz, Christian. 2002–2003. *Lexikon der ägyptischen Götter und Götterbezeichnungen*. 8 vols. Orientalia Lovaniensia Analecta 110–116, 129. Leuven.

Meltzer, Edmund S. 2001. "Horus." In *Oxford Encyclopedia of Ancient Egypt*, ed. Donald B. Redford, vol. 2:119–122. Oxford.

Montanari, Franco, ed. 2015. *The Brill Dictionary of Ancient Greek*. Leiden.

Morenz, Ludwig D. 2004. "Apophis: On the Origin, Name, and Nature of an Ancient Egyptian Anti-God." *Journal of Near Eastern Studies* 63, no. 3:201–205.

Nagy, Gregory. 1979. *The Best of the Achaeans: Concepts of the Hero in Archaic Greek Poetry*. Baltimore, MD.

Noegel, Scott B. 2004. "Apollonius' *Argonautika* and Egyptian Solar Mythology." *Classical World* 97, no. 2:123–136.

———. 2021. *"Word Play" in Ancient Near Eastern Texts*. Ancient Near East Monograph Series 26. Atlanta, GA.

———. Forthcoming. "Eyelids of the Dawn." In *Biblical Job in the Literary Network of the Ancient Near East*, ed. Andreas Johandi, Kasion-Publikationen zur ostmediterranen Antike, Münster.

Preisendanz, Karl. 1928–1931. *Papyri Graecae Magicae: Die griechischen Zauberpapyri*. 2 vols. Leipzig.

Ritner, Robert K. 1993. *The Mechanics of Ancient Egyptian Magical Practice.* Studies in Ancient Oriental Civilization 54. Chicago.

Ritner, Robert K., and Foy Scalf. 2019. "Anubis, Archer Figures, and Demotic Magic." *Göttinger Miszellen* 259:185–212.

Robert, André, and Raymond Tournay. 1963. *Le Cantique des Cantiques: Traduction et commentaire.* Paris.

Sauneron, Serge. 1989. *Un traité égyptien d'ophiologie: Papyrus du Brooklyn Museum no. 47.218.48 et. 85.* Bibliothèque Générale 11. Cairo.

Schenkel, Wolfgang. 1977. "Horus." *Lexikon der Ägyptologie* 3:14–25.

Segert, Stanislav. 1983. "Parallelism in Ugaritic Poetry." *Journal of the American Oriental Society* 103, no. 1:295–306.

Selden, Daniel L. 1998. "Alibis." *Classical Antiquity* 17, no. 2:289–412.

Sethe, Kurt. 1906–1909. *Urkunden des ägyptischen Altertums.* Vol. 4, *Urkunden der 18. Dynastie.* Parts 1–16. Leipzig.

Shnider, Steven. 2006. "Psalm XVIII: Theophany, Epiphany Empowerment." *Vetus Testamentum* 56, no. 3:386–398.

———. 2016. "The Winged Sun Disc in Psalm 18." *Revue Biblique* 123, no. 3:438–442.

Stähli, Hans-Peter. 1985. *Solare Elemente im Jahweglauben des Alten Testaments.* Fribourg.

Stephens, Susan A. 1998. "Callimachus at Court." In *Genre in Hellenistic Poetry,* Hellenistica Groningana 3, ed. M. Annette Harder, Remco F. Regtuit, and Gerry C. Wakker, 167–185. Groningen.

———. 2002. "Egyptian Callimachus." In *Callimaque: Sept Exposés Suivis de Discussions; Vandoeuvres-Genève, 3-7 Septembre 2001,* Entretiens sur l'Antiquité classique 48, 235–270. Geneva.

———. 2003. *Seeing Double: Intercultural Poetics in Ptolemaic Alexandria.* Hellenistic Culture and Society 37. Berkeley, CA.

———. 2015. *Callimachus. The Hymns.* Oxford.

Streck, Michael P. 2007. "Der Parallelismus membrorum in den altbabylonischen Hymnen." In *Parallelismus membrorum,* Orbis Biblicus et Orientalis 224, ed. Andreas Wagner, 167–181. Fribourg.

Tait, W. John. 1980. "Letter from the Priests of Aphrodite to Apollonios." In *Greek and Demotic Texts from the Zenon Archive: P. L. Bat. 20,* ed. Pieter W. Pestman, Papyrologica Lugduno-Batava 20, 188-194.

Taylor, John G. 1993. *Yahweh and the Sun: Biblical and Archaeological Evidence for Sun Worship in Ancient Israel.* Sheffield.

Teeter, Emily. 1997. *The Presentation of Maat: Ritual and Legitimacy in Ancient Egypt.* Studies in Ancient Oriental Civilization 57. Chicago.

Tigay, Jeffrey H. 1986. *You Shall Have No Other Gods: Israelite Religion in the Light of Hebrew Inscriptions.* Harvard Semitic Monographs 31. Atlanta, GA.

Tov, Emanuel. 2001. *Textual Criticism of the Hebrew Bible.* 2nd ed. Minneapolis, MN.

Waterfield, Robin, trans. 1988. *The Theology of Arithmetic: On the Mystical, Mathematical and Cosmological Symbolism of the First Ten Numbers; Attributed to Iamblichus.* Grand Rapids, MI.

Watson, Wilfred G. E. 1984/1986. *Classical Hebrew Poetry: A Guide to Its Techniques.* Journal for the Study of the Old Testament: Supplement Series 26. Sheffield.

———. 1985. "Internal Parallelism in Classical Hebrew Verse." *Bib* 66, no. 3:365–384.

———. 1989. "Internal or Half-Line Parallelism in Classical Hebrew Again." *Vetus Testamentum* 39, no. 1:44–66.

West, Martin L. 1997. *The East Face of Helicon: West Asiatic Elements in Greek Poetry and Myth.* Oxford.

Westendorf, Wolfhart. 1980. "Horusauge." *Lexikon der Ägyptologie* 3:48–51.

Whitley, John B. 2015. "הפיע in Amos 4:13: New Evidence for the Yahwistic Incorporation of Ancient Near Eastern Solar Imagery." *Journal of Biblical Literature* 134, no. 1:127–138.

Wiggins, Steve A. 1996. "Yahweh: The God of Sun?" *Journal for the Study of the Old Testament* 21, no. 71:89–106.

Wilkinson, Richard H. 1991. "The Representation of the Bow in the Art of Egypt and the Ancient Near East." *Journal of the Ancient Near Eastern Society* 20:83–99.

Williams, Frederick. 1978. *Callimachus: Hymn to Apollo; A Commentary.* Oxford.

UCALEGON AND THE GAULS

AENEID 2 AND THE *HYMN TO DELOS* REVISITED

ROBERT COWAN

J AMES DIGGLE HAS RECENTLY OBSERVED, with admirable brevity, that Aeneas's statement that his (or possibly Deiphobus's) "neighbor Ucalegon was burning" (*proximus ardet / Vcalegon*) alludes to the almost identical phrase γείτονος αἰθομένοιο in Callimachus's *Hymn to Delos*. He suggests that there is therefore no need to posit, with Fraenkel, a common Ennian antecedent for the Virgilian phrase and its doublet in Horace (*paries cum proximus ardet*).[1] Diggle is surely right about the Callimachean allusion, though accepting it does not necessarily exclude the Ennian one. However, the brevity of Diggle's note means that his only comment on the echo's intertextual significance is that the Callimachean phrase occurs "also in the context of an enemy incursion."[2] This observation, though important, scarcely does justice to the level of allusive engagement one would expect when one of the most learned of Roman poets echoes the paragon of Alexandrian *doctrina*. This article will show that the engagement is both more extensive and more significant than Diggle's note gave him space to explore and that it is enriched and complicated by further engagement with the *Iliad* and the *Homeric Hymn to Apollo*.

This article was researched and written during a period of leave granted by the University of Sydney Faculty of Arts and Social Sciences Special Studies Programme in 2021, for which I am very grateful. I am indebted to *HSCP*'s anonymous reader for their helpful comments and suggestions. I retain responsibility, of course, for all remaining errors and flights of fancy.

[1] Diggle 2020, citing Verg. *Aen.* 2.311–312, Callim. *Hymn* 4.180, Hor. *Epist.* 1.18.84, Fraenkel 1957:319n1. "Whether *p[roximus]* means 'next to Aen[eas]', or 'next to Deiph[obus]', or both is not, need not be, clear" (Horsfall 2008:265).

[2] Diggle 2020:905.

I. TWO INTERTEXTS AND THEIR CONTEXTS

Virgil's detailed and sophisticated intertextuality with Callimachus's poetry—undoubtedly far more extensive than the fragmentary survival of all but the *Hymns* and *Epigrams* allows us to judge—is well known and needs little rehearsal here. Scholars have, moreover, identified several places where the *Aeneid* engages in a complex and ideologically charged manner with the *Hymn to Delos* itself and particularly with Apollo's second prophecy, in which the phrase γείτονος αἰθομένοιο occurs. On the smallest scale, Anchises' poignant apostrophe of the shade of Augustus's nephew and possible heir-apparent, *tu Marcellus eris,* gains added poignancy from its similarity to and crucial difference from Apollo's ἐσσόμενε Πτολεμαῖε: he will be Marcellus, but he will not "be his best self"; he will not fulfill his kingly potential as Ptolemy Philadelphus will.[3] Panning out, Hunter has suggested that the prophecy of the Callimachean Apollo as a whole significantly influenced that of the Virgilian Jupiter in *Aeneid* 1.[4] Most extensively, Barchiesi's discussion of Apollo's prophecy on Delos at *Aeneid* 3.73–98 demonstrates how the "constellation of Apollo, Delos, the Ptolemies, Cos, and Alexandria is a model for the constellation of Apollo, Delos, the Julians, Troy and Rome, and Callimachus helps the *Aeneid* to shape a dynastic project through time and geography."[5] Particularly pertinent for the current discussion is Barchiesi's observation of how Apollo's virtual quotation of *Iliad* 20.307–308 is embedded in and accessed through the wider Callimachean allusion.[6] Virgil's depiction of the sack of Troy engages, with a similar degree of complexity and ideological significance, with Callimachus's "prediction" of the Gallic attack on Delphi.

---

[3] Verg. *Aen.* 6.883; Callim. *Hymn* 4.188; Acosta-Hughes and Stephens 2012:239; Stephens 2015:211; 2018:105–106. This apostrophe of Ptolemy occurs a mere three lines after the end of Apollo's "prediction" of the Gallic attack on Delphi.

[4] Hunter 2006:53.

[5] Barchiesi 1994:438, building on Heyworth 1993's treatment of the presence of the *Hymn to Apollo* in the same passage; cf. Miller 2009:103–111.

[6] Barchiesi 1994:441.

Before we explore the relationship between the two passages, we should quote them more fully and put them into context.[7] The Virgilian passage follows Aeneas's visitation by the ghost of Hector and his subsequent response to the sounds of the Greek attack, which is compared to a herdsman hearing the noise of a bushfire or flash flood (2.309–317):

> tum uero manifesta fides, Danaumque patescunt
> insidiae. iam Deiphobi dedit ampla ruinam
> Volcano superante domus, iam proximus ardet
> Vcalegon; Sigea igni freta lata relucent.
> exoritur clamorque uirum clangorque tubarum.
> arma amens capio; nec sat rationis in armis,
> sed glomerare manum bello et concurrere in arcem
> cum sociis ardent animi; furor iraque mentem
> praecipitat, pulchrumque mori succurrit in armis.

> Then indeed the proof was clear, and laid bare were the
> Danaans'
> tricks. Now the house of Deiphobus, substantial as it was,
> collapsed
> as Vulcan overcame it, now his neighbor burned,
> Ucalegon; the Sigean straits reflect the fire far and wide.
> There arises both the yell of men and the blare of trumpets.
> Weapons I mindlessly grab; and there is insufficient reason in
> weapons,
> but my heart burns to gather a band for war and to charge to
> the citadel
> with my comrades; frenzy and rage drive my mind
> headlong, and it occurs to me that it is glorious to die in arms.

The Callimachean passage is from the fetus of Apollo's second prophecy *in utero*, in which he urges his mother Leto not to give birth to him on Cos, because Ptolemy II is destined to be born there and will defeat the Gauls in Egypt as Apollo himself will at Delphi. A brief description

---

[7] The text of Virgil is Conte 2019, of Callimachus Stephens 2015, of Homer West 2000, and of the *Homeric Hymns* Richardson 2010. All translations are my own.

of the Gauls, comparing them in number to snowflakes or stars, is
followed by a lacuna of two lines before the text resumes as follows
(*Hymn* 4.178–185):

... καὶ πεδία Κρισσαῖα καὶ Ἡφαί[στο]ιο φάρ[αγγ]ες
ἀμφιπεριστείνωνται, ἴδωσι δὲ πίονα καπνόν
γείτονος αἰθομένοιο, καὶ οὐκέτι μοῦνον ἀκουῇ,
ἀλλ' ἤδη παρὰ νηὸν ἀπαυγάζοιντο φάλαγγας
δυσμενέων, ἤδη δὲ παρὰ τριπόδεσσιν ἐμεῖο
φάσγανα καὶ ζωστῆρας ἀναιδέας ἐχθομένας τε
ἀσπίδας, αἳ Γαλάτῃσι κακὴν ὁδὸν ἄφρονι φύλῳ
στήσονται·

... and the plains of Crisa and the glens of Hephaestus
are crowded round on all sides, and they see substantial smoke
of a burning neighbor, and no longer only by report,
but already by the temple they see phalanxes
of hostiles, already beside my tripods
swords and shameless baldrics and loathed
shields, which will set up an evil road for the Galatians
that mindless tribe.

Before discussing the two intertexts' relationship, we must first address
some issues surrounding the context of this second passage.

Although the general context is perfectly clear, the two-line lacuna
in the manuscripts between lines 176 and 178 makes some details
uncertain. Unfortunately, lines 177a–177b are also badly damaged in
POxy 2225, leaving only the incomplete words παιδ[and δωρι[at the
start of the respective lines and even less illuminating scraps toward
their ends. The content of these lines has provoked a degree of contro-
versy. Pfeiffer suggested that the lines referred to the septennial
Septerion festival, which included a procession by Dorian youths (the
truncated παῖδ[ες ... Δωρί[ης) to Tempe, bringing back a laurel wreath
for use in the Pythian games.[8] Mineur objected that the timing of that
procession in summer 278 did not match the traditional dating of the
Gallic attack to winter 279/278, a dating supported by the equally

8   Pfeiffer 1953:24.

traditional snowstorm—divine or natural—that helped to foil it.[9] He suggested as an alternative that the παῖδες are more metaphorical "sons of the Greeks," designating defenders of the Delphic sanctuary, and that δωρι[conceals a reference to the region of Doris.[10] However, Bing argued in turn that the chronological problem could be solved if the Dorian procession were depicted as leaving Delphi at the time of the attack rather than returning to it from Tempe.[11] More importantly, he showed that Callimachus would have had a good poetic reason for manipulating the chronology (one of Mineur's objections), since the Septerion commemorated and even reenacted Apollo's victory over Python, a key mythic parallel for his victory over the Gauls.[12]

It remains possible that lines 177a–177b contained other phrases echoed in *Aeneid* 2. The παῖδες performing the Septerion ritual perhaps might be connected with the Trojan boys and unmarried girls singing ritual songs around the wooden horse as it is dragged into Troy.[13] In addition, one feature of the Septerion ritual mentioned by Bing—the burning of a hut representing Python's lair by youths—could resonate with Callimachus's "burning neighbor."[14] More importantly, *POxy* 2225 makes clear that the παῖδες, whether processing youths or sons of Greece, are the subject of ἴδωσι and they, not the late-born Titans of line 174, saw the rich smoke of the burning neighbor. From this it can be inferred that the smoke comes from the embers of a city sacked by the Gauls rather than, as earlier critics assumed, the altars of Delphi.[15] This inference is further supported by the phrase's echo of the Homeric ἄστεος αἰθομένοιο ("burning city," *Il.* 21.523), which will be discussed below. From the more detailed narratives of the Gallic expedition, the most probable candidate for the burning neighbor is the Aetolian city of Callion. Pausanias narrates its destruction at some length, specifying

---

[9] Mineur 1979, 1984:172–173.
[10] Mineur 1979:126.
[11] Bing 1988:129–130n67, restated and endorsed by Ukleja 2005:241–244.
[12] Bing 1988:130–131.
[13] *pueri circum innuptaeque puellae / sacra canunt*, 2.238–239.
[14] Bing 1988:130–131, citing Ephorus *FGrHist* 70 F 31b = Strabo 9.422 and Plut. *De def. orac.* 417e–418d.
[15] Cahen 1961:272 translates, "la grasse fumée sur les autels du dieu voisin," but also admits that the lacunae and the oracular style make the sense unclear.

that the Gauls burnt the city (ἐνέντες πῦρ ἐς τὸ Κάλλιον, Paus. 10.22.6), slaughtered men, raped women, and even cannibalized babies.[16] The name of Callion may or may not have already been sufficiently established in the traditions about the Gallic attack to come to the minds of Callimachus's readers. Nevertheless, it is clear that the "burning neighbor" to which he refers is either Callion itself or a city that was similarly sacked and burnt.[17] It is equally clear that, in the minds of Virgil's readers, this forges a connection with Ucalegon's burning house in the sack of Troy.

II. BEYOND THE BURNING NEIGHBOR: FURTHER ECHOES

The echo of γείτονος αἰθομένοιο in *proximus ardet* is the most direct point of contact between the two passages, but it is by no means the only one. Moreover, the prominence of this clear correspondence sensitizes the reader to other connections. She is particularly cued to think of the phrase that completes line 180 and thus stands in an intertextually privileged position: καὶ οὐκέτι μοῦνον ἀκουῇ. Echoes of this phrase in Aeneas's narrative will then have particular resonance. As noted, his first intimations of the sack are purely and explicitly auditory: *diuerso ... luctu* (2.298), *clarescunt sonitus* (301), *horror* (301, *OLD* s.v. 3b), *arrectis auribus* (303), *accipiens sonitum* (308, of the herdsman in the simile). Line 309 marks a shift from sound to vision, as he no longer only hears far-off noises but sees with his own eyes the burning houses of Deiphobus and Ucalegon.[18] The shift to autopsy is explicitly articulated by *tum uero* and the emphasis on sight underlined by *manifesta fides* and *patescunt*. These phrases correspond to the Callimachean ἀλλ'

---

[16] Paus. 10.22.3–4. Pausanias even offers his own epic parallel, presumably thinking of the alleged cannibalism: Καλλιεῦσι δὲ ... δεινὰ οὕτω παθοῦσιν ὡς μηδὲ τὰ ὑπὸ Ὁμήρου πεποιημένα ἔς τε Λαιστρυγόνας καὶ ἐς Κύκλωπα ἐκτὸς εἶναι δοκεῖν ἀληθείας ... ("The Callians who endured such terrible sufferings that not even the things attributed by Homer to the Laestrygonians and the Cyclops seem to be beyond the truth ..."), 10.22.7.

[17] For convenience, I shall refer to Callion and the Callians throughout, but the argument stands if Callimachus is referring to another sacked town whose name has not survived or even to an emblematic but nonspecific one.

[18] "[A] glance is enough to make plain the effect of Sinon's tale, and of the T[rojan] H[orse] as Aen[eas] passes from sounds to sights" (Horsfall 2008:264); "hearing gives way eventually to sight" (Nelis 2015:34).

ἤδη ... ἀπαυγάζοιντο, while expanding the underlying idea of καὶ οὐκέτι μοῦνον ἀκουῇ to cover the range of threatening noises that Aeneas, the tenor of the simile, and his vehicle the herdsman "only heard" in the preceding lines.[19] The Callimachean original is wittily—though, of course, not humorously—adapted, since ἀκουῇ is most naturally taken as meaning "by report," "by hearsay," or "by stories that they had heard" rather than, as it is expansively glossed in the *Aeneid*, "by the invisible sounds of warfare that they had heard."[20] At the same time, Aeneas has also just "heard" that Troy was burning from the ghost of Hector.[21] Indeed, Virgil may be playing an even more elaborate game, since Aeneas used the phrase *Danaum insidiae* earlier, when introducing Sinon into the narrative, to invite Dido and the Carthaginians to "hear now the tricks of the Danaans" (*accipe nunc Danaum insidias*, 2.65). Now, with the vivid *enargeia* of his description, his audience can imagine that it is no longer experiencing these tricks only by hearing (οὐκέτι μοῦνον ἀκουῇ) but that they are visible before its eyes (*Danaumque patescunt / insidiae*).

Sensitized by these more prominent echoes, the reader may also notice other, subtler correspondences.[22] The phrase πίονα καπνόν is a striking and unexpected one. The *iunctura* is unique in extant Greek. In a different context it could conceivably—if boldly—evoke κνῖσα (the smoke arising from the burnt fat of a sacrifice), and that was indeed how it was taken before the discovery of *POxy* 2225. In the

---

[19] Aeneas's reintroduction of the sonic dimension in 2.313 (*exoritur clamorque uirum clangorque tubarum*) does not undermine the connection since, if any reader wishes to press the details hard, Callimachus's οὐκέτι μοῦνον positively suggests that the παῖδες continued to hear the Gauls *as well as* beginning to see them.

[20] Incidentally, these details about hearsay and autopsy in Callimachus's narrative sit awkwardly with Bing's solution to the chronological objection in having the παῖδες set off for, rather than return from, Delphi, but his thematic justification for a more radical distortion of the timeline still stands.

[21] 2.289–295. I am indebted to *HSCP*'s anonymous reader for this excellent point.

[22] It is tempting to imagine some connection between the metonymic Vulcan who overwhelms Deiphobus's house (*Aen.* 2.311) and the glens of Hephaestus that may be crowded round on all sides (Ἡφαί[στο]ιο φάρ[αγγ]ες, *Hymn* 4.178). However, the reading of line 178 is much contested, with many rival suggestions threatening to displace Hephaestus (see Bousquet 1973), and in any case the mismatch of the two references to the god (metonymic/topographical, hostile/defensive) would make it a very subtle and complex allusion indeed.

context of burning Callion, however, it demands to be read differently. Its very uniqueness is a reflection of its oxymoronic quality. Smoke is axiomatically insubstantial, thin, anything but πίων. Patroclus's ghost is "like smoke" (ἠΰτε καπνός, *Il.* 23.100), and the scholia gloss this as "on account of its being thin and airy" (διὰ τὸ λεπτὸν καὶ πνευματῶδες, Σ bT ad loc.). The Cloud chorus inspires Strepsiades to "quibble about smoke" (περὶ καπνοῦ στενολεσχεῖν, Ar. *Nub.* 320) "because," the scholia explain, "smoke is thin and feeble and weak" (στενὸς γὰρ καὶ ἀμενηνὸς καὶ ἀσθενὴς ὁ καπνός, Σ RM ad loc.).[23] The word that the reader is more likely to find πίων qualifying at the end of a hexameter is δῆμος, in the sense of land or community. It does so five times in the *Iliad* (plus once after the medial diaeresis), five times in the *Odyssey*, twice in the *Theogony*, and once in the *Homeric Hymn to Artemis* (referring, as it happens, to Delphi).[24] Callimachus takes the early epic formula, with its connotations of wealth, fertility, and amplitude, and turns it to smoke, just as the Gauls do to Callion. The πίων δῆμος is reduced to πίων καπνός, an obliteration so complete that the δῆμος is erased from the landscape and from the poem.

In *Aeneid* 2, the reference to Deiphobus's *domus* as *ampla*, though less striking, is a sufficiently arbitrary detail to stand out and encourage the reader to look for some more-than-surface significance. As commentators have noted (or rather implied), the juxtaposition of *ampla* with *ruinam* emphasizes the totality and magnitude of the collapse: even though the house was large and magnificent, it still fell and fell in its entirety.[25] A large house becomes a large fire, and as it collapses (*ruinam*) it will be reduced to no more than a large cloud of smoke. Virgil does not spell out that there will be *amplus fumus* where Deiphobus's house once stood, just as Callimachus does not mention that Callion was once a πίων δῆμος. Rather, he learnedly indicates

---

[23] Cf. the tragic topos of the doubly insubstantial "shadow of smoke" (καπνοῦ σκιά): Aesch. fr. 399.2 Radt; Soph. *Ant.* 1170, *Phil.* 946.

[24] Line end: *Il.* 16.437, 514, 673, 683, 20.385; *Od.* 13.322, 14.329, 17.526, 19.271, 399; Hes. *Theog.* 477, 971; Hom. *Hymn Art.* 14. After medial diaeresis: *Il.* 5.710.

[25] This seems to be the implication of the elusive observations of Austin 1964:140 ("The juxtaposition of *ampla* with *ruinam* is good") and Horsfall 2008:264 ("A substantial residence, and the placing of the adj. suggests that it is, all of it, in flames").

his awareness of what Callimachus has left unsaid. Virgil presents his reader with the substantial property (perhaps with a further nod toward πίονα οἶκον at *Od.* 9.35, which corresponds even more closely to *ampla ... domus*) and leaves her to supply the Callimachean smoke that it will become. Only later, looking back, will Aeneas see "the whole of Neptune's Troy smoking from the ground" (*omnis humo fumat Neptunia Troia*, 3.3).[26]

III. TROY, CALLION, ROME, DELPHI, ACTIUM

This extensive engagement with Callimachus's description of the Gallic attack on Delphi, and particularly on Callion, invites Virgil's reader to make connections between it and the Greek sack of Troy that go well beyond the broad similarity that both are "in the context of an enemy incursion." The defeat of the Gauls at Delphi was memorialized, appropriated, and exploited for a wide range of political ends by Aetolians, Alexandrians, Pergamenes, and others in festivals, poetry (perhaps including Callimachus's own elegiac *Galatea*), and art, most famously the great Pergamene altar.[27] Readers have long understood Gallomachy's importance to the ideological imagery of the *Aeneid*, as well as its parallelism with Gigantomachy and Titanomachy, a correspondence explicitly anticipated in Callimachus's description of the Gauls as ὀψίγονοι Τιτῆνες ("late-born Titans," 174).[28] Incidental references to Romans defeating Gauls pepper the *Heldenschau*, and there is one reciprocal mention of the Gallic victory at the Allia.[29] However, the Gauls' most prominent appearance is on the shield of Aeneas (8.652–666), which represents their repulsion from the Capitol in 390 BCE. The implicit parallelism in Augustan culture between this (partial) victory over Gallic barbarians and the Gauls' defeat at Delphi a century later

---

[26] "Each word contributes to the picture of utter destruction: the whole city has been levelled to the ground and reduced to smoke" (Heyworth and Morwood 2017:84). Cf. Sen. *Tro.* 17: *omnisque late fumat Assaraci domus.* Horsfall 2006:41 adds Aeschylean and Euripidean parallels.

[27] Nachtergael 1977; Weber 1993:303–311; Marszal 2000; Barbantani 2001; Rebeggiani 2018:69–72.

[28] Hardie 1986:120–143.

[29] Decii: 6.824; Torquatus and Camillus: 6.825; Marcellus: 6.855–859; Allia: 7.717.

can be inferred, not only from the retrojection of the name of the Galatian commander Brennus onto the conqueror of Rome but also from the ideologically charged depiction of the Delphic victory on the doors of the Temple of Palatine Apollo, as alluded to by Propertius.[30]

In the *Hymn to Delos*, the parallel (ξυνός τις ἐλεύσεται ἄμμιν ἄεθλος, 171) between Apollo's victory over the Gauls at Delphi and Ptolemy Philadelphus's suppression of the revolt by Gallic mercenaries on the Nile has clear political implications, as the Galatians' "defeat in Greece and in Egypt is seen as righting the cosmic order."[31] In the *Aeneid*, the parallelism of the Roman victory over the Gauls in 390 and that of the young Caesar at Actium is less explicit, but, triangulated with that at Delphi—in both its Attalid and Ptolemaic reception—its implications are no less clear: "The sequence of danger triumphantly averted, followed by ceremonial celebration, is shared with the final, Augustan, scenes of the Shield, a correspondence which reinforces the parallelism between the Gallic assault on the Capitol and the Battle of Actium."[32]

However, both narratives of Gallomachy, as well as that of cataclysmic civil war preceding the Augustan Golden Age, are sequences, not simply of danger triumphantly averted but also of disaster and destruction actually suffered—the burning of Callion, the capture of Rome, the fratricidal battles of Pharsalus, Philippi, and many others—and followed by miraculous rebirth and a rise to greatness.[33] Indeed, if one accepts Horsfall's argument, recently revived by Herbert-Brown, that the shield of Aeneas alludes to (at least one version of) the Ennian tradition whereby the Capitol was captured by the Gauls, then

---

[30] *altera* [sc. *ualua*] *deiectos Parnasi uertice Gallos*, Prop. 2.31.13. On the Temple of Palatine Apollo, with further bibliography, see Pandey 2018:83–141, esp. 92–108 on Prop. 31/32, and 99–101 on the Gauls.

[31] Barbantani 2011:181. The parallel victories also correspond to the similarly cosmic defeats of Python by Apollo and, as part of the depiction of Ptolemy as manifesting Pharaonic virtues, of Seth by Horus: Bing 1988:130–134; Stephens 2003:117–119. In addition, Ukleja 2005:250–251 notes similarities between the Gauls and the Scythians of *Hymn to Artemis* 251–258, while Giuseppetti 2012:486–489 parallels the Persian attack on Delphi in 480.

[32] Hardie 1986:125. Cf. "the episode is chosen as an instance of the city and state of Rome surviving extreme danger" (Harrison 1997:72).

[33] Cf. Morgan 1998, 1999 on "constructive destruction," though his emphasis is more on the acknowledgment of the brutal violence inflicted than on the suffering endured.

·

it depicts total, unaverted disaster, leading only later to recovery and supremacy.[34] The fall of Troy leading to the rise of Rome is of course the most important example of this arc in the *Aeneid*. It is in this respect that Callimachus's destruction of Callion, which precedes Apollo's triumph at Delphi, parallels Virgil's sack of Troy, which precedes Aeneas's victory in Latium and the young Caesar's at Actium. The parallelism between the Trojan and the (fourth-century) Gallic sack has been well explored by Kraus but mainly with emphasis on how Livy makes the fall of Rome resemble that of Troy.[35] Virgil's allusion to the *Hymn to Delos*—textually echoing and chronologically foreshadowing, in future reflexive mode—makes the sack of Troy resemble the Gallic sack.[36]

IV. A WINDOW ON THE *ILIAD*

The case for a parallelism between the sacks of Rome and Troy, mediated through that of Callion, is supported by a further allusion. Diggle includes (parenthetically and even more briefly) an additional detail about Callimachus's γείτονος αἰθομένοιο: "(itself echoing Hom. *Il.* 21.523 ἄστεος αἰθομένοιο)."[37] This echo was already noted by Mineur, but he too was content to do no more than note it.[38] An examination of the Homeric phrase's context reveals both that Callimachus's evocation of it was significant and that Virgil's window allusion to *Iliad* 21 through the *Hymn to Delos* creatively annotated the relationship between the Greek texts.[39] The phrase occurs in a simile that comes at the transition from the theomachy back to the human level and Priam's evacuation

---

[34] Horsfall 1981; Herbert-Brown 2019, offering a radical reading in which Virgil glorifies the Gauls throughout the *Aeneid* as, in part, a celebration of his own occluded Gallic identity.

[35] Kraus 1994:274–278.

[36] For future reflexive: Barchiesi 1993. The temporal interplay is further complicated by the Delphic narrative's being an *ex eventu* prophecy by the unborn Apollo, long preceding even the sack of Troy. Sordi 1964 argues for the Gallic attack on Rome as a model for the whole of the Trojan-Latin struggle of the second half of the *Aeneid*.

[37] Diggle 2020:905.

[38] Mineur 1984:174.

[39] On window allusions (a.k.a. window references or double allusions): Thomas 1986:188–189; McKeown 1987:37–45; Cowan 2014.

of the Trojan troops from the plain into the city.[40] While the other gods return bickering to Olympus, Apollo takes measures to ensure that Troy does not fall to the onrushing Achilles before its fated time (*Il.* 21.514–516). The direct intervention of Apollo to defend a beloved city from being sacked provides a contextual link between Homer's Troy and Callimachus's Delphi to complement the verbal echo at line 523. However, the very specification that Apollo is taking care "lest the Danaans sack [Troy] beyond fate <u>on that day</u>" (μὴ Δαναοὶ πέρσειαν ὑπὲρ μόρον ἤματι κείνῳ, 21.517) reinforces for the reader the ineluctable fact that there will be a later day when, in accordance with its fate, Troy will actually fall. The salvation of Delphi and the destruction of Callion are combined in this moment when the very fact of Troy's not falling foreshadows the day when it will.

The sack is adumbrated even more heavily by the astonishing simile that follows (Hom. *Il.* 21.520–525):

αὐτὰρ Ἀχιλλεύς
Τρῶας ὁμῶς αὐτούς τ᾽ ὄλεκεν καὶ μώνυχας ἵππους·
ὡς δ᾽ ὅτε καπνὸς ἰὼν εἰς οὐρανὸν εὐρὺν ἱκάνει
ἄστεος αἰθομένοιο, θεῶν δέ ἑ μῆνις ἀνῆκεν,
πᾶσι δ᾽ ἔθηκε πόνον, πολλοῖσι δὲ κήδε᾽ ἐφῆκεν,
ὣς Ἀχιλεὺς Τρώεσσι πόνον καὶ κήδε᾽ ἔθηκεν.

But Achilles all the same
destroyed the Trojans, both the men themselves and their
single-hoofed horses;
as when the smoke comes up to wide heaven
of a burning city, which the wrath of the gods has sent forth,
and it has laid toil on all, and cast cares on many,
so did Achilles lay toil and cares on the Trojans.

The simile is noteworthy for the lack of distance between its tenor and vehicle. The wrath of the gods imposing toils and cares on the people

---

[40] Tantalizingly, the penultimate exchange in the theomachy is between Hermes and Leto, followed by the latter's gathering of Artemis's fallen bow (21.497–504), but the connection to Callimachus's pregnant Leto is surely too tangential.

of a sacked city (surely Troy) is compared to Achilles imposing toils and cares on the Trojans as he approaches the city and threatens to sack it. The exceptional verbatim repetition of πόνον … κήδε᾽ ἐφῆκεν underlines how near to indistinguishable are the actions, actors, and victims of tenor and vehicle, narrative and simile.[41] Muellner points to the passage's implications for the depiction of Achilles: "[t]he hero with *mēnis* has become a hero *like mēnis*, as the grammatical and verbal parallelism of the last two lines in this passage seem to stress."[42] Others note that the role of the "wrath of the gods" (θεῶν … μῆνις, 523) in the simile matches the reason for Troy's fall and thus marks the sack as an act of divine punishment.[43] However, the comparison most notably constitutes a virtual prolepsis of the sack of Troy, that act which Achilles' onslaught resembles and anticipates, but cannot constitute.[44]

Callimachus's allusion to this simile is no less remarkable. The echo of ἄστεος αἰθομένοιο by γείτονος αἰθομένοιο, which shares the same *sedes* and the context of Apollo defending a city, could draw parallels between the Gallic sack of Callion and the Greek sack of Troy in a fairly bland intertextual manner. However, by alluding to a simile that only implicitly refers to the sack of Troy, he makes his own imitation serve the same connotative function as the source text: his burning Callion is like but is not actually the sack of Troy, just as are the burning ἄστυ in the simile and the routed Trojans whom Achilles pursues. By means of a window allusion to *Iliad* 21 through the *Hymn to Delos*, Virgil too does not merely link the Trojan and Gallic sacks but learnedly signals his apprehension that Callimachus has already made this move in depicting the destruction of Callion.

---

[41] "[T]he repetition is unusual, and may be intended to emphasize the comparison" (Richardson 1993:97).

[42] Muellner 1996:168 (original italics).

[43] Moulton 1977:110–111; Edwards 1987:106; Richardson 1993:97.

[44] "Although the resumptive clause makes clear that the simile is intended to depict Achilleus' slaughter of the Trojans, the vehicle portion focuses our attention not at all on Achilleus but on the sack of Troy, an event that Achilleus helps bring about but in which he does not participate" (Ready 2011:259).

V. WHO CARES ABOUT UCALEGON?

What of Ucalegon, who is, after all, the Virgilian burning neighbor? It seems certain that Virgil is alluding to his sole appearance in the *Iliad* (or indeed anywhere in extant Greek literature) as one of the old men standing alongside Priam on the walls by the Scaean Gate, debating whether to return Helen to the Greeks (*Il.* 3.148). As Bliss has noted, several of the other old men from the teichoscopy also have significant cameos in *Aeneid* 2: Thymoetes (perhaps treacherously) advocates the introduction of the wooden horse into Troy and, in the scene immediately following the one under discussion, Panthus desperately flees with the Penates. Priam's own appearance can scarcely be termed a cameo. Perhaps equally significant is the absence of a cameo by a man paired with Ucalegon in the teichoscopy and, sometimes, with Aeneas as an alleged traitor, Antenor, though he was mentioned by Venus in book 1.[45]

Whether or not Ucalegon was already a speaking name in the *Iliad* (though this too is probable), Virgil is almost certainly either evoking or tendentiously suggesting its etymology from οὐκ ἀλέγων, either "not worrying" or "not regarding."[46] This etymologizing could in turn suggest that Ucalegon is willfully negligent and lacks due anxiety about the enemy threat.[47] As discussed in the appendix below, this is how Horace interprets the name at *Epist.* 1.18.85. The only other extant occurrence of the name Oukalegon (not including Juvenal's allusion to

---

[45] Bliss 1996:51; Thymoetes: 2.32–34; Panthus: 2.318–338; his death is reported at 429–430; Priam: 469–558; Antenor: 1.242–249. The three sons of Laomedon (as they are designated in the identical 20.238), Lampus, Clytius, and Hicetaon, all grouped together in *Il.* 3.147, do not appear in the *Aeneid*, though (presumably a different) Thymoetes, *son* of Hicetaon, is fighting in Latium at *Aen.* 10.123, closely followed by Acmon, son of Clytius (10.128–129), in a cluster curiously redolent of the Homeric teichoscopy.

[46] Speaking name in Homer: Kirk 1985:283; Krieter-Spiro 2015:67; Kanavou 2015:77; in Virgil: Kraggerud 1960:37; Gantar 1971:1–2; Bliss 1996; O'Hara 1996:132; Horsfall 2008:265; Casali 2017:204. *HSCP*'s anonymous reader attractively suggests that there may be a deliberate irony in Virgil's requiring his readers to take so much care in teasing out the many intertextual implications of a passage about the man who does not care, but the level of intertextual complexity here, though high, is far from exceptional in the Virgilian corpus.

[47] Paschalis 1997:107.

Virgil) is as that of a satyr or silen on a sixth-century column krater depicting the return of Hephaestus.[48] Homeric and Virgilian (and, for that matter, Juvenalian) scholars have not to my knowledge mentioned this satyr, doubtless because he is unrelated mythologically to Homer's Trojan elder. However, he does offer further evidence for the name's etymologizing potential, as his careless posture and gaze correspond to its meaning.[49] Alternatively, the Homeric Ucalegon's name could resonate with the phrase θεῶν ὄπιν οὐκ ἀλέγοντες ("those who do not care about the eye of the gods," *Il.* 16.388) to brand him as one of the impious Trojans who failed to honor Zeus Xenios and the will of the other gods by rightfully restoring Helen to Menelaus.[50] Finally, Ucalegon may be set in antithesis with his neighbor Deiphobus, the man who exhibits rational fear of the enemy (δήϊος + φόβος), the pairing demonstrating the indifferent mercilessness of the gods who send all alike to their destruction.[51] Or both may represent the due exaction of divine justice on impious Trojans, since Deiphobus (Helen's third husband) was as guilty of ignoring the will of the gods as Ucalegon.[52]

Unlike the burning city in the simile from *Iliad* 21, the figure of the Homeric Ucalegon standing on the walls by the Scaean Gate appears not to be connected with the Callimachean depiction of the Gallic attack on Delphi. If we accept that Virgil is alluding to the Homeric Ucalegon, this seems not to be a window allusion, or even a combinatorial allusion, but rather a creative juxtaposition of two discrete literary antecedents, producing a new connection between them instead of illuminating an existing one. However, if Virgil is indeed activating the etymological

---

[48] New York 1997.388a–eee. See Moore 2010:30–32 for a detailed description of the satyr.

[49] "[N]o figure bearing the personal name 'I don't care' is more appropriately so called than the silen on the fragmentary New York krater, who relaxes on a cushion, blithely drinking his wine, enjoying the exotic raw flesh that he stole from the maenads, oblivious to the resolution of the Olympian conflict occurring around him" (Hedreen 2016:215); cf. Hedreen 2004:41.

[50] Bliss 1996.

[51] Kraggerud 1960:37.

[52] Bliss 1996. Gantar 1971:5 sees the contrast as between the absent Antenor and the burning Ucalegon: "il timore degli dei, l'ospitalità e la saggezza dell'uno venivano ricompensate mediante la conservazione della casa, mentre l'empietà, l'indifferenza, la spensieratezza dell'altro veniva punita con l'incendio della casa."

implications of Ucalegon's name, then he could possibly, in addition to the allusion to *Iliad* 3, be evoking a passage which contains the phrase οὐκ ἀλέγων and to which Callimachus is already alluding in the *Hymn to Delos*. Just such a passage occurs in the Homeric *Hymn to Apollo*. Readers have long observed Virgil's knowledge of and detailed engagement with the *Homeric Hymns*, in particular the disturbing echoes of the *Hymn to Aphrodite* in the encounter between Aeneas and his disguised mother, and Cacus's imitation of Hermes' tricks in the latter's *Hymn*.[53] Most pertinently for the current argument, Barchiesi has also shown how, by the use of *colitur* at *Aen.* 3.73, Virgil evokes both Leto's prophecy in the *Homeric Hymn to Apollo* that Delos will be honored and that prophecy's fulfilment in the *Hymn to Delos*, triangulating the three poems.[54]

The *Homeric Hymn to Apollo* is widely acknowledged as a privileged intertext for the *Hymn to Delos*.[55] Within it, the speech in which the river-nymph Telphousa disingenuously advises Apollo to build his temple not at her spring but at Delphi instead is a particular model for the fetal Apollo's speech advising Leto to give birth not on Cos but on Delos. As Hunter puts it, Apollo's speech "functions as a positive rewriting of the negative 'not Telphousa, but Delphi' episode."[56] Persuaded by Telphousa's words, the young god travels on toward Delphi (*Hom. Hymn Ap.* 277–286):

ἔνθεν δὲ προτέρω ἔκιες ἑκατηβόλ᾽ Ἄπολλον,
ἷξες δ᾽ ἐς Φλεγύων ἀνδρῶν πόλιν ὑβριστάων,
οἳ Διὸς οὐκ ἀλέγοντες ἐπὶ χθονὶ ναιετάασκον
ἐν καλῆι βήσσηι Κηφισίδος ἐγγύθι λίμνης.
ἔνθεν καρπαλίμως προσέβης πρὸς δειράδα θύων,
ἵκεο δ᾽ ἐς Κρίσην ὑπὸ Παρνησὸν νιφόεντα
κνημὸν πρὸς ζέφυρον τετραμμένον, αὐτὰρ ὕπερθεν
πέτρη ἐπικρέμαται, κοίλη δ᾽ ὑποδέδρομε βῆσσα

---

[53] *Hom. Hymn Aph.*: Olson 2011; Gladhill 2012; *Hom. Hymn Herm.*: Clauss 2016:66–73.
[54] Barchiesi 1994:439n4.
[55] Bing 1988:110–120; Vestrheim 2000:64–65; Ukleja 2005; Klooster 2012:22–29; and see Mineur 1984 and Stephens 2015:159 and 179–232, *passim*.
[56] Fantuzzi and Hunter 2004:355 (chapter authored solely by Hunter). Cf. Giuseppetti 2012:472.

τρηχεῖ· ἔνθα ἄναξ τεκμήρατο Φοῖβος Ἀπόλλων
νηὸν ποιήσασθαι ἐπήρατον εἶπέ τε μῦθον·

From there you went forward, far-darting Apollo,
and you came to the city of the Phlegyans, insolent men,
who live in that land not regarding Zeus
in a lovely glen near the lake of Cephisus.
From there you proceeded rapidly
to the ridge with eager haste,
and you came to Crisa under snowy Parnassus
a spur facing to the west, but from above
a rock hangs over it, and a hollow glen runs underneath
rough; there the lord Phoebus Apollo decided
to make his lovely temple and spoke a speech.

In a privileged intertext, Apollo's journey toward Crisa and on to Delphi parallels (or, if Bing is correct, reverses) that of the Callimachean παῖδες performing the Septerion. On that journey, he performs a literal *praeteritio*—physical, poetic, cultic—passing by the Phlegyans, who neighbor Crisa and who do not regard Zeus.[57]

Callimachus himself may have engaged, learnedly and polemically, with *Hom. Hymn Ap.* 279 elsewhere in his *oeuvre*. At *Aetia* fr. 75.64–66, in the summary of Xenomedes' history of Ceos that concludes the Acontius and Cydippe episode, Callimachus reports that "the old man set down on his writing tablets insolence and death-by-thunderbolt, those sorcerers the Telchines and Demonax who foolishly did not regard the blessed gods (ἐν δ' ὕβριν θάνατόν τε κεραύνιον, ἐν δὲ γόητας | Τελχῖνας μακάρων τ' οὐκ ἀλέγοντα θεῶν | ἠλεὰ Δημώνακτα γέρων ἐνεθήκατο δέλτ[οις]). Callimachus's younger contemporary (or immediate successor) Euphorion and the far later Nonnus preserve a tradition in which the inhabitants of Ceos were not Telchines but Phlegyans.[58] While both the *Homeric Hymn* and the *Aetia* probably

[57] On literal *praeteritio*, see Miller 1986:31 on Leto's passing of possible sites for Apollo's birth at *Hom. Hymn Ap.* 30–44, and more generally Cowan 2011, esp. 161–162n4 for further references.
[58] Euphorion fr. 115 Powell = 105 Lightfoot = Serv. *ad Aen.* 6.618; Nonn. *D.* 18.36–37. *SH* 443 fr. 3.11 = fr. 191 B fr. 3.11 Lightfoot (*POxy* 2526), tentatively assigned to Euphorion,

218   *Robert Cowan*

look back to the description of the cyclopes at *Od.* 9.275–276,[59] the scene may gesture toward and polemically correct the rival tradition in Callimachus's assertion that the inhabitants of Ceos were indeed οὐκ ἀλέγοντες, like the Phlegyans in the *Homeric Hymn*, but were not actually Phlegyans. Whether or not Callimachus is alluding to the *Homeric Hymn* in *Aetia* 3, the close contextual link between Apollo's itinerary after consulting Telphousa and the vision of the youths celebrating the Septerion in the *Hymn to Delos* is itself sufficient to motivate Virgil to signal the connection between the latter two passages. Virgil connects the οὐκ ἀλέγοντες Phlegyans of the *Homeric Hymn* with the burning neighbor of the *Hymn to Delos* by giving his own burning neighbor the *redende Name* Ucalegon.

Virgil connects the Phlegyans and the burning neighbor, but what is the nature of that connection? For the reader who wishes to map one text precisely onto the other, the Phlegyans correspond to the Callians (people living in the vicinity of Delphi) who are destroyed by fire, as the Phlegyans were in various traditions.[60] These in turn correspond most neatly to Ucalegon, the man who is οὐκ ἀλέγων, who lives in the vicinity of Aeneas and who is, along with the house that he metonymically represents, destroyed by fire. Indeed, the association between the Φλεγύαι and the γείτων αἰθόμενος could also play on the former's etymological link (real or imagined) with the verb φλέγειν.[61] However, the wider tradition about the Phlegyans, to which the *Homeric Hymn* clearly gestures with its mention of insolence and impiety, depicts them in terms that correspond far more closely to the invading Gauls than to their Callian victims. The Phlegyans were not only generally hubristic but specifically attacked Apollo's sanctuary at Delphi and

---

also refers to the Phlegyans being (euphemistically) laid to rest: Φλεγύηισι σὺν ἀνδράσιν εὐνηθε[ῖ]σα. Huxley 1965:240–241; Harder 2012:646; but see Fermi 2012 for an argument that the island on which Euphorion locates the Phlegyans in fr. 115 is in fact Euboea.

[59] Richardson 2010:122; Harder 2012:649.

[60] Paus. 9.36.3. Callion lies about 60 km west-northwest of Delphi, whereas Lake Copais in Phocis, which either equates to or is near the λίμνη Κηφισίδος, is approximately the same distance to the east. However, neither Virgil nor Callimachus need be identifying Callion as the actual home of the mythical Phlegyans. Their shared status as Delphi's neighbors is sufficient to connect them.

[61] For the etymology, Fontenrose 1959:25; Kajava 2010.

were as a result destroyed by the direct intervention of the god.[62] The fullest account is in Pausanias, but versions of the story were manifestly current in Augustan Rome.[63] Ovid has Ceyx travel to the oracle at Claros because Phorbas and his Phlegyans make Delphi inaccessible.[64] Although this sounds more like the variant whereby the Phlegyans attacked travelers on their way to Delphi rather than the shrine itself, the epithet *profanus* gestures toward a more directly impious assault. Virgil himself famously places their eponymous king Phlegyas in Tartarus, warning mortals to learn justice and not to disregard the gods, but he gives no indication of the ruler's crime.[65] Servius explains that he burnt Apollo's temple at Delphi in revenge for the god's rape of his daughter Coronis. The motivation is more specific, and it is not clear whether the other Phlegyans helped him, but the attack on Delphi, its divine punishment, and the motif of disrespecting (*temnere* ~ οὐκ ἀλέγειν) the gods are all present and correct. If the *Homeric Hymn*'s οὐκ ἀλέγοντες Phlegyans also correspond to Callimachus's Gauls, how are we to read Virgil's Ucalegon? To answer this question, we must reconsider the whole intertextual relationship between the *Aeneid* and the *Hymn to Delos*, as well as their further intertexts.

Up to this point, I have mostly taken the relationship between Virgil's sack of Troy and Callimachus's sack of Callion as broadly in line with a triumphalist depiction of Gallomachy as the ultimate victory of order over chaos, albeit one that lays more emphasis on the destructive aspect of constructive destruction and on the dangers that are not averted but recovered from on the path to empire. However, that relationship contains more disturbing crosscurrents which many readers could find unsettling. The sustained, immersive, and all-consuming trauma of Troy is thrown into greater relief by the contrast with the fleeting, distant glimpse of the collateral damage at Callion. This makes it hard for the reader to focus on the reassurance that the gods will

---

[62] On the Phlegyans and their complex relationship with Phlegyas, Phorbas, and other figures, see esp. Fontenrose 1959:25–27, with a full list of sources.

[63] Paus. 9.36.2–3.

[64] *nam templa profanus / inuia cum Phlegyis faciebat Delphica Phorbas*, Ov. *Met.* 11.413–414.

[65] *Phlegyasque miserrimus omnis / admonet et magna testatur uoce per umbras: / "discite iustitiam moniti et non temnere diuos,"* 6.618–620.

eventually deliver Aeneas and a select group of Trojans. Callimachus's brief vignette of burning Callion is immediately followed by the reassuring "collapse [of] the temporal framework: the invading army ... are imagined as menacing and simultaneously captive."[66] The Gauls are beside Apollo's temple (παρὰ νηόν, 181) and their weapons beside his tripods (παρὰ τριπόδεσσιν ἐμεῖο, 182), but with the ease and instantaneity of divine (and Pharaonic) action they are defeated the moment they arrive.[67]

In contrast, Virgil's vignette of burning Ucalegon is followed by the breathless entrance of his fellow teichoscopist Panthus, the priest of Apollo of the citadel (*arcis Phoebique sacerdos*, 2.319). The priest slips away from the enemy's weapons rather than setting them up as trophies (*telis ... elapsus Achiuum*, 318); he smuggles the sacred objects away rather than leaving them to stand proud and unscathed beside their daggers (*sacra manu ... trahit*, 320–321) and carries gods that are not conquering, like the Callimachean Apollo, but conquered (*uictosque deos*, 320); and he is out of his mind like the defeated Gauls rather than the delivered Delphians (*amens*, 321 ~ ἄφρονι, 184). Delphi will be delivered, but this is the last day for Troy (324–325) because the gods, so far from defending the city against its impious attackers, have themselves handed it over to them (*ferus omnia Iuppiter Argos / transtulit*, 326–327). Of course, one might interpret the sack of Troy as a Callion writ large, which foretells the *imperium sine fine* already promised by Jupiter and later expanded on in the *Heldenschau*, on the shield, and in the so-called reconciliation of Juno. However, the Trojan apocalypse could as easily be read as a dark inversion of a Delphic victory rather than a poignant harbinger of an Augustan one.

Panthus's declaration that Jupiter has handed everything over to the Greeks also raises the question of roles and identity within the two episodes. It may seem an obvious and even banal point that, in the intertextual mapping of Virgil's Troy onto Callimachus's Callion

---

[66] Stephens 2015:210; Stephens 2003:139 went further in positing a depiction of "the ranks of the defeated enemy as they would be traditionally represented along the temple walls *after* the victory" (original italics).

[67] On this aspect of Egyptian kingship and its reflection in Callim. *Hymn* 1.87–88, see Stephens 2003:112.

and Delphi, the Greeks play the role of the Gauls. However, this is a more ideologically charged inversion than may at first appear. It is not simply that Callimachus's victims become Virgil's aggressors. The political and cosmic connotations of Apollo's and Ptolemy's paired victories over the Gauls are closely and explicitly bound up with their status as victories of Greeks over barbarians. The struggles will come "when against Greeks the late-born Titans raise up their barbarian dagger and Celtic Ares" (ὁππόταν οἱ μὲν ἐφ᾽ Ἑλλήνεσσι μάχαιραν | βαρβαρικὴν καὶ Κελτὸν ἀναστήσαντες Ἄρηα | ὀψίγονοι Τιτῆνες, 172–174). Casting the ordered, civilized Greeks as chaotic, barbarian Gauls thus constitutes a significant inversion. The impiety of the Greek army at the sack of Troy was an established topos, even in Greek literature. Indeed, there may even be a further verbal echo of Callimachus's Gauls in Virgil's depiction of the victorious Greeks, not in book 2 but in book 1. Juno's indignant complaint about Athena's wielding of Jupiter's thunderbolt against Ajax son of Oileus describes the sacrilegious rapist stranded on a rock in the middle of the sea, "breathing out flames" (exspirantem ... flammas, 1.44). Critics have rightly taken this as a polemical riposte to Lucretius's rationalizing claim that this is precisely what the gods do not do to sinners.[68] However, the phrase, especially the prefix, closely resembles Callimachus's description of the Gallic mercenaries killed on an island by Ptolemy, "breathing out [sc. their last breath] in fire" (ἐν πυρί ... ἀποπνεύσαντας, 186). Virgil's "correction" of Lucretius is backed up with corroboration from Callimachus. More broadly, the Gallic-Greek equation can be fitted into the Aeneid's overall strategy of asserting the superiority—both moral and military—of Rome to Greece and aetiologizing its attainment of that superiority, not least through Aeneas's victory over Argive Turnus in the Latian replay of the Trojan War.

However, the Aeneid—and especially book 2—does not preserve clean distinctions, even when it inverts them. Virgil's sack of Troy is a famously confused event, in which both Greeks and Trojans pay the

---

[68] cur quibus incautum scelus auersabile cumquest / non faciunt icti flammas ut fulguris halent / pectore perfixo, documen mortalibus acre ... ? ("Why do [the gods] not see to it that whichever people have not guarded themselves against committing avoidable crime are struck and breathe out the flames of a thunderbolt, their breast pierced, a bitter lesson to mortals ... ?" Lucr. 6.390–392).

penalty with their blood (366–369), where disguise and friendly fire turn resistance into inadvertent civil war (420–430), where civilization and barbarism, piety and impiety, trustworthiness and deception, are ceaselessly contested, claimed, assigned, and denied to each side in turn. In such a maelstrom, the reader cannot straightforwardly map Virgil's Greeks onto Callimachus's impious, barbarian enemies of Greece and Virgil's Trojans, with their notorious barbaric gold (504) and Laomedontian perfidiousness (4.542), onto their Aetolian and Phocian victims. Virgil's Greeks are both civilized and barbaric and so are his Trojans. Both Aeneas and the band (*manum*, 315) of Trojans that he cobbles together to pursue a glorious, futile death are mindless (*amens*, 314), lacking in reason (*nec sat rationis*), burning (*ardent*, 316), and driven headlong by frenzy and rage (*furor iraque*). This mindless band is less like the unfortunate Callians than the mindless tribe (ἄφρονι φύλῳ, 184) of Gauls. With this we come back to Ucalegon. Ucalegon is a victim of impious aggression, a burning neighbor like the Callians. But he is also οὐκ ἀλέγων, like the Phlegyans, those rather different burning neighbors, whose burning was divine punishment for their impious attack on Delphi. Reading *Aeneid 2* with the *Hymn to Delos*, and especially with a further window allusion to the *Homeric Hymn to Apollo*, generates a complex and even contradictory picture which corresponds perfectly to Virgil's presentation of the essential question about the sack of Troy: was it a just punishment for those who did not regard the gods or a barbaric atrocity against an undeserving people (*gentem / immeritam*, 3.1–2) that the gods did not prevent and even assisted?

VI. CONCLUSION

Virgil's engagement with Callimachus's depiction of the sack of Callion in the *Hymn to Delos* enriches and complicates his own depiction of the sack of Troy, as well as adding layers of complexity to the source text. He connects the Gallic sacks of Callion and Rome with the Greek sack of Troy, along with all the ideological associations that Gallomachy, Titanomachy, Gigantomachy, and Pythonomachy carried in Ptolemaic Alexandria and Augustan Rome, while also annotating that Callimachus had already linked Callion and Troy through his allusion to the *Iliad*

21 simile. Less securely, Virgil's inclusion of the figure of Ucalegon from *Iliad* 3 may also evoke the οὐκ ἀλέγοντες Phlegyans from the *Homeric Hymn to Apollo*, who disturbingly resemble both the Callian and Trojan victims and the Gallic and Greek aggressors. The intertextual relationship(s) can be read as part of a teleological narrative of Rome's rise from Trojan disaster to Augustan supremacy but also leaves room to hear some of the *Aeneid*'s famous further voices.

VII. APPENDIX: FRAENKEL'S UNNECESSARY ENNIUS?

What of Fraenkel's passing thought that *Aeneid* 2.311 alluded to Ennius? As has been suggested, Diggle's rejection of Fraenkel's idea on the grounds that Virgil and Horace were alluding to Callimachus instead could be considered a little hasty. The identification of an extant, common model undoubtedly reduces the need to hypothesize a lost one elsewhere, but it does not constitute positive evidence that such an additional intertext did not exist. Is there, then, any good reason to believe Fraenkel's hunch, and does our greater appreciation of the Callimachean intertext make it more plausible or less?

We must first address the significance of the Horatian occurrence of *proximus ardet*, since the existence of two parallel passages prompted Fraenkel's suggestion of a common source. However, the passages are probably not actually parallel and, allowing for the circulation of drafts of the *Aeneid* among the circle of Maecenas well before the publication of *Epistles* 1 in 20 BCE, it seems overwhelmingly likely that Horace is alluding to Virgil rather than that both are to Ennius or Callimachus. Cucchiarelli suggests that, by the time *Epistles* 1 was published, the phrase had already become proverbial for a neighbor in danger, which is just possible, though, even for the instant classic that was the *Aeneid*, it must have taken a little time for its tags to become axiomatic.[69] A direct, marked allusion is surely more likely. Such an allusion is made more likely—and more pointed—by Kenney's acute observation, reported by Mayer, that the well-established etymological interpretation of Ucalegon as οὐκ ἀλέγων (discussed above) neatly fits with

---

[69] Cucchiarelli 2019:495–496.

Horace's advice to Lollius to avoid dangerous friends who can damage him by association, like a burning neighbor whose housefire gains strength if it is "not taken care of" (*neglecta*, 1.18.85).[70] *Aeneid* 2.311–312 therefore seems sufficient in itself to account for the Horatian phrase and the combination of the distinct elements of the burning neighbor motif and the etymology of Ucalegon points very much in that direction. It is not impossible that Horace is also performing a window or combinatorial allusion that encompasses Callimachus and a lost passage of Ennius. However, it is hard to see much intertextual engagement with the *Hymn to Delos*. Any relationship to the *Annales* remains in any case purely speculative. If Horace is alluding directly to Virgil, and not even to Callimachus, we have even less positive impulse to indulge in such speculation.

Even if Horace is alluding solely to Virgil, and Virgil is alluding to Callimachus (and Homer), that still does not rule out the possibility that Virgil is also alluding to Ennius (perhaps himself alluding to Callimachus). Considering the triangulation of Callion, Troy, and Rome that we have seen Virgil creatively constructing, the most obvious candidate for such an Ennian intermediary would be a reference to the Gallic sack of Rome in the *Annales*. The only trace of a narrative treatment from book 4, where the events of 390 would have been located in the chronological sequence of the poem, is the possible assignment of fr. 154–155 Skutsch to Camillus's speech against abandoning Rome. Absence of evidence is not evidence of absence, but it is hard to justify hypothesizing a largely unattested Gallic narrative and then hypothesizing a specific phrase within it. Ennius did refer to the Gallic sack, apparently in an analeptic comparison with the events narrated in *Annales* 7, probably the First Punic War. Virgil probably engaged with this flashback in his description of the Gauls on the shield of Aeneas.[71] He may also have done so in his depiction of the sack of Troy. However, there is little positive reason to think that he did, especially when there is another episode that is more positively attested to have been an intertext for *Aeneid* 2, and it is to this that we now turn.

---

[70] Mayer 1994:253, crediting E. J. Kenney (presumably *pers. comm.*).
[71] On Virgil and fr. 227–228 Skutsch, see Norden 1915:102–110.

Although the equal brevity of Diggle's shorter note and Fraenkel's footnote allows neither the space to raise the issue, the latter's suggestion of an Ennian intertext was probably not totally arbitrary. Servius claimed that Virgil's whole description of the sack of Troy was based on Tullus Hostilius's destruction of Alba Longa, and Norden deduced that Servius means by this Ennius's depiction of Alba's demolition in the *Annales*.[72] More specifically, Servius linked *Aeneid* 2.313, two lines after the "burning neighbor," to Tullus and hence implicitly to Ennius. This at least provides some positive reason to think that there might be another allusion in the close vicinity. Moreover, the phrase *proximus ardet* would fit very neatly the destruction of Rome's neighboring metropolis. Perhaps some such unexpressed idea also lays behind Fraenkel's musing. If—and it remains a highly speculative if—Ennius alluded to Callimachus's burning of Callion in his destruction of Alba, it would color the latter as an impiously barbaric sack. If Servius is right, Virgil retrojected such an interpretation onto Ennius's Alba by imitating it in his Troy.[73] It is just possible that, at *Aeneid* 2.311, Virgil acknowledged that Ennius had already made the same move, signaling this by means of a window allusion to Callimachus that brought the burning neighbor back to a brutal sack.

THE UNIVERSITY OF SYDNEY

WORKS CITED

Acosta-Hughes, Benjamin, and Susan A. Stephens. 2012. *Callimachus in Context: From Plato to the Augustan Poets.* Cambridge.

Austin, R. G. 1964. *P. Vergili Maronis Aeneidos Liber Secundus.* Oxford.

Barbantani, Silvia. 2001. *Φάτις Νικηφόρος: Frammenti di elegia encomiastica nell'età delle Guerre Galatiche; Supplementum Hellenisticum 958 e 969.* Milan.

[72] Serv. *ad* Verg. *Aen.* 2.486; "Zwar ist der Name des Ennius an keiner der beiden Stellen des Servius genannt, aber ... diese Angaben des Servius nur unter der Voraussetzung Sinn haben, wenn dadurch Ennius als das Vorbild Vergils bezeichnet werden sollte." Norden 1915:154, crediting Columna and Merula for the observation.

[73] *Contra* Goldschmidt 2013:176: "in the *Aeneid* the trauma of the destruction of Alba ... is implicitly transferred to the Greeks, while Tullus' proto-civil war ... is silently elided."

————. 2011. "Callimachus on Kings and Kingship." In *Brill's Companion to Callimachus*, ed. Benjamin Acosta-Hughes, Luigi Lehnus, and Susan Stephens, 178–200. Leiden.

Barchiesi, Alessandro. 1993. "Future Reflexive: Two Modes of Allusion and Ovid's *Heroides*." *Harvard Studies in Classical Philology* 95:333–365.

————. 1994. "Immovable Delos: *Aeneid* 3.73-98 and the Hymns of Callimachus." *Classical Quarterly*, n.s., 44:438–443.

Bing, Peter. 1988. *The Well-Read Muse: Present and Past in Callimachus and the Hellenistic Poets*. Göttingen.

Bliss, Francis. 1996. "Ucalegon and the Scaean Gate." *Vergilius* 42:50–54.

Bousquet, Jean. 1973. "Callimaque, Hymne à Délos, v. 178." *Revue des Études Grecques* 86:ix.

Cahen, Émile. 1961. *Callimaque*. 5th ed. Paris.

Casali, Sergio. 2017. *Virgilio. Eneide 2: Introduzione, traduzione e commento*. Pisa.

Clauss, James J. 2016. "The Hercules and Cacus Episode in Augustan Literature: Engaging the *Homeric Hymn to Hermes* in Light of Callimachus' and Apollonius' Reception." In *The Reception of the Homeric Hymns*, ed. Andrew Faulkner, Athanassios Vergados, and Andreas Schwab, 55–78. Oxford.

Conte, Gian Biagio. 2019. *Publius Vergilius Maro. Aeneis: Editio altera.* Berlin.

Cowan, Robert. 2011. "Passing over Cephisos' Grandson: Literal *Praeteritio* and the Rhetoric of Obscurity in Ovid *Met.* 7.350–93." *Ramus* 40:146–167.

————. 2014. "Fingering Cestos: Martial's Catullus' Callimachus." In *Flavian Poetry and Its Greek Past,* ed. Antony Augoustakis, 345–371. Leiden.

Cucchiarelli, Andrea. 2019. *Orazio. Epistole I.* Pisa.

Diggle, James. 2020. "Ucalegon (Verg. *Aen.* 2.311–12) and Other Burning Neighbours." *Classical Quarterly*, n.s., 70:904–905.

Edwards, Mark W. 1987. *Homer: Poet of the Iliad.* Baltimore.

Fantuzzi, Marco, and Richard Hunter. 2004. *Tradition and Innovation in Hellenistic Poetry.* Cambridge.

Fermi, Damiano. 2012. "Un' isola per i Phlegyai: Euph. *CA* fr. 115 e [Apollod.] 3.5.5 (41 W.)." *Lexis* 30:414–431.

Fontenrose, Joseph Eddy. 1959. *Python: A Study of Delphic Myth and Its Origins.* Berkeley.

Fraenkel, Eduard. 1957. *Horace.* Oxford.

Gantar, Kajetan. 1971. "Ucalegonte in Virgilio, Omero e Giovenale." *Atti e memorie della R. Accademia Virgiliana di Mantova* 39:1–6.

Giuseppetti, Massimo. 2012. "Mito e storia nell'*Inno a Delo* di Callimaco." In *Mythe et pouvoir à l'époque Hellenistique,* ed. C. Cusset, N. Le Meur-Weissman, and F. Levin, 469–494. Leuven.

Gladhill, C. W. 2012. "Sons, Mothers, and Sex: *Aeneid* 1.314-20 and the *Hymn to Aphrodite* Reconsidered." *Vergilius* 58:159–168.

Goldschmidt, Nora. 2013. *Shaggy Crowns: Ennius' Annales and Virgil's Aeneid.* Oxford.

Harder, Annette. 2012. *Callimachus. Aetia.* Vol. 2, *Commentary.* Oxford.

Hardie, Philip R. 1986. *Virgil's Aeneid: Cosmos and Imperium.* Oxford.

Harrison, S. J. 1997. "The Survival and Supremacy of Rome: The Unity of the Shield of Aeneas." *Journal of Roman Studies* 87:70–76.

Hedreen, Guy. 2004. "The Return of Hephaistos, Dionysiac Processional Ritual, and the Creation of a Visual Narrative." *Journal of Hellenic Studies* 124:38–64.

———. 2016. *The Image of the Artist in Archaic and Classical Greece: Art, Poetry, and Subjectivity.* Cambridge.

Herbert-Brown, Geraldine. 2019. "Gauls on Top: Provincials Ruling Rome on the Shield of Aeneas." In *The Alternative Augustan Age,* ed. Kit Morrell, Josiah Osgood, and Kathryn Welch, 247–265. Oxford.

Heyworth, S. J. 1993. "'Deceitful Crete: *Aeneid* 3.84ff. and the *Hymns* of Callimachus." *Classical Quarterly,* n.s., 43:255–257.

Heyworth, S. J., and J. H. W. Morwood. 2017. *A Commentary on Vergil Aeneid 3.* Oxford.

Horsfall, Nicholas. 1981. "From History to Legend: M. Manlius and the Geese." *Classical Journal* 76:298–311.

———. 2006. *Virgil. Aeneid 3: A Commentary.* Leiden.

———. 2008. *Virgil. Aeneid 2: A Commentary.* Leiden.

Hunter, Richard L. 2006. *The Shadow of Callimachus: Studies in the Reception of Hellenistic Poetry at Rome.* Cambridge.

Huxley, George. 1965. "Xenomedes of Keos." *Greek, Roman, and Byzantine Studies* 6:235–245.

Kajava, Mika. 2010. "Φλεγυᾶν and the Phlegyans, with a Note on μόρφνος φλεγύας (Hes. *Sc.* 134)." *Arctos* 44:123–132.

Kanavou, Nikoletta. 2015. *The Names of Homeric Heroes: Problems and Interpretations.* Berlin.

Kirk, G. S. 1985. *The Iliad: A Commentary.* Vol. 1, *Books 1-4.* Cambridge.

Klooster, Jacqueline. 2012. "Visualizing the Impossible: The Wandering Landscape in the *Delos Hymn* of Callimachus." *Aitia* 2. http://journals.openedition.org/aitia/420.

Kraggerud, Egil. 1960. "Einige Namen in der *Aeneis*." *Symbolae Osloenses* 36:30–39.

Krieter-Spiro, Martha. 2015. *Homer's Iliad: The Basel Commentary; Book III.* Trans. Benjamin W. Millis and Sara Strack. Berlin.

Marszal, John R. 2000. "Ubiquitous Barbarians: Representations of the Gauls at Pergamon and Elsewhere." In *From Pergamon to Sperlonga: Sculpture and Context*, ed. Nancy T. de Grummond and Brunilde S. Ridgway, 191–234. Berkeley.

Mayer, Roland. 1994. *Horace: Epistles, Book I.* Cambridge.

McKeown, James C. 1987. *Ovid. Amores.* Vol. 1, *Text and Prolegomena.* Liverpool.

Miller, Andrew M. 1986. *From Delos to Delphi: A Literary Study of the Homeric Hymn to Apollo.* Leiden.

Miller, John F. 2009. *Apollo, Augustus, and the Poets.* Cambridge.

Mineur, W. H. 1979. "The Boys and the Barbarians: Some Remarks on Callimachus *H.* 4.77." *Mnemosyne* 32:119–127.

———. 1984. *Callimachus. Hymn to Delos.* Leiden.

Moore, Mary B. 2010. "Hephaistos Goes Home: An Attic Black-Figure Column-Krater in the Metropolitan Museum." *Metropolitan Museum Journal* 45:21–54.

Morgan, Llewelyn. 1998. "Assimilation and Civil War: Hercules and Cacus (*Aen.* 8.185-267)." In *Vergil's Aeneid: Augustan Epic and Political Context*, ed. Hans-Peter Stahl, 175–197. London.

———. 1999. *Patterns of Redemption in Virgil's Georgics.* Cambridge.

Moulton, Carroll. 1977. *Similes in the Homeric Poems*. Göttingen.

Muellner, Leonard. 1996. *The Anger of Achilles: Mênis in Greek Epic*. Ithaca.

Nachtergael, Georges. 1977. *Les Galates en Grèce et les Sôtéria de Delphes: Recherches d'histoire et d'épigraphie hellénistiques*. Brussels.

Nelis, Damien. 2015. "Vergilian Cities: Visions of Troy, Carthage and Rome." In *Cityscaping: Constructing and Modelling Images of the City*, ed. Therese Fuhrer, Felix Mundt, and Jan Stenger, 19–45. Berlin.

Norden, Eduard. 1915. *Ennius und Vergilius: Kriegsbilder aus Roms großer Zeit*. Leipzig.

O'Hara, James J. 1996. *True Names: Vergil and the Alexandrian Tradition of Etymological Wordplay*. Ann Arbor.

Olson, S. Douglas. 2011. "Immortal Encounters: *Aeneid* 1 and the Homeric *Hymn to Aphrodite*." *Vergilius* 57:55-61.

Pandey, Nandini B. 2018. *The Poetics of Power in Augustan Rome: Latin Poetic Responses to Early Imperial Iconography*. Cambridge.

Paschalis, Michael. 1997. *Virgil's Aeneid: Semantic Relations and Proper Names*. Oxford.

Pfeiffer, Rudolf. 1953. *Callimachus*. Vol. 2, *Hymni et Epigrammata*. Oxford.

Ready, Jonathan L. 2011. *Character, Narrator, and Simile in the Iliad*. Cambridge.

Rebeggiani, Stefano. 2018. "Buried Treasures, Hidden Verses: (Re)appropriating the Gauls of Pergamon in Flavian Rome." In *Rome, Empire of Plunder: The Dynamics of Cultural Appropriation*, ed. Matthew P. Loar, Carolyn MacDonald, and Dan-El Padilla Peralta, 69–81. Cambridge.

Richardson, Nicholas. 1993. *The Iliad: A Commentary*. Vol. 6, *Books 21-24*. Cambridge.

———. 2010. *Three Homeric Hymns: To Apollo, Hermes, and Aphrodite*. Cambridge.

Sordi, Marta. 1964. "Virgilio e la storia romana del IV Sec. a. C." *Athenaeum* 42:80-100.

Stephens, Susan A. 2003. *Seeing Double: Intercultural Poetics in Ptolemaic Alexandria*. Berkeley.

———. 2015. *Callimachus. The Hymns*. Oxford.

———. 2018. *The Poets of Alexandria*. London.

Thomas, Richard F. 1986. "Virgil's *Georgics* and the Art of Reference." *Harvard Studies in Classical Philology* 90:171–198.

Ukleja, Karina. 2005. *Der Delos-Hymnus des Kallimachos innerhalb seines Hymnensextetts*. Münster.

Vestrheim, Gjert. 2000. "Meaning and Structure in Callimachus' Hymns to Artemis and Delos." *Symbolae Osloenses* 75:62–79.

Weber, Gregor. 1993. *Dichtung und höfische Gesellschaft. Die Rezeption von Zeitgeschichte am Hof der ersten drei Ptolemäer*. Stuttgart.

West, M. L. 2000. *Homeri Ilias: Volumen alterum rhapsodias XIII–XXIV et indicem nominum continens*. Munich and Leipzig.

AKTIA AND ISAKTIOI AGONES

GREEK CONTESTS AND ROMAN POWER

CHRISTOPH BEGASS

AFTER DEFEATING Marcus Antonius and Cleopatra at Actium, Octavian commemorated his victory by dedicating the area close to the bay in Western Epirus where the sea battle had been fought. In ca. 28 or 27 BC, he joined several smaller towns by a forced *synoikismos* into a new city called Nikopolis[1] and established a new era that started with the date of the victory on September 2.[2] Finally, he founded a festival called τὰ Ἄκτια.[3] All these measures were intended to commemorate and to celebrate the victory which eventually ensured Augustus's sole reign over the Roman Empire.

Epigraphic corpora are abbreviated according to the *AIEGL*'s list; see a full list of abbreviations at the end of this article. I wish to thank the anonymous reviewer for helpful suggestions and Prof. Charlotte Roueché for supplying me with a high-resolution photograph of the Aphrodisias inscription. After this article was accepted for publication, Jean-Yves Strasser's monumental book on the *Mémoires de champions* was published, and I have included references to his study throughout.

[1] Kienast 2009:458n25; Lange 2009:96–106; Spawforth 2012:33–36, 160–162. For the Egyptian Nikopolis cf. Gurval 1995:72–74; Kienast 2009:458n459.

[2] Kienast 2009:247 with n140a; 249n144.

[3] Cf. Langenfeld 1975:238; Lämmer 1986/1987; Gurval 1995:74–81; Klose 1997; Spawforth 2007:384–385; Pavlogiannis, Albanidis, and Dimitriou 2009; Guerber 2009:217–218; Lange 2009:97–98; Calomino 2011:27–40; Blanco-Pérez 2018:13; Strasser 2021:10, 562; not treated, however, by Graf 2015. For the pre-Augustan games in honor of the Actian Apollo, cf. Strabo 7.7.6, 325C: ἤγετο δὲ καὶ πρότερον τὰ Ἄκτια τῷ θεῷ, στεφανίτης ἀγών, ὑπὸ τῶν περιοίκων· νυνὶ δ' ἐντιμότερον ἐποίησεν ὁ Καῖσαρ (I follow Radt's 2002–2011 edition); Habicht 1957:98–109; Sarikakis 1965:146; Lämmer 1986/1987:28; Pavlogiannis, Albanidis, and Dimitriou 2009:81–82, 101; Nielsen 2018:59, 114, no. 17.

I. ACTIAN GAMES IN THE ROMAN EMPIRE

I examine here the Actian games and their impact on Greek agonistics during the first three centuries AD. Due to their prominence, we know much about Actian games in the Eastern Mediterranean, but we lack a comprehensive catalogue.[4] I begin, then, with an overview. Besides the *Aktia* at (1) Nikopolis, Actian games were held in the Greek cities of (2) Perinthos (Thracia),[5] (3) Thessalonike (Macedonia),[6] and (4) Cos;[7] in Asia Minor in (5) Neocaesarea (Pontus),[8] (6) Hierapolis (Phrygia),[9]

---

[4] Leschhorn 1999:40 counted Actian or isactian games in fifteen cities, without offering sources or differentiating between the two types; see also Klose 1997:32, 35. Though far from being complete, the *Lexicon of Greek Coin Inscriptions* offers numismatic evidence (Leschhorn and Franke 2002:33–34). The best account of *Aktia* throughout the empire is still Harl 1987:68–69; the survey by Gurval 1995:78n151, who accepted contested attestations while dismissing reliable sources, is problematic.

[5] *I.Perinthos* 31 (*IGR* 1.802; Strasser 2021:375–376, no. 154), line 2: Ἄκτια ἐν Περίνθῳ. *I.Perinthos* 30, lines 3–4: ἀγωνοθετήσαντα | [τῶν μεγάλων] οἰκουμενικῶν Ἀκτίω[ν]; *I.Ephesos* 2072, line 9 (Strasser 2021:213–214, no. 81, line 10): Ἄκτια ἐν Περίνθῳ; Robert 1970:20 = 1989a:661 = 2007:259 (Strasser 2021:343–344, no. 137), line 19: Ἄκτια ἐν Περίνθῳ β΄; Adak 2016:178 (Strasser 2021:363, no. 146), line 16, with Adak's commentary (181). The contest's name is restored in *I.Ancyra* 1.146, lines 16–17 (Strasser 2021:349–350, no. 140, lines 15–16): [Ἄκτια?] ἐν | Περίνθῳ ε΄; the numismatic evidence is discussed by Schönert 1965:46–51; see also Wallner 1997:83–85, Burrell 2004:236–242, and Adak 2016:181.

[6] Touratsoglu 1988:304, no. 3 (Valerianus): ΠΥΘΙΑ ΑΚΤ–ΙΑ; cf. the commentary at Touratsoglu 1988:78.

[7] *IG* 12.4.2.938 (Strasser 2021:53–54, no. 7), lines 3–4 (Cos): [Ἄκ]τια τὰ μεγάλα Καισάρηα ἀγενεί[ου]ς πένταθλον πρᾶτον Κώιων. In contrast, two other Coan inscriptions refer to the contests of Nikopolis; cf. *IG* 12.4.2.947, line 5 (*SEG* 51.1067; cf. Strasser 2021:447–448, no. 195, line 4): [– – – Ἄ]κτια ἱερά and *IG* 12.4.2.1166 (Strasser 2021:84–85, no. 26), lines 4–5: νει|κ[ήσα]ντος Ἄκτια, Κλαυδεῖα ἐν Ῥόδωι, where we have to distinguish between the Ἄκτια of Nikopolis and Κλαυδεῖα of Rhodes; cf. the discussion by Strasser 2015b and *SEG* 63.662.

[8] Moretti, *I.agonistiche* 87 (*F.Delphes* 3.1.555; Strasser 2021:392–394, no. 163), line 21: Ἄκτια ἐν Νεοκαισαρείᾳ.

[9] For a complete collection of the numismatic evidence, see Johnston 1984:65, no. 8 (*RPC* 6.5437); 70, no. 39; 71, no. 46 (*RPC* 6.5445); 74, no. 61 (*SNG von Aulock* 3636; *RPC* 6.5479); 76, no. 74; 78, no. 81. Leschhorn and Franke 2002:34, however, refer only to *SNG von Aulock* 3637 (like no. 3636, see above) and 8382. Yet the inscription on these coins, Α ΠΥΘΙΑ, does not refer to Α(ΚΤΙΑ) ΠΥΘΙΑ but, as Burrell 2004:137n22 notes, to "'first', either in rank or in order of celebration"; this contest is epigraphically attested in *I.Aphrodisias Performers* 69 (Strasser 2021:392–394, no. 163), line 28: Ἄκτι[α ἐν Ἱερα]πόλει. For the *Aktia* at Hierapolis, cf. von Papen 1908:175–181; Harl 1987:180n143; Wallner 1997:102–103 who,

(7) Sardeis (Asia),[10] and (8) Tarsos (Cilicia);[11] in Syria perhaps in (9) Antiochia on the Orontes,[12] for certain in (10) Tyros,[13] (11) Bostra (Ἄκτια Δουσάρια),[14] and in (12) Damascus.[15] Whether the "pentaeteric contest" of Alexandria to which several inscriptions refer was in fact called Ἄκτια remains an open question, but the phrase παῖδες Ἀκτιακοί, which possibly appeared in some inscriptions, may not prove the contest's status.[16] Several more cities must have hosted Actian

---

following von Papen 1908 and Johnston 1984, argues that the right to celebrate *Aktia* was granted to the city first by Elagabal, when the emperor honored Hierapolis as *neokoros*, but it was abolished due to his *damnatio* in 222. For the first *neokoria*, see Burrell 2004:135–138; for the assumed withdrawal see Burrell 2004:138–140. Under Gordian III or, more plausibly, Philip the Arab the city regained the *neokoria* and the games were reinstated; cf. Wallner 1997:102–103; Burrell 2004:140. It remains uncertain whether the *Aktia* should be identified with the "neokorate games," as already von Papen 1908:163, 179 had assumed; see also Burrell 2004:137 with further discussion.

[10] *Aktia Koraia: SNG München* 527: ΚΟΡΑΙΑ ΑΚΤΙΑ CAP–ΔΙΑΝΩΝ Β ΝΕΩΚΟ–ΡΩΝ (Caracalla); cf. Harl 1987:180n140.

[11] Ziegler 1985:25, no. A 20 (Valerian); cf. 25n29, 32. For the third *neokoria*, see Burrell 2004:217.

[12] *IG* 14.747 (*IGR* 1.446; Moretti, *I.agonistiche* 68; *I.Napoli* 1.51; Strasser 2021:115–116, no. 40), lines 23–24, *I.Ancyra* 1.146, lines 31–32 (Strasser 2021:349–350, no. 140, lines 30–31), and below, notes 20 and 74.

[13] The games are referred to as *Aktia Herakleia* on coins (cf. Harl 1987:180n140; Bru 2011:232–235), but simply as Ἄκτια ἐν Τύρῳ in inscriptions; cf. Moretti, *I.agonistiche* 87 (*F.Delphes* 3.1.555; Strasser 2021:384–385, no. 159), line 22 and *I.agonistiche* 90 (*IG* 2³.4.629; Strasser 2021:419–420), line 29.

[14] Epigraphically attested only at Ostia; cf. *ILS* 5233 (Strasser 2021:340–341, no. 133), line 1: *Actia aput Bo[s]|tram*. The numismatic evidence is discussed by Harl 1987:69 and 180n144; cf. Wallner 1997:106, Wallner 2000:103n40, Körner 2002:226–227. For a general account, see Bru 2011:236–238.

[15] *I.Aphrodisias Performers* 69 (Strasser 2021:392–394, no. 163), lines 30–31: Ἄκτι[α ἐν ... Δα]μά|σκῳ. For the agonistic life of Damascus, see Bru 2011:241–242 who, however, does not discuss the *Aktia*.

[16] Contest at Alexandria: Moretti, *I.agonistiche* 65, lines 7–8: ἐν Ἀλεξανδρέᾳ τῇ κατ' Αἴγ[υπτον] | πενταετηρικόν ...; in his recent edition, Strasser 2021:81–82, no. 24 restores the lines as ἐν Ἀλεξανδρέᾳ τῇ κατ' Αἴγυπτον, τὸ]ν | πενταετηρικόν ἐν Ἀντιοχείᾳ, which is also possible; *IG* 14.746 (*IGR* 1.445; Moretti, *I.agonistiche* 67; *I.Napoli* 1.50; Strasser 2021:101–102, no. 35), lines 14–15: ἐν Ἀλεξανδρείᾳ τὸν ἱερὸν πενταετη[ρικόν]; *IG* 14.747 (*IGR* 1.446; Moretti, *I.agonistiche* 68; *I.Napoli* 1.51; Strasser 2021:115–116, no. 40), line 27, where παῖδες Ἀκτιακοί may be restored; for context, see Gurval 1995:78n151; Lange 2009:98; Remijsen 2010:425.

games—for example, Caesarea Stratonis[17] and at least two unidentified cities—in one of which *Philippia Aktia* were celebrated.[18] In a victors list from Ancyra, Ἄκτια ἐν Ἀντιο‖[χείᾳ] are mentioned.[19] As two contests at Syrian Antioch are mentioned shortly before (lines 26–28: πρὸς Δάφνην), Sofie Remijsen has concluded "that the *Aktia* took place in a different Antioch."[20] Though this seems plausible, the victors list is too loosely organized to draw far-reaching conclusions. Despite some references in scholarly literature, there is no evidence for *Aktia* in Nikomedeia[21] or in Keryneia on Cyprus.[22]

The question of whether we can also trace Actian games in Rome is hotly debated. When Nero's wife, Poppaea Sabina, gave birth to Claudia Augusta in January 63, the euphoric emperor celebrated a *certamen ad exemplar Actiacae religionis*.[23] Though the character of this festival remains unclear, it was apparently modeled after the games held at Nikopolis, i.e., in honor of Apollo.[24] According to the *Res gestae, ludi*

[17] *I.Aphrodisias Performers* 69, lines 31–33 where the name is supplemented: [Ἄκτια? ἐν] Και‖[σ]αρε[ίᾳ τῆς Στρ]ατω‖νος; rejected by Strasser 2021:392–394, no. 163. For this city's history, see Isaac 2011. In late antiquity, ἀγῶνες ἱεροί are attested on a cup (now in the Louvre); cf. *CIIP* 2.1138 with detailed discussion.

[18] Moretti, *I.agonistiche* 87 (*F.Delphes* 3.1.555; Strasser 2021:384–385, no. 159), line 20: Φιλίππια Ἄκτια ἐν τῇ πατρίδι. Regarding the athlete's *patris*, Moretti, *I.agonistiche*, p. 258 voted for a location in Bithynia; see the recent discussion by Strasser 2021:386. Remijsen 2010:424n42 and Strasser 2021:386 voted for a connection of this festival to Philippus Arabs; not discussed by Körner 2002. For two other unknown host cities, see *I.Aphrodisias Performers* 69 (Strasser 2021:392–394, no. 163), line 29: Ἄκτι[α ἐν ...] and *IG* 2³.4.630 (Strasser 2021:406–407, no. 165), line 17: [- -Ἄκ]τια ἐ[ν - -].

[19] *I.Ancyra* 1.146, lines 30–31 (Strasser 2021:349–350, no. 140, lines 15–16).

[20] Remijsen 2010:424n41. For the *Aktia* of Antiochia at the Orontes, see note 74; for the ἀγὼν Εὐκράτους, see note 76.

[21] *Pace* Sarikakis 1965:156n6, following Reisch 1894:1214 (both without references). For the agonistic activities in Nikomedeia, cf. Bosch 1935:232–235 and Robert 1977:30–35 = 1989b:240–245 = 2007:695–700.

[22] Based solely on a fragmentary honorary inscription (*editio princeps*: T. Reinach in Contoléon, Reinach, and Reinach 1904:213; Fujii 2013:164), Mitford 1980:1326 identified the ἐπινίκια of Keryneia as "Actaean Games [which] were celebrated in honour of Augustus' victory," but see now Fujii 2013:70, 128 and Blanco-Pérez 2018:13. Kantiréa 2008:100–101 has proposed that the ἐπινίκια refer to a later Augustan victory, perhaps over the Parthians in 20/19 BC.

[23] Tacitus *Annales* 15.23.2.

[24] Cf. Herz 1978:1165.

votivi pro salute Caesaris were celebrated in Rome every fourth year since 28 BC. [25] In this year, Octavian established a festival "which had been voted in honor of the victory won at Actium" [26] and which seems to have been directly connected to the inauguration of the temple dedicated to Apollo Palatinus. [27] Theodor Mommsen's assumption that these two festivals were two separate events sparked debate as to the nature of these Roman games in memory of the victory at Actium. [28] Though Dio claims that the πανήγυρις ἡ ἐπὶ τῇ νίκῃ τῇ πρὸς τῷ Ἀκτίῳ γενομένῃ was to be held every four years, and our sources do attest celebrations in 20 and 16 BC, [29] these games seem to have disappeared by the time when Nero's daughter was born. In contrast to the Actian games of Nikopolis, not a single victor of these enigmatic Roman games is known. This festival was evidently exceptional and may not be regarded as a Greek *agon* but merely as a *spectaculum* for the people of Rome.

II. *ISAKTIOI AGONES* IN THE ROMAN EMPIRE

Besides these Actian games, we know that several cities held contests classified as *isaktioi agones*. The *Aktia* and *isaktioi agones* differed only in name. While the label "Actian" directly referred to the festival Augustus held near Nikopolis, the designation of games as isactian referred only to their status and to their prize, which was modeled after the crown awarded at Nikopolis. [30] This does not imply, however, that all known

[25] *Res gestae divi Augusti* 9.1 (I follow the text of Scheid 2007): *vota p[ro salute mea susc]ip̣i p̣[er con]ṣuḷeṣ et ṣacerḍotes qu̱[in]to qu[oque anno decre vit senatus. Ex iis] votis s[ae]pe fecerun̠t vivo m[e ludos aliquotiens sacerdot]um q̱ua̱ttu̱o̱r amplissima colle[gia, aliquotiens consules.]* – εὐχὰς ὑπὲρ τῆς ἐμῆς σωτηρίας ἀναλαμβάνειν διὰ τῶν ὑπάτων καὶ ἱερέων καθ' ἑκάστην πεντετηρίδα ἐψηφίσατο ἡ σύγκλητος. ἐκ τούτων τῶν εὐχῶν πλειστάκις ἐγένοντο θέαι, τοτὲ μὲν ἐκ τῆς συναρχίας τῶν τεσσάρων ἱερέων, τοτὲ δὲ ὑπὸ τῶν ὑπάτων.

[26] Cassius Dio 53.1.4: καὶ τὴν πανήγυριν τὴν ἐπὶ τῇ νίκῃ τῇ πρὸς τῷ Ἀκτίῳ γενομένῃ ψηφισθεῖσαν ἤγαγε μετὰ τοῦ Ἀγρίππου, καὶ ἐν αὐτῇ τὴν ἱπποδρομίαν διά τε τῶν παίδων καὶ διὰ τῶν ἀνδρῶν τῶν εὐγενῶν ἐποίησε.

[27] Cassius Dio 53.1.3. For the identification of Apollo Palatinus with Apollo Actius, see the discussion in Gurval 1995:257n19.

[28] Mommsen 1883:42–43; Rieks 1970:107–108n3; Langenfeld 1975:257; Gurval 1995:122; Scheid 2007:42.

[29] The celebration every four years is attested by Cassius Dio 53.1.5, 54.19.8 (celebration in 16 BC) with Gurval 1995:122. For the celebration in 20 BC, see Scheid 2007:42.

[30] See below, note 73.

Actian games or *isaktioi agones* were established under Augustus's reign. On the contrary, most of them seem to have been established in the third century.[31]

Actian and isactian games were the third most common type of contest in imperial times, after Olympian and isolympian games (the most widespread) and Pythian and isopythian games (the second most common).[32] As an honorary decree of a prominent yet recently deceased athlete reveals, there must have been several contests classified as *isaktioi* between the first and the third century AD.[33] The decree was passed by the *synodos* of the athletes at Naples, but the only known copy was put up in the vicinity of the deceased's hometown, Elaia; it confirms that the late athlete had "brilliantly won several sacred and *isaktioi agones*" (ὡς πλείστους | ἀγῶνας καὶ ἱεροὺς καὶ ἰσακτίους ἐπιδό|ξως κατορθῶσαι, lines 8–10). Although this inscription neither specifies these games nor mentions any host cities, it proves that *isaktioi agones* must have been both numerous and well established in Italy and in the Greek part of the Roman Empire. This impression is corroborated by the epithet of a M. Aurelius Silvanus who, acting as ἄρχων νομοδίκτης at Oxyrhynchus in AD 273/274, signed an official document of the Dionysian synod as τρισπυθιονείκης ("three-time winner of Pythian games"), δεκαολυμπιονείκης ("ten-time winner of Olympian games"), and δωδεκααακτιονείκης ("twelve-time winner of Actian games"). As Peter Frisch has observed, it seems impossible that Silvanus won the *Aktia* at Nikopolis so many times, and thus his title must refer to different Actian games or *isaktioi agones*.[34]

---

[31] Ziegler 1985:118; Mitchell 1993: vol. 1, 219.

[32] Cf. Leschhorn 1999:40; see also the numbers in Klose and Stumpf 1996:97, which are also based on Leschhorn: *Olympia* (no. 38), *Pythia* (no. 33), *Aktia* (no. 15), *Capitolia* (no. 9).

[33] *Editio princeps*: Bean 1965:588–591, no. 2 (*non vidi*); Merkelbach 1975:146–148 = 1997:434–436 emendates line 5 and incorporates Robert's correction of line 39 (cf. Robert 1968:406–417 = 1989b:93; Robert and Robert 1968; Robert and Robert 1969). Mauritsch et al. 2012:342–343, no. 240 reprint Bean's text, while offering a German translation; cf. now Stauber 2022:102–104, no. 830, also with German translation and short commentary.

[34] *Pap.Agon.* 1.23 with Frisch's commentary (42).

As we still lack a critical survey of the evidence on *isaktioi agones*,[35] it seems useful to first discuss the scattered sources—mostly numismatic and epigraphic—that mention them, before we place the isactian festivals into their historical context.

II.1. BEROIA

From the late first century onward, the Macedonian *koinon* celebrated a festival in Beroia during which contests were also held. Under Nerva, Q. Popillius Python gained permission from the emperor to sponsor the festival and become the first *agonothetes*.[36] Thus, the contests were almost certainly part of the imperial cult.[37] Around the mid-third century, these contests were called τοῦ κοινοῦ | τῶν Μακεδόνων ἀγῶνος Ἀλεξανδρείου, ἱεροῦ, οἰκουμενικοῦ, ἰσελαστικοῦ, ἰσα[κτίου.[38] The reading of ἰσα[κτίου is confirmed by an *invitatio ad munera* from Thessalonike, dated to AD 252.[39] As the *titulus* for Popillius Python shows, the games were not promoted to a higher status but rather had been established as an *isaktios agon* right from the beginning.[40]

II.2. HERAKLEIA PONTICA

As we learn from a victor's inscription from Aphrodisias, an *isaktios agon* in honor of Hadrian was held at Herakleia Pontica. In this text, the contest, which was called ἐν Ἡρακλε[ί]|ᾳ τῇ πρὸς τῷ Πόντῳ

---

[35] Reisch 1894:1214, in his otherwise still valuable article on the *Aktia*, discusses only two *isaktioi agones*, in Caesarea and Herakleia (below, note 41 and note 70). Leschhorn and Franke 2002:154 offer only numismatic attestations from Neocaesarea (Pontus) and Soloi-Pompeiopolis (Cilicia), respectively. The best survey is still that of Sarikakis 1965:156.

[36] Robert 1939:131, no. 2 = 1969:1284, no. 2 (*I.Beroia* 117), line 13: εἰσακτίους ἀγῶνας; Robert 1939:132 = 1969:1285 (*I.Beroia* 118); for Q. Popillius Python, cf. Bartels 2008:148.

[37] Cf. Leschhorn 1998:404–405.

[38] *I.Beroia* 69, lines 6–8 (AD 228): [ἀγωνο]]θέτης τοῦ κοινοῦ τῶν Μακεδόνων ἀγῶνος Ἀλεξανδρείου ἱεροῦ, οἰκουμενικοῦ, ἰσελαστικοῦ, ἰσα[κτίου Λ(ούκιος) Σε]]πτίμιος Ἰνστεϊανὸς Ἀλέξανδρος καὶ Αἰλ(ία) Ἀλεξάνδρα ἡ γυνὴ αὐτοῦ. For a thorough interpretation, cf. Herz 2008:118–119.

[39] AE 1999.1425; SEG 49.815; Hatzopoulos 2000; now IG 10.2.1 Suppl. 1, 1073, lines 5–6: τοῦ κοινοῦ τῶν | Μακεδόνων ἀγῶνος ἱεροῦ οἰκουμεν[ικ]οῦ εἰσελαστι[κοῦ ἰσακτ]ίου Ἀλεξανδρείου.

[40] Cf. Robert's correct reading of line 13: εἰσακτίους ἀγῶνας instead of εἰς Ἀκτίους ἀγῶνας (Robert 1939:132 = 1969:1285).

Ἀδρι<ά>νηο[ν] | Ἡράκλειον ἰσάκτ<ι>ον, is mentioned twice, as the victor had won both the παίδων δόλιχον and the ἀνδρῶν δόλιχον (lines 17–19 and 30–31, respectively).[41] After the death of Antinoos on October 24, 130,[42] Antinoeia contests were held in several cities across the Empire, but the new cult's center was Antinoos's hometown of Bithynion-Hadriane (formerly Claudiopolis) in Bithynia.[43] In the inscription discussed above, a contest in this city is mentioned, but the crucial right edge of the stone is damaged (lines 15–17; see figure 1):

> [ἐ]ν Ἀδριανήᾳ τῆς Βειθυνία[ς – –]
> 16   ὸν Ἀδριάνειον Ἀντινόειο[ν]
> παίδων δόλιχον.

Calder and Cormack, in their edition for the Monumenta Asiae Minoris Antiqua (MAMA) project, restored the relevant passage as ἰσάκτι]|ον, but Luigi Moretti corrected the adjective to ἰερ?]|ὸν and was followed by Charlotte Roueché:[44]

> [ἐ]ν Ἀδριανήᾳ τῆς Βειθυνία[ς ἰερ]-
> 16   ὸν Ἀδριάνειον Ἀντινόειο[ν]
> παίδων δόλιχον.

Besides the simple fact that ἰσάκτι]|ον is far too long for the lacuna, it is indeed more likely that the status of these games, being an important part of Antinoos's cult, was that of a ἰερὸς ἀγών; but only new sources can potentially solve this problem. We may assume that Calder and Cormack were simply misled by the isaktios agon Hadrianeia Herakleia at Herakleia of Pontus.

---

[41] Moretti, I.agonistiche 80 (MAMA 8.521; I.Aphrodisias Performers 70; Strasser 2021:356–357, no. 142). For a date, see Moretti, I.agonistiche, p. 236. For agonistic motifs on the city's coins, see Leschhorn 1999:33.

[42] Cf. Birley 1997:247; for a recent discussion of the date, see Brennan 2018:110.

[43] For Antinoeia contests, see Leschhorn 1999:36. For the cult in Bithynia, see now Begass 2022:766–770.

[44] Moretti, I.agonistiche 80 (MAMA 8.521; Roueché, I.Aphrodisias Performers 70; I.Aphrodisias 2007, 12.215; Strasser 2021:356–357, no. 142), lines 15–17.

Figure 1. Moretti, *I.agonistiche* 80 (*MAMA* 8.521; *I.Aphrodisias Performers* 70; *I.Aphrodisias* 2007, 12.215; Strasser 2021:356–357, no. 142), upper part, lines 1–19. Photo by Mossman Roueché (1976), used with permission of Charlotte Roueché.

II.3. ANCYRA

In the same inscription, Calder and Cormack also suggested restoring the status of the *Asklepieia* of Ancyra (Galatia) as follows:[45]

ἐν Ἀ[ν-]

12   [κ]ύρα τῆς Γαλατίας εἰσ[άκτιον]

[Ἀ]σκλήπειον παίδων δόλιχ[ον].

It may seem plausible that isactian games were held in Ancyra, given that the city houses an inscription of the *Res Gestae divi Augusti*, which were originally set up in Rome and "have nothing directly to do with

---

[45] Calder and Cormack, *MAMA* 8.521, lines 11–13. For games held in Ancyra, the best account is still Robert 1960:350–368, but see now Mitchell and French, *I.Ancyra* 1:13.

the province of Galatia or Ankara itself ";[46] however, restoring an *isaktios agon* in Ancyra is less appealing than it seems. Firstly, the supplement is too long for the limited space left on the right edge of the stone; secondly, it is, as far as I see, not supported by any other evidence. Furthermore, Αὐγούστεια Ἄκτια are not attested in Ancyra before the mid-third century.[47] Without any earlier evidence, the Αὐγούστεια Ἄκτια do not seem to have any tradition reaching back to the time of Augustus[48] but were established under Valerian and Gallienus, probably together with the city's second *neokoria* in AD 253/4.[49] In Moretti's edition, however, the lines run:[50]

> ἐν Ἀ[ν]-
> 12   κύρα τῆς Γαλατίας εἰσ[ελαστικὸν?]
> [Ἀ]σκλήπειον παίδων δόλιχ[ον].

This supplement must seem even more strange, as Moretti has correctly noted on another occasion that the festival in honor of Asclepius, first celebrated under Caracalla in AD 215, was an *agon isopythios*.[51] Attested in various inscriptions and on coins, the isopythian status of the festival is beyond doubt. It came about because Asclepius was the son of Apollo, who was in turn the lord of the Pythian sanctuary at Delphi.[52] Even if it is thus tempting to restore εἰσ[οπύθιον] |

---

[46] Cf. Mitchell and French, *I.Ancyra* 1:12.

[47] *I.Ancyra* 1.116, lines 5–8: ἀγω|νοθετήσαντα τῶν μεγά|λων Αὐγουστείων Ἀκτί|ων; *SNG von Aulock* 6199 (Arslan 2004:231, no. 223): ΑΚ-ΤΙΑ ΠΥ-ΘΙΑ ΜΥ-ϹΤΙ-ΚΟϹ (minted under Gallienus's wife Salonina); cf. Robert 1960:366–367; Touratsoglu 1988:78n178.

[48] *Pace* Mitchell and French in *I.Ancyra* 1:34 and 285; but cf. Burrell 2004:173: "Though Ankyra was likely *neokoros* for the temple of Augustus and Rome, the cult for which it got the second honor must remain uncertain. The *Asklepieia Sotereia*, though founded under Caracalla, may have honored the god rather than the emperor; *Augousteia Aktia* could have been granted as late as the time of Valerian."

[49] Cf. the discussion at *I.Ancyra* 1:285. For the date of the second *neokoria*, see *I.Ancyra* 1:14, 34 and Burrell 2004:173–174.

[50] Moretti, *I.agonistiche* 80, lines 11–13.

[51] Moretti, *I.agonistiche*, p. 209; *I.Ancyra* 1:34. For contests at Ancyra, see Robert 1960:350–368; for the *Asklepieia Sotereia isopythia*, see Robert 1960:362–365.

[52] Inscriptions: Ἀσκλήπεια Σωτήρια ἰσοπύθια: *IGR* 3.204 (*I.Ancyra* 1.96), lines 10–12: τῶν ἱερῶν ἀγώνων | τῶν μεγάλων Ἀσκληπι|είων ἰσοπυθίων; *I.Ancyra* 1.97, lines 11–13; 98, lines 8–10; 99, lines 8–9; 100, lines 9–10; 101, lines 7–9 (suppl.); 102, lines 8–9. For the coins,

[Ἀ]σκλήπειον παίδων δόλιχ[ον], one letter at most, if any, is missing after ΕΙΣ. Charlotte Roueché has given the correct text,[53] though the problem of a proper interpretation of ΕΙΣ[-] remains.[54] Despite these difficulties, however, we have to remove Ancyra from the list of host cities of *isaktioi agones*.

II.4. NEOCAESAREA

At the beginning of the third century, an actor was honored in his hometown, Side, with a statue that was accompanied by a large inscription. The list of his victories includes a contest called κοινὸν Πόντου ἰσά|κτιον ἐν Νεοκαισαρείᾳ.[55] This competition is also known from a coin minted at Neocaesarea (Pontus) under Severus Alexander (234/5).[56] On the reverse, which shows a prize table with an agonistic crown and a palm branch,[57] the legend along the edge reads: ΚΟΙ ΠΟΝΤΟ ΜΗ ΝΕΟΚΕ (sic) ΕΤ ΡΟΑ (κοινοῦ Πόντου, μητροπόλεως, νεοκώρος, ἔτους ροα΄). The inscription ΙCΑ–ΚΤΙ–OC (sc. ἀγών), between the legs of the prize table, is clearly related to the contest celebrated by the Pontic *koinon*.[58] This confirms the evidence given by the Side inscription, without providing any further information about the contest or its name. As the victor was an actor, the contest, however, must have included a *mousikos agon*.

Several years later, *Aktia* were founded by the city. As several coin series with agonistic motifs and ΑΚΤΙΑ on the reverse first appear in AD

---

see Arslan 2004:216–217, nos. 147 and 150–154. For the date of the first celebration, see *I.Ancyra* 1:32 and 268. Roueché 1981:119 discusses numerous foundations of Pythian games in third-century Asia Minor.

[53] Roueché, *I.Aphrodisias Performers* 70 (*I.Aphrodisias 2007*, 12.215), lines 12–14: ἐν Ἀ[ν]|κύρα τῆς Γαλατίας ΕΙΣ[·] | [Ἀ]σκλήπειον παίδων δόλιχ[ον].

[54] Recently, Strasser 2021:356–357, no. 142 has proposed the reading εἰσ[ελ<αστικὸν>] and supposed that the mason made an error.

[55] *I.Side* 2.130 (Strasser 2021:336–367, no. 131), lines 8–9 (for a date between AD 205 and 212, see J. Nollé's commentary at *I.Side* 2.130). The contest is also attested in Moretti, *I.agonistiche* 87 (*F.Delphes* 3.1.555; Strasser 2021:384–385, no. 159), line 21: Ἄκτια ἐν Νεοκαισαρείᾳ. Marek 2003:95–100 offers a survey of agonistic activities in Pontus.

[56] Klose and Stumpf 1996:112, no. 206; Çizmeli 2006:52, no. 271; *RPC* 6.6544 (temporary number; rpc.ashmus.ox.ac.uk/coins/6/6544); cf. also Marek 2003:98, Abb. 144a–b.

[57] For this widespread iconography, cf. Klose 2005:130; Specht 2007.

[58] Correctly observed by Klose and Stumpf 1996:122.

241/2 (ET POH = 178 of the city's era),[59] Kenneth W. Harl has proposed that these *Aktia* were founded and celebrated for the first time on the occasion of Gordian III's visit to Neocaesarea in this very year.[60] Are, then, the *Aktia* of Gordian the same as the *koinon's isaktios agon* attested on coins minted under Severus Alexander? The answer is difficult as the sources draw a very distorted picture. It thus seems helpful to go through the evidence chronologically.

Already in 226/7, Neocaesarea had received the privilege of a second *neokoria* from Severus Alexander—proudly presented as ΔΙC ΝΕΩΚΟΡΟC on coins—and thus had the opportunity to celebrate a second ecumenical contest.[61] As we have seen above, the only known competition is the *isaktios agon* celebrated in Neocaesarea by the Pontic *koinon*. But one coin type, which depicts two crowns above a temple, suggests the existence of a second, hitherto unattested contest.[62]

Under Gordian III, the *Aktia* were promoted insistently as the *koinon's* games[63] on coins, and they were still celebrated under Gallienus in AD 262/3.[64] But, as Axel Jürging has observed, only one of the two contests was, from Severus Alexander onward, classified as a ἱερὸς ἀγών.[65] On the coins dating to AD 226/7 discussed above, the city is called ΔΙC ΝΕΩΚΟΡ, and the two crowns refer to these two *neokoriai*, but the legend ΙΕΡΟΥ (viz., ΙΕΡΟC) is always in singular form.[66] Jürging's conclusion that the *Aktia* were the only "sacred" contest must be accepted, even if I cannot verify his reading of ΙΕΡΟC on the AKTIA

---

[59] The coins dated to 241/2 with the reverse legend AKTIA are Çizmeli 2006:55, no. 295; 56, nos. 303–304; 59, nos. 321–323, 325, 333; 60, no. 335; 61, nos. 340–341; 62, nos. 350–351; 62–63, no. 356; AK[TIA] can be supplemented in 59, no. 324; the following coins have A(KTIA): 55, no. 298; 56, no. 305; 61, nos. 347–348.

[60] Harl 1987:69; followed by Mitchell 1993: vol. 1, 222 and Wallner 1997:85n333. The evidence is discussed by Harl 1987:180n146.

[61] Cf. Ziegler 1985:65n263; Jürging 1991:45; Burrell 2004:208; Çizmeli 2006:120–122. The coins are listed in Çizmeli 2006:47–54.

[62] Cf. Ziegler 1985:65n263; Jürging 1991:45. For an example of this coin type, see Çizmeli 2006:48, no. 247.

[63] See above, note 58.

[64] Jürging 1991:44, no. 2; Çizmeli 2006:75, no. 448a, but see n67.

[65] Cf. Jürging 1991:46–47.

[66] Çizmeli 2006:48, nos. 247 and 250.

coin he examines or on the other known example from the Cabinet de Médailles in Paris.[67] The most probable explanation is that Neocaesarea, as host city of the Pontic *koinon*, celebrated an *isaktios agon* under Septimius Severus, which might have been abolished due to this emperor's *damnatio memoriae* after his death in 235.[68] Under Gordian III, the *koinon* gained the emperor's permission to hold *Aktia* again. Gordian's *Aktia* were most likely a refoundation of the previous *isaktios agon*. This might explain why a single coin type from Neocaesarea, minted under Gordian III in AD 241/2, reads ΜΗΤΡΟ(πολις) ΝΕΟΚΑΙCΑΡΙΑC, ΕΤ(ους) ΡΟΗ, ΙCΑΚΤΙΟC on the reverse.[69] Given the enormous output of AKTIA emissions in that very year, this type might be interpreted either as a prototype or as a mistake by the city's coin magistrate. In sum, we might conclude that in Severan times, the Pontic *koinon* used to celebrate an *isaktios agon* in Neocaesarea which was probably refounded, maybe after a short period of abolition (ca. AD 235–241), as *Aktia* with Gordian III's permission in AD 241/2.

II.5. Caesarea Panias

As his *palmarès* claim, a boy boxer won ἐν Καισαρείᾳ ἰσάκτιον (sc. ἀγῶνα) around the mid-third century.[70] The Caesarea mentioned in the inscription has been identified as Caesarea Panias in Syria, though we hardly know anything about the city's agonistic activities, besides a festival for Pan (Πάνεια).[71]

---

[67] Jürging 1991:44, no. 2: "Auf der Preiskrone: IEPOC, auf dem 'Altar' AKTIA"; Çizmeli 2006:75, no. 448a reads AKTIA only between the legs of the crown. For the Paris coins, cf. Çizmeli 2006:75, no. 448b and the images available online (catalogue.bnf.fr/ark:/12148/cb41808985m). For the problem of the very small and hardly legible legends on the crowns, see Ziegler 1985:24–25 with n29.

[68] For the *damnatio*, see Kienast, Eck, and Heil 2017:172. Burrell 2004:209, however, doubts that the contest was revived shortly after Alexander's consecration in 238.

[69] *RPC* 7.2.2828.

[70] Moretti, *I.agonistiche* 85 (*IGR* 3.1012; *IGLS* 4.1265 [with misleading interpunction]; Strasser 2021:352–353, no. 141), line 11.

[71] Moretti, *I.agonistiche* 72, line 43 (Strasser 2021:166–167, no. 61b, line 26–27). According to Robert 1960:443, the Πάνεια mentioned in *I.Didyma* 179 (Strasser 2021:512–513, no. 254), lines 8–9 refer to those of Caesarea Panias, rather than those of Panopolis; cf. also Frisch, *Pap. Agon.*, p. 64–65; but see now Slater 2012:158.

II.6. Soloi-Pompeiopolis

A similar case is known from Soloi-Pompeiopolis in Cilicia Trachea. Under Commodus, the city organized an *isaktios agon* which is only attested on a single coin. The reverse shows a crown around which the legend reads: [ΠΟΜ]ΠΗΙΠΟΛΕΙΤΩΝ ΙΣΑΚΤΙΟ[Σ].[72] On the basis of comprehensive numismatic and archaeological evidence, Klose has convincingly shown that the στέφανος is, in fact, a reed crown that was awarded at the Actian games.[73] As this isactian contest is not attested otherwise, we do not know anything specific about this competition or about the agonistic activities in Pompeiopolis.

II.7. Antioch at the Orontes

As mentioned above, sacred and "pentaeteric" games were also held at Syrian Antioch, but it is far from certain that these competitions were called *Aktia*: τὸν ἐν Ἀντιοχείᾳ ἱερὸν πεν[ταετηρικὸν ἀγῶνα] | Ἀκτιακῶν παίδων παγκράτιον.[74] The παῖδες Ἀκτιακοί, who are attested in Antioch and Alexandria in this inscription, have already been correctly identified by Reisch as boys "who are in the age-class of boy-contests at the *Aktia*."[75] This expression, however, does not verify that the name of the Antiochene festival was *Aktia*.

Besides this contest, an *isaktios agon* was also celebrated in Antioch: ἐν Ἀντιοχείᾳ | [τῆς Συρίας τὸν] Εὐκράτους ἰσάκτιον παίδων στάδιον.[76]

---

[72] Ziegler 1985:57, no. H 1; see the photograph in Klose 1997:37, Abb. 9; the coin is provisionally listed as *RPC* 4.3.10219 (temporary number; rpc.ashmus.ox.ac.uk/coins/4/10219) but is without a picture.

[73] Klose 1997:35–37. For the different types of crowns awarded in contests, see Rumscheid 2000.

[74] *IG* 14.747 (*IGR* 1.446; Moretti, *I.agonistiche* 68; *I.Napoli* 1.51; Strasser 2021:115–116, no. 40), lines 23–24; for παῖδες Ἀκτιακοί at Alexandria (Egypt), cf. line 27. Moretti, *I.agonistiche* proposes a date of ca. AD 110 (p. 187) and gives a brief discussion of the contests attested in Antioch (p. 176); cf. now the discussion by Strasser; for context, see also Remijsen 2010:425.

[75] Reisch 1894:1214, "Als παῖδες Ἀκτιακοί, d.h. Knaben, in dem für die Knabenagone der A[ktia] vorgeschriebenen Alter […] werden Ende des 1. Jhdts. die Knaben an den Agonen von Antiocheia und Alexandreia bezeichnet."

[76] *Suppl. Rodio* 67 (Robert 1960:444; Strasser 2004:162; Strasser 2021:323–324, no. 125), lines 2–3; cf. Slater 2012:151–152.

The status of the ἀγὼν Εὐκράτους, once a privately founded contest,[77] must have been raised at some point, as it was, by the time when this inscription was erected, an ecumenical contest.[78] On the basis of Strasser's redating of the Rhodian inscription to sometime around the beginning of the third century,[79] we might identify a possible occasion for this elevation. In an inscription from Smyrna, we hear of another athlete who had won the ἀγὼν Εὐκράτους and was therefore honored, as the text emphasizes, in a special way with a crown.[80] Louis Robert had thought of Lucius Verus who, while campaigning against the Persians, might have visited the contests at Antioch and personally crowned the athlete. In his reedition of this text, however, Georg Petzl restored the decisive lines (14–16) as follows: στεφανωθεὶς | ὑπὸ [τῶν κ]υρίων ἡμῶν | [αὐτοκρατόρων]. In contrast to the earlier reconstruction, two emperors crowned the athlete in 197/8 during their stay at Antioch. They may be identified, according to Petzl, as Septimius Severus and Caracalla. As the Rhodian inscription is the only text declaring the ἀγὼν Εὐκράτους an *isaktios agon*,[81] the sojourn of the emperors might have been an appropriate occasion for its rise in status. If the sacred contest discussed above was in fact called *Aktia*, Antioch would have been the only known city hosting both Actian games and an *isaktios agon* at the same time.

---

[77] The evidence for the ἀγὼν Εὐκράτους was collected by Robert 1937:144, to which must be added Gough 1952:128, no. 1 (Moretti, *I.agonistiche* 86; Strasser 2021:318–319, no. 123), lines 9–11, discussed below, note 81; cf. too Robert 1960:444n1.

[78] Strasser 2004:144, "date donc au plus tôt du tout début du IIIe s."

[79] Strasser 2004:144 and 2021:325, but cf. already Petzl, *I.Smyrna* 2.662: "Ende des 2., Anfang des 3. Jhs. n. Chr."

[80] Robert 1937:143 (*I.Smyrna* 2.662; Strasser 2021:326–327, no. 127).

[81] The other sources include an inscription from Tralles (Moretti, *I.agonistiche* 78; *I.Tralleis* 117; Strasser 2021:302–303, no. 114), dated by Robert 1937:144n3 "pas antérieur à Commode." Two texts from Delphi cannot be precisely dated; cf. *F.Delphes* 3.1.550 (Strasser 2021:381–382, no. 157), line 30 and Moretti, *I.agonistiche* 87 (*F.Delphes* 3.1.555; Strasser 2021:384–385, no. 159), line 25. See also the inscription from Anazarbus, Gough 1952:128, no. 1 (Moretti, *I.agonistiche* 86; Strasser 2021:318–319, no. 123), lines 9–11: Ἀντιόχειαν κατὰ | τὸ ἑξῆς τὸν Ἀδριάνειον καὶ τὸν Κομόδειον καὶ τὸν | Εὐκράτους. Moretti, *I.agonistiche* p. 254 dated this inscription after AD 229, but Strasser 2021:321 recently redated the career of the honored Demetrios to "ca. 190–210," the inscription to "205–212." As the contests of Antioch are only listed without giving further details about their status, this text does not offer any information in regard to the problem considered here.

Now that we have reevaluated the evidence, it is clear that *isaktioi agones* were held in the following six cities: (1) Beroia (Macedonia), (2) Herakleia at Pontus (Pontus), (3) Neocaesarea (Pontus), (4) Caesarea Panias (Syria), (5) Soloi-Pompeiopolis (Cilicia), and (6) Antioch on the Orontes (Syria). According to the decree for the deceased athlete from Elaia, however, there seem to have been more.[82]

III. GREEK CONTESTS AND ROMAN POWER

Throughout antiquity, small or newly founded festivals were often raised in status by a link to a festival of the *periodos*—i.e., the *Olympia* at Elis, the *Pythia* at Delphi, the *Isthmia* at Corinth, or the *Nemea* at Argos. Recent studies have shown, however, that games that had gained status as isolympian or isopythian did not have to offer the same agonistic or musical program as their Olympian or Pythian counterparts. The organizers were instead obliged to offer the same prizes and honors to the winners of these contests as in Olympia or Delphi, as we can clearly observe in a Hellenistic decree from Chalcis: τοῖς νικήσασιν Χαλκ[ι]δ[έων τ]ὸν ἀγῶνα τοῦτον διδό|ναι τὰ ἴσα ἆθλα, ὅσαπερ κ[αὶ] το[ῖς τὰ] Πύθια νικήσασιν.[83] From the archaic to Hellenistic periods, the agonistic world "knew a centre and a periphery," and Greece remained, as has been recently stated, "the unchallenged centre, boasting the most prestigious festivals."[84] And although the four "great" Greek festivals did remain, due to their age, the most prestigious games of the *periodos* even in Roman times, the Actian games—the most important agonistic foundation of the first Roman emperor—also became a reference to which an increasing number of smaller festivals were connected. Thus, in imperial times, the traditional *periodos* was "advanced" or "enhanced" by the *Aktia* at Nikopolis, the *Sebasta* at Naples, and the *Capitolia* at Rome.[85] This is underlined by the fact

---

[82] Cf. note 33.

[83] *Syll.*³ 561, lines 22–23; see too *Syll.*³ 558, line 19: ἰσοπύθιον ταῖς τιμαῖς. Cf. Chaniotis 2018:326; Mann 2018:471; already correctly observed by Bosch 1950/51:88.

[84] Fauconnier 2016:82.

[85] For the "advanced" *periodos*, see J. and L. Robert, *Bull. ép.* 1954, no. 57, Frisch, *Pap. Agon*, p. 42, and Frisch 1991. For the integration of the Actian games, see Pavlogiannis, Albanidis, and Dimitriou 2009:92–100. For the *Capitolia*, see note 89.

that one athlete was honored for having won all seven contests and thus was claimed to be "the first among mankind who was a full *periodonikes*" (περιοδονίκης τέλειος πρῶτος ἀνθρώπων).[86] Similarly to the *Sebasta* at Naples, which were also founded by Augustus in AD 2 and were classified as an *isolympios agon*,[87] the *Aktia* of Nikopolis were originally an ἀγὼν Ὀλύμπιος.[88] In contrast to the *Sebasta*, but comparable to the *Capitolia*, which were established by Domitian in AD 86,[89] Augustus's *Aktia* eventually became a model for many festivals in the Greek-speaking East.[90] All of the provincial *Aktia* and *Capitolia* were, like the *isaktioi* and *isokapitolioi agones*, primarily connected to the Roman emperor. On a more general level, the establishment or refurbishing of a festival as an *isaktios agon* reveals a tendency in Greek *poleis* of imperial times to adapt their own festivals to this new type of games, which were neither Roman nor Greek but rather a blend of a Greek *agon* and Roman imperial cult.[91] Referring to an inscription about a pancratiast's victories, Fergus Millar has observed that the "places in the Syrian region where his victories had been won, [...] represent a wholly Greek world, in which Roman colonization is invisible."[92] For this inscription only, Millar's observation is correct, as only the host cities are

---

[86] *Editio princeps*: Şahin 1991:145, no. 1 (*SEG* 41.1407A; Strasser 2021:318–9, no. 64A), lines 6–7; Şahin proposed a date AD 160–180, Strasser around 150. For the title, see Frisch 1991.

[87] *IG* 14.748a, lines 3–4 from which the supplement in the *Sebasta*'s foundation decree (*I.Olympia* 56, line 2) is taken; for the date of the foundation, see Frisch, *Pap.Agon.*, p. 118; for the *Sebasta*, cf. Miranda de Martino 2014:1166–1169 with further readings.

[88] Strabo 7.7.6, 325C: ἀποδέδεικται δ' ὁ ἀγὼν ὀλύμπιος τὰ Ἄκτια, ἱερὸς τοῦ Ἀκτίου Ἀπόλλωνος; cf. Langenfeld 1975:239; Lämmer 1986/1987:30–31; Spawforth 2007:385; Pavlogiannis, Albanidis, and Dimitriou 2009:84–85.

[89] The main source for the *Capitolinus agon* in Rome as a *quinquennale certamen* is Suetonius *Domitianus* 4.4 who confirms that it was held as a *triplex certamen* (*musicum, equestre, gymnicum*); for the *Capitolia*, see especially Caldelli 1993; cf. too Pleket 1975:68; Rieger 1999; Graf 2015:95–98; Strasser 2015a:66–71. For isocapitolian games, cf. Ziegler 1985:147–148; Wallner 1997:178n735; Leschhorn 1999:40.

[90] The different backgrounds of the *Sebasta* and the *Aktia* are stressed by Heinemann 2016:222n14.

[91] Cf. Aneziri 2014:428n25. On "upgrading" festivals, see van Nijf 2000:182.

[92] Millar 2006:165–166, referring to Moretti, *I.agonistiche* 72 (*I.Aphrodisias Performers* 91; Strasser 2021:166–167, no. 61b), from the 160s AD.

mentioned, without the festivals' names; but we know from another inscription that the contests were, most probably, called *Aktia*.[93] At the end of the third century, these two elements—Rome and Greece, in this particular order—were stressed in a law *de athletis* which settled the honors for athletes who won "in Rome or ancient Greece" (*Romae seu antiquae Graeciae*).[94] In contrast to the Hellenistic period, when the then newly founded festivals in Asia Minor and Ptolemaic Egypt were intended to stress the "Greekness" of their royal founders,[95] the festivals in imperial times labeled as isactian or isocapitolian, while explicitly linked to Rome and its emperors, were established not forcibly by Roman authorities but deliberately by the Greek cities themselves. While each Greek city likely had its own motivations for instituting these contests, we can identify two general reasons for this development. Firstly, quite a number of the cities' council members in imperial Greece and Asia Minor had a Roman background, and thus a strong connection to the emperor and his cult.[96] Secondly, styling a festival in the High Empire in this manner might have been not only an homage paid to Roman dominance but also an investment into the city's future. By stressing the relationship of the city with the emperors, new *Aktia* might have been seen as an opportunity to enhance the city's prospects to become *neokoros*.[97] Hereafter, the renewed festivals were imitated by smaller cities. The foundation of these blended Greco-Roman *agones* thus cannot simply be categorized as "Romanization of

---

[93] Cf. above, note 71.

[94] *Cod. Iud.* 10.54, issued by Diocletian and Maximianus. The law is undated, but from the emperors' reigns we can establish a date between 285/286 and 305. The offices held by the addressee, Hermogenes, are not specified; if we are to identify him with an otherwise attested person, the likeliest candidate is the later *praefectus urbis Romae* (cf. *PLRE* 1, 424 [Aurelius Hermogenes 8]), though he could be someone otherwise unknown.

[95] Cf. Parker 2004; Mann 2018:468 (with further readings). In a similar way, Millar 1993:316 considered the celebration of Greek festivals as "one of the central features of the communal life of Greek cities in the Imperial period." Unmatched is L. Robert's statement: "La diffusion de ces concours sous l'Empire marque la diffusion géographique de l'hellénisme" (Robert 1982:229 = 1989b:792).

[96] Cf. Alcock 1993:156; Halfmann 1979; Spawforth 2012:36–55. For a case study of Ephesos from the second century BC to the mid-first century AD, see Kirbihler 2016.

[97] For *neokoriai*, see Friesen 1993; Burrell 2004; for the quarrels, see Robert 1977 and Price 1984:126–132.

games," as Luigi Moretti once did.[98] In the last few decades, however, several studies have stressed the importance of festivals and agonistic contests to "constructions of Greek identity (on civic, regional, and individual levels)" without ignoring "the Roman response to Hellenic culture."[99] On a larger scale, these festivals can be taken as an important indicator for "a Romanisation of Greece ... through a process of 're-hellenisation' for which the impulse came from the west."[100] So, when a Greek city decided to found new *Aktia* or to refurbish a traditional festival as an *isaktios agon*, the polis placed itself at the crossroads of Greek tradition and Roman power.

UNIVERSITY OF MANNHEIM

LIST OF ABBREVIATIONS

AE = *L'Année épigraphique.* 1888–. Paris.

CIIP = *Corpus Inscriptionum Iudaeae/Palaestinae: A Multi-Lingual Corpus of the Inscriptions from Alexander to Muhammad.* 2010–. Berlin.

F.Delphes 3 = *Fouilles de Delphes.* 1909–1985. Vol. 3, *Épigraphie.* Paris.

I.Ancyra = Stephen Mitchell and David French, eds. 2012–2019. *The Greek and Latin Inscriptions of Ankara (Ancyra).* Munich.

I.Aphrodisias Performers = Charlotte Roueché. 1993. *Performers and Partisans at Aphrodisias in the Roman and Late Roman Periods: A Study Based on Inscriptions from the Current Excavations at Aphrodisias in Caria.* London.

I.Aphrodisias 2007 = Joyce Reynolds, Charlotte Roueché, and Gabriel Bodard, eds. 2007. *Inscriptions of Aphrodisias.* https://insaph.kcl.ac.uk/insaph/iaph2007/.

[98] "Romanizzazione degli Agoni" is the name of the fourth chapter of his collection, which covers inscriptions from the period 146 BC to AD 86: cf. Moretti, *I.agonistiche*, pp. 131–179. For recent discussions of the contested concept of "Romanization," cf., for example, Alcock 1997; Alcock 2002:36–98; Barrett 1997; Freeman 1997; Whittaker 1997:158; the collected articles in Schörner 2005; Spawforth 2012:26–33; Papaioannou 2016.

[99] Newby 2005:281 (for the quote); the best accounts are van Nijf 2000, Aneziri 2014, and Blanco-Pérez 2018; see also Price 1984:101–132; Klose 2005; König 2005:1–34; Pleket 2010:202–203; unsatisfactory, however, is Iddeng 2012. For a case study of the Isthmian games in Roman Corinth, see del Basso 2017.

[100] Spawforth 2012:28.

I.Beroia = Loukretia Gounaropoulou and Miltiades B. Hatzopoulos. 1998. Ἐπιγραφὲς Κάτω Μακεδονίας (μεταξὺ τοῦ Βερμίου ὄρους καὶ τοῦ Ἀξιοῦ ποταμοῦ). Vol. 1, Ἐπιγραφὲς Βεροίας. Athens.

I.Didyma = Albert Rehm. 1958. *Didyma.* Vol. 2, *Die Inschriften.* Edited by Richard Harder. Berlin.

I.Ephesos = *Die Inschriften von Ephesos.* 1979–1984. 7 vols. Inschriften griechischer Städte aus Kleinasien 11–17. Bonn.

I.Napoli = Elena Miranda, ed. 1990–1995. *Iscrizoni greche d'Italia.* 2 vols. Rome.

I.Olympia = Wilhelm Dittenberger and Karl Purgold, eds. 1896. *Die Inschriften von Olympia.* Berlin.

I.Perinthos = Mustafa Hamdi Sayar. 1998. *Perinthos-Herakleia (Marmara Ereğlisi) und Umgebung: Geschichte, Testimonien, griechische und lateinische Inschriften.* Wien.

I.Side = Johannes Nollé. 1993–2001. *Side im Altertum: Geschichte und Zeugnisse.* 2 vols. Inschriften griechischer Städte aus Kleinasien 43–44. Bonn.

I.Smyrna = Georg Petzl, ed. 1982–1990. *Die Inschriften von Smyrna.* 2 vols. Inschriften griechischer Städte aus Kleinasien 23–24. Bonn.

I.Tralleis = Fjodor B. Poljakov, ed. 1989. *Die Inschriften von Tralleis und Nysa.* Vol. 1, *Die Inschriften von Tralleis.* Inschriften griechischer Städte aus Kleinasien 36.1. Bonn.

IG = *Inscriptiones Graecae.* 1873–. Berlin.

IGLS = *Inscriptions grecques et latines de la Syrie.* 1929–. Paris.

IGR = *Inscriptiones Graecae ad res Romanas pertinentes.* 1906–1927. Paris.

ILS = Hermann Dessau. 1892–1916. *Inscriptiones Latinae selectae.* 3 vols. Berlin.

MAMA = *Monumenta Asiae Minoris Antiqua.* 1928–2013. 11 vols. London.

Moretti, *I.agonistiche* = Luigi Moretti. 1953. *Iscrizioni agonistiche greche.* Rome.

Pap.Agon = Peter Frisch. 1986. *Zehn agonistische Papyri.* Opladen.

PLRE = Arnold H. M. Jones, John R. Martindale, and John Morris, eds. 1971–1992. *The Prosopography of the Later Roman Empire.* Cambridge.

RPC = *Roman Provincial Coinage.* 1992–. London.

SEG = Supplementum Epigraphicum Graecum. 1923–. Leiden.

SNG München = Sylloge nummorum Graecorum: Deutschland; Staatliche Münzsammlung München. 1968–. Berlin.

SNG von Aulock = Sylloge nummorum Graecorum: Deutschland; Sammlung v. Aulock. 1957–1981. Berlin.

Suppl. Rodio = Giovanni Pugliese Carratelli. 1952–1954 [1955]. "Supplemento epigrafico rodio." *Annuario della Scuola Archeologica di Atene a delle Missioni Italiane in Oriente* 30–32: 247-316.

*Syll.*³ = Wilhelm Dittenberger. 1915–1924. *Sylloge inscriptionum Graecarum*. 3rd ed. 4 vols. Leipzig.

WORKS CITED

Adak, Mustafa. 2016. "Der Läufer Marcus Aurelius Nikomachos aus Erythrai." *Philia* 2:177–184.

Alcock, Susan. 1993. *Graecia Capta: The Landscapes of Roman Greece*. Cambridge.

———. 1997. "The Problem of Romanization: The Power of Athens." In *The Romanization of Athens*, ed. Michael C. Hoff and Susan I. Rotroff, 1–7. Oxford.

———. 2002. *Archaeologies of the Greek Past: Landscape, Monuments, and Memories*. Cambridge.

Aneziri, Sophia. 2014. "Greek Strategies of Adaptation to the Roman World: The Case of the Contests." *Mnemosyne* 67, no. 3:423–442.

Arslan, Melih. 2004. *Galatya Krallığı ve Roma Dönemi Ankyra Şehir Sikkeleri/ The Coins of Galatian Kingdom and the Roman Coinage of Ancyra in Galatia*. Ankara.

Barrett, John C. 1997. "Romanization: A Critical Comment." In Mattingly 1997, 51–64.

Bartels, Jens. 2008. *Städtische Eliten im römischen Makedonien: Untersuchungen zur Formierung und Struktur*. Beiträge zur Altertumskunde 242. Berlin and New York.

Basso, Lavinia del. 2017. "Greek Hellenic *Agones* in a Roman Colony: Corinth and the Return of the Isthmian Games." In *Strategies of*

Remembering in Greece under Rome (100 B.C. - 100 A.D.), ed. Tamara M. Dijkstra et al., 97–107. Leiden.

Bean, George E. 1965. "Inscriptions of Elaea and Lebedus." *Belleten* 29, no. 116:585–597.

Begass, Christoph. 2022. "On the Road Again: Hadrians Reise von Ägypten nach Athen (131) im Lichte neuer Quellenfunde." *Klio* 104, no. 2:750–789.

Birley, Anthony R. 1997. *Hadrian: The Restless Emperor*. London.

Blanco-Pérez, Aitor. 2018. "Epinikia: Celebrating Roman Victory in the Eastern Provinces of the Empire." *Tyche* 33:9–41.

Bosch, Clemens. 1935. *Die kleinasiatischen Münzen der römischen Kaiserzeit*. Vol. 2, *Einzeluntersuchungen*. Band 1, *Bithynien, 1 Hälfte*. Stuttgart.

———. 1950/51. "Die Festspiele von Nikaia." *Jahrbuch für kleinasiatische Forschung* 1:80–99.

Brennan, T. Corey. 2018. *Sabina Augusta: An Imperial Journey*. Women in Antiquity. Oxford.

Bru, Hadrien. 2011. *Le pouvoir impérial dans les provinces syriennes: Représentations et célébrations d'Auguste à Constantin (31 av. J.-C. - 337 ap. J.-C.)*. Culture and History of the Ancient Near East 49. Leiden and Boston.

Burrell, Barbara. 2004. *Neokoroi: Greek Cities and Roman Emperors*. Cincinnati Classical Studies, n.s., 9. Leiden and Boston.

Caldelli, Maria Letizia. 1993. *L'Agon Capitolinus: Storia e protagonisti dall'istituzione domizianea al IV secolo*. Rome.

Calomino, Dario. 2011. *Nicopolis d'Epiro: Nuovi studi sulla zecca e sulla produzione monetale*. BAR International Series 2214. Oxford.

Chaniotis, Angelos. 2018. *Age of Conquests: The Greek World from Alexander to Hadrian (336 B.C.- A.D. 138)*. Cambridge, MA.

Çizmeli, Zeynep. 2006. *Le monnayage de Néocésarée et du koinon du Pont*. Glaux 17. Milan.

Contoléon, A. E., Solomon Reinach, and Théodore Reinach. 1904. "Inscriptions des îles (Ios, Délos, Rhodes, Chypre)." *Revue des études grecques* 17, no. 75:196–214.

Fauconnier, Bram. 2016. "Athletes and Artists in an Expanding World: The Development of Ecumenical Associations of Competitors in the First Century BC." In *Athletics in the Hellenistic World*, ed.

Christian Mann, Sofie Remijsen, and Sebastian Scharff, 73–93. Stuttgart.

Freeman, Philip W. M. 1997. "Mommsen through to Haverfield: The Origins of Romanization Studies in late 19th-c. Britain." In Mattingly 1997, 27–50.

Friesen, Steven J. 1993. *Twice Neokoros: Ephesus, Asia and the Cult of the Flavian Imperial Family*. Religions in the Graeco-Roman World 116. Leiden and Boston.

Frisch, Peter. 1991. "Der erste vollkommene Periodonike." *Epigraphica Anatolica* 18:71–73.

Fujii, Takashi. 2013. *Imperial Cult and Imperial Representation in Roman Cyprus*. Heidelberger althistorische Beiträge und epigraphische Studien 53. Stuttgart.

Gough, Michael. 1952. "Anazarbus." *Anatolian Studies* 2:85–150.

Graf, Fritz. 2015. *Roman Festivals in the Greek East: From the Early Empire to the Middle Byzantine Era*. Cambridge.

Guerber, Éric. 2009. *Les cités grecques dans l'Empire romain: Les privilèges et les titres des cités de l'Orient hellénophone d'Octave Auguste à Dioclétien*. Rennes.

Gurval, Robert A. 1995. *Actium and Augustus: The Politics and Emotions of Civil War*. Ann Arbor.

Habicht, Christian. 1957. "Eine Urkunde des akarnanischen Bundes." *Hermes* 85, no. 1:86–122.

Halfmann, Helmut. 1979. *Die Senatoren aus dem östlichen Teil des Imperium Romanum bis zum Ende des 2. Jh. n. Chr.* Hypomnemata 58. Göttingen.

Harl, Kenneth W. 1987. *Civic Coins and Civic Politics in the Roman East, A.D. 180–275*. The Transformation of the Classical Heritage 12. Berkeley and London.

Hatzopoulos, Miltiade B. 2000. "Bulletin épigraphique." *Revue des études grecques* 113:526–528, no. 473.

Heinemann, Alexander. 2016. "Sportsfreunde: Nero und Domitian als Begründer griechischer Agone in Rom." In *Nero und Domitian: Mediale Diskurse der Herrschaftsrepräsentation im Vergleich*, ed. Sophia Bönisch-Meyer, Lisa Cordes, Verena Schulz, Anne Wolsfeld, Martin Ziegert, 217–263. Tübingen.

Herz, Peter. 1978. "Kaiserfeste der Prinzipatszeit." *Aufstieg und Niedergang der römischen Welt* 2.16.2:1135–1200.

———. 2008. "Überlegungen zur Geschichte des Makedonischen Koinon im 3. Jh. n. Chr." In *Festrituale in der römischen Kaiserzeit*, ed. Jörg Rüpke, 115–132. Tübingen.

Iddeng, Jon W. 2012. "What is a Greco-Roman Festival? A Polythetic Approach." In *Greek and Roman Festivals: Content, Meaning, and Practice*, ed. J. Rasmus Brandt and Jon W. Iddeng, 11–37. Oxford.

Ihm, Maximilian. 1907. C. *Suetonii Tranquilli opera.* Vol. 1, *De vita Caesarum libri viii.* Leipzig.

Isaac, Benjamin. 2011. "Caesarea." In *Corpus Inscriptionum Iudaeae/ Palaestinae.* Vol. 2, *Caesarea and the Middle Coast*, ed. Walter Ameling, Hannah M. Cotton, Werner Eck, Benjamin Isaac, Alla Kushnir-Stein, Haggai Misgav, Jonathan Price, and Ada Yardeni, 17–35. Berlin and Boston.

Johnston, Ann. 1984. "Hierapolis Revisited." *Numismatic Chronicle* 144:52–80.

Jürging, Axel. 1991. "Unedierte Stadtmünzen der römischen Kaiserzeit." *Mitteilungen der Österreichischen Numismatischen Gesellschaft* 31, no. 3:41–71.

Kantiréa, Maria. 2008. "Le culte impérial à Chypre: Relecture des documents épigraphiques." *Zeitschrift für Papyrologie und Epigraphik* 167:91–112.

Kienast, Dietmar. 2009. *Augustus: Prinzeps und Monarch.* 4th ed. Darmstadt.

Kienast, Dietmar, Werner Eck, and Matthäus Heil. 2017. *Römische Kaisertabelle: Grundzüge einer römischen Kaiserchronologie.* 6th ed. Darmstadt.

Kirbihler, François. 2016. *Des Grecs et des Italiens à Éphèse: Histoire d'une intégration croisée (133 a.C. - 48 p.C.).* Scripta Antiqua 88. Bordeaux.

Klose, Dietrich O. A. 1997. "Zur Entstehung der Preiskronen: Das Beispiel der Aktischen Spiele." *Jahrbuch für Numismatik und Geldgeschichte* 47:29–45.

———. 2005. "Festivals and Games in the Cities of the East during the Roman Empire." In *Coinage and Identity in the Roman Provinces*, ed.

Christopher Howgego, Volker Heuchert, and Andrew Burnett, 125–133. Oxford.

Klose, Dietrich O. A. and Gerd Stumpf. 1996. *Sport, Spiele, Sieg: Münzen und Gemmen der Antike.* Munich.

Koestermann, Erich. 1960. *P. Cornelii Taciti libri qui supersunt.* Vol. 1, *Ab excessu Divi Augusti.* Leipzig.

König, Jason. 2005. *Athletics and Literature in the Roman Empire.* Cambridge.

Körner, Christian. 2002. *Philippus Arabs: Ein Soldatenkaiser in der Tradition des antoninisch-severischen Prinzipats.* Untersuchungen zur antiken Literatur und Geschichte 61. Berlin and New York.

Lämmer, Manfred. 1986/1987. "Die aktischen Spiele von Nikopolis." *Stadion* 12/13:27–38.

Lange, Carsten Hjort. 2009. *Res publica constituta: Actium, Apollo and the Accomplishment of the Triumviral Assignment.* Impact of Empire 10. Leiden and Boston.

Langenfeld, Hans. 1975. "Die Politik des Augustus und die griechische Agonistik." In *Monumentum Chiloniense: Studien zur augusteischen Zeit; Kieler Festschrift für Erich Burck zum 70. Geburtstag,* ed. Eckard Lefèvre, 228–259. Amsterdam.

Leschhorn, Wolfgang. 1998. "Griechische Agone in Makedonien und Thrakien: Ihre Verbreitung und politisch-religiöse Bedeutung in der römischen Kaiserzeit." In *Stephanos nomismatikos: Edith Schönert-Geiss zum 65. Geburtstag,* ed. Ulrike Peter, 399–416. Berlin and New York.

———. 1999. "Die Verbreitung von Agonen in den östlichen Provinzen des römischen Reiches." In *Agonistik in der römischen Kaiserzeit,* ed. Manfred Lämmer, 31–57. St. Augustin.

Leschhorn, Wolfgang, and Peter Robert Franke. 2002. *Lexikon der Aufschriften auf griechischen Münzen.* Vol. 1, *Geographische Begriffe, Götter und Heroen, mythische Gestalten, Persönlichkeiten. Titel und Beinamen, Agonistik, staatsrechtliche und prägerechtliche Formeln, bemerkenswerte Wörter.* Denkschriften der philosophisch-historischen Klasse der Österreichischen Akademie der Wissenschaften 304. Vienna.

Mann, Christian. 2018. "Könige, Poleis und Athleten in hellenistischer Zeit." *Klio* 100, no. 2:447–479.

Marek, Christian. 2003. *Pontus et Bithynia: Die römischen Provinzen im Norden Kleinasiens.* Mainz.

Mattingly, David J., ed. 1997. *Dialogues in Roman Imperialism: Power, Discourse, and Discrepant Experience in the Roman Empire.* Journal of Roman Archaeology, Supplementary Series 23. Portsmouth, RI.

Mauritsch, Peter, Werner Petermandl, Harry Willy Pleket, and Ingomar Weiler. 2012. *Quellen zum antiken Sport: Griechisch/lateinisch und deutsch.* Texte zur Forschung 102. Darmstadt.

Merkelbach, Reinhold. 1975. "Der griechische Wortschatz der Christen." *Zeitschrift für Papyrologie und Epigraphik* 18:101–148. Reprinted in Merkelbach 1997, 393–436.

———. 1997. *Hestia und Erigone: Vorträge und Aufsätze.* Ed. Wolfgang Blümel, Bärbel Kramer, Johannes Kramer, and Cornelia E. Römer. Stuttgart and Leipzig.

Miranda de Martino, Elena. 2014. "Les *Sebasta* de Naples à l'époque de Domitien: Témoignages épigraphiques." *Comptes rendus des séances de l'Académie des Inscriptions et Belles-Lettres* 158, no. 3:1165–1188.

Millar, Fergus. 1993. *The Roman Near East, 31 B.C. – A.D. 337.* Cambridge, MA.

———. 2006. "The Roman *Coloniae* of the Near East: A Study of Cultural Relations." In *Rome, the Greek World, and the East.* Vol. 3, *The Greek World, the Jews, and the East,* ed. Hannah M. Cotton and Guy M. Rogers, 164–222. Chapel Hill.

Mitchell, Stephen. 1993. *Anatolia: Land, Men, and Gods in Asia Minor.* 2 vols. Oxford.

Mitford, Terence B. 1980. "Roman Cyprus." In *Aufstieg und Niedergang der römischen Welt* 2.7.2:1285–1384.

Mommsen, Theodor. 1883. *Res gestae divi Augusti ex monumentis Ancyrano et Apolloniensi.* 2nd ed. Berlin.

Newby, Zahra. 2005. *Greek Athletics in the Roman World: Victory and Virtue.* Oxford.

Nielsen, Thomas Heine. 2018. *Two Studies in the History of Ancient Greek Athletics.* Scientia Danica, Series H, Humanistica 8, 16. Copenhagen.

Nijf, Onno M. van. 2000. "Athletics, Festivals and Greek Identity in the Roman East." *Proceedings of the Cambridge Philological Society* 45:176–200. Reprinted in *Greek Athletics*, ed. Jason König (Edinburgh, 2013), 175–198.

Papaioannou, Maria. 2016. "A Synoecism of Cultures in Roman Greece." In *Beyond Boundaries: Connecting Visual Cultures in the Provinces of Ancient Rome*, ed. Susan E. Alcock, Mariana Egri, and James F. D. Frakes, 31–45. Los Angeles.

Papen, Ferdinand Gaudenz von. 1908. "Die Spiele von Hierapolis." *Zeitschrift für Numismatik* 26:161–182.

Parker, Robert. 2004. "New 'Panhellenic' Festivals in Hellenistic Greece." In *Mobility and Travel in the Mediterranean from Antiquity to the Middle Ages*, ed. Renate Schlesier and Ulrike Zellmann, 9–22. Münster.

Pavlogiannis, Onoufrios, Evangelos Albanidis and Minas Dimitriou. 2009. "The Aktia of Nikopolis: New Approaches." *Nikephoros* 22:79–102.

Pleket, H. W. 1975. "Games, Prizes, Athletes and History: Some Aspects of the History of Sport in the Greco-Roman World." *Stadion* 1:49–89.

———. 2010. "Roman Emperors and Greek Athletes." *Nikephoros* 23:175–203.

Price, S. R. F. 1984. *Rituals and Power: The Roman Imperial Cult in Asia Minor.* Cambridge.

Radt, Stefan. 2002–2011. *Strabons Geographika.* 10 vols. Göttingen.

Reisch, Emil. 1894. "Aktia." In *Paulys Realencyclopädie der classischen Altertumswissenschaft*, vol. 1, 1213–1214.

Remijsen, Sofie. 2010. "The Introduction of the Antiochene Olympics: A Proposal for a New Date." *Greek, Roman, and Byzantine Studies* 50, no. 3:411–436.

Rieger, Barbara. 1999. "Die *Capitolia* des Kaisers Domitian." *Nikephoros* 12:171–203.

Rieks, Rudolf. 1970. "Sebasta und Aktia." *Hermes* 98, no. 1:96–116

Robert, Louis. 1937. *Études anatoliennes: Recherches sur les inscriptions grecques de l'Asie Mineure.* Paris.

———. 1939. "Hellenica." *Revue de philologie de littérature et d'histoire anciennes* 13:97–217. Reprinted in Robert 1969, 1250–1370.

———. 1960. *Hellenica XI–XII: Recueil d'épigraphie, de numismatique et d'antiquités grecques.* Paris.

———. 1968. "Enterrements et épitaphes." *L'Antiquité Classique* 37, no. 2:406–448. Reprinted in Robert 1989b, 82–93.

———. 1969. *Opera Minora Selecta.* Vol. 2. Amsterdam.

———. 1970. "Deux concours grecs à Rome." *Comptes rendus des séances de Académie des Inscriptions et Belles-Lettres* 114, no. 1:6–27. Reprinted in Robert 1989a, 647–668 and Robert 2007, 247–266.

———. 1977. "La Titulature de Nicée et de Nicomédie: La gloire et la haine." *Harvard Studies in Classical Philology* 81:1–39. Reprinted in Robert 1989b, 211–249 and Robert 2007, 673–703.

———. 1982. "Une vision de Perpétue martyre à Carthage en 203." *Comptes rendus des séances de Académie des Inscriptions et Belles-Lettres* 126, no. 2:228–276. Reprinted in Robert 1989b, 791–839.

———. 1989a. *Opera minora selecta: Épigraphie et antiquités grecques.* Vol. 5. Amsterdam.

———. 1989b. *Opera minora selecta: Épigraphie et antiquités grecques.* Vol. 6. Amsterdam.

———. 2007. *Choix d'écrits.* Ed. Denis Rousset. Paris.

Robert, Jeanne, and Louis Robert. 1968. "Bulletin épigraphique." *Revue des études grecques* 81:504, no. 442.

———. 1969. "Bulletin épigraphique." *Revue des études grecques* 82:501, no. 489.

Roueché, Charlotte. 1981. "Rome, Asia and Aphrodisias in the Third Century." *Journal of Roman Studies* 71:103–120.

Rumscheid, Jutta. 2000. *Kranz und Krone: Zu Insignien, Siegespreisen und Ehrenzeichen der römischen Kaiserzeit.* Istanbuler Forschungen 43. Tübingen.

Şahin, Sencer. 1991. "Inschriften aus Seleukeia am Kalykadnos (Silifke)." *Epigraphica Anatolica* 17:139–166.

Sarikakis, Theodoros. 1965. "Ἄκτια τὰ ἐν Νικοπόλει." *Αρχαιολογική Εφημερίς* 104:145–162.

Scheid, John. 2007. *Res gestae divi Augusti: Hauts faits du divin Auguste.* Paris.

Schönert, Edith. 1965. *Griechisches Münzwerk: Die Münzprägung von Perinthos.* Deutsche Akademie der Wissenschaften zu Berlin, Schriften der Sektion für Altertumswissenschaft 45. Berlin.

Schörner, Günther, ed. 2005. *Romanisierung - Romanisation: Theoretische Modelle und praktische Beispiele.* BAR International Series 1427. Oxford.

Slater, William. 2012. "The Victor's Return, and the Category of Games." In *Epigraphical Approaches to the Post-Classical Polis: Fourth BC to Second Century AD,* ed. Paraskevi Martzavou and Nikolaos Papazarkadas, 139–163. Oxford.

Spawforth, Antony J. S. 2007. "*Kapetoleia Olympia*: Roman Emperors and Greek Agones." In *Pindar's Poetry, Patrons, and Festivals: From Archaic Greece to the Roman Empire,* ed. Simon Hornblower and Catherine Morgan, 377–390. Oxford.

———. 2012. *Greece and the Augustan Cultural Revolution.* Cambridge.

Specht, Edith. 2007. "Wreaths, Balls, and 'Crowns': Greek Imperial Coins and Athletics." In *Sport and the Construction of Identities,* ed. Bettina Kratzmüller, Matthias Marschik, Rudolf Müllner, Hubert D. Szemethy, and Elisabeth Trinkl, 799–804. Vienna.

Stauber, Josef. 2022. *Repertorium der griechischen und lateinischen Inschriften aus Mysien.* Denkschriften der philosophisch-historischen Klasse der Österreichischen Akademie der Wissenschaften 538. 2 vols. Vienna.

Strasser, Jean-Yves. 2004. "Inscription rhodienne pour un héraut sacré (Suppl. Epig. Rh. 67)." *Klio* 86, no. 1:141–164.

———. 2015a. "Inscriptions agonistique de Rhodes." *Philia* 1:57–76.

———. 2015b. "Un citharède de Cos (IG XII 4, 2, 1166)." *Revue des études grecques* 128, no. 2:659–672.

———. 2021. *Mémoires des champions: Corpus des palmarès d'Octavien à Valentinien Ier.* Bibliothèque des Écoles françaises d'Athènes et de Rome 395. Athens.

Touratsoglu, Ioannis. 1988. *Die Münzstätte von Thessaloniki in der römischen Kaiserzeit (32/31 v. Chr. bis 268 n. Chr.).* Antike Münzen und geschnittene Steine 12. Berlin and New York.

Wallner, Christian. 1997. *Soldatenkaiser und Sport.* Grazer Altertumskundliche Studien 4. Frankfurt am Main.

————. 2000. "Der olympische Agon von Bostra." *Zeitschrift für Papyrologie und Epigraphik* 129:97–107.

Whittaker, C. R. 1997. "Imperialism and Culture: The Roman Initiative." In Mattingly 1997, 143–163.

Ziegler, Ruprecht. 1985. *Städtisches Prestige und kaiserliche Politik: Studien zum Festwesen in Ostkilikien im 2. und 3. Jahrhundert n. Chr.* Kultur und Erkenntnis 2. Düsseldorf.

MYTH AND ACTUALITY AT THE SCHOOL OF RHETORIC

THE ENCOMIUM ON THE FLOWER OF ANTINOUS IN ITS CULTURAL AND PERFORMATIVE CONTEXT

CHIARA MECCARIELLO

I. INTRODUCTION

Among the papyri unearthed by the "Missione Archeologica" of the University of Milan during the 1934 excavations of Tebtynis is a square fragment from a roll bearing three columns written in small round handwriting. First published by Achille Vogliano in 1937 under the title "Frammento di antologia" (*P.Mil.Vogl.* I 20, second to third century CE[1]), it contains five self-standing prose pieces, each introduced by a heading and each identifiable—though with varying degrees of certainty—as a specific type of the preliminary rhetorical exercises

---

Some of the arguments of this paper were presented at the conference "Els noms i l'onomàstica en les pràctiques mitogràfiques," held in February 2020 at the Autonomous University of Barcelona. I would like to thank Jordi Pàmias (the conference organizer) and the other participants for the helpful discussion, as well as Daniela Colomo and Lucio Del Corso for commenting on an earlier version of this article. Editions of papyri are abbreviated according to the Checklist of Editions of Greek, Latin, Demotic, and Coptic Papyri, Ostraca, and Tablets available at https://papyri.info/docs/checklist. For all other abbreviations, please refer to the list at the end of this article.

[1] On the date see especially Colomo 2004:88n12, who compares P.Vat.Gr. 11v (Roberts 1956: no. 18b), assignable to the first half of the third century CE on the grounds of dated documents contained in the same roll (on these see now Ricciardetto 2015). Cavallo highlights the paleographic similarity between *P.Mil.Vogl.* I 20 and *P.Lond.Lit.* 192 and proposes to date both to the late third century CE, on the basis of *P.Lund* IV 13 (Roberts 1956: no. 23b, third quarter of the third century CE; see Cavallo *apud* Stramaglia 1996:138n215, and Cavallo 2005:186). However, as Prada 2012:628 has pointed out in his discussion of *P.Lond.Lit.* 192, solid second-century CE parallels exist, such as *P.Oxy.* VI 853 (Roberts 1956: no. 17a) and *P.Oxy.* XXXI 2536 (first hand, Turner and Parsons 1987: no. 61).

known as *progymnasmata*.[2] Brief and somewhat crude in their style, they read more like sketches of rhetorical compositions than fully fleshed-out pieces. Vogliano deemed them "di valore assai discutibile" in both content and style, and Körte highlighted their "billige mythographische und historische Weisheit" and their alleged "Gedankenlosigkeit."[3] More recent studies have elucidated several aspects of these pieces in light of progymnasmatic theory, thereby shifting the focus from their poor literary quality to their value for reconstructing learning practices.[4] The text in the papyrus shows several errors that appear to stem from copying (e.g., μεμνημαι for μεμύημαι at i.20, Σειδων for Σόλων at ii.4, δημαγωνα for δημαγωγία at ii.16): certainly not an autograph, it cannot be a student's original work. The regular handwriting, informal but carefully executed, and the well-organized layout, combined with the copying mistakes, point to the work of a scribe: this roll is likely, then, a professionally produced book used in school, rather than the direct product of a schoolroom.[5] At any rate, its intended users were individuals engaged in rhetorical training, and a teacher of rhetoric is a likely candidate for the authorship of the pieces.[6]

    [2] Körte was the first to see the school connection and to characterize the compositions as "das Machwerk eines namenlosen Schulmeisters, der seinen Schülern Skizzen zu rhetorischen Übungen diktierte" (1939:116; but dictation seems to be ruled out by copying mistakes, see below). More recently, scholars have proposed identifications of single pieces with specific types of *progymnasmata* (see especially Colomo 2004:2013 and Fernández Delgado and Pordomingo 2008); there can indeed be little doubt that the composition on Heracles at i.18–31 is an *ethopoeia*, the one on exile at ii.1–24 a *thesis*, and the one on the flower of Antinous an encomium (see also below, note 7). However, uncertainties remain about both the final, incomplete piece on the *himation* of Agathocles at iii.26–32 (perhaps an encomium or a *psogos*: Fernández Delgado and Pordomingo 2008:188–189) and the composition about the phoenix at i.1–17 (*diegema*: Gualandri 1974; ekphrasis: Stramaglia 2003, Pordomingo 2007, Fernández Delgado and Pordomingo 2008; see the rich discussion in Colomo 2013:66–68).
    [3] Vogliano 1937:175, Körte 1939:116.
    [4] Especially Colomo 2004 and 2013, Fernández Delgado and Pordomingo 2008.
    [5] See, for example, Bastianini 1992:93.
    [6] For the possibility that this papyrus belonged to a teacher's library, based on the text of the papyri with which it was discarded in antiquity, see Del Corso 2020:57–58. Colomo 2013:70 has the following suggestion regarding how *P.Mil.Vogl.* I 20 came into existence: "It is perhaps not implausible to think that one or more students may have given the notes taken during classes to a professional scribe in order to have a proper school book, although not a very refined one."

In this article I will focus on the fourth composition contained in the papyrus, a piece entitled "On the Flower of Antinous" (εἰς τὸ Ἀντινόειον ἄνθος), which occupies the bottom of the second and most of the third column. As indicated both by the heading and by formal traits, it is most likely an encomium.[7] The story of the flower of Antinous is reported by Athenaeus in Ulpian's discussion of various types of garlands: according to this account, the red lotus was labeled "flower of Antinous" on the initiative of the Egyptian poet Pancrates, who showed it to Hadrian when the emperor visited Alexandria in 130 CE.[8] The poet proposed to name the flower *Antinoeios* because it allegedly sprung from the earth "when it was drenched with the blood of the Mauretanian lion Hadrian had killed while hunting in the part of Libya near Alexandria."[9] Athenaeus equips the story with four hexameters by Pancrates in which the mention of several flowers, perhaps part of a landscape description, is followed by the line "for the flower named for Antinous had not yet appeared," which presumably justifies its absence from the description.[10]

---

[7] The use of εἰς is common in titles of encomia: see, e.g., Plut. *Demosth.* 1.1 (τὸ ... εἰς Ἀλκιβιάδην ἐγκώμιον), [Plut.] *X orat.* 838 B2 (εἰς Ἑλένην ἐγκώμιον), and the heading εἰς Ῥαδάμανθυν preserved in *P.Mil.Vogl.* III 123 + *P.CtYBR* inv. 4573, col. aII.30, a Hellenistic collection of encomia. The formal traits of encomia detectable in the composition on the flower of Antinous are analyzed by Fernández Delgado and Pordomingo 2008:182–188. A verse encomium on Antinous and Hermes, likely an autograph, is preserved in *P.Oxy.* L 3537v (third or fourth century); the other side of the papyrus contains a verse *ethopoeia* on Hesiod penned either by a different hand or in a different writing style by the same person.

[8] Ath. 15.677d–e = *FGrHist* 625 T 1. For the identification of this Pancrates with Pachrates, a prophet from Heliopolis who is associated with Hadrian in a magical papyrus (*Pap.Graec.Mag.* IV 2446–2455), see Ogden 2004, who also argues that the sorcerer Pancrates in Lucian's *Philopseudes* is modeled on the same individual.

[9] Ath. 15.677e, translated by Olson 2012.

[10] F 3 Heitsch, translated by Olson 2012. Two further fragments from Pancrates' work have been identified in *P.Oxy.* VIII 1085 (F 2 Heitsch), containing hexameters about the lion hunt involving Hadrian and Antinous, and *P.Lond.Lit.* 36 (F 1 Heitsch), which mentions both figures but is of less secure attribution. Another poetical fragment about the same lion hunt, *P.Oxy.* LXIII 4352, is a later composition dating to the reign of Diocletian, whom the poem celebrates. For the symbolism of the lotus in Egyptian tradition and its significance in the Antinous story, see Höschele 2019.

The composition in *P.Mil.Vogl.* I 20 presupposes the aition but does not refer to this story. Instead of outlining a plain praise of the named subject matter, or a description of the flower and its origin, the author discusses various flowers and plants that resulted from metamorphoses of mythical youths in the context of violent death or abduction. In a final syncrisis he concludes that the flower of Antinous is the most beautiful of all. This superiority seems to be based on the flower's (unmentioned) bright color as opposed to the pale color of two of the *comparanda*, the narcissus and the hyacinth, which reflects the tragic end of the corresponding characters.

While the overall reading and interpretation of the composition are uncontroversial, the text contains some oddities which were already highlighted in the first edition. In this article I will trace both the encomium's puzzling elements and its overall structure to the type of source that, I will argue, underlies its composition, namely, the mythographical catalogue. In the final section, I will examine the mythologization of Antinous and the praise of his flower as two complementary achievements of the encomium and set the composition in its envisioned performative context.

II. TEXT AND TRANSLATION

I report here the text of the papyrus with a brief apparatus and my translation.[11] The encomium is almost entirely preserved: the ends of all lines in col. iii are lost, but most of them can be easily supplemented.[12]

COL. II.25–33

εἰς τὸ Ἀντινόειον ἄνθος.
οὔ[τ]ε νάρκισσος ὁ Ἀθηναῖος,
οὔτε ὑάκινθος ὁ Λακεδαιμόνιος, οὔτε κρόκος ἐξ ἀρχῆς ἄνθος ἦν, οὐχ Ὕλας παῖς παρὰ Θραι-

---

[11] Images of the papyrus are available online as part of the *Photographic Archive of Papyri in the Cairo Museum* (http://ipap.csad.ox.ac.uk/).
[12] The supplements at iii.6, 15, and 20 are briefly discussed below.

ξίν, οὐ κυπάρισσος ἐν Κρήτηι   30
δένδρον, οὐκ ἀπ᾽ ἀρχῆς ἡ δά-
φνη φυτόν, ἀλλὰ Κρόκος μὲν ἦν
μειράκιον Κιλίκιον, Ὕλας

COL. III.1–25

παῖς καλὸς Θρᾶιξ, Κυπά[ρισσος παῖς
εὐειδής, Δάφνη νεᾶν[ις παρθέ-
νος, θυγάτηρ ποταμοῦ, Ṇ[άρκισ-
σος καλὸς παῖς Βοιώτιος, [Ὑάκιν-
θος Σπαρτιάτης ὡραῖο[ς ἔφη-   5
βος. Ὕλαν εἶ[χ]εν Ἡρακλῆς, [Διόνυ-
σος ἥρα· Κρόκος συνεβά[κχευε
Διονύσωι· Νάρκισσον ἥρ[πασαν
Νύμφαι, Ὑακίνθου καὶ Δ[άφνης
Ἀπόλλων ἥρα. Νύμ[φ]αι Κρ[όκον   10
ἀπέκτειναν, Ὕλαν ἥρπα[σαν
Νύμφαι, Κυπάρισσος κατ[ὰ πε-
τρῶν ἔρριψε ἑ[α]τόν, Δ[άφνην
φεύγουσαν ὑπεδέξατο γῆ· Ν[άρ-
κισσος ὑπερηφανείαι ἐρ[ασθεὶς   15
ἑαυτὸν ὡς ἄλλον ἀπώλεσ[εν· ἓν
δὲ μόνον τὸ τοῦ Ἀντινόου [ἄνθος
πάντων ἥδ[ι]ον διαφέρον, ο[ὐχ
ὡς νάρκισσος ὠχρόν, περὶ τῆς [ἁρ-
παγῆς λυπούμενον, οὐδὲ ὡς [ὑάκιν-   20
θος ὠχρόν, τὸ χρῶμα τοῦ π[τώ-
ματος μειμούμενον. τίς ἀ[ναπλέ-
ξεται στεφάνους πενθουμέ[νων
ὀνομάτων, κλαύσεται μᾶλλ[ον
τὴν ὥραν τῶν ἀπολομέ[νων.   25

fere omnia suppl. Vogliano ‖ ii 25 εἰς: ις pap. ‖ iii 2 <Κρὴς> εὐειδής Maas,
εὐειδὴς <Κρής> Vogliano ‖ 4 βυωτιου pap. ‖ 4–5 [Ὑάκιν]θος Castiglioni
‖ 6 εἶ[χ]εν vel εἶ[λ]εν Maas ‖ 6–7 [Διόνυ]σος Castiglioni ‖ 8 ἥρ[πασαν:
ἥι[τησαν Castiglioni ‖ 13 ερειψε pap. ‖ 15 ἐρ[εθισθεὶς vel ἐρ[ασθεὶς Maas
‖ 16 ἓν suppl. Maas ‖ 18 ηδ ex αδ corr. pap ‖ 19 ὠχρόν: ωχην pap. ‖ 21

θος: θον pap. ‖ 21-22 π[τώ]‖ματος Vogliano: π[ελιώ]‖ματος anonymus apud Hollis: nisi potius †ώχρόν† ... π[λήγ]‖ματος (e.g., πελιόν ... π[λήγ]‖ματος) ‖ 22 τίς scripsi: τὶς Vogliano ‖ 22-23 ἀ[ναπλέ]‖ξεται Colomo[13] : ἀ[ναλέ]‖ξεται Vogliano ‖ 25 απολωμε[pap.

ON THE FLOWER OF ANTINOUS

Neither the Athenian narcissus, nor the Spartan hyacinth, nor the crocus were flowers from the beginning, nor was Hylas, a boy of Thrace, nor was the cypress in Crete a tree, nor was the bay (*daphne*) originally a plant; but Crocus was a Cilician lad, Hylas a beautiful Thracian boy, Cypress a handsome [boy], Daphne a young virgin, daughter of a river, Narcissus a beautiful Boeotian boy, Hyacinth a youthful Spartan ephebe. Hylas was taken by Heracles and loved by Dionysus; Crocus reveled with Dionysus, Narcissus was abducted by the Nymphs, with Hyacinth and Daphne Apollo was in love. The Nymphs killed Crocus, Hylas was abducted by the Nymphs, Cypress threw himself down from the rocks, Daphne was welcomed by the earth while fleeing. Narcissus, who arrogantly fell in love (with himself), killed himself as (though killing?) someone else. But the flower of Antinous alone surpasses all others in pleasantness,[14] being neither pale like the narcissus, which was grieved by the abduction, nor pale

---

[13] I would like to thank Daniela Colomo for sharing with me a draft of her edition of P.Lips. inv. 1454v, forthcoming in *P.Lips*. III, where she proposes this supplement in a brief discussion of the encomium in *P.Mil.Vogl*. I 20.

[14] If the supplement at iii.16 is correct, the syntax of the sentence is elliptical, with the verb "to be" understood and πάντων governed *apo koinou* by ἥδ[ι]ον and διαφέρον: lit. "the flower of Antinous is the only one that excels among all, (being) sweeter (than all), (being) neither pale like the narcissus ... nor ..." Hollis 2003:12 translates "with respect to one thing the flower of Antinous alone, more delightful than all the others, is different from them" whereas Fernández Delgado and Pordomingo 2008:182 render "Pero una sola, la flor de Antínoo, destaca entre todas y es más agradable." Like the latter, I am inclined to take ἐν ... μόνον together as a nominative referring to τὸ τοῦ Ἀντινόου [ἄνθος] rather than separately, with ἐν as adverbial accusative and μόνον referring to the flower: ἐν ... μόνον is more likely to be a unit, and underlying the flower's uniqueness rather than the uniqueness of its distinguishing characteristic is more appropriate to the encomiastic context.

like the hyacinth, which imitates the color of a corpse. Whoever will weave garlands of mourned names, will weep even more for the young age of the dead.

III. ERRORS AND ODDITIES? A CATALOGIC HYPOTEXT

Vogliano and other scholars who contributed to his edition and commentary of *P.Mil.Vogl.* I 20 were puzzled by several traits of this composition, which they labeled "errori" and "stranezze."[15] Maas concluded that the text was heavily interpolated and sought to restore its original form by subtraction.[16] The main alleged interpolations were the indication of the geographical provenance of the flowers at ii.26–30 and, as tentatively suggested by Vogliano, the references to Hylas, who did not metamorphose into a plant, unlike all other characters. However, the very notion of interpolation is problematic in the context of a progymnasmatic composition, especially if the pieces are interpreted as sketches of model exercises:[17] as Körte put it, "Wer sich bemüht, die Wiederholungen und Widersprüche im einzelnen zu heben, verbessert eher den Verfasser als den Schreiber."[18] Still, these "Wiederholungen und Widersprüche," while not indicating a departure from a hypothetical original (a category that seems out of place in this context), can be valuable indicators of the rhetor's compositional procedure.

In what follows, I will show that positing a mythographical catalogue as the rhetor's immediate source for Antinous's *comparanda* provides a unifying explanation for these and other characteristics of the encomium. First, I will discuss the structural, syntactical, and linguistic elements of the composition that point to the influence of a mythographical catalogue (sections III.1–2); second, I will discuss

---

[15] Vogliano 1937:183.

[16] Maas *apud* Vogliano 1937:183.

[17] Even in the first edition, where the compositions are *not* interpreted as school texts, "interpolation" is left somewhat undefined, and it is unclear whether the editors suppose that the rhetor clumsily amplified a preexisting, logically "clean" composition or that the alleged interpolations are erudite but clumsy scribal additions.

[18] Körte 1939:117.

details of the text whose *raison d'être* becomes easier to understand if this derivation is accepted (sections III.3–7).

III.1. STRUCTURE AND SYNTAX

A striking feature of this encomium is the delayed appearance of its subject matter. After the title, the flower of Antinous is only mentioned in the conclusion of the piece (iii.17), and in an allusive manner that presupposes the reader's knowledge of its aition. Very little of the composition is about Antinous. The focus rests instead on other characters, who share with him a young age and a traumatic and premature end of their human life. A metamorphosis, in most cases into a flower or plant, is also a common trait of all their stories.[19] An overarching μέν ... δέ structure (μέν: ii.32, δέ: iii.17) conveys the opposition between these mythological characters and the singularity of Antinous. This balanced contrast accentuates the impression of the former as a compact block, which is instrumental to the main point of the encomium: the unique superiority of the flower of Antinous to the flowers originating from the metamorphoses of other mythical youths.

For this set of six largely homogeneous characters the same type of information is provided in four different sections:

1), 2) Name and geographical provenance (in the case of Daphne, the latter is substituted with a reference to her fluvial father), first at ii.25–32, where the characters appear as vegetation entities (with one exception, see below), and then at ii.32–iii.6, where they are mentioned as youths.

---

[19] Some of these characters are found together in other sources, including, e.g., Luc. *Ver. Hist.* 2.17 (Ὑάκινθός τε ὁ Λακεδαιμόνιος καὶ ὁ Θεσπιεὺς Νάρκισσος καὶ Ὕλας καὶ ἄλλοι καλοί), Hyg. *Fab.* 271 (Hyacinthus, Narcissus and Hylas are listed among *QVI EPHEBI FORMOSISSIMI FVERVNT*), *CIL* X 7567.5 (epitaph of Pomptilla, first or second century CE, mentioning Narcissus and Hyacinth in the context of postmortem floral metamorphosis), Procop. *Decl.* 4.37–39 Garzya/Loenertz (Narcissus and Hyacinth are singled out for their beauty and sad destiny). See also the iconographical items listed in *LIMC* s.v. Hylas, 579 and the Latin passages quoted in Mattiacci 2017:39n62. The hexametric composition on Antinous preserved in *P.Oxy.* LXIII 4352 also draws a parallel with Narcissus, Hyacinth, and perhaps Adonis (fr. 5 ii.3–7; on the possible relationship between this text and Pancrates' poem see Höschele 2019:231–232). The encomium in *P.Mil.Vogl.* I 20, however, is the only source to preserve an extensive tableau of metamorphosed characters.

3) Brief reference to a (semi)divine character variously involved in their stories—as lover, companion, or abductor (iii.6–10).

4) A condensed description of the end of their human existence (iii.10–16).

The names of the six characters are regularly mentioned, with no article and usually as the first element of a sentence, in each of these four sections; the overall structure is paratactic and almost always asyndetic (see especially ii.29–32, ii.33–iii.16). Moreover, the mythological characters follow a fixed order. The sequence Narcissus, Hyacinth, Crocus, Hylas, Cyparissus, and Daphne reappears in identical form, although with different starting points, in sections 1 (from Narcissus to Daphne), 2 (from Crocus to Hyacinth) and 4 (from Crocus to Narcissus; Hyacinth is omitted). The first two characters, Narcissus and Hyacinth, are mentioned again as flowers, in the expected order, in the conclusion of the encomium (iii.19–21). In section 3, the order is disrupted (Hylas, Crocus, Narcissus, Hyacinth, and Daphne), but the section overall has less regularity than the others, as two characters loved by Apollo are grouped together (Hyacinth and Daphne) and, if Castiglioni's supplement Ὕλαν εἶ[χ]εν Ἡρακλῆς, [Διόνυ]]σος ἤρα at iii.6–7 is correct, Cyparissus is missing and two segments are devoted to Hylas.[20] The sequence Hylas–Crocus in this case may have been prompted by Crocus's association with Dionysus: after starting with Hylas and proceeding, by association, with Crocus, the author would have started

---

[20] No connection between Hylas and Dionysus is attested, and Maas *apud* Vogliano 1937:183 believed [Διόνυ]]σος ἤρα to be the remains of an original Κρόκου Διόνυσος ἤρα, which would be a variant of the following Κρόκος συνεβά[κχευε] Διονύσωι. Notably, while—with this supplement—Hylas is the only character in this section to have two sentences devoted to him, Cyparissus is missing, and so it is tempting to suppose that this segment was originally devoted to him. We may speculatively think of an original Κυπαρίσσου Ζέφυρος ἤρα, corrupted to [Κυπάρισ]]σος ἤρα. The line length would still be within the expected range (between twenty-one and twenty-eight characters: cf. the irregular right-hand alignment in columns i and ii). On Zephyrus's involvement in the Cyparissus myth see Serv. *Aen.* 3.680 (*alii hunc Cyparissum Cretensem puerum pulcherrimum et castissimum fuisse <tradunt>, quem quidam ab Apolline, non nulli a Zephyro amatum volunt*) and Nonnus, *Dion.* 11.364–365 (incidentally, the Servius passage is also the only parallel on Cyparissus's Cretan provenance stated at ii.30; I have not been able to find parallels for the manner of death). This mythical variant would be in line with the absence of Cyparissus among Apollo's beloved at iii.9–10 (Ὑακίνθου καὶ Δ[άφνης]] Ἀπόλλων ἤρα).

again from the beginning (Narcissus and Hyacinth) and then continued (and ended) with Daphne by association with Hyacinth (iii.9–10, Ὑακίνθου καὶ Δ[άφνης] | Ἀπόλλων ἤρα), leaving aside Cyparissus.

Be that as it may, a homogeneous treatment of different mythological characters, in a mostly paratactic structure and with a fixed and repetitive pattern, could be a textbook definition of "mythographical catalogue," a textual typology of which several examples, in both Greek and Latin, are known from papyri of the Imperial period, from Hyginus's *Fabulae*, and from medieval manuscripts.[21] These catalogues range from bare lists of plain names to lists of names accompanied by geographical information or even expanded by brief narratives.

Mythographical catalogues of metamorphoses are preserved in both ancient papyri and medieval manuscripts.[22] One example is found in P.Mich. inv. 1447 (no. 70 van Rossum-Steenbeek), labeled by the first editor "a papyrus dictionary of metamorphoses."[23] A portion of col. ii is well preserved and consists of an alphabetical collection of names of relevant characters, each equipped with genealogical information, a brief metamorphic story, and often a reference to an author who treated the myth or mentioned the character. Here, as in other papyri, the various items are conspicuously separated through forked *paragraphoi*

---

[21] Mythographical catalogues on papyrus are collected in van Rossum-Steenbeek 1998: nos. 58–74, while a set of Greek catalogues known under the name of *Anonymus Florentinus* was published by Westermann 1839 (see below). On the contents, style, and layout of papyrus catalogues and on their relationship with Hyginus, see van Rossum-Steenbeek 1998:150–156.

[22] The topic was also treated in an Imperial-period prose collection of forty-one stories by the otherwise unknown mythographer Antoninus Liberalis. Conceptually, the boundaries between a catalogue such as the one in P.Mich. inv. 1447 and Antoninus Liberalis's collection are somewhat blurred (Delattre 2021:98–100 does treat the latter as a catalogue). A theoretically based classification lies beyond the scope of this article, but it will suffice to point out the two main features that distinguish what are here called "catalogues" from mythographical collections of narratives. First and foremost, names take priority: each catalogue entry starts with the name of the metamorphosed character; the narrative portions, when present, may be characterized as brief expansions. Second, the entries are brief and structurally homogeneous. Conversely, Antoninus Liberalis's stories are complex narratives that sometimes span several paragraphs and only about twenty percent of the stories start with the name of the metamorphosed character(s).

[23] Renner 1978.

and blank spaces. I report here the two shortest pieces as printed by van Rossum-Steenbeek with Renner's translation (adapted):[24]

COL. II.29–35

Ἀρέθουσα θυγατὴρ μὲν Ὑπέρ[ο]υ, Π[οσ]ει[δῶνι δὲ συν-
ελθοῦ[σ]α κατὰ τὸν Βοϊκὸν Εὔριπον, [εἰς κρήνην
ἠλλάγη ἐν Χ[αλκίδι] ὑπὸ [τῆς] Ἥρας, ὡς Ἡσίοδος ἱστορε[ῖ
>—
Αἴθυιαι Ἀλιάκμονος τοῦ Ἁλιάρτου θυγατ[έρες
ἑπτὰ τὸν ἀριθμὸν θρηνοῦσαι τὴν Ἰνὼ μ[ετε-
μορφώθησαν ὑπὸ Ἥρας εἰς .[.] .ρ[.]....[..].. [
παρ' Αἰσχύλωι καλοῦνται μισοκόρων[οι

Arethusa, daughter of Hyperos, having had [inter]course with Poseidon in the region of the Boeotian Euripus, was transformed [into a spring] in Chalcis by Hera, as Hesiod recounts.

The Aethyiae, daughters of Haliacmon the son of Haliartus, seven in number, while lamenting Ino were transformed by Hera into (birds) ... are called by Aeschylus "crow haters."

A similar catalogue of metamorphoses is found in a set of mythograph-ical extracts forming the so-called *Anonymus Florentinus*.[25] The relevant catalogue consists in a sequence of brief entries; each begins with the name of the main character, indicates the entity into which the char-acter was transformed, and provides a brief summary of the causes and circumstances of the metamorphosis. I report here a representative selection with Cameron's translation:[26]

[24] Van Rossum-Steenbeek 1998:336, Renner 1978:287 and 289.
[25] Westermann 1839:218–223. These texts are preserved in a small group of medieval manuscripts ultimately depending on a twelfth-century codex (*Laur. Gr.* 56.1). For the date of the manuscript and further information, see Cameron 2004:335–339.
[26] Cameron 2004:287.

Λυκάων ὁ βασιλεὺς μετεμορφώθη εἰς λύκον διὰ τὸ τῷ Διὶ
παραθεῖναι ἐπὶ τῆς τραπέζης κρέα ἀνθρώπινα παρ' αὐτῷ
ξενουμένῳ.

[…]

Κορώνη Κορωνέως θυγάτηρ τοῦ Φωκέων δυνάστου
φεύγουσα τὸν Ποσειδῶνος ἔρωτα εἰς τὸ ὁμώνυμον
μετέβαλεν ὄρνεον κατ' ἔλεον Ἀθηνᾶς.

Νυκτιμένη Κλυμένου θυγάτηρ φεύγουσα τὸν τοῦ πατρὸς
ἔρωτα κατ' ἔλεον Ἀθηνᾶς εἰς γλαῦκα μετεμορφώθη.[27]

King Lycaon was changed into a wolf because he placed
human flesh on the table before Zeus when he was a guest
at his house.

Corone the daughter of Coroneus the king of the Phocians,
fleeing the love of Poseidon, was turned into a bird [the
crow] through Athena's pity.

Nyctimene, the daughter of Clymenus, fleeing the love of
her father, was turned into an owl by the pity of Athena.

Besides showcasing structural aspects of the mythographical catalogue
that are reflected in our encomium, these examples also demonstrate
that metamorphic content was particularly appropriate for such catalogues: the topic itself, then, likely prompted the use of this type of
source.[28] Adding to the plausibility that such a source was employed,
both papyrological evidence and literary reuses indicate that the

---

[27] Westermann 1839:222.
[28] A catalogue of metamorphoses of women is also found in *P.Oxy.* LXII 4306 (fr. 1, col. 2,
17–28). For a survey of mythographical catalogues of metamorphoses, both self-standing
and embedded in literary works, see Guichard 2014 and the bibliography therein; for
metamorphic materials in *progymnasmata*, see especially Guichard 2014:17–18, and cf.
Menander Rhetor (2.3.4) on the inclusion of metamorphoses of plants and birds in public
speeches. On the relationship between *progymnasmata* and mythography more broadly,
see Gibson 2013 and Meccariello 2019:164–170.

genre was alive and well in the second century CE, when our rhetor probably wrote.[29]

III.2. στεφάνους πενθουμέ[νων] ὀνομάτων

A linguistic clue to the use of a catalogic source may be identified in the conclusion of the encomium, where a generalizing sentence encapsulates in a few words the ambiguous vegetal/human quality of the characters involved, their tragic end, and their youth. Here, the flowers of mythological origin are hinted at through the phrase στεφάνους πενθουμέ[νων] ὀνομάτων (iii.24–25). The use of the word ὀνόματα is particularly interesting in this context, as in its primary meaning of "names" or "named characters" it is often found in catalogues or in their paratextual elements. To quote a few examples, in the bilingual teaching handbook known as Pseudo-Dositheus's *Hermeneumata*, the phrase θεῶν καὶ θεάων ὀνόματα (Lat. *deorum ... et dearum nomina*) is used in the introduction to indicate the list of divine names contained in the second book. We can observe the same use in P.Mich. inv. 2458 (second or third century CE), where the Greek and transliterated Latin headings [θεάων ὀνόματα]/[δεαρου]μ νωμινα (line 12) can be reconstructed right above a bilingual list of goddesses. In P.Vindob.G 26727 (second century CE), which contains six brief sections about mythological characters and their genealogies, the sequence] ̣ν ὀνόματα followed by a blank space (clearly a heading) can be read at line 9, and the phrase [νυμ]φῶν ὀνόματα τῶν [ἐκ | Διός?] γενομένων recurs at lines 10–11. Similarly, but in a narrative context, ὀνόματα introduces the short catalogue of Nereids in Apollodorus's *Library*; and the Latin equivalent *nomina* is found many times in Hyginus's *Fabulae*.[30] Conceptually, a catalogue is in fact a sequence of names designating characters that share a certain trait, names that may or may not be accompanied by further information: a bare list of names and a list of names with nominal

---

[29] Some literary uses are discussed in section IV below.

[30] Apollod. *Bibl.* 1.11; Hyg. *Fab.* 181.3, 5, 182.2, 183.4, and 183 [heading] *EQVORVM SOLIS ET HORARVM NOMINA*. The text of Hyginus is quoted according to Marshall's *editio altera* (Marshall 2002). For the text of P.Mich. inv. 2458 and P.Vindob.G 26727 I have followed, respectively, Kramer 1983: no. 12 and Itgenshorst 1997.

or verbal specifications are both *onomata/nomina*. The alphabetical arrangement in the case of a "narratively expanded" catalogue such as the one in P.Mich. inv. 1447 quoted above indicates the same name-centrism, and the case of Hyg. *Fab.* 183, in which the *EQVORVM SOLIS ET HORARVM NOMINA* of the title are equipped with additional, often syntactically independent information, illustrates well the flexibility of a genre whose primary purpose was to list names.[31] Against this background, the rhetor's use of ὀνόματα can be understood as indicating the catalogic origin of the mythical characters listed in the encomium—be it an unintentional lapse or a subtle reference to the nature of the hypotext.

In the next sections I will illustrate several oddities and other traits of the encomium which the catalogic source I have reconstructed helps to explain.

III.3. FLOWERS WITH ETHNIC TERMS

As underlined in the *editio princeps*, the use of ethnic terminology at ii.26–32 is problematic. While encomia typically state a character's provenance at the beginning,[32] here the specifications "Athenian," "Spartan," "among the Thracians," and "in Crete," referring to νάρκισσος, ὑάκινθος, Ὕλας, and κυπάρισσος, respectively, defy the logic of the passage. These associations are obviously appropriate for the human characters from which the named flowers/plants are said to derive, but at this point the focus is on the flowers/plants as such, rather than their original human identity. (The geographical provenance is, in fact, repeated at ii.32–iii.6, where it is not out of place.) The papyrus perhaps references the geographic origin of each flower when it first appears because the encomium draws from a catalogue which features ethnic terms near the beginning of each entry. This is the case, for example, in the catalogues of Argonauts found in P.Oxy. LXI 4097, where each name is accompanied by a patronymic and place of origin (e.g., fr. 1.8, Κάστωρ καὶ Πολυδε[ύκης *vac.* Δι]ὸς *vac.* ἐκ Σπάρ[της), and

---

[31] On the importance of names in mythology and mythography, see Henrichs 1987:248–254. On catalogues vis-à-vis collections of narratives, see note 22 above.

[32] Fernández Delgado and Pordomingo 2008:187.

in Hyg. *Fab.* 14, where the geographical provenance of each character is indicated after the names of his or her parents (e.g., 14.2, *Polyphemus Elati filius, matre Hippea Antippi filia, Thessalus ex urbe Larissa*).

III.4. HYLAS

Hylas is thematically out of place among Antinous's *comparanda*, since the myth usually has him metamorphose into an echo or a spring, not into a flower.[33] Ausonius *Epigr.* 107 Green (*furitis procaces Naiades / amore saevo et irrito: / ephebus iste* [scil. Hylas] *flos erit*) is the only extant witness to Hylas's florification. Several editors have fixed this singularity by accepting Förster's emendation of *flos* to *fons*, and indeed the fact that this epigram is followed by two epigrams on Narcissus may have favored the corruption.[34] The youth is not named in the poem itself but only in its heading, *Nymphis quae Hylam merserunt* (unlikely to be Ausonius's),[35] which might presuppose a text with *fons* (cf. *merserunt*; the previous epigram, also on Hylas, does not mention this aspect of the story). Toll's edition printed the heading *Ad Nymphas Narcissum persequentes*, which fixes the problem of *flos* by identifying the *ephebus* with Narcissus;[36] Schenkl also removed the problematic reference to Hylas by expunging the segment *quae Hylam merserunt*.[37] At any rate, even if Ausonius wrote *flos* and this epigram conveyed an otherwise unknown floral transformation of Hylas,[38] the way in which our encomium refers to this character at his first appearance points to the rhetor's ignorance

---

[33] On Hylas's metamorphosis into an echo, see Heerink 2015:3. His transformation into a spring or stream is implied by the existence of a river and a spring named Hylas (Plin. *HN* 5.144, Hsch. s.v. υ 149) and by the reference to his sharing *fontis honores* in Val. Fl. 4.26–29; see Mattiacci 2017:38.

[34] Förster 1887, cf. Villani 1898:119; the correction is accepted by Pastorino 1971 and Green 1999.

[35] Cf. Schröder 1999:201–202.

[36] Toll 1671.

[37] Schenkl 1883.

[38] For a defense of the *paradosis* see Kay 2001:279, Mauerhofer 2004:300n7, and Mattiacci 2017:38–39. Kay's argument that "if Hylas did metamorphose into something watery like a spring, that would have suited the Naiads, whose *amor* need not then be *irritus*," does not take into account the fact that a transformation into a spring would still deprive the Naiads of the love of Hylas *qua ephebus*.

of such a version. In fact, the sequence οὐχ Ὕλας παῖς παρὰ Θραι|ξίν at ii.29–30 is embedded between οὔ[τ]ε νάρκισσος ... οὔτε ὑάκινθος ... οὔτε κρόκος ἐξ ἀρχῆς ἄνθος ἦν and οὐ κυπάρισσος ἐν Κρήτηι δένδρον, οὐκ ἀπ᾽ ἀρχῆς ἡ δάφνη φυτόν, and thus remains excluded both from the initial floral sequence and from the other vegetal categories. Taken up as it is, somewhat paradoxically, by its opposite Ὕλας παῖς καλὸς Θρᾶιξ at ii.33–iii.1, this segment indeed betrays the difficult integration of the character into the vegetal tableau.[39]

The appearance of Hylas in the encomium, I argue, is easily explained by his presence in the underlying catalogic source, which need not have consisted solely of stories of *vegetal* transformation. In this case, rather than of the "inclusion" of Hylas, we should more properly speak of his "failed exclusion": Hylas does share some characteristics with Antinous and the other figures of the composition, such as young age, a (semi)divine lover, a dramatic death, and a metamorphosis, and this "family resemblance" could have easily led the rhetor to retain the character even in the absence of a vegetal connection.[40]

III.5. Narcissus's Suicide

The segment on the death of Narcissus (iii.14-16, Ν[άρ]|κισσος ὑπερηφανείαι ἐρ[ασθεὶς] | ἑαυτὸν ὡς ἄλλον ἀπώλεσ[εν]) is syntactically problematic. The transitive ἀπώλεσ[εν] requires ἑαυτόν, and the phrase ἑαυτὸν ... ἀπώλεσ[εν] aligns this passage with Conon's version of the myth, in which Narcissus commits suicide rather than wasting away (*FGrHist* 26 F 1, 24). However, ὡς ἄλλον is odd in this context; and while it would be clearly apt to describe Narcissus's love for his own reflected image, which he mistook for another person (cf. Tzetz. *Chil.* 1.9.237, ἐρᾷ σκιᾶς τῆς ἑαυτοῦ καθάπερ ἄλλου νέου), the accusative would not work with ἐρ[ασθείς].[41] ἐρ[εθισθείς] (preferred by Fernández

---

[39] For the unusual Thracian provenance of Hylas, see *P.Oxy.* LIV 3723.ii.19 with Huxley 1989.

[40] Hylas and Antinous also share a connection with water if the composition of the encomium is to be placed after Antinous's death in 130 CE. That the aition presupposes his drowning is the overall argument of Höschele 2019.

[41] Cf. iii.9–10, Ὑακίνθου καὶ Δ[άφνης] | Ἀπόλλων ἤρα. The sequence [Διόνυ]|σος ἤρα at iii.6–7, which understands the object of Dionysus's love from the preceding Ὕλαν εἶ[χ]εν

Delgado and Pordomingo, with ὑπερηφανίαι interpreted as dative of agent) would suggest, somewhat paradoxically, that Narcissus's ὑπερηφανία instigated his suicide; conversely, ὑπερηφανίαι as an adverbial dative followed by ἐρ[ασθείς] would effectively encapsulate Narcissus's arrogant self-love. In the latter case, the problematic ἑαυτὸν ὡς ἄλλον ἀπώλεσ[εν], with ἐρ[ασθείς] left without an object, could be explained as a case of extreme syntactic compression, with ἑαυτόν depending ἀπὸ κοινοῦ on both ἐρ[ασθείς] and ἀπώλεσ[εν], but taking the case required by the main verb and dragging ὡς ἄλλον into the accusative despite its only being relevant to ἐρ[ασθείς]. This imperfect syntax could stem from the condensation of an already compressed catalogic entry.[42] The effect, not necessarily intentional, is to highlight the paradox of Narcissus's suicide, as he ends up killing not only himself but also his beloved.

III.6. MYTHICAL VARIANTS

In the encomium, Narcissus is said to hail from two different places: at ii.26, his first appearance, he is said to be Athenian, whereas at iii.4 he reappears as Boeotian. While Castiglioni and Vogliano considered Ἀθηναῖος a scribal mistake for Θηβαῖος, Fernández Delgado and Pordomingo suggested that the rhetor was aware of a mythical variant, since a river called Cephisus, the name of Narcissus's father, is found both in Attica and Boeotia (Polemon *FHG* 81 = fr. 4 Giannini = *Sch.* Eur. *Med.* 827; cf. Strab. 9.3.16).[43] Again, we may explain the inconsistency by supposing that the catalogue reported both versions.[44] A similar

---

Ἡρακλῆς, could indicate some flexibility in the treatment of this verb, but the sequence is otherwise suspicious (see above, note 19).

[42] Alternatively, the text might suggest that Narcissus killed himself by mistake, as he intended to kill the person he believed his own reflection to be. Such a version would not be entirely inconceivable, but the mechanics of the act would be rather paradoxical. I must note that, in this case, the supplement ἐρ[εθισθείς], indicating rage and jealousy as Narcissus's motive, could be reconsidered (Narcissus would be irritated by the existence of an equally beautiful competitor).

[43] Fernández Delgado and Pordomingo 2008:182.

[44] For mythical variants in catalogues, see, e.g., van Rossum-Steenbeek 1998: nos. 67, 73 and Hyg. *Fab.* 14.1, *Asterion Pyremi filius* [...] *ex urbe Pellene. alii aiunt Hyperasii filium, urbe Piresia* [...]; 14.3, *Eurytus et Echion* [...] *ex urbe Alope* [...]; *quidam auctores Thessalos putant.*

mechanism may explain the omission of any place of origin for Daphne: the existence of several variants for the name and geographic location of her fluvial father might have resulted, in the catalogue, in a longer sequence of alternatives, which the rhetor would have simply chosen to leave out.[45]

III.7. COLORS

The information on the color of the narcissus and the hyacinth, which is essential to the main point of iii.14–22 and, indeed, of the whole encomium, is unlikely to have figured in the posited catalogic source. Conversely, color is central to the story of the flower of Antinous in Athenaeus, who specifies that the lotus Pancrates showed Hadrian was not the common blue one (κυανέαν ἔχων τὴν χροιάν) but a variety of the color of the rose, that is, red or pink (ἡ μὲν τῷ ῥόδῳ ἐοικυῖα ... τὸν ῥοδίζοντα λωτόν).[46] In the encomium, color is crucial to the flower's excellence, because it is what makes it aesthetically superior both to the narcissus and the hyacinth, which are said to be "pale," since they reflect the tragic stories of the youths from whom they derive. Here, Antinous's death goes unmentioned; if presupposed, it is intentionally obliterated, since his case is *opposed* to those of his somber mythical *comparanda*: unlike the mythical characters, Antinous is not lamented but celebrated. This contrast probably owes to the fact that, unlike the other flowers/plants, the flower of Antinous was not said to derive from the person or blood of Antinous himself but from the blood of the merciless lion that Hadrian killed: in the words of the author of the hexameters preserved in *P.Oxy.* LXIII 4352, the flower was a "memorial of the hunt" and a "garland of victory" (ii.2), and thus a celebration of

---

[45] Cf. Fernández Delgado and Pordomingo 2008:183: "El silenciamiento del lugar de origen de Dafne [...] tal vez se deba [...] a un no querer comprometerse por parte del autor ante lo inestable del mito."

[46] Ath. 15.477d–e. The flower is commonly identified with the *Nelumbo nucifera*, see Grenier 2008:50n13. As for ῥοδίζοντα, a vivid indication of the color of the rose can be found in Ath. 13.604 b (about the adjective *rhododaktylos* used for Dawn in Homer): εἰ γάρ τις εἰς ῥόδεον χρῶμα βάψειε τοὺς δακτύλους, πορφυροβάφου χεῖρας καὶ οὐ γυναικὸς καλῆς ποιήσειεν <ἂν> ("because if someone dipped (the goddess') fingers in rose-colored pigment, he would produce the hands of a purple-dyer, not of a beautiful woman," translated by Olson 2011).

power and love.[47] However, there is no explicit reference to this in the encomium.

Interestingly, in construing the aesthetic opposition between the flower of Antinous on the one hand, and the narcissus and the hyacinth on the other, the rhetor ascribes to the hyacinth the adjective "pale" (iii.21, ὠχρόν). Regardless of the botanical identity of the flower, which is uncertain, in no other source is the hyacinth presented as a pale-colored flower; it is usually characterized as "purple"[48] and perceived as "dark."[49] Notably, a connection between spilled blood and the hyacinth is found in Ovid (*Met.* 10.210–213): the similarity of the two aitia in this respect, notwithstanding the different circumstances of the spillage, indicates that the hyacinth (or some varieties of hyacinth) and the flower of Antinous could be perceived as chromatically similar, which is in line with the use of πορφυρέην/*purpureus, rubens,* and *ferrugineus* for the former, and of ῥοδίζων for the latter.[50] But of course, the rhetor would not seek out this connection. It is not unusual for rhetorical compositions to stretch or manipulate facts to prove a point, and here the rhetor—provided that he knew the color of the hyacinth—might have adapted its botanical qualities to his own agenda.[51] At any rate,

---

[47] *P.Oxy.* LXIII 4352 fr. 5 ii.1–2, εὗρε δὲ τερπομένη ζωάγριον Ἀντιν[όοιο] | θήρης μνημοσύνην, νίκης θάλος.

[48] See, e.g., Dioscorid. 4.62 ἄνθους ... πορφυροειδοῦς and πορφυρέην in Pancrates fr. 3.2 Heitsch. In Latin we find *purpureus* (Ov. *Met.* 10.210–213, *ecce cruor, qui fusus humo signaverat herbas, / desinit esse cruor, Tyrioque nitentior ostro / flos oritur formamque capit, quam lilia, si non / purpureus color his, argenteus esset in illis*), *rubens* (Verg. *Ecl.* 3.63), and *ferrugineus* (Verg. *G.* 4.183).

[49] Cf. esp. Theoc. *Id.* 10.28: καὶ τὸ ἴον μέλαν ἐστί, καὶ ἁ γραπτὰ ὑάκινθος. Philostr. *Ep.* 3, ὑάκινθος μὲν οὖν λευκῷ μειρακίῳ πρέπει καὶ νάρκισσος μέλανι, offers a good indication of the chromatic polarity of the hyacinth and the narcissus. On the difficult botanical identification of the hyacinth, see Irwin 1990:214–215 and Amigues 1992. A useful discussion of the (related) intricacies of Greek color terminology can be found in Irwin 1974:27–30.

[50] Cf. above, note 44. The hyacinth might have come in different shades reflecting botanical variety (see LSJ s.v. B I 1–3); but of course one should not expect that each literary occurrence of the flower presupposes a precise botanical identity, or that the chromatic notations used always reflect botanical knowledge. Still, a pale hyacinth is unique to *P.Mil.Vogl.* I 20.

[51] See, for example, the general observations in Colomo 2011:48–50 and Russell 1983:106–107, 113–128.

after referencing the (rightfully[52]) pale narcissus, he has clearly added a second flower *ad abundantiam*; and in light of the catalogic source that we have reconstructed, we can surmise that his choice has simply fallen on the next flower in the list, regardless of its color.[53]

IV. MYTHOGRAPHICAL CATALOGUES BETWEEN SCHOOL AND LITERATURE

To sum up, the encomium on the flower of Antinous in *P.Mil.Vogl.* I 20 shows structural, stylistic, and lexical traits that strongly suggest a catalogic source. Further, the use of such a source explains a few puzzling aspects of the text, including oddities that induced the first editors to postulate interpolation. However, the use of a catalogue does not exclude the simultaneous reliance on other types of sources: in the realm of rhetoric, literary influence and poetic sources can often be detected, and should not be excluded for this very composition either. Indeed, Antinous is extremely unlikely to have featured in the postulated mythographical catalogue, and the rhetor might have known of the aition directly from Pancrates' poem, which would explain the centrality of color in the encomium and the "happy" premise of the flower's appearance on earth. Moreover, echoes of Herodotus

---

[52] Probably to be identified with the *Narcissus poeticus*, see Giesecke 2014:59. Cf. Stat. *Theb.* 7.340–342: *tu quoque praeclarum forma, Cephise, dedisses / Narcissum, sed Thespiacis iam pallet in agris / trux puer.*

[53] I have also considered the possibility that ὠχρόν might be a dittographic scribal mistake stemming from the use of the same adjective for the narcissus in the previous sentence. The supplement π[τώ]|ματος printed in the *editio princeps* at iii.21–22 could indicate a corpse, for which the pale color is appropriate (a dying Hyacinth is pale, for example, in Ov. *Met.* 10.185–186). However, if we posit that ὠχρόν is corrupted and that the text originally had another adjective (perhaps something like πελιόν, "livid," rather than πορφύρεον, which would be too close to the supposed color of the flower of Antinous), the supplement π[λήγ]|ματος, indicating a wound from a stroke, would be more suitable both to the story of Hyacinth, who was hit by a discus (see *LIMC* s.v. Hyakinthos, 546), and to the dark color of the flower. The supplement π[ελιώ]|ματος (keeping ὠχρόν), which Hollis 2003:12n44 found in the margins of an Oxford copy of *P. Mil.* I, points in the same direction.

and Homer have been securely identified in the composition on the phoenix with which *P.Mil.Vogl.* I 20 currently opens.[54]

Nor should this papyrus induce one to conclude that mythographical catalogues were used exclusively or primarily in advanced school contexts, or even that they were compiled with such contexts in mind. On the contrary, the genre is likely to have had a broader readership comprising general readers as well as literary authors.[55] Cameron, for example, has shown that a mythographical catalogue likely underlies the list of women seduced by Jupiter and Neptune under disguise in the sixth book of Ovid's *Metamorphoses*.[56] A similar source may be posited for Oppian's list of mythological characters that jealousy (ζῆλος) "arrayed against their own children" (*Cyn.* 3.244–248),[57] which seems to wink at a typology of catalogues documented, for example, by *P.Oxy.* LXII 4307 (mothers who killed their sons) and Hyginus's catalogue of *matres quae filios interfecerunt* (*Fab.* 239). Early Christian writers also resorted to such catalogues. In Clement of Alexandria's *Protrepticus*, to name just one example, the allegation that pagan deities lack self-restraint is substantiated by an extensive list of sexual partners of various gods and goddesses, which clearly presupposes lists of unions of deities and mortals comparable to the one preserved in *P.Mil.Vogl.* III 126.[58]

The catalogic source posited for the encomium on the flower of Antinous in *P.Mil.Vogl.* I 20 is thus in line with the broader employment of this textual typology among cultivated authors of the Imperial age. In this period, learning practices and literary production could draw on a common pool of subliterary aids, which provided precious orientation in a large and multifarious mass of mythological data. The employment of this textual typology, however, implies neither

---

[54] Colomo 2013:35–38, 41–42; on the use of literature at the school of rhetoric see especially Patillon 2007.

[55] Cf. van Rossum-Steenbeek 1998:156. Meccariello 2019 reaches a similar conclusion for mythographical handbooks.

[56] Cameron 2004:261–263 on Ov. *Met.* 6.103–122.

[57] Translated by Mair 1928.

[58] Clem. Al. *Protr.* 2.32–33. Catalogues also underlie Ps.-Clem. (of Rome) *Recogn.* 10.26.3 and *Hom.* 5.17.1–4, quoted in van Rossum-Steenbeek 1998:145.

the unavailability of other sources nor the unwillingness to directly engage with "proper" literature.

V. FLOWERS, MYTHOLOGIZATION, AND EPHEBIC CONTESTS

As I have already pointed out, the mythographical catalogue that constituted the source of the encomium in *P.Mil.Vogl.* I 20 is unlikely to have included Antinous. Neither does the encomium itself mention Antinous *qua* character. On the one hand, the suppression of the Antinous story bypasses the potential problem of imperfect parallelism—the flower of Antinous does not stem from the boy's metamorphosis and is not connected to his death—while simultaneously removing an unwanted somber component. On the other hand, it takes only a vague familiarity with the figure of Antinous and his fate to recognize that the encomium indirectly portrays him and his story through the mythological characters that are offered, *en bloc*, as *comparanda*, and with whom Antinous has in common youthful beauty as well as a premature and violent death. Through this mirroring, the encomium enforces the mythologization of Antinous, who is tacitly cast in a spatially and temporally remote dimension crowded with divine figures.

Conversely, the flower of Antinous is explicitly singled out and celebrated for its aesthetic superiority. While the story of its appearance on earth is not told, the emphasis is on its non-pale color, a physical trait pertaining to concrete human, sensory experience.

A convergence of clues allows us to link the composition to a specific occasion, or rather type of occasion, in which the flower might have been physically present and the mythologization of Antinous would have been particularly meaningful—namely, the ephebic contests that took place during the *Megala Antinoeia* instituted by Hadrian in the newly founded city of Antinoupolis, as well as the *Antinoeia* that were created, on their model, in other locations in Egypt and beyond.[59] Several aspects of these festivals are uncertain, but two elements are of interest here.

---

[59] For the connection between encomia, including progymnasmatic encomia on Antinous, and the *Antinoeia*, see Del Corso 2020:42–43. Hollis 2003:12, followed by Whitmarsh 2018, suggests a connection between Pancrates' poem and the inauguration

First, besides athletics, the ephebic contests that were part of the *Antinoeia* games included encomium contests: ephebic winners of encomia competitions at the Athenian *Antinoeia* are attested epigraphically and, according to the second-century inscription *IPortes* 10, a λογικὸς ἀγών, a "prose speech competition" which likely included encomia, took place at the *Megala Antinoeia* in Antinoupolis.[60] It is reasonable to assume that the encomium in *P.Mil.Vogl.* I 20 was conceived for such a context—if not to be performed at a specific competition, at least to provide the necessary training.

A second interesting piece of information comes from the Barberini Obelisk. This monument, which Hadrian dedicated to Antinous after his death, bears text in hieroglyphics on all of its four faces. The main topics are Antinous's death and apotheosis, the foundation of Antinoupolis and the *Antinoeia*, and the institution of a cult of Antinous-Osiris. The text on one of the faces describes the *Antinoeia* of Antinoupolis and mentions, among the winners' prizes, "crowns of flowers for their heads."[61] Notably, in the passage on Pancrates discussed above, Athenaeus mentions "Antinoeian *garlands*" made of red lotus:[62] if these were indeed used as prizes in *Antinoeia* competitions, the mention of "garlands" in our encomium (iii.32, στεφάνους) would acquire further significance. This element makes it even more plausible that an encomium on the Antinoeian flower such as we find

---

of the games in honor of Antinous in 131 CE. The *Antinoeia* were annual ephebic games, whereas the *Megala Antinoeia* were sacred games (also annual) which included both adult and ephebic competitions: see Remijsen 2014:193. *Antinoeia* are mentioned in a private letter from Tebtunys, the location where *P.Mil.Vogl.* I 20 was found (the letter is *P.Tebt.* II 592, third century CE).

[60] The relevant Athenian inscriptions are *IG* II² 2119, 2087 and 2116 (all from the second half of the second century CE). For the possible inclusion of encomia in the λογικὸς ἀγών of Antinoupolis cf. *IG* IX² 531, 43–45 (first century BCE or CE, from Thessaly), which records two distinct competitions, one ἐνκωμίῳ λογικῷ (in prose) and one ἐνκωμίῳ ἐπικῷ (in hexameters); papyri from Roman Egypt have preserved encomia of both types. On ephebic encomia competitions in the Greco-Roman world, see Pernot 1993:63–65.

[61] Grenier 2008:20, IIIa; Meyer 1994:55, IIIb, translated by Boatwright 1987:245.

[62] *Ath.* 15.677d, quoted above. Hollis 2003:12 already mentions the possibility that *Antinoeia* victors received red lotus crowns.

in *P.Mil.Vogl.* I 20—or rather a fuller and/or more polished version of it—
was conceived for this specific occasion.[63]

When read against the backdrop of rhetorical competitions within
the *Antinoeia* games, the encomium appears to achieve two goals: on
the one hand, it underlines the beauty of a tangible object that was
relevant to this performative setting; on the other, it mythologizes the
eponymous hero of the games by providing a familiar mythological
frame to interpret his recent history. Finally, the piece's emphasis
on the youth and beauty of the named characters—and, indirectly, of
Antinous—makes it particularly appropriate to ephebic competitions:
indeed, Crocus the μειράκιον, Hylas the παῖς καλός, Cyparissus the
[παῖς] εὐειδής, Narcissus the καλὸς παῖς, and Hyacinth the ὡραῖο[ς
ἔφη]||βος (ii.32–iii.6), together with the mythologized Antinous,
constitute the mythical counterparts of the competing boys.[64]

UNIVERSITY OF EXETER

LIST OF ABBREVIATIONS

CIL = *Corpus inscriptionum Latinarum.* 1863–. Berlin.

FHG = Karl Müller. 1841–1870. *Fragmenta historicorum Graecorum.* 5 vols. Paris.

FGrHist = Felix Jacoby. 1923–. *Die Fragmente der griechischen Historiker.* Leiden.

IG = *Inscriptiones Graecae.* 1873–. Berlin.

IPortes = André Bernand. 1984. *Les portes du désert. Recueil des inscriptions grecques d'Antinooupolis, Tentyris, Koptos, Apollonopolis Parva et Apollonopolis Magna.* Paris.

LIMC = *Lexicon iconographicum mythologiae classicae.* 1981–1999. 8 vols. Zurich and Munich.

[63] Similarly, encomia preserved in Oxyrhynchus papyri are likely to stem from gymnasium-based festival competitions: see Colomo 2014:81.

[64] For the characterization of Antinous as a handsome boy see especially the Barberini Obelisk, where he is described as a beautiful "youth" or "ephebe": the latter translation of the Egyptian ḥwn is by Grenier 2008:14, IIA, who compares an Athenian inscription mentioning a ἱερεὺς Ἀντινόου ἐφήβου (*IG* II² 2065.1.27).

LSJ = Henry George Liddell and Robert Scott. 1996. *A Greek-English Lexicon: With a Revised Supplement*. 9th ed. Oxford.

P.CtYBR = Yale Papyrus Collection.

P.Mich. = Michigan Papyrus Collection.

P.Vat.Gr. = Greek Papyri of the Vatican Library Collection.

P.Vindob.G = Greek Papyri of the Vienna Papyrus Collection.

WORKS CITED

Amigues, Suzanne. 1992. "*Hyakinthos*: Fleur mythique et plantes réelles." *Revue des études grecques* 105:19–36.

Bastianini, Guido. 1992. "Diogenes Cynicus." In *Corpus dei papiri filosofici greci e latini*, vol. 1.1**, 89–144. Florence.

Boatwright, Mary T. 1987. *Hadrian and the City of Rome*. Princeton.

Cameron, Alan. 2004. *Greek Mythography in the Roman World*. Oxford.

Cavallo, Guglielmo. 2005. *Il calamo e il papiro: La scrittura greca dall'età ellenistica ai primi secoli di Bisanzio*. Florence.

Colomo, Daniela. 2004. "Herakles and the Eleusinian Mysteries: P. Mil. Vogl. I 20, 18–32 Revisited." *Zeitschrift für Papyrologie und Epigraphik* 148:87–98.

———. 2011. "Euripides' *Ur-Medea* between *Hypotheseis* and Declamation." *Zeitschrift für Papyrologie und Epigraphik* 176:45–51.

———. 2013. "The *Avis Phoenix* in the Schools of Rhetoric: P. Mil. Vogl. I 20 and P. Lond. Lit 193 Revisited." *Segno e Testo* 11:29–78.

———. 2014. "5194. Encomium of the *Logos*." In *The Oxyrhynchus Papyri*, vol. 79, ed. W. Benjamin Henry and Peter J. Parsons, 79–88. London.

Delattre, Charles. 2021. "Textual Webs: How to Read Mythographic Lists." In *Lists and Catalogues in Ancient Literature and Beyond*, ed. Rebecca Laemmle, Cédric Scheidegger Laemmle, and Katharina Wesselmann, 81–106. Berlin and Boston.

Del Corso, Lucio. 2020. "Rhetoric for Beginners? Papyrological Evidence for Progymnasmata." In *Les Progymnasmata en pratique, de l'Antiquité à nos jours*, ed. Pierre Chiron and Benoît Sans, 42–66. Paris.

Fernández Delgado, José A., and Francisca Pordomingo. 2008. "PMilVogl I 20: Bocetos de *progymnásmata*." *Zeitschrift für Papyrologie und Epigraphik* 167:167–192. Reprinted in *La retórica escolar griega y su influencia literaria* (Salamanca, 2017), 91–134.

Flammini, Giuseppe. 2004. *Magister Dositheus. Hermeneumata Pseudodositheana Leidensia.* Leipzig.

Förster, Richard. 1887. "Zu Ausonius." *Jahrbücher für klassische Philologie,* n.s., 33:784.

Gibson, Craig A. 2013. "True or False? Greek Myth and Mythography in the *Progymnasmata.*" In *Writing Myth: Mythography in the Ancient World,* ed. Stephen M. Trzaskoma and R. Scott Smith, 289–308. Leuven.

Giesecke, Annette. 2014. *The Mythology of Plants: Botanical Lore from Ancient Greece and Rome.* Los Angeles.

Gow, Andrew S. F. 1952. *Bucolici Graeci.* Oxford.

Green, Roger P. H. 1999. *Ausonius. Opera.* Oxford.

Grenier, Jean–Claude. 2008. *L'Osiris Antinoos.* Montpellier.

Gualandri, Isabella. 1974. "Un papiro milanese: Lattanzio, Claudiano e il mito della fenice." *Rendiconti della classe di scienze morali, storiche e filologiche dell'Accademia dei Lincei* 29:293–311.

Guichard, Luis A. 2014. "Catálogos de metamorfosis de época helenística e imperial." In *Metamorfosi tra scienza e letteratura,* ed. Francesco Citti, Lucia Pasetti, and Daniele Pellacani, 15–39. Florence.

Heerink, Mark A. J. 2015. *Echoing Hylas: A Study in Hellenistic and Roman Metapoetics.* Madison.

Henrichs, Albert. 1987. "Three Approaches to Greek Mythography." In *Interpretations of Greek Mythology,* ed. Jan N. Bremmer, 242–277. London and Sydney.

Hollis, Adrian S. 2003. "Myth in the Service of Kings and Emperors." In *Mitos en la literatura griega helenística e imperial,* ed. Juan A. López Férez, 1–14. Madrid.

Höschele, Regina. 2019. "Two Lovers and a Lion: Pankrates' Poem on Hadrian's Royal Hunt." *Philologus* 163:214–236.

Huxley, George. 1989. "Thracian Hylas." *Journal of Hellenic Studies* 109:185–186.

Irwin, M. Eleanor. 1974. *Colour Terms in Greek Poetry.* Toronto.

————. 1990. "Odysseus' 'Hyacinthine Hair' in *Odyssey* 6.231." *Phoenix* 44:205–218.

Itgenshorst, Tanja. 1997. "Das mythologische Fragment P. Vindob. Gr. 26727: Eine neue Lesung." *Zeitschrift für Papyrologie und Epigraphik* 119:189–192.

Kay, Nigel M. 2001. *Ausonius. Epigrams.* London.

Kayser, Carl L. 1977. *Flavii Philostrati opera.* Leipzig.

Kiessling, Theophilus. 1826. *Historiarum variarum chiliades.* Leipzig.

Körte, Alfred. 1939. "Literarische Texte mit Ausschluss der christlichen." *Archiv für Papyrusforschung* 13:78–176.

Kramer, Johannes. 1983. *Glossaria bilinguia in papyris et membranis reperta.* Bonn.

MacLeod, Malcolm D. 1972. *Luciani opera.* Vol. 1. Oxford.

Mair, Alexander W. 1928. *Oppian, Colluthus, Tryphiodorus.* Cambridge, MA.

Marshall, Peter K. 2002. *Hyginus. Fabulae.* 2nd ed. Munich.

Mattiacci, Silvia. 2017. "Miti acquatici in miniatura: Ila, Narciso, Ermafrodito negli epigrammi di Ausonio." In *Il calamo della memoria: Riuso di testi e mestiere letterario nella tarda antichità; Raccolta delle relazioni discusse nel VII Incontro internazionale di Trieste, Biblioteca statale, 29–30 settembre 2016,* ed. Lucio Cristante and Vanni Veronesi, 21–50. Trieste.

Mau, Jürgen. 1971. *Plutarchus. Moralia.* Vol. 5.2.1. Leipzig.

Mauerhofer, Kenneth. 2004. *Der Hylas-Mythos in der antiken Literatur.* Berlin.

Meccariello, Chiara. 2019. "Impulso mitografico e mitografia nelle pratiche educative greche antiche." *Polymnia* 4:147–175.

Meyer, Hugo. 1994. *Der Obelisk des Antinoos: Eine kommentierte Edition.* Munich.

Mynors, Roger A. B. 1969. *P. Vergili Maronis opera.* Oxford.

Ogden, Daniel. 2004. "The Apprentice's Sorcerer: Pancrates and His Powers in Context (Lucian, *Philopseudes* 33–36)." *Acta Classica* 47:101–126.

Olson, S. Douglas. 2011. *Athenaeus. The Learned Banqueters.* Vol. 7, *Books 13.594b–14.* Cambridge, MA.

————. 2012. *Athenaeus. The Learned Banqueters.* Vol. 8, *Book 15.* Cambridge, MA.

Pastorino, Agostino. 1971. *Opere di Decimo Magno Ausonio*. Turin.

Patillon, Michel. 2007. "Les modèles littéraires dans l'apprentissage de la rhétorique." In *Escuela y literatura en Grecia antigua: Actas del Simposio Internacional Universidad de Salamanca, 17–19 de noviembre de 2004*, ed. José A. Fernández Delgado, Francisca Pordomingo Pardo, and Antonio Stramaglia, 511–521. Cassino.

Pernot, Laurent. 1993. *La rhétorique de l'éloge dans le monde gréco-romain*. Vol. 1. Paris.

Pordomingo Pardo, Francisca. 2007. "Ejercicios preliminares de la composición retórica y literaria en papiro: El encomio." In *Escuela y literatura en Grecia antigua: Actas del Simposio Internacional Universidad de Salamanca, 17–19 de noviembre de 2004*, ed. José A. Fernández Delgado, Francisca Pordomingo Pardo, and Antonio Stramaglia, 405–453. Cassino.

Prada, Luigi. 2012. "For a New Edition of P. Lond. Lit. 92: Current Research on the Greek Version of the Myth of the Sun's Eye." In *Actes du 26e Congrès international de papyrologie, Genève 16–21 août 2010*, ed. Paul Schubert, 627–634. Geneva.

Remijsen, Sofie. 2014. "Appendix: Games, Competitors, and Performers in Roman Egypt." In *The Oxyrhynchus Papyri*, vol. 79, ed. W. Benjamin Henry and Peter J. Parsons, 190–206. London.

Renner, Timothy. 1978. "A Papyrus Dictionary of Metamorphoses." *Harvard Studies in Classical Philology* 82:277–293.

Ricciardetto, Antonio. 2015. "Les documents administratifs du recto du *P. Vat. gr. 11*." In *Le Traité Sur l'exil de Favorinos d'Arles: Papyrologie, philologie et littérature*, ed. Eugenio Amato and Marie-Hélène Marganne, 49–64. Rennes.

Roberts, Colin H. 1956. *Greek Literary Hands, 350 B.C.–A.D. 400*. Oxford.

Rossum-Steenbeek, Monique van. 1998. *Greek Readers' Digests? Studies on a Selection of Subliterary Papyri*. Leiden.

Russell, Donald A. 1983. *Greek Declamation*. Oxford.

Schenkl, Karl. 1883. *D. Magni Ausonii opuscula*. Berlin.

Schröder, Bianca-Jeannette. 1999. *Titel und Text: Zur Entwicklung lateinischer Gedichtüberschriften; Mit Untersuchungen zu lateinischen Buchtiteln, Inhaltsverzeichnissen und anderen Gliederungsmitteln*. Berlin and New York.

Shackleton Bailey, D. R. 2003. *Statius. Thebaid*. Vol. 1, *Books 1-7*. Cambridge, MA.

Stramaglia, Antonio. 1996. "Fra 'consumo' e 'impegno': Usi didattici della narrativa nel mondo antico." In *La letteratura di consumo nel mondo greco-latino: Atti del convegno internazionale, Cassino, 14-17 settembre 1994*, ed. Oronzo Pecere and Antonio Stramaglia, 97–166. Cassino.

———. 2003. "Amori impossibili: PKöln 250, le raccolte proginnasmatiche e la tradizione retorica dell'"amante di un ritratto."" In *Studium declamatorium: Untersuchungen zu Schulübungen und Prunkreden von der Antike bis zur Neuzeit*, ed. Bianca-Jeanette Schröder and Jens-Peter Schröder, 213–239. Munich and Leipzig.

Tarrant, Richard J. 2004. *P. Ovidi Nasonis Metamorphoses*. Oxford.

Thilo, Georg. 1881. *Maurus Servius Honoratus. In Vergilii carmina commentarii*. Leipzig.

Toll, Jakob. 1671. *D. Magni Ausonii Burdigalensis opera*. Amsterdam.

Turner, Eric G., and Peter J. Parsons. 1987. *Greek Manuscripts of the Ancient World*. 2nd ed. London.

Villani, Luciano. 1898. "Per la critica di Ausonio." *Studi Italiani di Filologia Classica* 6:97–119.

Vogliano, Achille. 1937. *Papiri dell'Università di Milano* [= *P.Mil.Vogl.* I]. Milan.

Westermann, Anton. 1839. *ΠΑΡΑΔΟΞΟΓΡΑΦΟΙ: Scriptores rerum mirabilium graeci*. Braunschweig.

Whitmarsh, Tim. 2018. "Pancrates." In *Oxford Classical Dictionary*, ed. Tim Whitmarsh and Sander Goldberg. https://doi.org/10.1093/acrefore/9780199381135.013.8244.

Ziegler, Konrat. 1994. *Plutarchus. Demosthenes et Cicero*. Leipzig.

SUMMARIES OF DISSERTATIONS FOR THE DEGREE OF PHD

REBECCA DEITSCH—*Constructing Goddesses: Gender & Politics in Flavian Epic*

THIS DISSERTATION EXAMINES how Flavian sociopolitical policies are reflected and refracted in the gendered reevaluation of goddesses in epic. The Flavian emperors, especially Domitian, revived Augustan moral reforms targeting elite Roman women, and, I argue, imperial numismatic and sculptural programs showcased sanitized versions of goddesses as models of proper feminine behavior. This renewed discourse about gender roles triggered a shift in the construction of female divine identity in the epics of Valerius Flaccus, Statius, and Silius Italicus. Unlike in the earlier Greco-Roman epic tradition, Flavian goddesses are expected despite their divine status to conform to *mortal* gender norms, and misbehaving female divinities exhibit animalistic behaviors once confined to mortal women and monsters.

While my project furthers our understanding of gender in Flavian epic, it also combines literary, glyptic, numismatic, and sculptural evidence to establish the value of goddesses as an interface between literature and politics. Thanks to the variation allowed by centuries of literary, cultic, and political usage, goddesses are fruitful vehicles for social dialogue about the nature of imperial power, the desirability of moral reform, and the construction of femininity. Studies to date have explored gender *or* ideology in Flavian epic, but my focus on female divinity as the intersection between the two constitutes an important new contribution.

My introduction sets the scene with an overview of the lives of women in the Flavian period and a detailed analysis of Flavian moral reforms. Chapter 1 then uses Diana's eviction from the battlefield in *Thebaid* 9 as a programmatic example of the imposition of mortal gender roles in the divine sphere. Diana's virginity makes it inappropriate for her to intervene in the male-coded space of battle (despite her divine status). Chapter 2 reviews literary and material evidence to demonstrate that both divine and mortal women were valuable to the imperial household primarily for their iconic, legitimizing function as guarantors of virtue and security. Flavian writers contribute to such socially sanctioned images, but they also capitalize on the disparity between idealized versions of goddesses and their more problematic mythological iterations, as I argue in chapters 3 to 6 (dedicated to Venus, Minerva, Diana, and Juno). All four goddesses are linked with instability—marital, social, and/or imperial—and thus reveal a fundamental pessimism about the future of the empire and the dynasty.

MARINA HAWORTH—*Desiring Athletes: The Meaning of Athletic Imagery on Red-Figure Athenian Symposium Pottery*

THIS DISSERTATION EXPLORES the iconography of athletes on Athenian red-figure pottery of the late sixth and fifth centuries BCE, a period in which athletic imagery pervaded the homes, marketplaces, and sanctuaries of ancient Greece. While these ceramic images have been examined in the past for details about sporting practice in ancient Greece, scenes set in the gymnasium often do not show sporting events, but rather individuals preparing for exercise, washing, grooming, and dressing. I suggest certain common athletic motifs may have been interesting to symposiasts because of their humorous and erotic subtexts.

Each chapter discusses a different iconographic topic. Following my introduction (chapter 1), chapter 2 examines the connections between the gymnasium and the symposium. Humor and desire form the backdrop of the imagery that contrasts the gymnasium with self-referential images of the symposium itself, the *kômos*, and the world of Dionysos. Chapter 3 interprets another athletic motif, the *apoxyomenos*, as embodying a civic ideal of everlasting glory tantamount to immortality. I suggest the Athenians may have been in the midst of a Bourdieusian "bronze habitus," taking inspiration from the bronze-casting innovations resulting in hollow-cast immortal bronze victor statues. My dissertation then turns, in chapter 4, to depictions of pet dogs in the gymnasium. By examining the use of canines as a metaphor in Greek comedy, epic, and other textual sources, I reveal that these images of dogs may represent the older man desiring the young athlete. Chapter 5 explores scenes that pay particular attention to dressing, undressing, and the folding of the *himation*; in doing so, I draw on theories of desire and striptease. In addition, this chapter examines possible visual puns involving the multivalent word "*kolpos*," which can refer to a hollow, a gap or gulf (including between the legs and other intimate parts), or a fold in a cloth. Finally, chapter 6 looks into the different ways athletes are shown tying themselves, or being tied: victors bound with fillets, the practice of *kunodesmê*, boxers binding their wrists with the *himas*, and athletes tying their sandals. I argue that many of the scenes contain references to wedding iconography, and the fillets, being bound onto the athlete by *erastês* figures, indicate a claiming of the boy as his *erômenos*.

Overall, athletic imagery on symposium vessels is revealed to function within the pederastic practice of classical Athens and the custom's relationship to the social politics of the city.

PAUL GEORGE JOHNSTON—*The Worlds of Roman Literature: Bilingual Culture, Imperial Power and Literary Tradition in the Ancient Mediterranean*

THIS DISSERTATION EXPLORES bilingual cultures of reading, writing, and patronage among the elites of Rome as an important context for understanding the Greek and Latin literatures of the Roman world. Drawing on approaches from comparative literature and translation studies, I interrogate the ways in which Roman literature has traditionally been conceptualized as an object of study and develop an alternative framework which situates Rome's Latin literature within the broader multilinguistic literary landscape of the Roman Empire. At the core of this study is the question of what political, linguistic, and cultural circumstances produced, and are reflected in, the particular body of Latin and Greek texts from the Roman period that survive to the present day. I argue that the bulk of the texts that survive from the Roman Mediterranean, including practically everything traditionally studied under the disciplinary umbrella of classical studies, must be understood as the product of a definitionally bilingual cultural system closely connected to the state apparatus of Rome, in which writers in both of the empire's major literary languages belonged to interconnected social milieux and addressed readerships that significantly overlapped. In other words, the extant (non-Christian) Greek and Latin texts from the time of the Roman Republic and early Empire, from Polybius and Plautus to Aelius Aristides and Apuleius, are effectively a record of a single cultural system that had the Roman administrative classes at its center. This new approach to Roman literature provides the tools for studying canonical Latin texts in dialogue with other, less well-studied materials from the same period that were composed from different linguistic, religious, and geographical perspectives, enabling scholars to move beyond an inherited stereotype of an almost exclusively one-directional influence of (older) Greek texts upon Latin literary production.

This dissertation advances significant reinterpretations of the major turns of Roman cultural and literary history, analyzing the changing linguistic and literary dynamics of Rome and its territory on a largely chronological basis. The story of Rome's development of a Latin literature, I argue, is equally a story of the city's rise to prominence as a gravitational "literary capital" within the Greek world. I show that the Greek writers of the Augustan period have been systematically and unjustifiably excluded from accounts of the literature and cultural politics of this pivotal moment in Roman history, and explore how our understanding of Augustus's reign and its impact is affected by incorporating Greek texts more fully. I demonstrate how the geographical horizons of Roman literature expand over the first and second centuries CE, from a literature of the city of Rome into a literature of the empire as a whole, as its administrative classes became increasingly diverse and geographically dispersed. The appearance in the textual record of the huge body of Greek texts representative of the "Second Sophistic" beginning at the turn of the second century as well as the emergence of provincial Latin authors, like Florus, Fronto, and Apuleius, can be understood as a function of these developments, a reflection of the changing ethnic and geographic makeup of the Roman administrative classes. I explore how the emergence of imperial panegyric as a distinctive genre in the second century illuminates some of the broader features of literary culture in the High Empire.

I also account for how other streams of literary activity, including those associated with the empire's Jewish and Christian communities, can be understood in terms of this model, as products of the same world as the "classical" canon but associated with somewhat distinct social and institutional contexts. This facilitates a better understanding of how the rise of Christianity reshaped the literary landscape of the Roman Empire and how the bilingual literary cultures of the early Empire eventually faded away. Throughout, I also demonstrate how changes in the empire's literary dynamics are related to broader cultural and political trends.

JOSÉ FELIPE SOZA LARRAIN—*The Antigonid Imperial System: Sovereignty and Politics of Empire in the Pre-Modern Mediterranean*

THIS DISSERTATION INVESTIGATES how the Antigonid dynasty constructed an imperial project to pursue supremacy over the communities of mainland Greece, Macedonia, and the Western Aegean after the collapse of Alexander the Great's empire. I examine the formation, consolidation, contraction, and breakdown of the Antigonid imperial system through which the dynasty ruled over their subjects and territories from the late fourth century until the Roman conquest of Macedonia in 167 BC. I demonstrate how the Antigonids built an empire that rested on a thalassocracy, linking ports and capitals through maritime corridors instead of territorial absorption, and a Pan-Hellenic ideology that presented the dynasty as leaders of the Greek world. Chapters 1 and 2 explore the origins of the Antigonid empire, particularly through the occupation of coastal cities, a thalassocratic ideology, and the appropriation of the kingdom of Macedonia. Chapters 3 and 4 analyze the system through which the dynasty ruled over their possessions in order to promote the integration of the imperial realm. The main characteristic was the military, administrative, and ideological interdependence of its parts. Chapters 5 and 6 focus on the retraction and subsequent collapse of the Antigonid imperial system after the Roman intervention in Greece. I argue that the Antigonid empire became a territorially bounded kingdom only late in its life, which finally turned it into a Macedonia-based polity.